Life in the Ghettos During the Holocaust

Religion, Theology, and the Holocaust
Steven T. Katz, *Series Editor*

Other titles in Religion, Theology, and the Holocaust

Act and Idea in the Nazi Genocide. Berel Lang

Christian Responses to the Holocaust: Moral and Ethical Issues
Donald J. Dietrich

The End of Days: A Memoir of the Holocaust
Helen Sendyk

Exodus Affair: Holocaust Survivors and the Struggle for Palestine, 1947
Aviva Halamish; Ora Cummings, trans.

Himmler's Jewish Tailor: The Story of Holocaust Survivor Jacob Frank
Jacob Frank, with Mark Lewis

The Last Lullaby: Poetry from the Holocaust
Aaron Kramer, ed.

The Man Who Stopped the Trains to Auschwitz: George Mantello, El Salvador, and Switzerland's Finest Hour David Kranzler

The Meeting: An Auschwitz Survivor Confronts an SS Physician
Bernhard Frankfurter, ed.; Susan E. Cernyak-Spatz, trans.

My War: A Memoir of a Survivor of the Holocaust
Edward Stankiewicz

New Dawn: The Triumph of Life After the Holocaust
Helen Sendyk

Nightmares: Memoirs of the Years of Horror Under Nazi Rule in Europe 1939–1945
Konrad Charmatz

Second Generation Voices: Reflections by Children of the Holocaust
Alan L. Berger and Naomi Berger, eds.

Sun Turned to Darkness: Memory and Recovery in the Holocaust Memoir
David Patterson

Survival: The Story of a Sixteen-Year-Old Jewish Boy
Israel J. Rosengarten

Three Homelands: Memories of a Jewish Life in Poland, Israel, and America
Norman Salsitz, with Stanley Kaish

War in the Shadow of Auschwitz: Memoirs of a Polish Resistance Fighter and Survivor of the Death Camps
John Wiernicki

Who Will Say Kaddish? A Search for Jewish Identity in Contemporary Poland
Larry Mayer, text; Gary Gelb, photographs

Will to Freedom: A Perilous Journey Through Fascism and Communism
Egon Balas

Life in the GHETTOS During the HOLOCAUST

Edited by Eric J. Sterling

With a Foreword by John K. Roth

Syracuse University Press

Syracuse, New York 13203-5160

First Edition 2005

05 06 07 08 09 10 6 5 4 3 2 1

The paper used in this publication meets the minimum requirements of American National Standard for Information Sciences—Permanence of Paper for Printed Library Materials, ANSI Z39.48-1984.∞™

Library of Congress Cataloging-in-Publication Data

Life in the ghettos during the Holocaust / edited by Eric J. Sterling; with a foreword by John K. Roth.—1st ed.
p. cm.—(Religion, theology, and the Holocaust)
Includes bibliographical references and index.
ISBN 0-8156-0803-9 (pbk. : alk. paper)
1. Holocaust, Jewish (1939–1945) 2. Jewish ghettos—History—20th century. 3. Jews—Europe, Eastern—Social conditions—20th century. 4. Holocaust, Jewish (1939–1945)—Personal narratives. I. Sterling, Eric, 1963– II. Series.
D804.3.L535 2004
940.53'185—dc22 2004030460

Manufactured in the United States of America

To my grandfather, Gunter Kamm,
a brief resident of Buchenwald and
the Hongkew ghetto in Shanghai,
to my grandmother, Carla Kamm,
and
to my parents—Marianne, a brief resident
of a prison in Nazi Germany and of the
Hongkew ghetto in Shanghai, and Robert

Contents

Illustrations

Maps

Foreword

How to Live in the Interim?

JOHN K. ROTH

> *"Death was a given. How to live in the interim was not."*
>
> —Michael Berenbaum

All the people who read this book will die. Those who do not read it will meet the same fate. Death is a given. Therefore, time after time, "How to live in the interim?" is a question that human beings confront. One way or another, we answer it.

True though those generalities are, they were not primarily what the Holocaust scholar Michael Berenbaum had in mind when he wrote the words that serve as the epigraph for this foreword. Berenbaum's comments come from his contribution to Eric Sterling's volume, which is among the most important studies of a massively destructive chapter in Holocaust history, but they were provoked by an interview he conducted in the spring of 2001. While working on *Uprising,* a film about the 1943 Warsaw Ghetto Uprising, Berenbaum spoke with Marek Edelman, a Jewish officer whose survival of that resistance defied the odds. As they discussed what resistance meant in that place, Edelman stressed that it entailed a definitive choice: namely, "how to live in the moments before we died." Berenbaum understood Edelman to be saying, not in general, but with specific reference to the Warsaw ghetto in the spring of 1943, "Death was a given. How to live in the interim was not."

The historian Wendy Lower, another contributor to this book, correctly states that "[t]he history of Nazi ghettoization practices across Europe is one of significant regional variations." Whether this volume's studies focus on the largest ghettos—Warsaw, Vilna, Łódź, and Theresienstadt—or, as Lower does, on the comparatively short-lived and obscure ghettos in occupied Ukraine, they document that, whatever the variations may have been, Berenbaum's observations do not pertain only to the Warsaw ghetto in 1943 any more than they are merely universal judgments about human existence in general. Wherever Nazi power established ghettos, death became a given for the Jews who were trapped within them. In the ghettos, the question—perhaps unclear at first but ever sharper over time, perhaps articulated infrequently but present nonetheless—became, as Edelman put it, "how to live in the moments before we died." Repeatedly, the responses were forms of resistance that also revealed significant variations. Some of those responses led to survival. In the ghettos, however, survival was much less likely than death by disease, starvation, shooting, or deportation that took European Jews to death through work, if not to gas chambers, in the Nazi camps for which the ghettos became way stations.

"How to live in the moments before we died?" *Life in the Ghettos During the Holocaust* shows how anguished the variations on that theme could be. Adam Czerniakow (1880–1942), a balding engineer in his early sixties, illustrates one of them. For nearly three years, he headed the Warsaw ghetto's Judenrat (Jewish Council). Almost daily he wrote in his diary, which eventually consisted of nine pocket-sized notebooks. The fifth is missing, but it remains unclear how this important diary survived at all. Rosalia Pietkiewicz, a Warsaw ghetto survivor, purchased it from an unidentified source in 1959. The original copy has been in Jerusalem at Yad Vashem, the Israeli Martyrs' and Heroes' Remembrance Authority, since 1964.

Czerniakow's reports—many beginning with the morning temperature—reveal him to be a modest man who worked against impossible obstacles to save Jewish lives. Dated July 23, 1942, his last entry states: "It is 3 o'clock. So far 4,000 are ready to go. The orders are that there must be 9,000 by 4 o'clock."[1] The numbers refer to the daily quota of Jews that the Nazis required the Judenrat to assemble for "resettlement."

Approximately 99 percent of the Warsaw ghetto's half-million Jews perished in the Holocaust. A majority were deported to Treblinka and gassed. Especially distressed by his inability to save the ghetto's children, Czerniakow committed suicide on July 23, soon after writing his diary's final words.

Czerniakow gave no warning about what he knew. His response to a version of Edelman's question remains controversial. The same can be said of the decision taken some time later in a different ghetto by another Jewish man, Herbert Bierhoff, a person less well known than Czerniakow but no less tragic. Bierhoff came to my attention through a ghetto survivor named Sigi Ziering, who succumbed to brain cancer on November 12, 2000.[2] Born in Kassel, Germany, Ziering was eleven when his father, Isaac, who had fled to England from Nazi Germany, was unable to find refuge for the rest of his Jewish family. Trapped with his mother, Cilly, and his older brother, Herman, Sigi Ziering was among the German Jews deported to the ghetto in Riga, Latvia, in 1941. Amazingly, all three survived the Holocaust.

Herman and Sigi, along with their mother, were reunited with their father in London. In 1949, the Zierings immigrated to New York. Sigi Ziering's scientific training and business ability eventually enabled him to lead the Diagnostic Products Corporation, an international enterprise that specializes in medical tests and instruments that are increasingly important for human health. Many people knew Ziering because of his philanthropic generosity, but he was best known to me because he wrote a play, *The Judgment of Herbert Bierhoff.* As Ziering explains in the preface to the privately published script he completed in 1999, the play is based on Holocaust experiences, testimonies, and memories that "have stayed with me for these many years, usually buried in my subconscious, but surfacing from time to time, especially as I watched my children, and now my grandchildren, growing up." Ziering's play, which is based on actual events, emphasizes that the Holocaust's core included the destruction of Jewish families and homes, which were and are essential for the vitality of Jewish life.

German forces occupied the Baltic state of Latvia and Riga, its capital city, during the summer of 1941. With the help of local collaborators, the Germans had killed about 90 percent of the country's ninety-five thousand Jews by the end of that year, including most of the approximately thirty thousand Latvian Jews who were initially confined in the Riga ghetto. The clearing of that ghetto made its space available to concentrate Jews who were deported eastward from Germany and Austria during the winter of 1941–42. By November 1943, the Riga ghetto had been "liquidated" as part of Nazi Germany's genocidal campaign to make Europe *judenrein*—Jew-free.

Ziering's narrative about the Bierhoff family and about his own life reflects this history. The Bierhoffs—Herbert, Ruth, and their daughter, Ellen, who was not yet six in the early autumn of 1943—were German Jews. They were deported from Kassel, their hometown, to Riga on December 9, 1941. Until the early autumn of 1943, her parents had successfully hidden Ellen from the "selections" that were rapidly thinning the Riga ghetto's already reduced population as the Germans' collapsing eastern military front led them to kill the remaining Jews or to relocate those who could still be exploited as slave laborers. As an "unproductive" Jewish child, Ellen Bierhoff was worse than useless to the Germans in Riga during the autumn of 1943. Hiding was unlikely to save her life much longer. No deliverance awaited her family; instead, death was becoming a given—but in the interim, agonizing decisions about how to live needed to be made.

Ziering makes his audience consider the unbearable dilemmas that Nazi domination forced on the Bierhoff family. If that responsibility gives his audience almost more than it can bear, one can scarcely imagine what the actual ghetto circumstances must have been for Herbert, Ruth, and Ellen, their precious child. The cast of Ziering's play includes a survivor named David who sums up what happened. As a member of the Jewish ghetto police, Herbert Bierhoff knew that the Nazis were about to launch yet another *Aktion* to murder more of the Riga ghetto's diminished Jewish population. Ellen would surely fall into the brutal and murderous arms of Nazi strangers. Bierhoff would be unable to save her. He faced a decision that no parent should ever have to consider. Ellen's father, David tells us, "chose the only way open to him, the mercy killing of his beloved daughter, in order to avoid an infinitely more brutal killing by the SS."

Before Bierhoff gave his daughter the poison that killed her, he did what fathers often do. With reassuring words spoken to give a child comfort in her particular circumstances—"tomorrow you are going on a trip where you'll have many oranges, and all the food you can eat"—he said good night to Ellen. It was the last time he would do so. It was not even his fate to remember that night for long because when the Germans discovered what he had done to Ellen, they shot him dead. Meanwhile, Ruth survived her daughter and husband, but not the Holocaust. Her experiences in the Riga ghetto were too much to bear. As she lay dying, she charged Shimon, the Bierhoffs' friend, to find "competent judges who will declare that Herbert was merciful and right in giving Ellen the pill." Part of the Holocaust's oral testimony, this wrenching story came to Ziering, whose play and cast put Herbert Bierhoff's heartbreaking predicament before us.

Was Herbert Bierhoff merciful and right when he gave Ellen that pill? In the play, the survivor named David says yes. Kurt, another survivor, is not so sure. There was always the chance, somehow, that Ellen might survive. Stranger things happened in the Holocaust. Kurt also wonders why Ellen's father did not take his own life after he took hers. In addition, there is the question of whether Herbert Bierhoff should have consulted with Ruth, his wife, before he made the decision that he seems to have made alone. Esther, a third survivor, listens to David and Kurt. She feels the agony of the quandary, but she has fewer "answers" than the men. Rejecting closure, she emphasizes that the survivors should simply "record and tell in a factual way, without embellishments, our personal experiences and the events which we witnessed." Sigi Ziering gives the play's last word to Shimon, the survivor who seeks to fulfill Ruth Bierhoff's last wish. Herbert Bierhoff, says Shimon, "did the right thing." But then Shimon pauses and delivers the last line to the audience: "Or did he?" *The Judgment of Herbert Bierhoff* asks us to consider the judgment a Jewish father made and then to make a judgment about his decision. How can we accept this challenge? But how can we not respond to Shimon's hard question?

First and foremost, there is no closure, at least none that I can or should attempt to provide. If I jump to a conclusion, I do not allow the Bierhoffs' anguish to be fully expressed, for full expression requires not only a giving of testimony, but a receiving of it as well. Ziering's play tells an unsettled story. It is not for me to "settle" what should remain unsettling.

I acknowledge that Ellen, somehow, might have survived, but I also believe that Herbert Bierhoff acted out of love, driven by the desperate choice he faced. I do not say that he did the "right" thing, and certainly I do not say that he did a "good" thing. The words *right* and *good* can scarcely apply to the situation that the Bierhoff family faced, which was definitely not of their own choosing. However, I do say that Ellen's father acted out of fatherly love, determined to keep his daughter from falling into the hands of strangers hellbent on her destruction. As a Jewish father in the Riga ghetto during the autumn of 1943, committed to doing the best he could for his priceless daughter, Herbert Bierhoff may have had but one loving choice—choiceless though it was—once the option of poisoning his child to death presented itself in those unrelentingly brutal circumstances.

I wonder about Ruth. I tend to think that Herbert should have shared his intentions and obtained Ruth's consent, if not her help, in taking their daughter's life. But of that I am far less sure than of the moral fact that looms largest in Ziering's play. That fact does not pertain primarily to the decisions Jews had to make in the Riga ghetto, but to those decisions the Germans made in establishing that place and the murderous policies that governed the vast ghetto network of which Riga was only one part. Those decisions and policies were wrong—or nothing could be. Like virtually every chapter of the book you are reading now, Ziering's play focuses attention on the anguished dilemmas faced by countless ghettoized Jewish families during the Holocaust. Nevertheless, that focus, crucial though it is, will be misplaced unless it motivates post-Holocaust audiences to resist the ideologies and conditions, the leaders and followers, that may again bring about the home-destroying conditions that the Bierhoffs encountered in the Riga ghetto in the autumn of 1943 or that Adam Czerniakow confronted in the Warsaw ghetto in the summer of 1942.

People study the Holocaust because it happened, but not only for that reason. We study it, teach about it, and try to learn from it primarily for ethical reasons that are rooted in a deep longing for a safer and more humane world. That deep longing has everything to do with remembering, just as the remembering can change lives and encourage us to make the longing good. The remembering does that by leading us to encounter the details of the Holocaust. *Life in the Ghettos During the Holocaust* abounds in that particularity.

Study of the Holocaust, I believe, aims to give us good memories, which is a paradoxical statement that calls for explanation. Of course, I do not mean that the *content* of those memories is good. With the exception of the cases of rescue that were too few and far between, most of the content of Holocaust-related memories is bereft of goodness. In that sense, Holocaust scholar Lawrence Langer rightly reminds us that "there is nothing to be learned from a baby torn in two or a woman buried alive."[3] Nor do I mean that the "good" memories Holocaust study aims to create consist only of figures, dates, and facts, important though those details surely are in that it is through such detail, especially when we focus on what happened to particular people in specific places, that we are helped to learn from the Holocaust.

What I do mean is that as we learn about and from the Holocaust, our memories will become good in the sense that they will not let us forget what is most important. The Holocaust can and should make us see differently. In such a rapid manner and in such devastating ways, the Holocaust swept away good things—basic ones that every person needs, such as a home, safe and secure—that too often are taken utterly for granted. The Holocaust teaches that good judgment must be honed "at memory's edge," to borrow the title of James Young's fine book about Holocaust memorialization.[4] That edge is at the border between honest loss of memory and forgetting, on the one hand, and the distortion, falsification, and even denial of memory, on the other. Memory's edge must be kept sharp, clear, keen, alert, and true. Eric Sterling and the contributors to his book about the Holocaust's ghettos take significant steps in that direction. By helping to show how and why death was a given in those destructive places, they move us to inquire about the past and more. They put history in the service of humanity. By enabling us to consider life in the ghettos during the Holocaust, they also summon us to reconsider how to live in the time, the interim, that is ours.

Acknowledgments

An endeavor such as this book cannot be completed without the help of many wonderful people. I thank the contributors for sharing their hard work, their excellent essays, their experiences, and their dedication with me and with the readers of this volume. I also thank them for their patience. Perhaps the most gratifying aspect of editing this book has been the wonderful interactions and dialogues I have enjoyed with these colleagues throughout the United States and abroad.

I thank Ellen Goodman, acquisitions editor at Syracuse University Press, for her help in making this book a reality. I am grateful to her and the selection committee at Syracuse University Press for believing in this volume. I also thank Peter Webber and John Fruehwirth of the Press. I am grateful to Annie Barva for her outstanding editing of this book. Her skillful and meticulous editing greatly enhanced the book.

I thank Wendy Lower, Stephen Feinstein, and Charlotte Opfermann for sharing photographs and images with me and for helping me select which ones to include in the book. Leslie Swift of the Photo Archives of the United States Holocaust Memorial Museum was very helpful in making it possible for me to acquire photographs for the book. I also wish to thank John K. Roth for his encouragement and collegiality as I worked on this project. I am truly indebted to John for his assistance.

Fariba Deravi and the Auburn University Montgomery (AUM) Research Council have aided this project by awarding me an AUM Grant-in-Aid, which enabled me to conduct research at the United States Holocaust Memorial Museum in Washington, D.C. I thank them for their generosity and support.

I have greatly benefited from the expertise of the librarians and staff members at the AUM Library. Dean Rickey Best has done a wonderful job of ensuring that the library possesses a fine collection of books regarding the Holocaust. Barbara Dekle, Carolyn Johnson, Tim Bailey, and others helped me find the resources that I needed. Carolyn Johnson has helped me immensely over the years by acquiring sources through interlibrary loan that I needed for my own essay in the volume and for the editing of the other chapters. In all my years of academia, I have never seen someone so skillful at securing interlibrary loan materials and so dedicated to helping library patrons find the sources they need, no matter how obscure. I also thank Jeannette Lessels, who is always very helpful and very enthusiastic about assisting library patrons.

I thank the Pucker Gallery for permission to include the image of Samuel Bak's *Ghetto*; the Los Angeles Museum of the Holocaust for permission to use Eli Leskley's image *Jewish Antisemitism in the Ghetto*; the United States Holocaust Memorial Museum for permission to reproduce the eight photographs that appear in the book; the Penguin Group for permission to include in chapter 12 sections from *Łódź Ghetto: Inside a Community under Siege,* edited by Alan Adelson and Robert Lapides; award-winning Israeli playwright Joshua Sobol for his very kind permission to include excerpts from my interview with him, as well as quotations from his play *Ghetto*; James R. Ross for permission to include his revised excerpts from *Escape to Shanghai*; and Brooklyn Films for permission to quote from Michael Berenbaum's interview with Marek Edelman and Simcha Rotem, which appeared in the documentary *Uprising* (2001). I also thank Ben Giladi, a survivor of Piotrków, for providing me with the Polish names of the streets and for permission to use the Piotrków ghetto map, which I received from him and William Samelson.

I am fortunate to have a superb and very supportive department head, Alan Gribben, who has helped me a great deal and who answered adeptly and patiently my many questions over the course of this project. Alan is an outstanding administrator, a great teacher, and a great friend. I also thank dear friends in the Department of English and Philosophy who have helped me much more than they realize: Joe Crowley, Anne Little, Jeff Melton, and David Walker. I have also benefited greatly from wonderful conversations about photos and images of the Holocaust with Craig Sheldon, whose vast knowledge and intellectual curiosity are inspirational. Several AUM faculty members tendered guidance, including Vice Chancellor Roger A. Ritvo (himself a Holocaust scholar) and Assistant Vice Chancellor Judd Katz.

I owe a great debt to my dear friends Bob Evans and Ruth Evans, the godparents of my children and the most wonderful people I have ever met. They have added so much to the lives of the members of the Sterling family, and they mean a great deal to us. In addition, Bob answered many of my questions concerning the editing of this book and made helpful suggestions regarding my essay on Joshua Sobol's play *Ghetto.*

My thanks also go to my brother, Sheldon; his wife, Michelle; and Brian and Marcy.

I thank my wonderful wife, Jill, and my two magnificent children, Scott and Sarah, for their love and support. I also appreciate their understanding during the many hours I needed to be alone in my office, working on this book.

I thank my terrific grandmother, Carla Kamm, who has always shown much love for and confidence in me. She also shared with me the story of my maternal grandfather, Gunter Kamm, who was interned for a month in Buchenwald but was fortunate enough to escape Germany and subsequently live in the Hongkew ghetto in Shanghai. When Gunter was taken to Buchenwald, my grandmother (Irene) left my mother (who was approximately eleven months old) with a nurse and went to Berlin, where she obtained a visa to Manila for the family. Armed with the visa, she was fortunate enough to obtain my grandfather's release from Buchenwald, with the understanding that upon his deliverance he would leave Germany immediately. Irene then found that while she was in Berlin, my mother and her nurse had been placed in a prison because the house where they were living had been identified as one belonging to Jews; my grandmother was able to obtain their release with the help of a bribe. Finding upon Gunter's release from Buchenwald that they were unable to use the visa to Manila, Gunter and Irene, along with my mother (also my paternal great-grandparents, Isadore and Julia, and my maternal great-grandfather Herman—Herman's wife, Lydia, had already died) escaped Germany by sailing to Shanghai, the only place in the world that would accept them. Although

I had already reached the age of fourteen when Gunter died, my grandfather perhaps felt too scarred by his experiences during the Holocaust to share them with his grandson. Furthermore, for many years, Gunter Kamm, in his capacity as the director of the United Restitution Organization (URO) in New York, had listened to the painful and horrific stories of Holocaust survivors. The URO provides legal help to Holocaust survivors in their claims against Germany. My grandfather's experiences have inspired me to write about the Holocaust.

Finally, I wish to thank my parents for their love and support. It is to my late grandfather Gunter, to my grandmother Carla, and to my parents that I dedicate this book.

Contributors

Michael Berenbaum is a writer, lecturer, and teacher consulting in the conceptual development of museums and the historical development of films. He served as president and chief executive officer of the Survivors of the Shoah Visual History Foundation and as director of the United States Holocaust Research Institute at the United States Holocaust Memorial Museum. From 1988 to 1993, he served as project director of the museum, overseeing its creation. He is the author and editor of twelve books, including *The World Must Know* (1993), and is an adjunct professor of theology at the Academy of Jewish Religion.

Deirdre Burke is a senior lecturer in religious studies at the University of Wolverhampton. She spent many years teaching religious education in schools in England and has a strong commitment to exploring religious issues with students. She earned her Ph.D. in 1998, with a dissertation entitled "Holocaust Education: Teacher and Learner Perspectives," and she has continued to research religious, ethical, and pedagogical issues in relation to the Holocaust.

Tim Cole teaches history at the University of Bristol, United Kingdom, where he coordinates the master's program in contemporary history. He is the author of *Selling the Holocaust* (1999) and *Holocaust City: The Making of a Jewish Ghetto* (2003). He is currently writing a social history of the Holocaust in Hungary.

Daniel Feierstein is a faculty member at the University of Buenos Aires and the National University "Tres de Febrero" of Argentina. He has published widely on the Holocaust. In particular, he focuses on resistance in the ghettos, sociology of the camps, and the comparison between different genocidal processes. He was the executive director of the National Institute Against Discrimination, Xenophobia, and Racism. He is one of the very few Holocaust scholars working south of the Rio Grande and is one of the first scholars to study Nazi documents stored in Argentina.

Stephen C. Feinstein received his Ph.D. in Russian and European history from New York University in 1971 and taught at the University of Wisconsin, River Falls, for thirty years, where he is now professor emeritus. He is the director of the Center for Holocaust and Genocide Studies at the University of Minnesota. His publications include *Witness and Legacy: Contemporary Art about the Holocaust* (editor, 1994, rev. ed. 2000); "Mediums of Memory: Artistic Responses of the Second Generation," in *Breaking Crystal,* edited by Efraim Sicher (1997); *Confronting the Holocaust: A Mandate for the 21st Century—Proceedings of the 27th Annual (1996) Scholars Conference on the German Churches and the Holocaust* (coeditor, 1998); "Art after Auschwitz," in *Problems Unique to the Holocaust,* edited by Harry James Cargas (1999).

Lawrence H. Feldman, born in New York City in November 1942, earned his Ph.D. in anthropology from Pennsylvania State University in 1971. He taught at Gettysburg College in 1972 and the University of Missouri from 1973 to 1984. Since 1984, he has been freelancing in Europe, North Africa, and Central America, with an emphasis on the southern Maya highlands. His emphasis has been on the Szinca people of southeast Guatemala in the colonial era, but he also works on other projects, including the escape of Jews through Spain during the Holocaust.

Susie Jans-Thomas is a professor of education at Mount Mary College in Milwaukee, Wisconsin. She has designed a series of graduate courses around the theme of oppression, using literature as the basis for instruction. The courses include: "Remembering the Holocaust Through Literature," "Women of the Holocaust," "Holocaust Survivors' Stories," "Literature of the Holocaust," "Censorship," "Civil Rights," and "From Camelot to Chaos: The Upheaval of the 1960s." In addition to her teaching and work with student teachers, she serves as the book review editor of the *Journal for the Wisconsin Council for Social Studies.*

Agnes Kadar, professor emerita of State University of New York, Nassau Community College, Garden City, New York, is a survivor of the Budapest ghetto. Most of her family perished in the Holocaust. She immigrated to the United States in 1957 and earned a master of science degree from New York University in 1966. She taught at various colleges within the State University of New York system, for twenty-nine years at Nassau Community College. She received the Chancellor's Award for Excellence in Teaching in 1998. Since retirement, she has presented a paper at the Twenty-ninth Annual Scholars' Conference on the Holocaust and the Churches about the history of the Budapest ghettos and at the Holocaust Memorial and Educational Center of Nassau County Teachers Conference about scientific principles used to justify the Holocaust.

Alexander Kimel was born in a little shtetl called Podhajce in eastern Poland. His childhood was saturated with intensive schooling: heder, Hebrew school, Polish public school. He survived the Holocaust in the small town of Rohatyn. Facing the violence, deprivation, and hunger, he matured very quickly. In his eyes, the whole community was torn to pieces and eradicated. Out of ten thousand Jews there, one hundred survived. Although he faced many dangerous moments in the ghetto, his most memorable was hiding for two months, without food or water, undetected in a German Military Police compound. After the liberation, he entered the "civilized" world and concentrated on getting an education. After many years of struggles, he graduated with a master's degree in electrical engineering, moved to Israel and later to the United States, where he worked as a consulting engineer.

Wendy Lower received her Ph.D. from American University, Washington, D.C. She has taught and lectured on the Holocaust at Georgetown University, the University of Vermont, the University of Konstanz (Germany), and the United States Holocaust Memorial Museum. In 2002, Lower's research on the Holocaust in Zhytomyr, Ukraine, appeared in the journals *German Studies Review* and *Holocaust and Genocide Studies.* Her monograph *Nazi Empire-Building and the Holocaust in the Ukraine, 1941–1944* will appear in 2005, and she is editing an essay collection, *The Holocaust in Ukraine.* Dr. Lower was the director of the Visiting Scholars Division, Center for Advanced Holocaust Studies, United States Holocaust Memorial Museum, and is currently assistant professor of history at Towson University, Maryland.

Charlotte Guthmann Opfermann survived twelve years of Nazi persecution, more than two years of which she spent imprisoned in ghettos and concentration camps. After many years in Texas, writing and teaching about World War II, in particular the Holocaust and its effects on our lives, Charlotte died on November 22, 2004.

David Patterson holds the Bornblum Chair in Judaic Studies at the University of Memphis. He has published more than ninety journal articles. A winner of the Koret Jewish Book Award, Dr. Patterson has written numerous books, including *In Dialogue and Dilemma with Elie Wiesel* (1991), *The Shriek of Silence* (1992), *Pilgrimage of a Proselyte* (1993), *Exile* (1995), *When Learned Men Murder* (1996), *Greatest Jewish Stories* (1997), *Sun Turned to Darkness* (1998), and *Along the Edge of Annihilation* (1999). He is coeditor of the *Encyclopedia of Holocaust Literature* (2001) and translator of *The Complete Black Book of Russian Jewry* (2003).

Diane Plotkin has been an adjunct professor of Holocaust studies and world literature at Brookhaven College for the past nineteen years. Her publications include *Sisters in Sorrow: Voices of Care in the Holocaust* (1998); "Medicine Fifty Years after Nuremberg," in *Problems Unique to the Holocaust,* edited by Harry James Cargas (1999); and "So I Won't Forget . . . From the Memoirs of Ellen Loeb," in *The Pall of the Past: The Holocaust, Genocide, and the 21st Century,* edited by Marilyn F. Nefsky (2000). She has presented papers at the Annual Scholars Conference on the Holocaust and the Churches, at an international meeting of Holocaust scholars at the Yidisher Visenshaftlikher Institut (YIVO, Institute for Jewish Research), and at an International Scholars Conference in Kraków.

James R. Ross is an associate professor of journalism and one of the founders of the Jewish studies program at Northeastern University in Boston. He has served as a visiting professor at Shanghai International Studies University and as a Fulbright professor in Ecuador. He is the author of three books, *Caught in a Tornado: A Chinese-American Woman Survives* *the Cultural Revolution* (1994), *Escape to Shanghai: A Jewish Community in China* (1994), and *Fragile Branches: Travels Through the Jewish Diaspora* (2000).

John K. Roth is the Russell K. Pitzer Professor of Philosophy at Claremont McKenna College, where he has taught since 1966. In addition to service on the U.S. Holocaust Memorial Council and on the editorial board for the journal *Holocaust and Genocide Studies,* he has published hundreds of articles and reviews and more than thirty books, including *Approaches to Auschwitz* (with Richard L. Rubenstein, 1987), *Different Voices: Women and the Holocaust* (with Carol Rittner, 1993), *Ethics after the Holocaust* (1999), and *Holocaust Politics* (2001). In 1988, Roth was named U.S. National Professor of the Year by the Council for Advancement and Support of Education and the Carnegie Foundation for the Advancement of Teaching.

Stephen A. Sadow is a professor of modern languages at Northeastern University in Boston. In 1999, his *King David's Harp: Autobiographical Essays by Jewish Latin American Writers* (1999) was awarded the National Jewish Book Award. He is the translator of Ricardo Feierstein's *Mestizo—A Novel* (2000) and, with J. Kates, of poetry by Feierstein, Ce'sar Tiempo, Isaac Goldemberg, Teodoro Ducach, and Angelina Muniz-Huberman.

William Samelson was born in Poland and lived there until the age of eleven, when he was interned in various Nazi labor and concentration camps throughout Poland and Germany for the duration of World War II. He is visiting professor of Holocaust and genocide studies at the University of Texas at San Antonio. Dr. Samelson has written extensively on the Holocaust and lectured widely on a variety of topics. Among his many publications are the memoirs *All Lie in Wait* (1969) and *One Bridge to Life* (1989). His latest work, *Warning and Hope* (2003), is a concise history of the Holocaust.

Eric J. Sterling (Ph.D., Indiana University) is Distinguished Research Professor at Auburn University Montgomery (in Montgomery, Alabama). His publications include articles on Arthur Miller's *Incident at Vichy* in *Publications of the Arkansas Philological Association* (1994); Shimon Wincelberg's *Resort 76* in *Literature and Ethnic Discrimination,* edited by Michael J. Meyer

(1997); Joshua Sobol's *Adam* and the death of Vilna resistance hero Yitzhak Wittenberg in *Resisting the Holocaust,* edited by Ruby Rohrlich (1998); bystanders as accomplices in *Moral Problems Unique to the Holocaust,* edited by Harry James Cargas (1999); Denise Levertov's "During the Eichmann Trial," in *Denise Levertov: New Perspectives,* edited by Anne Little and Susie Paul (2000); Peter Barnes's *Auschwitz,* in *European Studies Journal* (2000–2001); and Diane Samuels's *Kindertransport,* in *Children and War,* edited by James Marten (2002). His essay on Martin Sherman's *Bent* and homosexuals during the Holocaust, in *Journal of European Studies* (2002), won the Association of College English Teachers of Alabama's Calvert Award for best paper by an English faculty member in Alabama and the University of Wyoming's Amy and Eric Burger Award for best essay on drama and theater.

Introduction

ERIC J. STERLING

Although many books have appeared in print concerning the concentration camps during the Holocaust, far less has been published about the ghettos. A book-length study of the ghettos is also important because Jews were confined in them during a pivotal time in their lives—the intermediate period between normal life and the agony they experienced in the concentration camps, between hope and despair, between life and death. The Nazis created the ghettos as part of their plan for the destruction of world Jewry. The ghettos played an instrumental role in their "Final Solution" because by enclosing the Jews within small, confined locations, they were able to control and monitor the Jews and subsequently to deport them to the concentration camps in an organized and methodical way.

By imprisoning and isolating the Jews in ghettos, the Nazis could also freely plunder their homes and strip them of their material wealth. This enclosure and isolation, furthermore, affected "Aryan" public opinion concerning Jews: it was easier for Nazi propaganda and ideology to convince ordinary "Aryan" citizens that Jews were evil and thus deserving of their removal from society. The Nazis were also able to treat the Jews more harshly because the general public did not encounter any Jews while conducting their everyday activities in shops, streets, schools, and apartment buildings. Public sympathy for Jews therefore waned, for there were no Jews living near Gentiles to contradict the anti-Semitic propaganda that the Nazis spread. The removal of Jews to the ghettos from ordinary society also appealed to some Gentiles because it opened up more job and housing opportunities for them; in other words, some people did not object to the ghettoization of Jews because the process helped them socioeconomically.

Before the Holocaust began, Jews had, of course, no conception of the unprecedented horror that would occur; they lived, for the most part, autonomously and peacefully. Jews in eastern Europe dwelled primarily in an unassimilated manner, whereas Jews in western Europe were more mainstreamed into the dominant culture. Although discrimination and anti-Semitism existed before the Nazis seized power in Germany, the problems were obviously quite minor compared to the atrocities that occurred during the Holocaust. European Jews thus enjoyed freedom and autonomy before the Holocaust, in marked contrast to when they were imprisoned in the concentration camps and existed under the complete control of the Nazi guards, who starved them, worked them to death, and murdered them arbitrarily—with impunity. But in between these two radically demarcated types of life—freedom and imprisonment—there existed a transitional life in the ghettos, where many Jews maintained their hope, their faith, and their culture while enduring harsh and atrocious conditions.

The Jews lived in a paradoxical world: they enjoyed some control over their lives via the Judenrat (Jewish Council) and the Jewish police, yet suffered helplessly under the Nazi regime's tyranny. Food was quite scarce in many of the ghettos (in Warsaw, Vilna, Kovno, Budapest, and Łódź—the complete list is, of course, quite numerous), but living conditions there were still far better than in the concentration camps, where the Nazis deported the Jews after liquidating the ghettos. Hospitals existed in ghettos in order to heal the sick and to preserve lives; in the concentration camps such as Dachau, in contrast, the hospitals were often used for medical experimentation on healthy Jews: the purpose of the concentration camp hospitals was sometimes not to treat patients or to learn from them, but simply to torture them, as was the case with the sadistic doctor Josef Mengele in Auschwitz. The Bialystok ghetto contained a gynecological clinic, yet obviously no such clinic existed in the concentration camps because the male and female prisoners were separated, and pregnancy (some women entered the camps pregnant) usually led to death for both mother and baby. The hard work in the factories that people in the Łódź ghetto thought would allow them ultimately to preserve their lives and achieve their freedom was replaced in Auschwitz by the haunting and sadistically ironic phrase on the gates: *Arbeit Macht Frei*—"Work will make you free." In the Hongkew ghetto in Shanghai, created by the Japanese most probably upon the Nazis' demand, the Jews possessed the freedom to leave the ghetto in order to work, yet they were nonetheless at the mercy of Kanoh Ghoya and Subinspector Okura, mercurial and cruel Japanese officials who administered the pass program—or did not, depending on their mood that day. Ernest G. Heppner remarks that Ghoya sometimes slapped Jews who applied for job passes, and Okura occasionally threw ghetto inhabitants into lice-filled prison cells (lice sometimes infected with typhus) when they requested job permits.[1] Despite the manifold hardships, life in the Shanghai ghetto was still far superior, of course, to the fate that would have awaited those who had not escaped to Shanghai from Germany. Life in the ghettos, therefore, though often wretched, was preferable to life in the camps.

Many of the Jews in the ghettos had not heard about the dangers of Auschwitz and the other camps; others, such as members of the Judenrat in Vilna, had heard of the terrors but refused to believe them, perhaps because they incorrectly deemed that cultured people were incapable of inflicting such atrocities on their fellow human beings.[2] Because most Jews either had not heard or had failed to believe the veracity of the stories of the atrocities—horrors in store for some of them—they often felt hopeful about their future. In the ghettos, Jews often looked toward the future, anticipating, in Łódź and Vilna for instance, that they would be rescued by the Russian army arriving from eastern Europe. Consequently, they actively maintained their culture. Otto Dov Kulka observes that Theresienstadt, a ghetto in the northwestern section of Czechoslovakia, housed many artists and writers, which resulted in an abundance of Jewish "cultural activities, with several orchestras, an opera, a theater troupe, and both light and satiric cabarets. Lectures and seminars were held, and a sixty-thousand-volume library was established, with special emphasis on Jewish subjects. For many, this library provided their first opportunity to gain an understanding of their Jewish identity."[3] Shanghai became a significant harbor for European Jewish refugees, who established schools, a theater, and newspapers after their arrival. In Vilna, Lithuania, Herman Kruk opened a library almost immediately upon the creation of the ghetto. According to Yitzhak Arad, the ghetto library began in September 1941 with forty-five thousand volumes, but by December 1942 had lent one hundred thousand books.[4] The ghetto theater was packed with patrons every night. Schools created within the ghetto taught the children. The Jews in the Vilna ghetto dreamed of better times; these dreams would cease when the ghetto was liquidated by Gestapo officer Bruno Kittel—after he discovered the existence of an organized resistance group—and the Jews were deported.

Armed resistance, although extremely rare in the concentration camps, occurred in several ghettos; the difference concerned a degree of autonomy that Jews enjoyed to some extent in the ghettos but not in the camps. Jews in the Warsaw ghetto rebelled against the Nazis on April 19, 1943, primarily using pistols and grenades that they had acquired from underground Polish military organizations.[5] The fact of the Warsaw Ghetto Uprising subverts the misconception that during the Holocaust Jews went meekly to their deaths without a struggle. From April 19 to May 16, 1943, the Warsaw ghetto inhabitants held their ground against Nazi forces despite being at a great disadvantage in terms of manpower, ammunition, and military experience. The Jewish fighters' valor and initial success shamed and embarrassed the Nazis while forcing them to expend ammunition and manpower, both in short supply, to quell the uprising. The revolt, furthermore, preoccupied the soldiers, preventing them for several weeks from going elsewhere to round up and murder other Jews.

It is not widely known that the Warsaw Ghetto Uprising was influenced in part by the United Partisan Organization (UPO), also known as the Fareynegte Partizaner Organizatskye (FPO), in Vilna. Jews in Vilna smuggled weapons into the ghetto as they prepared for an armed uprising. According to Abraham Foxman, the Jews in the Vilna ghetto, primarily those who worked in the German ammunition factory and depot in Burbiszki, smuggled in "fifty machine guns, fifty grenades, thirty revolvers, a few rifles, and a few thousand bullets."[6] As the Jews in Vilna prepared for their rebellion, couriers (such as Henryk Grabowski) traveling between Warsaw and Vilna informed the Jews in Warsaw about the massacres at

Ponar and about the UPO in order to convince them to revolt as well; when people living in the Warsaw ghetto learned that tens of thousands of Vilna Jews had been murdered in the Ponar mountains during the summer of 1941 (Yehuda Bauer claims that forty thousand were slain),[7] they feared for their own safety, which is one of the reasons why they decided to organize their own resistance. The fact that the Vilna Jews could slip in and out of the ghetto and smuggle in weapons manifests that some autonomy did in fact exist in the ghetto.

The UPO spent nineteen months in preparation for the rebellion in Vilna, gathering weapons and planning their attack, but the plan disintegrated before being carried out when Kittel, a specialist in liquidating ghettos, learned about the organization and arrested its leader, Yitzhak Wittenberg, at the home of ghetto leader Jacob Gens. A significant distinction between the outcome of the resistance in the Warsaw and Vilna ghettos is that in the former ghetto, the resistance supplanted the Judenrat and the Jewish police, but in the latter the Judenrat and police subdued and helped to destroy the resistance movement.

The Judenrat, the governing body consisting of prominent men within the Jewish community, played a significant role in ghetto life. It exemplified the conflicting and ambiguous situation that existed in the ghettos in terms of political autonomy: it provided a semblance of self-governance. The Jews lacked the freedom of self-government that they had enjoyed in their communities before the Holocaust, but at least the Judenrat, along with the Jewish ghetto police, allowed them to maintain limited authority and power over their lives. Judenrat leaders such as Mordechai Chaim Rumkowski (Łódź); Jacob Gens (Vilna); Efraim Barasz (Bialystok); Jacob Edelstein, Paul Eppstein, and Rabbi Benjamin Murmelstein (Theresienstadt); and Adam Czerniakow (Warsaw) enacted some ghetto policies such as food rationing, but in other respects they proved to be mere figureheads controlled by the Nazis. When Nazi officials demanded selections, requiring primarily the young, the elderly, and the infirm to be deported to the concentration camps, the Judenrat leaders were powerless and could not refuse the demands. Rumkowski, Barasz, and Gens reluctantly handed over Jews from their ghettos, knowing full well the fate that awaited these constituents. Isaiah Trunk observes that the

Nazi authorities "forced the Councils to make all the preliminary preparations for 'resettlements' on their behalf. . . . Beset by the impending ordeal, a sizable number of Councils fearfully came to the conclusion that since not all the Jews could be saved, it was better to deliver to the Nazi Moloch those ghetto dwellers with little or no chance of survival in order to save others."[8] Czerniakow, contrariwise, decided that he would not participate in these selections and have Jewish blood on his hands; he committed suicide. Warsaw ghetto victim Chaim A. Kaplan remarked that by refusing to sign the deportation decree, Czerniakow "perpetuated his name by his death more than by his life. His end proves conclusively that he worked and strove for the good of his people, that he wanted its welfare and continuity even though not everything done in his name was praiseworthy."[9] Although Czerniakow's suicide may be considered noble and selfless, it nonetheless failed to ameliorate the desperate situation, thus demonstrating his powerlessness.

The ambivalence surrounding the Judenrat (its members' power or powerlessness and their relationship with their ghetto constituents) can perhaps best be exemplified by a brief discussion of Łódź chairman Mordechai Rumkowski. Rumkowski has earned a mixed reception from survivors of the Łódź ghetto as well as from historians. Even those who hated him admitted that he skillfully organized and ran the ghetto factories. Some admire Rumkowski for his diligence and valiant attempts to save the lives of Jews who survived the selections imposed by the Nazis. Rumkowski supporters laud him for trying to save those who worked in the factories, even though he saved some lives at the expense of others; they assert that if the Jewish leader had not agreed to Nazi demands for selections, the ghetto would have been liquidated immediately. In a speech to the inhabitants of the Łódź ghetto on September 4, 1942, Rumkowski remarked:

> The ghetto has been dealt a grievous blow. They [the Nazis] demand that we give them that which is most precious to it—the children and old people. I was never privileged to have a child of my own, and therefore I devoted my best years to children. I lived and breathed together with the children. I never imagined that my own hand would have to bring the

> sacrifice to the altar. In my old age I am compelled to stretch out my hand and beg: "My brothers and my sisters, give them to me! Fathers and mothers, give me your children." . . . Yesterday I was ordered to deport more than twenty thousand people from the ghetto; otherwise, I was told, "We'll do it ourselves." . . . I must carry out the grim, bloody surgery, I must amputate limbs to save the body! I must take away children, and if I do not, others too may be taken. (Piteous wailing erupts).[10]

Rumkowski agreed to relinquish the Jewish children to the Nazis even though it was generally accepted that he loved children (before his appointment as ghetto leader, he presided over an orphanage in Helenowek). The Łódź ghetto, which existed for four and one-half years, was not liquidated until August 30, 1944, surviving longer than any other ghetto during the Holocaust; this fact is especially noteworthy when one considers the food shortages and the unsanitary conditions that led to a typhus epidemic. Furthermore, some believe that if the Russian army had made its way to Łódź several months earlier, many Jews would have been rescued and Rumkowski might have been considered a hero. These supporters also maintain that Rumkowski possessed only limited power and did all that he could to save lives, but that he was forced to adhere to Nazi demands in order to prevent the liquidation of the ghetto.

Rumkowski's critics, however, paint a markedly different picture of the Jewish leader, calling attention to his pride, selfishness, and illusions of grandeur; for instance, he arranged for the ghetto currency and postage to bear his picture, and he rode throughout the ghetto while sitting in his horse-drawn carriage and wearing his black boots (which resembled those worn by Gestapo officers). Lucille Eichengreen, who knew the Judenrat leader and lived in the Łódź ghetto, describes Rumkowski as a sinister megalomaniac in her biography of the man, entitled *Rumkowski and the Orphans of Łódź*. She portrays Rumkowski as a corrupt man who ruled over the ghetto while drunk with power and possessing a vengeful streak. Those who angered Rumkowski or questioned his authority were expeditiously deported by the Nazis to the death camps. Furthermore, Eichengreen quotes several ghetto inhabitants and speaks from personal experience to prove that Rumkowski was unquestionably an insatiable sexual predator—

a pedophile who regularly molested the girls in the orphanage and in the ghetto. In fact, an investigation of Rumkowski's frequent sexual molestations of girls in the orphanage was under way when the war began and the Nazis, for reasons still unknown, selected him as ghetto leader. Eichengreen also observes how the Jews disdained Rumkowski for the selections:

> When he was through [with the aforementioned speech], Rumkowski was pelted with stones as he passed by in his horse-drawn carriage. . . . He had made it only too clear that he would cooperate with the Germans for the sake of "the ghetto's good." The Jews of Łódź repeated his words with anger, to no effect. . . . He had asked us to cooperate with the Germans, and he had asked us to surrender our aged and our young—but these "requests" were beyond the reach of understanding. We seethed in outrage, but we did not revolt. Incomprehensible as it may seem, no one dared oppose Rumkowski.[11]

Rumkowski's decision to agree to the selections violates the words of Maimonides in the Mishnah Torah: "if pagans should tell them [the Jews], 'Give us one of yours and we shall kill him, otherwise we shall kill all of you,' they all should be killed and not a single Jewish soul should be delivered."[12]

Complicity is another controversial issue regarding ghetto life. One must remember that times were desperate, which led some Jews who had heretofore conducted their lives in a benevolent and honorable fashion to act in a selfish and egocentric manner. But if one was not there, one must take into account the circumstances before judging the people—or judging at all. Some Jews attempted to save their own lives and the lives of their family members by aiding the Nazis. In *Am I a Murderer?* Calel Perochodnik details his life as a ghetto policeman in Otwock, Poland; he reluctantly joined because he heard that those Jews who became policemen and helped the Nazis with the deportations would have their families spared.[13] Some Łódź ghetto survivors and historians accuse Rumkowski of being an accomplice because he insisted that the Jews manufacture various materials, including military equipment, for the Nazi war effort. Rumkowski has also been accused of permitting the deportations so that he and his wife could be saved; he was spared until the end, riding on the last railcar that left Łódź for Auschwitz. In Auschwitz, he was murdered—not by Nazi guards, but rather by a Jew from the Łódź ghetto who detested him for being an accomplice.

The essays in this book consist of personal accounts by eyewitnesses and scholarly accounts of life conditions, struggles to maintain one's faith under unprecedented adversity, and armed resistance. The book covers a multitude of locations, which is crucial, for life in the ghettos during the Holocaust varied markedly because conditions differed from one ghetto to another and according to different stages of a particular ghetto's existence. In the Vilna ghetto in Lithuania, for instance, life changed dramatically after the capture and murder of Yitzhak Wittenberg and the concomitant disbanding of the UPO. Because of the marked distinctions between ghettos, this book attempts to include various types of essays, although no one book, of course, can completely cover all aspects of life in every ghetto.

Life in the Ghettos During the Holocaust begins with John K. Roth's poignant foreword in which he relates the moving story of Herbert Bierhoff, a Jew living in the Riga ghetto who loved his daughter so much that he poisoned her so that she would not be mercilessly tortured and murdered by the Nazis. Roth employs this story in response to a statement deriving from Michael Berenbaum's essay: "Death was a given. How to live in the interim was not." The essay contributions to this book initiate with narrations by eyewitnesses—survivors themselves. William Samelson's essay concerning the Piotrków ghetto describes life in the first ghetto set up in Nazi-occupied Europe; Samelson's account of what happened to his family and what he witnessed in Piotrków is descriptive, trenchant, and comprehensive. Michael Berenbaum's essay concerns decisions made during the Warsaw Ghetto Uprising and includes significant discussions with uprising survivors Marek Edelman and Simcha Rotem. Charlotte Opfermann's contribution relates her eyewitness account of life in Theresienstadt, including the infamous Red Cross visit to the Theresienstadt ghetto; she also tells of her reactions when she revisited Theresienstadt in 1993. Alexander Kimel's autobiographical account of his life in the ghetto is riveting and powerful; he relates how he survived the Rohatyn ghetto in Poland. Agnes Kadar describes the historical and political situations that led to the construction of the ghettos in Hungary and provides several moving interviews of people who survived ghetto life in Hungary. The contribution by Lawrence H. Feldman consists of an interview of a Polish man who lived in the Warsaw ghetto until July 1942. The interview derives from the files of the U.S. Organization for Strategic Services (OSS).

James R. Ross writes of conditions in the Hongkew ghetto in Shanghai, providing an account of life in the ghetto during the Holocaust; this essay serves a significant role in the book because it is the only article about a ghetto outside of Europe, and it is important that readers realize that Hitler's victims suffered in places other than Europe and that the effect of Nazi terror reverberated throughout the world. Thousands of Jews escaped to Shanghai in order to save their lives; it became a haven to Jews who fled from Hitler because it was at one point the only place where Jewish refugees could gain entry without a visa. The Hongkew ghetto has special meaning to me because my mother and her family survived the Holocaust by gaining entry into Shanghai from Nazi Germany (please see the acknowledgments for the story of how my grandmother obtained the release of my mother from a German prison and of my grandfather from Buchenwald).

Diane Plotkin's essay focuses on smuggling in the ghetto; smuggling was, of course, an integral aspect of ghetto life because of the food shortages prevalent during the Holocaust. Her essay also contains interviews of three survivors of different ghettos. Historian Wendy Lower, formerly of the United States Holocaust Memorial Museum and now a professor at Towson University, delineates the different stages of ghettoization in Ukraine from 1941 to 1942; readers will learn how the ghettos in Ukraine differed from others during the Holocaust. Tim Cole's contribution concerns life conditions in the Hungarian ghettos; his work describes, for instance, housing problems Jews encountered during their ghettoization and forced relocations. David Patterson's contribution concerns the theme of death in the ghetto; Dr. Patterson's passionate and moving essay treats death not only with regard to the physical loss of life but also with regard to Judaic law. Deirdre Burke also writes about death in the ghettos, but from another perspective. She discusses death rituals, the recording of deaths, and other aspects of death in the ghettos, using a more historical and less spiritual approach than Patterson does. Stephen C. Feinstein's essay focuses on art during the Holocaust. Discussing objects such as the design of postage stamps in Łódź, Feinstein provides the reader with a profound sense of cultural artifacts in the ghettos. Daniel Feierstein's essay concerns Jewish resistance in the ghettos—a significant but sometimes overlooked part of Jewish activity during the Shoah; Feierstein shows that Jewish groups were in fact quite active in resistance movements. My own essay portrays life in the Vilna ghetto, including the political situation involving Jacob Gens, the collaboration of Mr. Weiskopf (the tailor who controlled the clothing factories), the desire to maintain Jewish culture through theater, and, ultimately, the liquidation of the ghetto. The essay focuses on Joshua Sobol's drama *Ghetto* but also includes documented history. Susie Jans-Thomas's essay focuses on her experiences at Mount Mary College in Milwaukee in teaching other instructors how to teach their own students about the ghettos. She discusses her methodology, which employs Tadeusz Pankiewicz's *The Cracow Ghetto Pharmacy.* Her contribution is significant to the book because many instructors want to know more about how to teach students about the Holocaust in an effective manner; the article is also important because as survivors grow older, there is a greater need to teach younger generations about the Holocaust so that decades and centuries from now people will remember and say, "Never again."

Life in the Ghettos During the Holocaust

1. Piotrków Trybunalski

My Ancestral Home

WILLIAM SAMELSON

The Germans began their invasion of Poland on September 1, 1939. They entered Piotrków Trybunalski on September 5 of the same year. Although it was only the first week of the Nazi invasion of Poland, the invaders set fires to the homes in the predominantly Jewish section of the city and shot dead those Jews who tried to escape the fire. This act indicated what events were to come and put fear into the hearts of the Piotrków Jews. All of Poland was occupied by Hitler's minions within the month of September, the fall of its capital Warszawa (Warsaw) occurring at the end of that month.

In accordance with Reinhard Heydrich's orders, toward the end of October 1939, the second month of the Third Reich's occupation of Poland, the Piotrków ghetto was established. It was the first ghetto in the Nazi-occupied territories of Europe. Without warning, the Nazis accomplished the deed during the night. When a major portion of Piotrków's Jewry awoke from their uneasy sleep, they found themselves encircled by multiple bales of heavy barbed wire. The Jewish section of the town was designated as ghetto territory, and its periphery was guarded by surrogate Schutzstaffel (SS) sentries of Lithuanian, Ukrainian, Latvian, and Estonian origin. All Jews who lived outside the ghetto area had been forced to leave their homes and move into the ghetto. The huge and rapid changes this entailed is reflected in the following table, which shows Piotrków Trybunalski street names before, during, and after the German occupation.

Original Polish Names	German Occupation Names	Current Polish Names
Litewska	Litaurschestrasse	Litewska
Wschodnia	Ostlandstrasse	Pitsudskiego
Zamkowa	Schlossgasse	Zamkowa
Staro-Warszawska	Alte-Warschauerstrasse	Staro-Warszawska
Garncarska	Topfergasse	Garncarska
Jerozolimska	Jerusalemstrasse	Jerozolimska
Nadrowy	Grabenstrasse	No longer exists
Szpitalna	Lillenstrasse	Szpitalna
Zamurowa	Mauerstrasse	Zamurowa
Plac Lipowy	Linden Platz	No longer exists
Plac Zydowski	Judenplatz	Plac Czarníeckiego
Rycerska	Ritterstrasse	Rycerska
Pereca	Feuchte-gasse	Pereca
Swinski Rynek	Schweine Mark	Swinski Rynek

Source: Thanks to Ben Giladi for the original and current Polish street names.

Toward the end of October 1939, the Germans, in their quest for *lebensraum,* announced the creation of the Generalgouvernement (General Government). This territory covered the central part of Poland, including the three major cities with the largest concentration of Jews: Warsaw, Łódź, and Kraków. Dr. Hans Frank was appointed governor of that territory. He was directly responsible to his führer, Adolf Hitler.

Piotrków's Jews had long occupied a section within the Christian Polish town in which they had enjoyed a kind of self-governing autonomy—a government within a government. They seldom moved outside their own environment, and only the very wealthy were able to assimilate into the Christian sector of the town. These factors explain the facility and alarming swiftness with which the Nazi occupiers were able to concentrate the Jews of Piotrków within a designated ghetto area. In one blitz sweep during the night of October 30, 1939, all of the Jews living outside the Jewish quarter were united with their Jewish brethren inside the newly formed ghetto.

At first, ghetto life did nothing to interrupt the long tradition of Jewish social and cultural endeavors of Piotrków. There were religious groups, including Hasidic sects, each with its unique *shteeble* (worship locale), as well

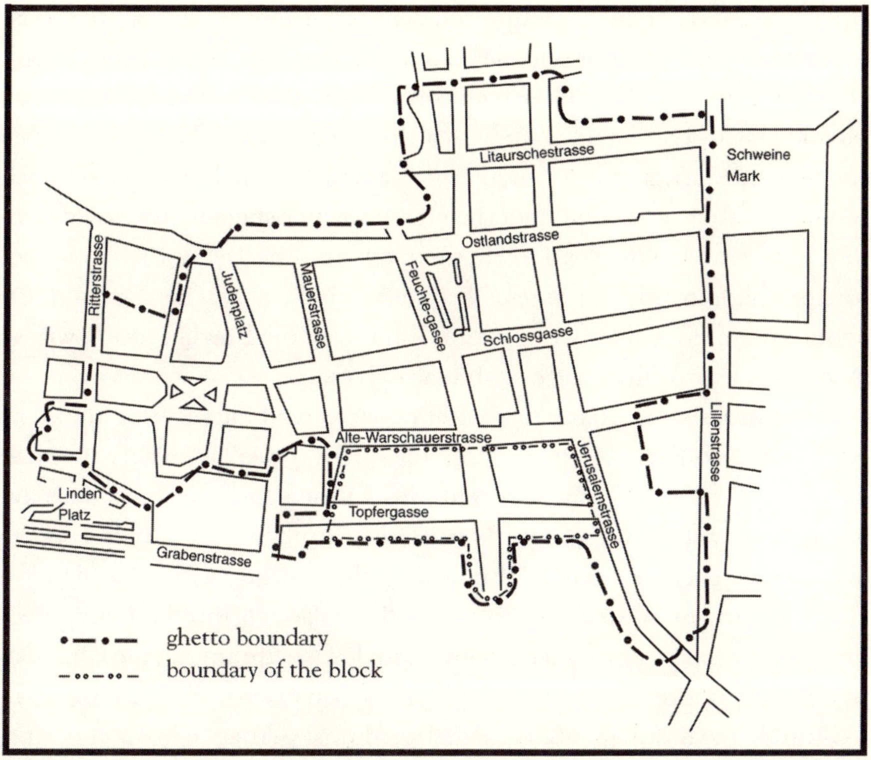

The ghetto in Piotrków Trybunalski. A map of the ghetto in which the streets are given German names. Based on German sources of 1942.

as secular groups. The town within a town possessed small property owners, artisans, wealthy merchants, and manufacturers as well as ordinary folk. It also included many of the needy who depended on the charitable institutions supported by the community.

The community was governed by the Community Council, which had the authority to levy and collect taxes. Zaman Tennenberg was the deputy chairman of the council, and other members were Mikhail Hertz, Avraham Samelson (my cousin on my father's side), Moshe Nordmann, Bunim Kaminski, Simcha Blachman, and Fischel Lubliner. Five more members were added later, forming a twelve-men council, as proscribed by the order of the Generalgouvernement on October 12, 1939. The council's primary function involved taking care of religious needs, public health, education, and welfare. An added duty was to be responsive to the Nazis' demands, which ranged from the collection and delivery of ransom monies to the assignment of forced labor brigades. And, yes, there existed a judicial system, consisting of the rabbinate, which was headed by the town's chief rabbi, Moshe Hayim Lau-Lavi. There was a ritual bath, the *mikvah,* with a male and female staff; a ritual slaughterhouse and kosher butchers; a Jewish cemetery and its staff and undertaker; a Jewish hospital with its own doctors, nurses, and midwives. Finally, there was also the Talmud Torah school for the children, which possessed some of the best teachers around. Of course, there existed also a Chevra Kaddisha (Holy Brotherhood), whose members devoted themselves to burial activities.

The preexisting quasi-state-within-a-state made it easy for the Nazi governor to concentrate the targeted Jews in the one place where they had been settled for more than four centuries. Difficult as it was to make a living in the Jewish sector of Piotrków before the ghetto days, their daily life deteriorated even more and very quickly with the onset of Nazi occupation and the many new "decrees" to follow. It is also worth mentioning here that in the years prior to the Nazi invasion, Jewish life among the Christian populace of Piotrków was not easy. The Christian authority was hostile in its attitude toward the Jews. It carried an almost perpetual boycott against Jewish goods, levied high taxes, and generated anti-Semitism that rivaled the medieval mind-set. It was a fertile ground in which the Nazis would continue their own brand of persecution of the Jewish people.

On that memorable Sabbath morning of September 1, 1939, with the first sounds of the wailing sirens and the onslaught of the Stuka dive bombers, the Jews of Piotrków sensed the coming of momentous changes in their lives. We hurried to the cellar. The night was lit up in spectacular flashes and fires. The children lay on the ground between their parents, pillows and feather bedding piled on top of them all. Prayers could be heard throughout. Sustained bombardment lasted more than an hour. Only when we emerged from our shelters were we able to survey the extent of the damage done.

That was to be the first experience of death for all of us. Bodies of men, women, and children lay strewn about in great disarray. As I looked at their faces, I gleaned in most of them evidence of surprise—a puzzled grimace caught at the moment of death. Others lay mortally wounded, crying out for help, moaning with pain, with head wounds or limbs torn from their bodies. Blood was everywhere. Buildings were on fire, many from their foundations all the way to the rooftops. Restoration would take much time and great effort.

The German Wehrmacht soldiers marched in goose step on the cobblestone streets. They were young and happy in their victory. Soon they were gone, and in their place came the Einsatzgruppen, units charged with the business of exterminating the *Untermenschen,* "subhumans." They, in turn, were joined by the Gestapo and the SS bureaucrats. Things changed quickly. The first of the many *Bekanntmachungen* (public announcements) was posted on walls in the ghetto. It read:

> PUBLIC NOTICE! Mandated by the Führer and by the order of the Gauleiter, all Jews will wear an identification armband on the right forearm displaying the Star of David. The armband is to be made of white cloth, ten centimeters wide, and the blue star one centimeter thick and eight centimeters in diameter, which must be positioned in the center of the armband. This order is effective immediately. Jews found not wearing identification will be severely punished!

The announcement gave cause for great concern, even as an entire new industry came into being overnight: the manufacture of armbands. Kids and grownups hawked them in the ghetto streets; every store carried them. Until then, we were able to traffic in the Christian section of the town relatively free of such basic restrictions. Now, we as Jews would be identified on sight by the star, the mark of Cain. Persons who were caught not wearing an identity armband would face the death penalty.

The newly established Jewish Militia ("Order-Keeping Police," or Ordnungsdienst, OD for short) was relentless in its attempts to implement the rules laid down by the German authorities. The militia's duties included the task of supplying workers for the Nazi war machine, most of the time forcibly. Also, a new breed of informers laid the foundation for distrust and fear among families and the best of friends. Motivated by incentives ranging from half a liter of vodka and a pound of spicy sausage to monetary awards, the informers delivered "violators" to the Seventh Bureau.

Following their arrest, these victims were never seen or heard from again. The disappearance of so many people was noticed in the community, so the Judenrat, Jewish Council of the Elders, expressed its concerns to the Gestapo. The latter denied knowledge of the captives' whereabouts. The council representatives dared not mention that in some cases the armbands had been ripped off the sleeves of the arrested Jews by the Christian militiamen who delivered them to the Gestapo.

Yet despite the generous bounty offered for the head of a Jew, the informers' treachery, and the fatal consequences of betrayal, the Jews risked their lives daily as they ventured into the countryside to negotiate a few potatoes or the luxury of a fresh egg. They bartered whatever valuables they possessed after having run out of money. The peasants came upon some very valuable properties in that manner, none they could have otherwise afforded.

Two glass factories on the outskirts of town, the Hortensia and Kara, had been taken over by the German war industry, Höbler Glass Enterprises, to produce glassware for the storage of medications needed at the front. Able-bodied Jews from the ghetto, regardless of age, were assigned work in the factories. It was our first experience with slave labor, for we were not paid for the work we performed. Each day the workers assembled on the streets of the ghetto; they were collected by the Jewish Militia and marched to the gates of the ghetto, there to be handed over to the surrogate SS ghetto sentries. The latter led us through the Christian part of the town to work, not without some harassment and baiting at the hands of our Christian compatriots. With every step, we heard the cry, *"Jude verrecke!"* (Jew croak) as Gentile children threw rocks at the marching column and grownups lined the streets to gloat at our misfortune. Needless to say, there were some who stayed away from the spectacle, and a lesser number stood by silently, on occasion shedding a tear for a friend seen humiliated among the marching ranks.

It was at that time that we became familiar with the expression *judenfrei* (free of Jews). Under the guise of recruitment for some highly regarded jobs that required a considerable degree of formal education, the Gestapo began a systematic deportation of the Jewish intelligentsia, for the most part young men. Most of them were rounded up during the night, "for resettlement into work camps," as their families were told. Those left behind would be reunited with their loved ones "at the earliest possible time," the Gestapo told us. Because the Germans used euphemisms to disguise the real purpose of the deportations, no one could have guessed the tragic outcome of their actions.

Being a part of the Judenrat and the ghetto militia allowed for certain privileges: temporary safety for the family, freedom from harassment, better living quarters, and so on. The few affluent Jews were willing and eager to buy those privileges. In grateful acknowledgment of those favors, those in charge of the ghetto's infrastructure saw to it that all Gestapo requests, no matter how bizarre or harmful to the community, were carried out with a minimum of resistance. This Jewish institution became the willing tool in the implementation of the Nazis' cultural agenda and sinister designs for the Jewish people. The Gestapo's simple prison psychology paid off as it used the Jew to betray the Jew. The promise of survival amidst dismal squalor was all too tempting to refuse the offer of servitude.

Most promising in the assumption of an administrative responsibility—even at some expense, both material and spiritual—was the illusion of being able to shield loved ones from the dangers that confronted ordinary ghetto inhabitants on a daily basis. As early as the winter of 1940, transports of resettled Jews from the West had begun to arrive and fill the ghetto beyond its physical capacity. Already tight quarters had to be shared with the new arrivals from Germany, Denmark, France, Holland, and Belgium. The resettled Jews were not only Jews from abroad, but also Jews from such Polish cities as Warsaw, Poznan, and Radome, among others. A grave housing shortage developed, and food became even scarcer than we had imagined. Famine became a reality.

Almost one year from the outbreak of the war, the Jewish population of Piotrków had grown from the eighteen thousand prewar inhabitants to almost twice that number. Trainloads were unloaded daily, and the ghetto council was told to maintain an accurate census. New arrivals were recorded for health, age, profession or trade, and, most important, personal property. The militia was especially concerned with the latter before assigning new quarters. By the time the refugees had become settled, few were left with little if any means of support.

The Polish Jews considered their German coreligionists equal to the Goyim (Gentiles) and dreaded having one of their families settled in their homes. The German Jews, likewise, bore a strong dislike for the eastern Jew, the Hasid. Some blamed the Hasidim for the dismal fate they had suffered, having been rejected as rightful citizens of their beloved Germany. "Had it not been for your peculiar deportment and unmistakably Jewish appearance, the Führer might have been kinder to all of us," some remarked.

My grandfather's second cousin on his mother's side, Josele Lazar, was a man of considerable influence at the Gestapo headquarters. He made custom-fitted boots for the administrative head of the ghetto, Sturmbannführer Paul Schröder. He also made boots for the commandant's wife and their two teenage sons, Egon and Bert. Grandfather Srulko knew that his cousin's influence would last for as long as the supply of leather afforded him a margin of usefulness with the Gestapo hierarchy. What he didn't know was the extent to which cousin Josele would be willing to accept some initiative on behalf of the family. First and foremost, as was the accepted norm during those critical times, Josele had his own immediate family to think of.

When Josele's great skill had reached the powerful *Brigadeführer,* the district commandant, in Łódź, he had become quite possibly the most influential Jew in Piotrków. Indeed, his influence eclipsed that of the entire Jewish Council.

"I have them eating out of the palm of my hand," he boasted to Grandfather Srulko.

"Then, Josele, you will have the Mandels move in with us?" my grandfather inquired. "So we won't have to share our home with the Yekkes," he said, using the derogatory expression with which eastern Jews labeled their German brethren.

Josele hesitated. "I'll try, Srulko," he smiled; "you know how hard it is to get concessions from the Nazis. All I can say is that I'll do my best."

"You know, Josele," my grandfather said, addressing his cousin with that familiar grin of condescension that Josele dreaded, "the trouble with you is that you're beginning to sound like the masters you're working for. You even look like them in those shiny boots you're wearing."

Grandfather's reference was on the mark. Many Jews who were in the servitude of the Nazis adopted the latter's mannerisms in their attempt to please their masters. Thus, most of the OD members made every effort to dress and carry themselves with the arrogance characteristic of their masters. At times, they gave the impression of having forgotten their roots altogether. Be that as it may, when the time arrived for "resettlement," each contingent of the resettled Jews was accompanied by a proportionate number of the Jewish Militia. The latter's fate was as much sealed as that of their charges, although it came to them as a total surprise.

The Mandels—Max, his thirteen-year-old son Hayim, and his niece Nora—moved in with us. It was a bit crowded, but we shared our home with our own—*haymishe,* as we referred to them. Now grandfather was able to arrange frequent meetings of the Hasidim, with Max's Talmudic knowledge being a great contribution to their heated scholarly arguments regarding the intricate laws of the Talmud, the Mishnah, and the Gomorrah.

Ghetto life continued unabated for some time, even as the daily routine of resettlement transports gathered momentum and rumors of an extermination camp at an obscure village called Treblinka persisted. Conditions in the ghetto worsened with the famine and the frequent collection of starved bodies at our doorsteps. A detail of lorries arrived each day to collect the deceased as they lay on the sidewalks naked, stripped of their clothing by the living, who had regarded their own needs of greater importance than the modesty of those departed.

It was also during this time that we had learned that the Germans recruited young women for the purpose of establishing a "comfort house" to service the SS, the Gestapo, and the local Wehrmacht garrison. The comfort women were a mixture of nationalities and ethnicity and were attracted mostly by the promise of relative safety and better living conditions. The "house" was situated quite inconspicuously on the outskirts of the ghetto.

On the eve of Rosh Hashanah in September 1940, the newly appointed Piotrków mayor, Oberbürgermeister Hans Drexel, arrived at the ghetto and the Jewish Council meeting to present his demand for "hostesses." He was met with silence. Drexel left the premises with a cynical grin on his face and a word of admonishment: "You Jews had better realize what's good for you. After all, we're here to stay, and you must serve our needs."

At the same time, forced labor activities increased, and a high tax was levied on the ghetto Jews by the new municipal administration. The Jews coped bravely and provided the labor details, but raising the money was well-nigh impossible, as their resources had been greatly depleted by time and the prevailing hardships.

By the winter of 1940–41, severe overcrowding caused sanitary conditions to worsen considerably. The deterioration was not owing to the Jews' negligence in observing strict hygienic rigors. The water supply was routinely cut off in the ghetto, and the meager rations did not suffice to keep everyone free of lice and other infectious parasitic insects. We were soon visited by a terrible typhus epidemic. A special sanitary service, comprising four young men, came into being and was assigned the duty of containing the epidemic as best they could. Wherever early symptoms were discovered, whole apartments were put under quarantine, and the entire family underwent a disinfection process at the *mikvah*. The local gym was converted into a "hospital." All available ghetto physicians, under the able guidance of Dr. Yakubowicz from Łódź, were enlisted to fight the epidemic.

Lacking proper medication, the ghetto physicians did their very best to administer aid to the people whose symptoms were discovered early on. Still, the death toll was staggering, and the pickup lorries worked overtime to transport the dead to the cemetery for internment. This, by the way, was also the duty carried out by the "sanitary service department." Soon the trucks were so overburdened with the transport of the dead that common droshkies were frequently seen taking up the slack.

In May 1941, the military units stationed in Piotrków began to evacuate their headquarters. Rumor had it that the Reich was preparing for an invasion of the Soviet Union. By then, the population of the ghetto had been reduced to approximately eight thousand inhabitants, consisting of those who worked at the two glass factories, their families, and others who one way or another had managed to endure in the ghetto till then.

On June 22, 1941, the Germans attacked their former ally, the Soviet Union. The invasion went under the name "Operation Barbarossa." This action of war between Nazi Germany and the Soviet Union caused conditions to worsen for the Jews in the ghetto as well as in the occupied territories. News circulated of killing factories, death camps, that the Germans had established in places we hadn't heard of before: Belzec, Majdanek, Sobibor, and others. Hitler's plan, which went by the designation Endlösung ("Final Solution"), became evident. The Einsatzgruppen activities intensified, but so did those of the partisan groups fighting the occupation. The latter found many recruits among the young in the ghettos. However, for each SS killed by the Underground, the Germans took ghetto hostages and hanged them in public places in full view of everyone. They hung placards round the necks of the executed as a warning to the living.

The Einsatzgruppen received clear orders from the chief planners of Jewish annihilation at the conference at Wannsee to make Europe *judenrein.* They took their jobs seriously. Transport after transport left the Piotrków ghetto. Their destination was the Treblinka extermination camp, northeast of Warsaw.

By the winter of 1941, only a few months from the initial Nazi successes on the eastern front, their campaign suddenly came to a stop. This wasn't owing to the Russians' valiant attempts to stop the onslaught. It was the severe winter weather that halted the German war machine's victorious march eastward. As their campaign stalled in frozen mud and snow, life in the shtetl ghetto worsened as well.

A new announcement established the curfew for all ghetto inhabitants. Only working parties would be allowed to leave the ghetto, accompanied by a cordon of sentries. They left at 5:00 A.M. and returned at 5:00 P.M., the curfew time. Another shift would leave at 5:00 P.M. and return at precisely 5:00 A.M. All male ghetto inhabitants caught outside the ghetto past curfew were given the "genital test" to determine their ethnicity. In their medieval mind-set, the SS and the Gestapo held the stereotypical notion as truth; only Jewish males were circumcised. The rest was obvious: some Polish (Christian) males from more enlightened homes had also been circumcised. If accused by anyone of being Jewish, they, too, underwent the "test" and failed miserably, to the delight of their enemies, who for some reason or another had pointed the finger in their directions.

Whatever joy invaded our hearts at the irony provided by the genital test, we huddled behind curtained windows each night as we watched our neighbors and friends being driven away from their homes. The Gestapo officer's voice could be heard throughout the neighborhood as he announced, "You are being resettled! Come out onto the street immediately! Each person can carry fifty pounds of luggage. You will leave all of your other belongings here. You will find better accommodations at your destination. You will work and receive pay for your work. Come out! You are being resettled!"

People filed out of their homes onto the street. Many were unable to carry any luggage whatsoever because their arms were weighed down with the small children and infants they carried. Some young people carried their elders and the feeble by piggyback onto the cattle cars waiting for them at the freight railway station. Neighbors were quickly rounded up and herded through the streets in orderly columns. The Jewish Militia was on its exemplary behavior as it aided the SS mercenaries in completing their task.

For the most part, the Jews were ready and resigned in their attitude. There was nothing they could do at this late hour. Each was burdened with his or her immediate family's safety; their prevailing thought during these crucial moments was "every man for himself." Some resisted, but they were quickly quieted with the butt of a rifle or a well-aimed bullet. There were also those who went into hiding in places they had prepared for their loved ones in cellars and false walls of their homes. They, too, were quickly discovered by especially trained dogs. The hunters stopped long enough to molest the more attractive women and young girls. The hunt went on for several hours. Shouts of pain, fear, and anguish resounded throughout the neighborhood as homes were looted and women were violated.

The rest of us were helpless with rage. Our family was still unmolested and safe from deportation. Only a block away, our friends and acquaintances were being driven from their homes, robbed, and raped, but we remained passive onlookers. The mere thought that the search might not end there but spread to the location of our dwelling inspired terror in our hearts. When the noise had died down and the columns of the newly condemned distanced themselves from the ghetto, we thanked the Almighty for another day together with family.

The winter of 1941 was one of the severest in memory. The Siberian winds came howling from the East, and deep snow blanketed the countryside as far as the eye could reach. Nature seemed to shrink into itself, and man followed its example. We ran out of coal to fire our stoves, and everyone was stealing what wood there was available. Wooden fences and staircases had begun to disappear. Soon we skipped three at a time to climb from one story to another. The water we carried from the well was frozen into ice by the time we returned home.

With the arrival of milder weather during the first signs of spring, the ranks of the workforce diminished because of the many runaways. People were joining the growing resistance movement as the Nazi war machine was gathering momentum on the eastern front once again. The Nazis were furious, and reprisals followed exponentially, but desertion did not abate. It was now either starve in the ghetto or take a chance in the forests and die honorably. Still, those prospective partisans whose families remained intact stayed behind, afraid reprisals would only jeopardize the safety of their loved ones.

Meanwhile, my whole body assumed the "aspect" of hunger. As I regarded my face in the mirror, I made a startling discovery: when I ran my fingers over my skin, I was able to feel the contours of my cheekbones. The skin was drawn tightly over the bones, and I was able to distinguish each and every one of them. It was only then that I looked carefully at the faces of those near me; they, too, had assumed the appearance of hunger: hollow eyes, stooped shoulders, their feet barely leaving the ground on which they walked with a strange shuffle. This appearance denoted a final resignation to one's fate and an utterly resigned embrace of death.

On the eve of the Passover holidays, the ghetto council received one more "request" from the commandant. Although the Nazis were aware that the ghetto had by then shrunk to several thousand inhabitants, the request was quite explicit: the Jews had to deliver twenty-five thousand zlotys within twenty-four hours. Furthermore, the council had to submit a supplementary list of young women considered suitable to serve the needs of the SS garrison stationed in Piotrków. As the Gestapo put it, "We have in Piotrków a garrison of healthy young men who unfortunately suffer from lack of sexual gratification. On occasions, they find relief with the women of the street. The result is an alarming rise in venereal diseases. Your women are known for exemplary cleanliness. They will be properly rewarded for their services."

Once again the Jews refused to comply with the Nazis' demand. The ghetto expected the worst of reprisals. In addition, rumor had it that the Germans had suffered serious reversals on the eastern front. "News" began arriving from killing camps in the East, the most urgent from Treblinka, the destination of the transports from the Piotrków ghetto. Indeed, the feelings of expectant tension and agony in those days were justified when the commandant of the district declared the Nazi intent to make Piotrków *judenrein.* This action was to be executed under the name of Operation Reinhard, bearing the name of one of Hitler's infamous architects of Judeocide.

The remaining ghetto population of some six thousand, save those performing forced labor at the two glass factories, assembled on the streets of the ghetto. The Nazis planned their *Aktion* to the minutest detail. Aided by the surrogate Lithuanian and Ukrainian SS as well as by the Jewish OD, they combed all of the abandoned dwellings. Anyone found inside was summarily shot, their bodies dumped unceremoniously on the sidewalks. They would be picked up later to be burned in a common pit; the service of the Chevra Kaddisha for a proper burial at the Jewish cemetery was no longer available.

Some weeping, others steeped in prayer, families stood together in bitter sorrow and fear. Men, women, the elderly, the children—no one was spared the agony of *Selektion.* The cynical SS officer positioned himself at the head of the crowd, and the process began. As the people filed in front of him, they presented documents attesting to their labor qualifications. Some were selected to remain at the two glass factory camps. Many concealed their documents in order to remain with their families. The tear-filled, anguished good-byes of those separated from their loved ones could be heard far and wide.

The Nazis loaded the Jews of Piotrków into the awaiting freight train, but not before they conducted a thorough body search and stripped them of all property. In some cases, more than one hundred people were loaded into a car that was clearly marked "maximum load, thirty persons or six

Survivors visit the Jewish cemetery in Piotrków Trybunalski, Poland. Photo and caption courtesy of the United States Holocaust Memorial Museum.

head of cattle." Once inside, the hapless victims discovered that the Nazi assassins had made no provisions for the passage to their undisclosed destination: no facility to relieve oneself, no water, no needed supplies of nourishment. It was then that the Jews realized the hopelessness of their situation. "Why would these highly efficient technocrats forget to make all those provisions?" everyone wondered.

It took three trains filled over their capacity to transport the Piotrków ghetto Jews on their terminal journey. Many died a terrible death on the way, but when the train reached its destination, they did not have to undergo the wrenching process of gassing.

By the end of 1942, with the beginning of the Soviet counteroffensive, the Nazi commandant received orders to transport the remaining Jews of the Hortensia and the Kara glass factories farther into Germany. During the transport, some managed to escape into the forest and join the partisans. If they were fortunate enough to find the Communist-affiliated Armia Ludowa (people's army), they would survive, but if they fell into the hands of the Armia Krajowa (National Army partisans), their fate might have been sealed as it would had they fallen into the hands of the Nazis.

Thus ended a glorious era of a thriving Piotrków community. As the war came to a close, the remnants were liberated at different times and from many camps during the spring of 1945. The survivors, only several hundred of us out of so many thousands, were freed by the Allies. We welcomed our freedom with a promise "never to forget, never to forgive" the murderous Nazi assassins. Eyewitnesses to a most heinous crime in the course of human history and beaten in the flesh, we remain an example of the indomitable spirit of humankind. Piotrków lives forever in our work and in our memory.

2. Some Clarifications on the Warsaw Ghetto Uprising

Based on Interviews with Marek Edelman and Simcha Rotem

MICHAEL BERENBAUM

We now understand that ghettos were a transitional measure between the 1939 conquest of Poland and of its Jewish communities and the implementation of the "Final Solution to the Jewish Problem" in 1941–42 with the creation of the death camps. In essence, the killing of Jews underwent a development in the East; beginning on June 22, 1941, Einsatzgruppen, mobile killers, were sent to stationary victims in the German-occupied Soviet Union with the assignment to slaughter Jews one by one, bullet by bullet. Then, beginning in the winter of 1942, Jews were shipped to killing centers on trains—mobile victims were transported to stationary death camps—with the precision of a factory assembly line. As the camps came on line, the ghettos of Poland and other parts of eastern Europe were emptied, and their inhabitants were killed.

In retrospect, this transitional function is clear. But it was anything but clear to the inhabitants. As Raul Hilberg and Walter Laqueur have pointed out, the Germans employed a language of deception to mask their overall aims, and the deception worked far longer and far better than we who were not there can easily imagine.

Professor Berenbaum would like to thank Brooklyn films for the permission to use material from the documentary *Uprising* in his essay.

Long ago I concluded that resistance was an act of desperation, a last stand commencing when ghetto leaders understood and inhabitants surmised that death for all was imminent—a matter of days and weeks, not months and years. By the time resistance broke out, there were no illusions. Death for the ghetto inhabitants, though not necessarily for any single individual, was all but certain.

Late in the spring of 2001, I traveled to Bratislava to participate in the filming of *Uprising,* a Jon Avnet film that was aired on NBC television in November of that year. Avnet had invited Marek Edelman, the highest-ranking surviving commanding officer of the Warsaw Ghetto Uprising and Simcha Rotem (Kazik), a foot soldier in the uprising whose book *Memoirs of a Warsaw Ghetto Fighter: The Past within Me* (New Haven, Conn.: Yale Univ. Press, 1994) was a source for the fictionalized account of the uprising. They were on the set to inspire the actors who were playing them and frankly to confirm for the director the sense that the film was being faithful to their experience. They were also there to be interviewed for a documentary that was planned to coincide with the admittedly fictionalized account. Being in their presence permitted me to clarify several important questions that had long troubled me.

First and foremost I asked: "What did you know about Treblinka, and how did you learn it?"

Edelman corrected me. The issue was not Treblinka. It was Chelmno, where gassing began on December 8, 1941, a full eight and one-half months *before* the deportations. Two men escaped from Chelmno, and they reported on what they had seen: mobile gas vans killing people with exhaust fumes. Warsaw Judenrat leader Adam Czerniakow knew what was happening. But he suspected, or so Edelman was told, that the gassing concerned small towns and that "it was impossible that such a thing could happen in Warsaw." In Łódź, Judenrat leader Mordechai Chaim Rumkowski also was informed of what was happening in Chelmno. Nevertheless, he continued to send Jews to Chelmno, reasoning that he had to sacrifice some to save more.

The "street," to use Edelman's term for the ghetto, was not convinced about gassings at Chelmno. "People didn't believe in such a thing at all.

'There is a war,' they were saying. 'Germans need a big labor force. Jews are a free labor force. There is no reason to kill them.' " In short, logic dictated that the Jews be kept alive. But the killing of the Jews was ideological, which overrode the logic of the war.

Nevertheless, I pressed on Treblinka.

Kazik's recollection was specific, dare I say even poetic. When the deportations of July 22 began, the Underground was anxious—perhaps *desperate* is the more appropriate word—to learn about Treblinka, the destination point of the transports leaving the ghetto. Zygmunt Frydrych, a member of the resistance who had connections with railway men through the Bund (Jewish Workers Party), was able to board one of these trains and to head toward Treblinka. He could not enter the camp, but rather reached the Malinka stop, where he proceeded to speak with the railway men. Trains were arriving daily, he was told. This bit of information he already knew. The trains were filled with Jews. That, too, he knew. They arrived in the station filled; they left empty. No food was brought into the camp, and no wells had been dug to provide water. This information was new. It confirmed his suspicions.

The trains were arriving full, leaving empty, with no provisions made for the passengers—*cargo* might be the more appropriate word—who had arrived at their destination. They were being left without food and water. At best, they would be starving. Ghetto inhabitants had also starved. In 1941, one in ten Jews in the Warsaw ghetto died of starvation, malnutrition, disease, and despair even before the first bullet was fired and before the deportations had begun. Starvation was passive violence, eliminating those who were unfit without being forced to take any direct action.

"The camp was silent," Frydrych was also told. Tens of thousands arrive. They enter. There are no provisions for their survival, and they make no noise.

In retrospect, we clearly know how to piece together each bit of information, but Frydrych's assignment was to learn what had happened to the Jews, to do so directly so that he could be clear—dare one say certain?—in his report to the ghetto about the fates of those who had been forcibly evacuated. Still, he had not seen with his own eyes what was happening. He "did not know," to use Laqueur's distinction between knowledge and information. Information could be pieced together, but the fragments were still not revelatory.

Early the next morning, as Kazik described it, Frydrych wandered around Malinka and saw a dazed man in his underwear, walking around, yet wearing no clothes.

Edelman added, "It turned out that he was his friend. He was the director of a housing cooperative; his name was Walach." Walach told of his escape from Treblinka on one of the trains that had brought Jews to the camp. He described in detail the gassing and the killing, so Frydrych had finally gotten his eyewitness report. Still he wanted more.

How was he to know what had happened, to know directly, to convince those who were skeptical back in Warsaw or those so desperate that they would still then deny what was happening?

"Take a deep breath," Frydrych was told. The smell of burning flesh was unmistakable, undeniable. Frydrych had his confirmation. With this, he could return home to bear witness, to assume the task of convincing his colleagues that resettlement was death and Treblinka an extermination center. Walach and Frydrych took off to Warsaw together.

This information was not uncontested. Formal delegates of Warsaw Jews were sent to two other camps—nonkilling centers—to report back on what they saw. They issued contrasting reports, so German propaganda had scored again.

"People didn't want to believe. Because it is so incredible that simply . . . one doesn't want to believe," Edelman noted. There are natural reasons for denying unhappy information. For the same reasons, otherwise intelligent women walk around with lumps in their breast and do not go to see a doctor, and people believe that shooting pains in their arms and chest are signs of indigestion and thus do not go to the emergency ward. But denial is costly, sometimes even perilous.

My second question concerned the mission Kazik led: the escape into the sewers. As students of the Warsaw Ghetto Uprising might recall, the Jews fielded two fighting forces in the Warsaw ghetto: one that united the Zionist left and center with the Bund was the Żydowska Organizacja Bojowa (ŻOB, Jewish Fighting Forces), and the other was composed of the followers of Ze'ev Jabotinsky and the Zionist right, called the Żydowski Związek Wojskowy (ŻZW). We know that each group differed as to how the Jewish future would be constituted, a future they had every reason to assume they would not live to see. The Bund believed that the Jews should enjoy minority rights and remain an integral part of Poland. The Zionists were firm that the Jewish future should be centered in Palestine, with the Socialists and the Jabotinskyites differing on the social and economic construction of the Jewish homeland.

Some attributed the failure to agree on a strategy question—whether the uprising was to be a last stand or there would be a planned escape route out of the ghetto—to the disunity between the two forces. Given the overwhelming imbalance between German power and Jewish resources, the ŻOB leaders were convinced that the ghetto uprising was the last stand, a fight unto death, with death all but certain. So the escape to the sewers, which was so central to Kazik's memoirs, seems counter to this strategy and the ŻOB leaders' views.

Edelman's account as to why there were two forces was straightforward. Nothing as grandiose as strategy or ideology was at stake. It was simply a disagreement between the ŻZW and the ŻOB as to who was to assume command. Given the fact that several ŻZW leaders had military experience, they felt that they should be given command, a position that was unacceptable to the ŻOB leaders, who formed the majority of the fighting forces. Even under those most dire of circumstances, these differences could not be negotiated. No compromise presented itself that would permit the fielding of one fighting force.

Kazik's account of how the escape to the sewers came about is straightforward and rather simple: "We found ourselves alive on April 26 [seven days after the April 19 uprising began], much to our surprise. So the leadership approached me and told me to go to the other side to see if there was a way out of the ghetto." Kazik followed orders and returned several days later, having found a path out through the sewers and helping to secure a truck that would transport the fighters to the forests, where they could reconstitute themselves to continue the fight and perhaps even survive.

Kazik recalled: "The fact was that after four or five days of fighting in the ghetto against the powerful forces, a majority of the fighters stayed alive. A 'tragedy' occurred, and then we realized that there is no sense in committing suicide. Against the cannons, against the gasses, against the bombardment, we didn't have anything. So we tried . . . to rescue somehow all the fighters that were still alive."

The matter-of-factness of the words "we found ourselves alive" and the passivity of the voice clearly indicate the frame of mind. Little did he, or perhaps even his leaders, imagine that they would hold out for a week against the German onslaught. They fully expected to be dead and had made no plans for life after the uprising or even for an escape route outside of the ghetto. The uprising was to be the last stand, with the fighters determined to live with honor and to die with honor.

Marek Edelman corrected me when I repeated to him my own well-documented conclusions that resistance was not a decision as to whether to live or to die, but a determination to make a statement with one's death, to exact a price. I was not alone in my conclusions that because resistance meant all but certain death for all within the ghetto, it could only enjoy widespread support—and the only issue was how to face the reality of impending death. "Professor," Edelman said with barely concealed disdain that fighters have toward those who have never been in combat, *"Professor, resistance was a choice with how to live in the moments before we died."*

Death was a given. How to live in the interim was not.

Also there were different types of death. Edelman said: "I am only telling you one thing: it is better to die being hit by the bullet than in the gas chamber. This is already egotistical."

It was the distinguished literary scholar Lawrence Langer who first introduced us to the concept of "choiceless choices," a description of the victims' situations and of our own inability to make moral judgments regarding the victims' behavior in the world of the camps. Langer reiterates the statement of Andrzej Wirth, who, commenting on Tadeusz Borowski's work *This Way to the Gas, Ladies and Gentlemen,* said: "The tragedy lies not in the necessity of choosing but in the impossibility of making a choice."[1] Choiceless choices, Langer understands, do not reflect options between good and bad, life and death, but between one form of abnormal response and another, both impossible, imposed by situations not of the victims' own choosing.

Kazik's experience in the sewers is a vivid illustration of Langer's point. Kazik was responsible for finding an escape route through the sewers and then for guiding the remaining survivors through the sewers. Transportation had to be arranged for the group emerging from the sewers because, given their appearance—the filth of the excrement in which they had stood and the stench that remained with them after they emerged—they would be unable to blend in with the Polish population on the "Aryan" side. They had to be transported from Warsaw to the forests. As they emerged, they had a few moments in which to board the truck and get out before they would be discovered and killed. Not all of those who were in the sewers came out at once, so Kazik faced the choice between remaining on the spot with the truck, endangering all the survivors, or leaving some of the group behind to a fate he could well imagine. The drama of his difficult circumstances was intensified by the fact that Zivia Lubetkin, who both outranked him in the resistance movement and, though only a few years older than Kazik, had been a motherlike figure to the young man, ordered him to stay. She had given her word that she would wait and not abandon those in the sewers. His response was immediate: "You're not my commander here." However, his guilt was enduring. Rescuer and savior, he had saved some, but he had also abandoned others not only to death, but perhaps even to the foulness of death by drowning within the sewers of Warsaw.

Survivors' attitudes change with time—at least some attitudes. Kazik was less angry and more forgiving of established Jewish leadership fifty-eight years after the uprising than he was initially and even in his earlier written testimony. He was uncertain why. Perhaps he had mellowed; perhaps, having assumed the responsibilities of family and children, he now understood the burdens and compromises of leadership. A young man's criticisms, when the world seems simpler and the morality much more basic, come more easily.

Edelman remained unforgiving. Adam Czerniakow, the German-appointed leader of the Warsaw Judenrat (the twenty-four-man Jewish

Council), had committed suicide on July 23, 1942, rather than sign the deportation order that would doom his community. In a moment of despair—perhaps even lucidity—he might have understood that all his efforts of the past three years were for naught, that working with the Germans would not allow him to preserve the bulk of the ghetto population, most especially the children, and that the ghetto was doomed. Many regarded his suicide as an act of personal integrity. However, Emanuel Ringelblum, the distinguished ghetto chronicler, who had organized the Oneg Shabbos group to compile a historical record of the ghetto, was less charitable in his assessment of the suicide. He wrote in his diary, "Suicide of Czerniakow—too late, a sign of weakness—should have called for resistance—a weak man."[2]

Even almost six decades later Edelman was bitter: "But instead of committing suicide, he could have said, 'Jews, you're going to be murdered.' Because after all, this suicide was . . . I demanded from him not a personal death, you know, but I demanded from the leaders of four hundred thousand people to be put on their legs."

Kazik interrupted: "[Shmuel] Zygielbojm [the representative of the Bund in London] committed suicide; it was known internationally. It was public. That was everything you think Czerniakow should have done. The reaction to the world . . . equaled zero."

Edelman was unrelenting: "If he had left a letter just like Zygielbojm did, he would have been the world's hero."

Pressed further, Edelman conceded that Czerniakow was "reluctantly decent, which had little impact. . . . He was trying to do as much as he could. He was beaten; he had pride; and he knew how to behave. His biggest mistake was that, first of all, he never wanted to have anything in common with the underground movement, and all the people were coming to him for support. . . . He wasn't as bad as Rumkowski who [in Łódź] was sending people to the camps and killing them [Rumkowski knew that in Chelmno Jews were being gassed in mobile gas vans], but his collaboration with the Germans was supposed to help him survive. You can have such an opinion; I have nothing against it, but when it came to the point where he [Czerniakow] knew that they were killing the Jews, and he knew it very early because he knew it in 1941, [he should have spoken out]."

Czerniakow was not linked to any of the social movements in the ghetto. According to Edelman, he was "disinclined to all conspiratorial work. He was a philanthropist. To give the pack of chocolate to every kid in an orphanage from his own money, but to form a social movement, this he was incapable of."

Edelman protested: "But Czerniakow, who was an authority, had he said, 'People, you are going to your deaths. Don't surrender. Defend yourselves with,' as they say, 'hands, legs, and whatever you have against the deportation,' this would have had colossal importance."

"It was his private matter that he didn't want to take responsibility for the death of three hundred thousand to four hundred thousand people."

Kazik was troubled by the morality of the uprising. He asked: "Did we have any right to shorten the lives of all these people? That we quickened their deaths is a fact. Possibly they would have died one week later, and that is one week in a man's life. You should know, as a doctor, how important that is."

Edelman answered: "Throughout all my life I've been taking responsibilities. I take responsibility for human life both in the ghetto and here."

"We [Yitzhak Zuckerman, Mordecai Anielewicz, and Edelman] knew that no one was going to survive." Still, they were ready to make the choice, to take the responsibility.

Both Edelman and Kazik protested the label *hero.*

"Are you a hero?" I asked.

Edelman responded, "Of course not. A hero is a fool. They tell him: 'Onward in the name of Stalin.' He jumps out of the trench and gets killed. The one who jumps is the hero, and those who did the real work, those are invisible."

"How would you describe yourself?"

"A fighter, yes, a fighter." The word is big.

"A freedom fighter?" I asked.

"Without freedom, without freedom, this will happen again."

3. Beware of Answered Prayers

Ghetto–Concentration Camp Theresienstadt/Terezin

CHARLOTTE GUTHMANN OPFERMANN

The perpetrators of the Final Solution claimed that the destinations of the deportation trains were work camps, resettlement camps, labor detail, and other similar euphemisms. We knew better. Surely none of the blind deportees from my hometown of Wiesbaden on September 1, 1942, expected to be engaged in antitank trench digging or similar work. None of the mothers of newborn infants of the earlier deportation on June 10, 1942, believed that anything other than death awaited them at the other end of the line. That is why half the bodies buried in the Jewish cemeteries in my birthplace of Wiesbaden between 1938 and 1945 are those of suicide victims.

No other camp or ghetto has received so much false publicity—from perpetrators and from survivors—as Theresienstadt, the two-hundred-year-old garrison village some sixty kilometers to the north of Prague. Long before Steven Spielberg introduced the world to such a camp with his film *Schindler's List,* Adolf Eichmann and his colleagues of the Reichssicherheitshauptamt (RSHA) decided to demonstrate to the German movie-going public, with a Fox *Tönende Wochenschau* newsreel, just where all these Jews were *supposedly* sent and how they passed their time—at leisure, attending concerts and lectures, reading, knitting, gossiping, with little children playing happily in sandboxes or on swings in well-landscaped parks.

The intent of this newsreel was not to put anyone's conscience at ease (there was no objection of consequence to the Jews' fate), but to contrast the *supposed* comfortable Jewish lifestyle in the midst of the war with the suffering and hardships endured by the German population. The film was intended to stimulate further anti-Jewish sentiment. Production started in 1942, and by 1945 two reels, several hours in length, were completed.

In truth, the Jewish inmates of Theresienstadt had only a portion of the old garrison at their disposal. When I arrived at this camp in June 1943, there were many guarded barricades and wooden fences, with entire streets off limits everywhere. The garrison was originally designed to house two or three thousand soldiers in barracks, plus a small contingent of support personnel in some two hundred small, one- and two-story houses.

Most of the time, forty to fifty thousand inmates were crowded into only a portion of the garrison. We were assigned approximately six feet by one yard of space per person. Appropriately, this is about the size of a coffin. Our dead comrades were granted even less space than that: theirs was a box measuring roughly six-by-eight inches, subsequently replaced by a more economical paper sack, the size of a school child's lunch bag. These containers held the ashes of our departed friends and neighbors, carefully marked with given name and a few details. In the end, even this dignity was taken away: in spring 1945, all of these containers (about thirty-five thousand) were unceremoniously dumped into the nearby River Eger in order to prevent the advancing Soviet army from finding proof of our suffering.

I lived in the attic of the Hamburger Kaserne, sleeping on the dirty, naked stone floor, sharing this area with roughly six thousand women who had been brought here from the four corners of the Reich. Most of the inmates at that time (June 1943) were from the Protektorat Böhmen und Mähren, Czechoslovakia. Most were young and at work in the many production programs with which the internal camp administrators hoped to persuade the German masters that this camp could be useful to the German war economy. The vain hope and intent of the various production programs (such as crates for use by the Wehrmacht and split mica for the Luftwaffe) was to persuade the *Kommandantur* that we should continue to live and not be deported to the dreaded East.

When elderly and infirm prisoners began to arrive from Germany in the summer and fall of 1942, this influx was perceived as a threat to the work camp concept, and thus the new prisoners were far from welcome for a number of reasons. There was no way to care for the sick or to accommodate elderly prisoners. To no one's surprise, fully two-thirds (more than twenty thousand) of the camp's dead were prisoners from Germany. The German veterans from World War I, who were also a part of this German contingent, were considered too patriotic, too much like the enemy, so there was a great deal of friction within the camp's prisoner population. I countered this problem as best I could by learning to speak Czech. Most of my fellow inmates preferred to speak their native tongue and did not speak German very well or at all.

Our daily life consisted of long hours of hard work, enduring hunger and suffering from thirst. Most prisoners lost approximately one-third of their body weight within the first two or three months of internment. The constant redeportations to the East were a fact of life, like the sun rising in the morning and night falling at the end of each day. Taking leave from friends and family members (even from spouses) became routine.

Word of the massacre of Jews at the hands of the Nazis had reached the outside world almost from the very beginning. We knew of the intended killing of the Polish and stateless Jews from Germany to Poland as early as October 27, 1938. Details had been broadcast to the free world over the years. But little was done with this knowledge.

The Red Cross inspection in June 1944 was made possible thanks to the initiative of the Danish king Christian X, the cooperation of the president of the German Red Cross (from the Schutzstaffel [SS], Brigadeführer Dr. Ernst Robert Grawitz, who was responsible for many of the medical experiments performed on concentration camp prisoners), Reichsführer Heinrich Himmler, Sturmbannführer Adolf Eichmann, and other major players. They all participated in the charade. Likewise, many inmates and internal leaders of the camp were forced to help.

In June 1944, Maurice Rossel, then working for the Geneva office of the International Red Cross, wrote a glowing report after a brief visit to the camp. The Red Cross archives did not release this report and Rossel's pictures until 1992, almost fifty years later. I am one of the children captured in several of his photographs. Quite possibly, the institution was embarrassed by its content. The Pamatnik Terezin (i.e., the Gedenkstätte Theresienstadt Museum) and Yad Vashem, Jerusalem, have a copy of this report. Almost all of the seemingly happy children and their caregivers whom

Rossel photographed in June were dead within weeks after his visit. He did not understand that they had been carefully clothed in special garments and coached at great length concerning what to do and what to say for this special occasion.

We were "issued" special clothes for the occasion that had to be returned to the *Kleiderkammer* after the visitors had left. For my use, I received a navy blue pleated skirt and a spiffy white blouse, plus a necktie of sorts. The children shown with me in the picture had been imprisoned for most of their lives and did not own clothes such as the ones they are wearing in the snapshots. They usually wore a bibbed blue-jean version that we created from the bedsheets of our dead and departed or deported friends and comrades, dyed with the ingenious use of a disinfection powder that did double duty in this way.

Along the preplanned route, several buildings had been painted in cheerful colors, with flowers planted along the way. A special children's playground was constructed, and children who normally would have been at work were taught how to play. There was a music pavilion. Many of the internal walls, barricades, and confining fences were torn down. Most of the prisoners were under strictly enforced house arrest and had to keep away from windows in order to hide the pitifully overcrowded conditions. For many months, the visit was planned in every conceivable detail. It was over in a few minutes.

As a result, there was no improvement of the horrible conditions in Theresienstadt. On the contrary, when a second such inspection was taken under consideration, 18,406 prisoners were deported, with most of them being killed in preparation.

The documentary film *Bericht aus der jüdischen Siedlung Theresienstadt* had been a work in progress since 1942. It was completed in 1944. Most of the film disappeared into Soviet archives when Soviet soldiers entered the camp in May 1945, but some twenty minutes of excerpts are available at various archives. The film is now known by its postwar title *The Führer Makes the Jews the Gift of a City.*

From June 1943 until mid-June 1945, even after our liberation by the Soviet army, I was a prisoner in this camp. Our normal daily life consisted of hard physical labor, very little food, many deliberate deprivations—

even of drinking water. We all suffered endless infectious illnesses, vermin infestation, dehydration, and low morale. We knew that we were going to be killed, even if we were to survive the endless illnesses and epidemics (typhus, encephalitis, and many others).

There were constant deportations "to the East," which—and we knew this very well—meant death. We did not know the details of the killing processes in other camps, but we knew that life expectancy in most concentration camps was a matter of weeks, a few months at best.

In October 1993, I was again in Theresienstadt, this time as a guest of the Prague Friedrich Ebert Stiftung, the Berlin Topografie des Terrors, the Prague Terezin Initiative, and the Wiesbaden Förderkreis Museum. For years, I have worked with this group—doing seminars, study groups, and Holocaust history lessons; collaborating on books, articles, and textbooks; and producing movies, audio and video presentations, and radio and television programs, much of it available from the German government's Amt für Politische Bildung in Bonn.

The purpose and agenda of the seminar in Theresienstadt in 1993 involved education. Most of the participants of the conference were curators from former concentration camp sites. Many had worked with one another previously, attended other conferences together, and knew each other for years.

Nearly fifty years earlier I had been housed in the airless and unlit attic of the Hamburger Kaserne, most of the time without food to eat and water to drink, and with a long walk down several flights of stairs to the nearest latrine. Then, we had been dimly aware of the fact that we had been brought here to die—eventually almost all of us did.

That October 1993, by contrast, I was housed in the former SS officer's club, built by the inmates for our captors' use. This building is now an official government guest house. Geographically, it is located within the garrison ramparts, but during my internment it had been barricaded off and was well outside the confines of the camp. The entire garrison Theresienstadt measures five hundred by seven hundred meters.

During my imprisonment, we did not have use of the entire garrison.

Many streets were off limits and barricaded, accessible only to German guards, Czech gendarmes, or members of the internal ghetto police. Today's visitors to this site are seriously mistaken when they view the village, sit in the lovely central market place, and view the fountain spewing (squandering) precious water or watch happy children playing catch. In our limited free time during our imprisonment, we moved about the crowded streets while ghetto guards at the doors of the various barracks reminded us to "keep to the right" in order to maintain the steady flow of foot traffic.

People were living in attics, cellars, and hallways. Hundreds were sleeping in the space that would normally accommodate two or three individuals. No one ever knew exactly how many prisoners were in Theresienstadt at any given time. Although there was intricate, elaborate record keeping, mandatory daily counts of the inmates in each nook and cranny, and artfully illustrated daily reports to the *Kommandantur,* none of these figures was accurate. Many of the numbers were routinely forged: the room elders, barrack elders, and house elders often refrained from submitting the names of recently deceased inmates in order to collect these dead prisoners' food ration cards or their allocated bread portions. Each job had its benefits, and the ability to obtain additional food in this manner was the benefit that went with that particular job.

In the camp in 1943, various work assignments had differing advantages: for a while, I worked in the *Zentralbad,* the community showers, which provided me an opportunity to wash myself *if* there was running water. The water supply was totally inadequate, and very often we could not draw a drop to wash or to drink. Working at the *Zentralbad,* I could take care of this essential need. This opportunity might well have saved my life.

Inmates among the working population were issued coupons and assigned a specific time (often weeks or months in the future) when they could go to the *Zentralbad* and take a shower, along with two or three dozen other bathers under the multiple shower heads. Men and women were scheduled at separate times.

Prisoners would queue up in front of the *Zentralbad,* patiently awaiting their turn while standing in the dusty, unpaved street in any kind of weather. Very often we had to inform them, "We have no water. Go home and await your next assigned schedule." This next schedule could be weeks or months in the future, by which time the ticket holder could have been dead or deported to a concentration camp and murdered. Desperate for a chance to wash, many prisoners would trade their bowl of soup or a portion of their bread ration for a shower ticket.

Working in the agricultural details was hard labor. The *Landwirtschaft* workers marched out of the camp, usually accompanied by a Czech guard, and tended the fields for the farmers in the surrounding villages. However, this work assignment meant that they could steal an occasional potato, a carrot, or a head of cabbage—always hoping that the guards who performed sporadic physical inspections upon reentry would not catch them with this loot.

At one time during the summer of 1943, I worked with a group of young women in such a field. We were given fists full of beans to plant in assigned, neat rows. While stooped over to do this work, I ate many of the beans, raw, whenever I thought the guard was not watching me. Chances are that not too many beans grew in that field during the following season.

The ever-present hunger and thirst were our worst enemies. Vermin and overcrowding contributed to the spread of many infectious diseases. Long hours of unpaid labor, seven days a week, consumed our strength and sapped our energy. The now much touted cultural life in this camp was not available for all prisoners, and most of us were much too tired, too hungry, and too dispirited to participate.

During the seminar in 1993, we were served reasonably good food, in adequate quantities. We ate in a pleasant communal dining room in the former SS Club House, seated at long tables with cheerful bouquets of wild flowers in the center of each table, next to salt and pepper shakers. We had paper napkins, tablecloths, plates, cups, saucers, and glasses for water—plenty of water. My fellow conference attendees raised their eyebrows in disbelief when I reminisced about how hungry we had been, how we suffered continually from thirst, vermin, depression, fear of redeportation to the even deadlier camps in the East.

In 1993, the cheerful waiters and waitresses were young recruits from the Czech army—the garrison served again its original military purpose then. This time I was permitted to come and go as I deemed fit, at any time of day or night, anywhere on and off the grounds—no curfews and no lights-out. Nothing was "off limits." All this took some getting used to. I suffered a severe case of disorientation—culture shock.

The gracious program planners in 1993 even provided a social evening in a rather formal setting: the erstwhile SS club's dining hall or ballroom, with several honored guests from Prague in attendance. Our servers were picturesquely attired in some striped pink-and-white uniforms for this occasion. They anxiously watched every bite we ate and every glass of wine we drank. Only later did I learn that they had been promised the leftovers from the feast for their own consumption. And they had promised their buddies at the barracks that they would throw a party after the official soiree was over.

My biggest shock came later in the evening when one of the fellow seminar attendees approached me and introduced herself: she was Frau Kypke, the widow of a wartime SS guard from Auschwitz. How and why she had ever found her way into this particular gathering was a mystery. Clearly, it was not a sack-and-ashes pilgrimage. I knew then that I had again landed in some forecourt of Dante's Inferno—for the second time. And it was to get worse.

During the following day, we all split up into several study groups. I attended a seminar discussing those of my former fellow prisoners who had—prior to their arrest for being Jewish—achieved fame in the fields of literature and the arts. This topic seemed appropriate because in 1944–45 I had been acquainted with several of them.

The leader of this particular seminar spoke only Czech, even though the official language for the conference was German. The translation for the seminar attendees was not high tech and simultaneous as it had been at some of the other sessions because the room we were using was not equipped to handle such an installation.

Frau Kypke, the SS guard's widow, was a member of this breakout session and took it all in with a benign smile as the various speakers spoke about writers, musicians, politicians, painters, soldiers, journalists, dancers, tenors, sopranos, and other greats who would have had much to offer the world if only they had been allowed to live.

Being naturally tactful about the painful reality of our topic, the speakers touched infrequently on the fact that all these people had died here of hunger, neglect, typhoid fever, encephalitis, tuberculosis, hepatitis, dysentery, and other diseases. Or that some had been redeported to other extermination camps. Some were beaten to death, shot, or hanged. Out of some 170,000 inmates, a few had been singled out for "special treatment" (i.e., killing) in the ghetto (the large garrison) or at the nearby penal colony Kleine Festung. One of these inmates was Dr. Paul Eppstein from Berlin, a one-time Theresienstadt elder, head of the Judenrat (the SS-appointed, internal Jewish administrative body). He was taken to the Kleine Festung and shot in a potato field nearby. He knew too much and had become an embarrassment.

Frau Kypke listened and smiled politely through it all. At one point, she raised her right hand like a good student and asked for specific details of the various writers' works while in Theresienstadt. "What papers," she wanted to know, "in the outside world did they write for while incarcerated here? Was any of this work preserved and available?"

I am sorry to admit that I lost my cool at that point. I had known all along that I wanted to kill that lady—and with her many other people who are afflicted with selective amnesia. Or even those who claimed ignorance, then and now, subtly denying the facts as I knew them to be.

I cut in with a brief nod toward the head table, speaking in German to make sure she would understand: "My dear lady, we did not have toilet paper for more than two years. We certainly did not have any paper for manuscripts. We were here to die and to be killed. Period." With that, I sat down. Relieved but also very much ashamed about my lack of self-control, I could sense that everyone around me was embarrassed. Fifty years of stiff-upper-lip post–World War II practice had suddenly proved vain.

Winston Churchill said, "It's exhilarating to have been shot at and missed." Having experienced twelve years of Nazi persecution, I appreciate life a little more each day.

4. Autobiographical Notes

ALEXANDER KIMEL

I was born in a small town, Podhajce, in Galizia. In 1939, my hometown was occupied by the Red Army, and a year later my family was thrown out of our house, and our business was "nationalized." Fearing that we would be sent to Siberia, my father moved the family to another small town, Rohatyn, where we survived the ghetto. Between 1941 and 1943, the Germans killed almost all the Jews. Out of ten thousand inhabitants, only one hundred survived. I personally have never been to a concentration camp.

The Killing Process

On March 21, 1942, the ghetto was raided by Einsatzgruppen, and thirty-seven hundred Jews—men, women, and children—were driven into a ditch about a mile from the ghetto and shot in cold blood. A few months later, about two thousand people were caught in a so-called *Aktion* (pogrom), loaded into cattle cars, and driven to the Belzec death camp for gassing.

Three months later, on the Day of Atonement, the Germans raided the ghetto, catching the people praying in makeshift synagogues. About fifteen hundred people were packed into cattle trains, without food and water, and taken to Belzec for gassing.

On June 8, 1943, the ghetto was liquidated, and all Jews who were caught were shot. The area was declared *judenrein,* "free of Jews," which meant that any Jews caught afterward were executed on the spot. I had personally escaped the ghetto a month earlier and hid in the forest and surrounding villages. After the liberation, I went back to school, and in 1959 I emigrated to the United States.

Fast Life

Life in the ghetto was dangerous and challenging. A day in the ghetto was like a month under normal conditions. A month was like a year, and a year was a lifetime. There was never a dull moment. Buying a quart of milk was wrought with danger. If the Nazis caught you, you were dead. One day they caught a Jewish family outside the ghetto, and the family was shot on the spot—a couple with two beautiful, cuddly daughters.

Another amazing thing was the unbelievable level of adaptation of the human species. The will to live was so strong. In between the spurts of danger, young people fell in love, women became pregnant, quarrels erupted between neighbors, and so on. Even parties were given in the ghetto. They used to call them *barbarki.*

One of my fondest memories from the ghetto relates to panics. Yes, panics. I loved panics. Whenever a German appeared in the ghetto, panic erupted. People were screaming, yelling, calling their children, and hiding in the bunkers. I usually stayed above ground and made myself . . . potato pancakes. In the ghetto, we suffered from chronic hunger. I always wanted to eat. How delicious those pancakes tasted.

Ghetto Life

Life in the ghetto was physically and emotionally draining. Almost every day I was sent on slave labor assignments, such as cleaning sewers, digging ditches, or working on the railroad. At night, we would dig bunkers, as the hideaways were called. The digging and disposing of the dirt had to be done in secrecy, from the neighbors and the Germans.

Rumors

The ghetto was full of rumors. We used to joke that the ghetto was running its own news service, called Jidden Willen Azoj (JIWO, "Jews Wish So").

The Germans confiscated all the radios, so without newspapers it was easy to float rumors. The news coming down the grapevine was very encouraging, for instance: Roosevelt declared that every Gentile who saved a Jew would be awarded five acres of land. Or a transport of Jews was intercepted in Przemysl by the German army. The army was rebelling against the killings.

General Staff

In the ghetto, we had our own General Staff, composed of old Jews sitting in a makeshift synagogue and planning the conduct of the war: "The British have to attack Italy." Another "general" suggested that Romania should be attacked. If only the Allies had listened to their advice. . . .

Punishment for Hitler

Another favorite pastime in the ghetto was devising a creative punishment for Hitler. The most favorite variant: Hitler would be caught, put into a mobile cage, and transported from town to town so that each Jew could spit into his face. Unfortunately, this punishment was never realized.

Despite all the killings, we believed that the Germans would lose the war and that we would survive. My guess is that a young healthy person cannot imagine that he will die, that the sun will stop shining, that the birds will be silent, or that darkness will prevail. Death is hard to imagine.

Will to Live and Resilience

The Jews in our ghetto showed an amazing emotional resilience. Despite all the tragedies, pain, and hopelessness, there was only one case of suicide. This was less than in normal times. It looks as if living in dangerous conditions has a therapeutic value. As it is written in the Talmud, *"Sakanath Nefesh Doche Hakol."* The danger of life overrides all other problems. The more life is unattainable, the more it is desirable, so the will to live became stronger and stronger.

Night Life

Believe it or not, there was an intensive night life in the ghetto. Every few houses maintained their own night watches to guard against a night or predawn raid by the Nazis. Going out meant keeping the night watches together. In the crowded conditions of the ghetto, young people had their chance for privacy.

Shame

One of my most painful memories is connected with my refusal to share bread with a hungry man. At that time, I was sixteen years old, working in a quarry. Every morning I got up at five o'clock in the morning and took an hour ride to the quarry. Splitting boulders with a twenty-pound hammer was exhausting. For our labor we received an additional ration of two hundred grams of stale bread. One day during the "lunch break," a neighbor of mine approached me and asked for a piece of bread. I refused because I was hungry myself. A few weeks later the neighbor was killed. This small episode has stayed with me all my life, always causing a feeling of shame.

Death of My Mother

A baby in the ghetto was a kiss of death, at least for my mother. Our neighbor, Ania, got pregnant and refused to have an abortion. In two adjacent houses, the Gutmans and the Achts shared a bunker and kept night watches together. The bunker was made from an old pickle cellar. The outside entrance door was bricked up, and a new camouflaged trap door was installed in the kitchen. The bunker had saved our lives in the previous two *Aktionen,* but now we faced a dilemma. Despite our pleas and threats, Ania was scared to have an abortion. There were no doctors in the ghetto. Soon she was so heavy that she could not pass through the trap door into the bunker. In case of an action, we all would get killed.

It was decided that Ania would slowly descend into the bunker and stay there until she gave birth. So poor Ania stayed alone in the dark, damp hole. My mother decided to help her and volunteered to sleep with her in the bunker. Because of the unsanitary conditions, my mother became infected with typhoid. Her heart condition, coupled with the lack of medication, caused her death. My mother died, but the baby who was born miraculously survived and lives in Israel now.

The Concert

One day I was invited to a violin concert in the ghetto. It was an event I will never forget. In a small dark room, about fifteen teenagers gathered to listen to a violin recital by one of our friends. I looked at those emaciated faces, wrinkled with pain, the downcast eyes revealing the distress of their souls. They were like withering branches cut off healthy trees.

The violinist played cheerful Russian songs such as "Katiusha, Capitan," and suddenly he switched the tune, and the known melody of the "Hatikva" filled the room: *"Od Lo Avda Tikvatejnu,"* our hopes are still alive. The tune and the words brought me to tears. I stood up, and through tears I looked at the beautiful youth condemned to death and asked myself a question: "Why? Why is this happening to us?" A scene from the Bible appeared before my eyes—the blinded Samson bringing down the Philistine Temple. At that moment, I would not have minded being blinded if only I could bring down this cruel world.

My Beliefs

I matured in the ghetto and grew up with the notion that danger of losing one's life is a normal state of being. I rarely experienced fear. I had this strong inner conviction that I would survive. To this day, I ask myself this question: Was I predestined to survive, or were my beliefs a self-fulfilling prophecy? I was caught twice by the Germans, and each time I calmly bluffed myself out. I acted calmly because I believed that I would survive. Sometimes I wonder if everybody else had the same feelings.

The Collapse of the Bunker

A few months after my mother's death, the family faced a major crisis—our bunker collapsed. We shared a small one-bedroom apartment with three spinsters. One night we were awakened by a loud rumbling, followed by a strong quake, and in a few seconds the outside wall collapsed—just like the walls of Jericho.

It turned out that the water from the melting snow had penetrated the ventilation shaft of the bunker, causing its collapse. During the next day, the Germans came to survey the strange phenomenon. Luckily, they accepted our explanation that the spring water had undermined the flimsy foundations.

We now did not have a place to live, and, worst of all, we did not have a bunker. Without a solid bunker, life was not worth living. Fortunately, my father found a solution. He promised to pay for the construction of a new bunker if the neighbors would squeeze us in, providing us with a small kitchen in which to live.

Soon, a master builder was hired, and the construction of a new, ultramodern piggyback hideaway started. The new entrance to the bunker complex was located in the cellar. Under an old piece of furniture, there was a masked entrance door to the first bunker, which was used for storing clothing and other valuables. Another trap door, located under a pile of dirty clothing, led to the main bunker. It was a long structure carved in clay, with benches also carved from clay. The arrangement resembled a streetcar.

Interestingly enough, the collapse of the first bunker saved our lives a few months later. During the last *judenrein Aktion,* the Germans discovered only the first bunker but did not find anybody there and left the door open. The other raiders assumed that the people inside were gone.

The Fortress: Sevastopol

Regarding the bunkers, the creativity and the determination of people trying to save their lives defy imagination. One megabunker, a marvel of ingenuity, was built in our ghetto and was called Sevastopol, after the Russian fortress on the Black Sea. Although everybody talked about it, only a few saw it. As it was rumored, Sevastopol contained a series of underground chambers, equipped with running water, electricity, and provisions for one year.

The bunker could hold about thirty people, who were the envy of the ghetto. As it turned out, Sevastopol survived about six months after the last *judenrein Aktion,* which took place in June 1943. Early in the winter days, a German gendarme who was patrolling the old ghetto area discovered a column of vapor rising from a hole in the ground, which turned out to be an outlet of a ventilation shaft.

After the discovery, the Germans tried to flush out the bunker's inhabitants by throwing hand grenades through the opening. They almost gave up when somebody suggested to flood the bunker. The Germans brought in a fire pumper and pumped water for two days, until the Jews emerged. I knew those people, and I often wondered how it felt to live underground and watch the water rising slowly, ready to engulf them.

Radical Medicine

"We have to stop the typhoid ravaging the ghetto. Please organize a hospital and transfer all sick people to this place." The Germans gave the Jewish Council two days to organize the hospital. On the third day, two Germans came and shot all the patients at point blank range. The Nazis practiced radical medicine.

Humiliation

I was often sent to work outside the ghetto, where I could get a piece of bread. I hated meeting some of my Gentile classmates. Seeing me, they usually exclaimed: "You are still alive?" I felt like a dead man walking.

Swollen Legs

As time went on, I saw people in the ghetto walking on funny legs. After a while, I realized that those people had swollen legs, caused by extreme hunger.

Worms

In the ghetto, I discovered that I had worms. Realizing that parasitic worms can kill a starving man, I decided to get rid of them by drinking a glass of kerosene. For a few months, my stomach was digesting and rejecting the kerosene. It almost killed me but had little effect on the worms.

Communal Disaster

When I look at the Holocaust survivors today, I am amazed by how well they adjusted to a new life. They all have settled down and thrive; I don't know any survivors who require public assistance. It is said in the Talmud, *"Tzarot Rabim Chatzit Nechama":* a disaster that strikes a community is easier to take.

Adjustment

In the ghetto, I often recalled my fear of academic examinations. "What a fool I was to be scared of exams." To my surprise, after the liberations, that fear of examinations returned. It seems that our reactions and phobias are very strong.

5. Historical Position of the Hungarian Jewry and Untold Ghetto Accounts

AGNES KADAR

Part of this work was originally presented at the Twenty-seventh Annual Conference on the Holocaust and the Churches, March 6–9, 1999, in Uniondale, New York. I am grateful to Ms. Roberta Levin, my husband, Ivan, and sons, Jerry and Danny, for help and encouragement with the development of this material. Many thanks to those who for the first time shared their harrowing experiences with me: Peter C., Elizabeth S., Irene W., Susan L., Ivan, Lilly, and Margot G. Reliving the darkest hours of our lives is not easier with time, but we all want our memories to teach the generations to come. This essay is a memorial for those who could not tell their stories.

Substantial Progress: Parallel Anti-Semitism

The history of Hungarian Jewry abounds in paradox: assimilation in the cities, orthodoxy in the rural areas. The first major moves to assimilate Jews (and Protestants) into the essentially Catholic Austro-Hungarian Empire was made by Joseph II in 1782, when he mandated that Jews join the army and adopt German family names.[1]

In 1867, Hungary and Austria finally settled the aftermath of the 1848 revolt, and, consequently, the Jewish population was emancipated. Jews became full citizens of the empire and were even permitted to own land.

At the same time, a well-known writer of the era, Kalman Mikszath, defined an "anti-Semite as a person who hates the Jews more than absolutely necessary and reasonable." By 1911, 58 percent of the medical doctors and 61 percent of the lawyers in the Austro-Hungarian monarchy were Jewish.[2] There were nine Jewish generals and fourteen generals of Jewish descent in the army.[3] Conversion to Catholicism was helpful but not necessary for advancement. Just like the assimilated Jews in Germany, a substantial portion of the Jews of Hungary professed to be Hungarians whose religion happened to be Jewish.

Repression Accompanied by Blindness of Jews Who Were Hungarian First, Jews Second

Dramatic changes occurred after World War I. The Austro-Hungarian monarchy disintegrated. Jews now represented a significant minority population in Hungary and were identified with the ill-fated and short-lived Hungarian Soviet Republic. The postwar right-wing regime under Admiral Miklós Horthy was anti-Semitic and anti-Communist. It was also antiliberal because it was the Western liberal democracies that had imposed the Trianon peace settlement in which Hungary lost two-thirds of its historical territory.[4] The protection of "Catholic Hungary" from its enemies became the political slogan of the 1920s. The Hungarian Parliament in 1920 passed its first anti-Jewish law, years before the German National Socialist (Nazi) movement began to promulgate such laws. The Numerus Clausus Law eliminated the equal rights of Hungarian Jews and limited the number of Jewish students admitted to Hungarian higher educational institutions.[5] Still, the assimilated Jews were not swayed. They were Hungarians first and last. They even objected to the League of Nations inquiry into the limitation of the rights of a minority. The Jewish leadership considered the Numerus Clausus Law an internal affair and defended the rationale espoused by the Hungarian government.[6] (Although the father of the Zionist movement, Theodore Herzl, was Hungarian born, Zionism had few followers in Hungary between the world wars). Subsequent Hungarian governments realized that Jews were needed if Hungary was to improve its economy and rebuild its banking system and industries. Therefore, rabid anti-Semitism was controlled for the time being.

The Downward Spiral

The Nazification of Germany and the birth of the Berlin-Rome Axis fueled the cry to decrease the number of Jews possessing influential positions in Hungary. Consecutive Hungarian governments, eager to regain territories lost with the Trianon Peace Treaty, positioned themselves to take advantage of the rapidly developing German expansionism. To solve the "Jewish question," the Hungarian Parliament passed the first Jewish law in 1938, which limited the number of Jews in white-collar jobs but did not define a Jew in racial terms. The second law, passed a year later, limited Jewish participation in Hungary's economic life. Under some circumstances, converts to Christianity were also classified as Jews. Objection to these laws came primarily from the Hungarian liberal intellectuals. A note of objection was signed by fifty-nine individuals, including Bela Bartok and Zoltan Kodaly,[7] and submitted to the Parliament. The leaders of the Christian churches—Justinian Seredy (the cardinal of the Roman Catholic Church), Laszlo Ravasz (the Protestant bishop), and Sandor Raffay (the Lutheran bishop)—objected only to the application of the anti-Jewish laws against those who had converted to Christianity, but they did not object to the laws in general. On the contrary, they declared the laws timely. The third "Jewish law," passed in 1941, was strictly a racial law. Much of the Jewish population did not comprehend its significance, but some felt an uneasy foreboding. The poet Miklós Radnoti wrote in a letter in 1942, "I do not deny that I am Jewish but I do not feel any need to belong to any Jewish religious group. Being Jewish is a problem, but I did not make it into one. It was forced on me. I am a Hungarian poet and it doesn't matter who says what, even if I will be killed for it."[8] (He was murdered during one of the death marches in 1944.)

As the Western democracies gave in to German expansionism, Hungary's attachment to Germany was rewarded by the return of part of the territories lost at the peace table. The citizenry rejoiced when, between

1938 and 1941, parts of Slovakia, Transylvania, and Yugoslavia became Hungarian territory again. According to the 1941 census, 67,876 Jews lived in the returned territories, so the Jewish minority in Hungary grew significantly. Jews from all over occupied eastern Europe tried to escape into "independent" Hungary, where conditions were better than in the German-occupied lands. These "foreign" Jews, including those who lived in the newly reconquered territories, added another facet to the "Jewish problem."

This is Irene's story:

> I was raised in Marosvasarhely, a predominantly Hungarian-speaking town in Transylvania, a province of Romania. I was the youngest in the family of six. My siblings were much older than I. My parents were retired artisans. By 1940, I was making a name for myself as a first-class seamstress. We were neither rich nor poor. We lived comfortably until the Hungarians "reconquered" the part of Transylvania where Marosvasarhely is located. Immediately, anti-Semitism skyrocketed. The Hungarian-owned stores would not serve Jewish customers, and the Hungarians would not shop in Jewish-owned stores. Life became much harder when we became part of the mother country.

Hungary was now indebted to the Third Reich, and one of the demands from Berlin was to solve "the Jewish question." Subsequent Hungarian governments seesawed between succumbing to pressure from Germany, internal pressures, economic common sense, and, at some level, aristocratic fairness. However, nothing could stop the downward spiral of Jewish suffering as World War II progressed.

Toward the "Final Solution"

In August 1941, the Hungarian government deported into German-held territories fifteen to eighteen thousand "foreign Jews" (mostly Polish). At this time, the German authorities were unable to deal with such a large number of Jews in a recently occupied area, so they simply murdered them in Kam'ianets'-Podil's'kyi. As the news reached Budapest, even the secretary of interior was shocked, and the deportation of foreign Jews ceased.[9] From this time forward, what would happen to Jews handed over to the Nazi authorities was evident to everyone who dared to consider the prospect.

From the beginning of the war, Jewish men were conscripted into labor battalions, where conditions were so bad that Secretary of Defense Vilmos Nagy, an honorable man, intervened for the Jewish labor battalions; consequently, the conditions temporarily improved. In April 1942, when the Hungarian army started for the Ukrainian front, it was augmented with fifty thousand Jews in the labor battalions. In 1943, only approximately six to seven thousand of these Jews returned to Hungary. Many who died were killed by their own officers; the rest had starved, were tortured, or had frozen to death. By 1943, it was clearly predictable that the Axis would not emerge victorious. The Hungarian governing class, looking for an "honorable" way out of the war, extended protection to its Jews even though Germany wanted Hungary to deport all of its estimated eight hundred thousand Jews to the East. Conditions were poor for Jews in Hungary, but they were allowed to live. Unfortunately, they became complacent and were unprepared for the impending German occupation.

On March 19, 1944, the German army marched into Budapest unopposed. The fate of Hungary's Jews was sealed by Adolf Eichmann's organizational and psychological skills, and by a Nazi-approved Hungarian government. The tactic that had worked in occupied Europe worked in Hungary, too. Jewish Councils were set up, and the Gestapo ruled through the councils' intimidated and often duped members. On April 5, 1944, Jews had to display the yellow Star of David on their outer garments. All Jews were registered. Outside of Budapest, they were forced into limited areas (ghettos) and swiftly deported. Eichmann's few hundred Gestapo men were successful because they enjoyed the whole-hearted cooperation of government agencies, such as the Grandarmerie, and the majority of the general public. The deportation of the Jews started in the reconquered territories on the assumption that the Jews were not really Hungarian. So those who considered themselves Hungarian between the wars while they were part of another country were easily discarded as "foreign Jews."

Irene's story continues:

We heard about the ghettos in Poland but considered it a nightmarish rumor.

One of my brothers lived in Paris. He and his wife sent their young daughter to stay with us to escape the persecution in German-occupied France. Lilly was a lovely outgoing child who made friends with everyone, including the policemen at the street corner close to our house. After the German occupation of Hungary on March 19, 1944, the robbing and annihilation of the Jews in the reconquered territories proceeded very rapidly. On May 3, 1944, while our Hungarian neighbors watched, more than seven thousand Jews were forced into a long, abandoned brick factory. Most of the factory had no roof, so we lived in makeshift tents. One day a policeman sought us out and offered to take Lilly out of the ghetto and raise her as his own child. The policeman, one of those whom Lilly had enchanted years before, risked his life for her but to no avail. My mother would not part from her grandchild, who had been entrusted to her years before by her son. A few weeks later, seven-year-old Lilly died with her grandmother, my mother, in the Auschwitz gas chambers.

The local authorities constantly searched for any valuables the Jews might still have. The town's Jewish jewelry store owner acted as an informer. He knew who had jewelry because most of it had been purchased from him. I presume that he was promised preferential treatment by the Nazi authorities, but he and his family ended up in Auschwitz also. He survived, but his family perished.

The first transport left town on May 27. Those of us who were left in the ghetto saw with horror all the belongings left behind by those deported before us. We were in the second transport, and the last group left for Auschwitz on June 8.

I survived as a slave laborer in a munitions factory in Germany until the American army liberated us. Miraculously, all of my siblings survived, but our parents and Lilly perished.

The deportation of the Jews in the provinces proceeded rapidly. This is Peter's story:

I lived east of Budapest in the town of Szolnok, where the restrictions on the Jews were more stringent than in the capital. By early April 1944, edicts had been posted in Szolnok ordering Jews to always wear a yellow star and restricting the time we could spend outside our homes to two hours each morning. As April came to a close, Jews were instructed to pack their baggage and be ready for transport to the newly created ghetto in town. The size of each person's bag was described in great detail. My mother packed for the two of us. Although she did not know where we were going, she packed, unpacked, and repacked the suitcases several times before she was satisfied that we had what we needed. At 10:00 A.M. on the day of transport, a policeman and a man with a pushcart knocked on our door. After placing our baggage on the cart, my mother and I followed the man with the cart. We were wearing our yellow stars and holding each other's hand. The policeman walked behind us. Our sad little procession attracted onlookers as we made the five-minute walk from our apartment to the newly constructed ghetto near the Orthodox synagogue. Some people just stared at us, but some made nasty, taunting remarks. My mother said a few people had tears in their eyes. I also had tears in my eyes as I was very scared and humiliated.

The Szolnok ghetto consisted of two buildings—the Orthodox synagogue and the Rakos family compound. The synagogue was a sprawling, one-story structure that contained a sanctuary, offices, classrooms, and a large courtyard. Across a little alley, on the side of the synagogue, was the Rakos house. The Rakos family was one of the richest in Szolnok. The contents of both the synagogue and the Rakos home had been completely removed by the Hungarian authorities prior to the opening of the ghetto. Hundreds of people were herded into the empty rooms. The floor space of each room determined the number of occupants assigned to it. A three-by-eight-foot area was allocated for each occupant. My mother and I placed our blankets on the floor so that the narrower end touched a wall and the opposite end terminated in the middle of the room. We put our pillows on top of the blanket against the wall and set our suitcase on the opposite end by our feet. Finally, we covered the area with another blanket. That piece of floor had become our home. Our room was in the Rakos house and had about twenty occupants. My mother, grandmother, aunt, and I formed a family unit, and we slept next to each other. There were three or four other families in the room with us. Toilet facilities were meager, and there was very little privacy. One person would hold up a blanket while someone washed behind it, using a basin of cold water. We ate starches, such as bread and potato soup and some vegetables. It is my dim recollection that the police dropped off the ingredients, but we were responsible for cooking the meals. We also supplemented our diet with food that we [had] brought into the ghetto, but that lasted only for a few days. We had nothing to keep us occupied. The old men played chess or cards. The women washed and mended clothes and talked. The children just hung around, improvised games, and fought with each other.

Our first Friday night service was conducted in the former summer kitchen, where it was impossible to separate the men from the women. The Orthodox men objected to the presence of women at the service. The conservative community was outraged and tried to reason with the Orthodox men. They said that under the circumstances we should not look for trouble but should come together and pray for our safe deliverance. The Orthodox men were unyielding, stating that the laws of Judaism are absolute and must be strictly observed in all circumstances. Heated words were exchanged, and, finally, the Orthodox men walked out and prayed at another location.

After a few days, we were ordered to line up in formation in the courtyard of the compound to meet the new commander of the ghetto. We were also instructed to select a ghetto council and designate somebody as its head. After we waited in formation for what seemed an interminable amount of time, the gates were swung open, and a young German officer and his sizable entourage marched through. The young officer faced us, struck an arrogant pose, and through an interpreter called for the head of the council. A respected member of the community stepped forward. He had gray hair and was probably in his late fifties. The officer sized him up and said, "I expect you to follow my orders." He removed his pistol from its holder and continued, "I have killed three or four Jewish Council leaders already because they did not do exactly what I told them to." The old man was visibly shaken and said in a halting voice, "I will follow your orders; we all will." The German officer's attempt at intimidation was only partly successful. We were scared but also outraged that a young man would address a man twice his age with such arrogance and disrespect. These feelings betrayed our naïveté. Then the officer delivered a short speech about our future. He informed us that in a few days, we would be transported to another location, where we would be required to work. We would be treated well as long as we did our jobs. Some of us believed the promise of good treatment for hard work, but most of us were skeptical and scared.

The next day we were ordered to pack all our belongings and report to the courtyard for inspection. We lined up in front of inspection stations where an "inspector" went through our belongings. He threw the items he confiscated to the right and the items he allowed us to take with us to the left. Then we were marched, under police guard, out the gates of the compound. As far as we could see, horse-driven carts were lined up waiting to transport us. The drivers of these carts were local peasants, mostly women. For a small payment, our neighbors and fellow citizens had volunteered to move the Jewish population out of town, perhaps permanently. About ten of us were crowded onto a wagon that took us to a sugar refinery that was temporarily abandoned because of the war (4,666 Jews were eventually deported from this site). We were taken to some empty factory rooms and ordered to set up our blanket beds in the same way as in the ghetto. We were instructed to dig a very large hole a hundred yards or so away from the building. This was our communal latrine—a low wooden fence served as a seat. The latrine was out in the open air and was used by both men and women. In some of the factory rooms, there were a number of industrial sinks. These rooms became our washrooms.

Things became more frightening by the hour. First, Jewish criminals serving time in the local jails were brought to the refinery. Then trains started to arrive on the refinery's spur line, bringing Jews from the region's small towns and villages. Most of us were paralyzed with fear. The wealthy members of the community were taken back to their former homes and ordered to show where they had hidden their gold and money. If they did not produce hidden treasure, they were beaten savagely. They were brought back into the camp beaten, bruised, and bloody.

The Jewish Council was asked to organize the people in the camp into two groups, A List and B List. The lists were widely distributed throughout the compound. We were on the B List. My grandmother noticed that all the wealthy people of the town were on the A List. She ordered my mother to ask some family friends who were on the council to move our family over to the A List. My reluctant and embarrassed mother obeyed her upset mother-in-law and approached one of her high school teachers and requested the transfer for our entire family group. The high school teacher was somber and said that he could not do it because too many people were involved. He would, however, move my mother and any family member with her last name to the A List. Consequently, Lili Z.; her son, Peter Z.; her mother-in-law, Hannah Z.; and her sister-in-law, Amalia Z., ended up on the A List with the wealthy Jews of the town. The rest of the family remained on the B List. Around June 25, two trains pulled in on the spur line. The people on the A List were loaded onto one train, and the people on the B List were loaded onto the other. The train carrying the A List went to Strasshof (near Vienna, Austria), where the people were eventually dispersed into small work camps. Most of the people on the A List survived the Holocaust. The train carrying people on the B List headed for Auschwitz. Most of these people, including my mother's family, perished in the Holocaust.

For the longest time, I was extremely naïve about these events. I actually believed that it was a random act of fate that my family ended up on the train to Austria rather than on the train to Auschwitz. I was in my twenties when my mother told me how my grandma had realized that people with money and influence were on the A List and how she had forced my mother to request a transfer to that list. I also realized how much sorrow and guilt my mother lived with for years because she was unable to save [the rest of] her family by transferring them to the A List.

One town after another was "freed" from the presence of Jews. This is Elizabeth's story:

I grew up in the town of Gyor, part of a working-class Orthodox Jewish family. My father was very proud of the decorations he had earned as a Hungarian soldier during World War I. We always felt that we were true Hungarians.

In 1943, I was in my early twenties and an active Zionist. The previous year we had lost my brother, who was serving in a labor battalion on

> the Ukrainian front. The Zionist leadership offered me and another active member temporary residence in Budapest and rapid transit to Palestine. I declined their offer, refusing to leave my grieving parents, and chose instead to stay and share their fate. My friend did not make it to Palestine either. The next time we met was in Auschwitz.
>
> By May 23, 1944, the Jewish population of Gyor (about forty-six hundred) and environs (about one thousand) was concentrated in the area around the Orthodox synagogue. My grandparents lived there in a small two-room apartment. When my family was forced to move in with them, ten people were living where two had lived before.

Baron Vilmos Apor, bishop of Gyor, in a courageous act, sent a strongly worded letter to the Hungarian secretary of interior, objecting to the mistreatment of the Jewish citizens of Gyor. He was threatened with jail but continued to voice his outrage.[10] Unfortunately, without support from the cardinal, his protests had no practical results.

During this period, the Jewish leadership of Gyor was duped by the Jewish Council at Budapest. The council accepted the Eichmann propaganda that if the Jews worked for the German war effort, they and their families would be safe; accordingly, they urged all the Jewish communities to follow orders. Even though the council and everyone in leadership positions knew about the extermination camps, they could not face their fellow Jews and tell the truth.

Elizabeth's story continues:

> The Germans and the local Hungarians in charge of deportation were interested primarily in the imagined or real wealth of the Jews. Threatening immediate death, they continually demanded that everything of value be turned over to them. At one point, everyone was marched to the school courtyard and ordered to strip—young and old, men and women—all out in the open and naked. Body searches followed. Midwives probed the women's private parts, searching for hidden jewelry. The loss of dignity and privacy still makes me shudder. We were moved to World War I–era barracks in early June. I can still hear the laughter and demeaning comments from the citizenry as they watched the Jews drag

their meager belongings through town. The Jews of Gyor were deported to Auschwitz between June 7 and 11, 1944. My family, in great foresight, obtained food that would not spoil easily, such as bacon, which is a Hungarian staple food. The first time in my life I ate nonkosher food was on the way to Auschwitz. Because I was young and strong, I worked and survived as a slave laborer in the AEG factory in Trautenau, making field mines. The Russian army occupied the town as the war ended on May 9, 1945.

This is Margot's story:

Our family lived in the eastern Hungarian town of Debrecen. I was the youngest of seven siblings. My parents were Orthodox Jews. My father was a grain merchant who traveled from farm to farm to purchase grain. It was a hard life during the depression, and we were not well off. We lived in a three-room apartment in the Jewish section of this historic town. We all attended Jewish schools. My mother was very keen on education, and father tried to make a living to support all of us.

After the German occupation of Hungary, as in other provincial towns, the Jews of Debrecen were called to City Hall and ordered to hand over their valuables. Those who were known to be wealthy were beaten and tortured until they revealed the hiding places they used to save their valuables.

On May 9, 1944, two areas were designated as ghettos. One was the part of town where most of the ultra-Orthodox Jews lived (the small ghetto), and the other was a larger area where we lived (the large ghetto). The two areas were separated by one of the main boulevards of the town, and Jews were not allowed to cross it. In five days, by May 15, all Jews had to reside in the ghetto. They had to find accommodations and move their belongings. My family did not have to move as we were already living in a building designated as part of the ghetto. Nine of us lived in a three-room apartment, so at first nobody moved in with us.

Both Debrecen's mayor, Dr. Kolcsey, and the town's prosecutor, Dr. Zold, lost their positions because they objected to the establishment of the ghetto. They were threatened with further repercussions over their stand.

Margot's story continues:

> Very soon the small ghetto was abolished, and all the ultra-Orthodox families had to move into the large ghetto. The family that moved in with us would not cook in our kitchen, as it was not kosher enough for them. They used the cooking facilities of another ultra-Orthodox family. Food was scarce—we had only what had been stored before the ghetto was sealed from the outside world on June 7. The Jewish Council had very limited resources to feed and care for the inhabitants of the ghetto.
>
> The Allied bombing, which started on June 2, was scary for everyone, especially for the children. But it also meant the end of the war was coming. While life was hard in the ghetto, we were at least in familiar surroundings. However, on June 21, we were moved to a brick factory on the outskirts of town. Jews from all the surrounding villages had also been brought there. On June 26, we were forced into cattle cars and began what we feared might be our last trip. For three days, the train moved slowly toward the east. Then suddenly it reversed direction, and we were taken back to Hungary. Even under these horrendous conditions, people rejoiced because they thought the war was over and they were going home. The train kept on going, and we ended up in Strasshof, Austria. Miraculously, all of my siblings and parents survived the deportation and built successful lives for themselves.

On May 15, 1944, the same day the deportation of the Jews from the provinces began, Vatican delegate Angelo Rotta, in a note to the Hungarian government, objected to the barbaric treatment of the Jews. Hungary was (and still is) a Catholic country, so the Vatican's wishes carried weight. Nonetheless, Hungary's Cardinal Seredy chose to speak out only for the converts who were persecuted. Thousands of Jews flocked to the Christian churches for conversion and protection. Some priests and nuns risked their lives to save Jews, in particular children, whom they placed in convent schools.

This is Susan's story:

Because my father was a decorated World War I veteran and a successful engineer, before and during the early part of the war, we lived in middle-class comfort in Budapest. The district we lived in was heavily blue collar. The children in the elementary school often hurled anti-Semitic remarks at me. In the summer of 1944, we had to move into a "Jewish house." We moved in with the family of my father's brother. My father was the titular head of both families because his brother had already perished in a labor battalion. My cousin Marika and I were good friends and about the same age—ten going on eleven. At this time, the Germans demanded Jewish laborers from the Hungarian government. Because all able-bodied men were gone by now, women, like my mother, were sent in forced marches toward what was then the Austrian Province of Germany. Eventually most of them died either on the long road or in the concentration camps. My mother was among the few who survived.

We had an aunt who was Christian not only in religion, but in spirit, too. She took my cousin and me to her apartment and hid us until, through her contact at the Swedish consulate, she was able to make arrangements for us to be taken to an orphanage operated by a Carmelite order of nuns. I remember the night when we were driven in a Swedish diplomatic car to the orphanage on the outskirts of Budapest. We were sitting on pillows so that from the outside of the car, we did not look like children. The nuns were kind and very careful because another house run by the same order had been betrayed; consequently, not only the Jewish children, but also all the orphans and the nuns were executed. We kept our first names but were given last names starting with the same letter as our real names. A nun would wake me up in the middle of the night, asking my name to make sure that even in my sleep I would give the appropriate answer. We did not know who was Jewish and who was not, so the chance of even accidental identification was reduced. Because the location of the orphanage was east of Budapest, the Russian army, after some horrendous bombardment, overran the area right after Christmas of 1944. For most of us, it meant liberation. But not for the kindly nuns, some of whom were raped in front of the children. The food supply, which kept us alive, was taken away, so we all started to starve. When the rest of Budapest was liberated, my father came to take us home.

> To thank the Carmelite order for saving our lives, when my father restarted his construction business, he rebuilt their bombed-out church. Sometimes I wonder what happened to the Jewish children in the orphanage who were never claimed by surviving family members because none had survived.
>
> I encountered a bigoted priest who taught me and my Jewish classmates the catechism and told us that he had no interest in saving our mortal bodies. However, if we converted, our immortal souls would be saved. Even as a frightened ten-year-old girl, I recognized the hypocrisy of this "Christian's" words and did everything to save my mortal body with its immortal soul attached to it.

Between May 15 and July 8, 1944 (after the Normandy landing on June 4, 1944), 427,400 Jews were deported from the Hungarian countryside to Auschwitz. Fewer than 5 percent survived. According to the Vrba-Wetzler report (an account of Auschwitz and Birkenau by escaped inmates Rudolf Vrba and Alfred Wetzler, intended to spread the word about Auschwitz and Birkenau and thus save Jewish lives), the Germans had been gearing up in Auschwitz for the expected influx of Hungarian Jews as early as January 1944.[11] This information and the purpose of Auschwitz were passed on to the Jewish Councils of Slovakia and Hungary and to the Zionist organizations in Switzerland, who communicated the information to the West. The Jewish Councils, for whatever reasons, did not make the information public. My future husband and I were both ten years old and easily remember the events of the period.

Ivan remembers:

> We still lived in our apartment in the summer of 1944 when a postcard arrived. It was sent from "Waldsee" and bore a simple message: "We are all well. I am working in my trade. They even gave me a brand new chisel and hammer.—With kisses, your brother Laci."
>
> We understood that Laci was telling us something, but we didn't know what. If he was working in his trade, "they" would have given him a concert piano because he was not a mason, but a concert pianist—a

> student of Bela Bartok, a graduate of the Hungarian Academy of Music, a composer of popular songs, and a famous band leader. When Jews no longer could be employed in the professions, he moved with his wife and daughter to Ungvar on the northeastern part of the reconquered territory of Hungary. During the summer of 1944, he and his family were deported. We knew about the deportation, so we scrutinized the message. We looked for "Waldsee" on the map with no success. We understood that he was not working in his trade. He and his family were probably not "well." More than that, we could not surmise. A boy in the house who collected stamps saw the card on our table and asked if he could soak off the stamp. We gave him the card, telling him to give it back after he took off the stamp. The next day he returned, his face ashen. He pointed to where the stamp had been and ran away without a word. Under the stamp there was a message: *Auschwitz. Sose latlak titeket,* meaning: "Auschwitz. I will never see you again." We were devastated. We did not know where or what Auschwitz was and could not find it on the map. But the message was clear and correct. All three of them perished.

Germans were willing to barter Jewish lives for money (approximately eighteen hundred Jews went to Switzerland instead of to Auschwitz) and for industrial property. On June 26, 1944, thirty-two members of the elite Jewish industrial families flew on a special Lufthansa plane to Lisbon, Portugal. As a survivor of the time and place, I cannot blame people for saving themselves and their families. It was not a time for altruism. Survival instincts took over.

By June 24, 1944, the remaining Jews in Budapest were forced to reside in houses designated by a "Jewish star." These houses were not in a closed area or ghetto, but a substantial portion was in the area that later became the ghetto.

Mounting outside pressures, combined with the Allied victories in Europe and in the Pacific, had a dampening effect on the collaboration of the Hungarian government with the Germans. On June 27, 1944, the three major Christian church leaders attempted to form a united front in order to protect the Jews who had converted. They planned to have a letter objecting to the inhuman treatment of all Jews read in the churches, but the plan was canceled on July 8. As a result of the Vrba-Wetzler report, the West put pressure on Admiral Miklós Horthy. On June 30, 1944, Admiral Horthy received a personal telegram from the Swedish king asking him to end the persecution of the Jews in order to preserve the good name of Hungary. Objection to the deportation of Jews came from neutral countries such as Turkey, Switzerland, Sweden, and fascist Spain. Finally, for good measure, on July 2, 1944, the Allied bombing of Budapest and other Hungarian cities commenced. On July 7, bowing to pressure, Regent Horthy stopped the planned deportation of the remaining Jews from Budapest. On August 1, President Franklin D. Roosevelt warned the Hungarian government about the consequences of the barbarous treatment of the Jews.

On October 15, 1944, Regent Horthy announced that Hungary was suing for a separate peace. For a few hours, Budapest Jews were jubilant: "We made it. It is over." However, the Hungarian army was not prepared to implement this separation from the German occupational forces. By nightfall, the ultranationalist Arrow Cross Party took over, and the bloodbath began.

Final Solution Coupled with Bloodbath

After October 15, 1944, the estimated three hundred thousand Jews still living in Hungary depended on instinct, daring, mental and physical stamina, and luck for survival. Most lived in Budapest, some were hiding, and some were forced laborers building roads and fortifications to stop the advancing Red Army. Ironically, the forced laborers were protected from the Arrow Cross Party's excesses because they were needed for defense. Foreign legations set up protected houses (the International Ghetto) and issued protection letters. Some neutral-power representatives were heroic and deserve our gratitude. Although Raoul Wallenberg stands out in our minds, there were other heroes. The value of the protection letters diminished, however, as their numbers increased. Some were originals, but many were fake. How did one obtain a letter of protection?

Here Ivan's story continues:

> My mother was an avid Esperantist. Esperantists thought that if everybody in the world spoke a common language, there would be no wars. An

> artificial language, Esperanto, was created, and Esperanto clubs were formed all over the world. In the 1920s, there was an Esperanto Congress in Budapest. During the congress, my mother guided two Esperantist students from Spain. My mother was beautiful, intelligent, and lively, so the two students were delighted to have her as their guide. When they returned to Spain, they sent her a lovely card that read: "Dear Erna, Thank you for your kindness. We had a great time in Budapest. Please come to see us in Madrid. We would be honored to have you as our guest." They signed the card and included their address. Although travel to Madrid was beyond my mother's means, she saved the card in a box with other memorabilia of the Esperanto Congress. When the dark times of 1944 came, Mother dug out this postcard, went to the Spanish embassy, asked to see the top official, and showed him the decades-old postcard. She said she wanted to go to Spain now with her family and needed the protection of the Spanish government until she could get a passport. The family was placed under the protection of the Spanish government and received the very highly coveted Spanish papers. Because Spain was neutral and fascist, these papers were respected even by the Hungarian Nazis and offered reasonable protection. A few houses in the International Ghetto where we lived were protected by the Spanish government and were real sanctuaries to the very end. The key to our survival were those two polite Spanish Esperantist students who had sent my mother an invitation to visit them in Madrid and my mother's inventiveness to use the invitation to save us.

Sometimes the key to survival was help from a Gentile. Some helped in exchange for money. Some helped because they had a conscience. Others helped because it was simply the right thing to do.

Ivan remembers Viki, a Righteous Gentile:

> After we were evicted from our home and before the establishment of the International Ghetto, we lived with friends in a "Jewish house." Father was away in a "work brigade," and mother had been taken to an abandoned brick factory in Obuda, where the transports to Germany and death started. Our friends did not want to take care of me—and I don't blame them—so they told me to go to a children's shelter located a few blocks away. Because I was a meticulous survivor, I packed myself a

giant rucksack with clothing and all the food I could scrounge up. I packed my first-aid kit with a box of powder to neutralize any mustard gas attacks! I still have that box. I also packed our only valuable, a small Persian rug that could be used as a bed. All in all, it was a well-stocked survival pack. However, it was so heavy that I barely could walk with it. During the time Jews were allowed out of their homes, I left for the children's shelter with my heavy pack and yellow Star of David on my coat. Near the shelter, before I could move away, I encountered a transport of Jews walking in the middle of the street. The Arrow Cross guard asked me where I was going. I told him that I was going to the children's shelter and showed him my Spanish protection paper. He was not impressed and pushed me into the transport. But I had great survival instincts. I showed the Spanish papers to an older German soldier. He did not look at the papers but pulled me over to the curb and shoved me away. He is one of the nameless Righteous Gentiles. The children's shelter was hell. We slept on the floor, had almost no food, and the few adults who tried to keep order were overwhelmed.

When I was growing up, the landlord and his family lived in an adjoining apartment. They had a live-in maidservant, Erzsi, who worked for them for many years. Erzsi had a girlfriend named Viki, a very strange person. She was a streetwise woman who lived in Angyalfold, a rough part of Budapest. When Viki visited Erzsi on her day off, they would ask me questions about history and geography and such. They were nice but uneducated women, and they got a kick out of talking to a young boy who knew the answer to so many of their questions. I was very surprised when I saw Viki wandering around in the children's shelter. "Viki! What are you doing here?" I asked. "Looking for you," she answered. "I am going to take you to your mother in the Spanish house." To this day, I don't know who found Viki and asked her to pick me up or how she found me. It remains a mystery. Viki asked for all my papers and shoved them under her panties while muttering some obscenities. Then she said, "Take off that coat with the yellow star and leave it here. Your name is fine because it is not a Jewish name. If anyone asks you, your mother died two years ago, and your father is a soldier; I am your father's girlfriend, and you live with me. Memorize this address. Now I know how smart you are. If anyone asks anything else, just shake your head. Play dumb. Let me do the talking." With that, we took off for the long walk to the Spanish house. We were stopped only once by an Arrow Cross patrol, but before they asked any questions, Viki asked them in her best Angyalfold dialect where could she find some food for us. They did not know, but hearing her was enough to let us go. This simple woman risked her life to take me to the Spanish house. She did not accept anything from us and thought nothing of the risks she was taking. Viki, whose last name I never knew, I salute you as a great human being, truly a Righteous Gentile.

After the Arrow Cross Party took over, disorganized terror commenced. Even the protected houses in the International Ghetto were often raided by teenage Arrow Cross Party members, and the inhabitants were robbed and taken away to their deaths. On October 21, 1944, papal legate Angelo Rotta requested that the passports of neutral states be honored. Leader of the Arrow Cross Party, Prime Minister Ferenc Szálasi demanded the recognition of his government before he would look into the matters presented by the Vatican's envoy.[12] It was difficult even for the Germans to deal with Szálasi. He did not dispatch the first transport of twenty-five thousand Jews for forced military labor in Germany until November 1, 1944. Added to these convoys, all walking toward the Austrian border about two hundred kilometers away, were old people, sick people, and young children.[13] Those who did not perish on these death marches almost certainly died in the concentration camps.

This is my personal story:

October 15, 1944, found me, my stepmother, and my one-year-old sister living with a cousin, her pregnant mother, and grandmother in a two-room apartment in one of the designated Jewish houses. One morning everyone was ordered down to the courtyard. All women under forty-five years of age without children under a year old were ordered to take a three-day supply of food and clothing and report back to be taken to "work" in Germany. My stepmother handed me my fourteen-month-old sister. She picked up her knapsack and was marched out of the building with the other women. Friends who encountered her on the long march reported that she went insane worrying about her baby. She died in the

> Bergen-Belsen Camp. When my stepmother was taken away, I took my sister to the Red Cross children's shelter, but the conditions were so poor that we returned home, where we were not wanted. My stepmother's sister had married a Gentile and converted. They were hiding out in a summer bungalow with their eighteen-year-old daughter. I sent them a card, and they came and took my sister back with them. They told everyone that she was their daughter's illegitimate child. My sister survived but is scarred for not ever knowing a loving mother. She is a well-known neuropsychologist in Hungary today.

The deportation from Budapest slowed but did not stop until the middle of December 1944, when the Red Army closed the circle around Budapest. By November 15, 1944, the organization of the large ghetto started for all Jews in Budapest. The Jewish Council worked feverishly to solve the housing problems of the ghetto, to obtain food and some sort of medical care. Help came from the International Red Cross, some of the neutral nations, and, surprisingly, the Hungarian government, which contributed money to feed the people. The sixty-five thousand Jews sealed in the ghetto by mid-December were either very young or very old, the remnants of the once vibrant Jewish community of Budapest.

Back to my story:

> After my sister went to live with relatives, I needed a place to stay and someone to care for me. I found my maternal grandmother living with her daughter-in-law and her family in a suburb of Budapest. Unfortunately, the Arrow Cross men had just ordered them to vacate the building before nightfall. For good measure, they surrounded the house. I still remember seeing those middle-aged ladies selecting the doodads they wanted to take with them. I told my grandmother that we could take only a small bundle because we had to climb out a basement window to avoid the Arrow Cross men. It made sense to her, but not to the other women. She was one of the pluckiest women I ever knew. We walked away. The rest of the family was shot that night. I still don't allow myself to get attached to things. I still want to be able to walk away. Grandmother and I walked to the ghetto and found refuge in her sister's two-room apart-

> ment, which was shared with twenty-six people—most of them strangers. By Christmas of 1944, the Red Army completely closed the ring around Budapest, and the siege began. I overheard people in the apartment saying that Uncle Joe would arrive soon. Joe was my favorite uncle's name. I did not know how he would solve the problem of no food, heat, or water, but I knew that if anyone could, certainly it was Uncle Joe. Much to the adults' amusement, I looked for my uncle Joe every day. It was too dangerous to tell me that we were actually waiting for Joe Stalin's army to save us. Meanwhile, the bombs were raining down on us, and the ghetto was sealed off from the outside almost completely until the Red Army liberated it on January 18, 1945. The first familiar face I saw after the liberation was my uncle Joe's!

This last story is about my aunt, Lilly:

> Lilly was born and raised in Burgenland, Austria. After the Anschluss in 1938, her family escaped to Hungary. The siege of Budapest found her and her future husband (my uncle Bandi) hiding out under false papers in an air-raid shelter with many people who did not know Lilly and Bandi were Jewish. As the Red Army advanced, the Russian soldiers went from air-raid shelter to air-raid shelter, looking for German and Hungarian soldiers. Two Russian soldiers entered the shelter where Lilly and Bandi stayed. Bandi tried to get some information from them about the front situation. One of them spoke something that sounded German, so Lilly joined the conversation. She realized that the Russian soldier was speaking Yiddish, not German. She was afraid to tell him that they were Jews because if the Germans returned, the others in the shelter would give them up. The Russian was in a hurry and told Lilly that the ghetto was to be blown up by a German-Hungarian contingent, and his group was supposed to prevent it. So, with much trepidation, my uncle drew them a map showing all the shortcuts to the ghetto, and Lilly translated the directions.

Was the ghetto really mined? Was there a last-minute effort to blow it up? No evidence was ever found of this plan, but Lilly's story is true.

About seventy thousand Jews survived in the two Budapest ghettos. Individual survival depended on a combination of luck and self-preservation skills, mental even more than physical. Self-pity did not help, and asking for mercy was futile. Many Hungarian Jews survived simply because the German occupation of Hungary came close to the end of the war. Surprisingly, Regent Horthy helped by ordering some protective measures. Help from the international community came late but at a crucial time. Many survived because the Budapest ghetto was sealed only a few weeks before the Red Army's victory over the German forces holding Budapest.

6. An American in Poland

Eyewitness to the Holocaust

LAWRENCE H. FELDMAN

In March 1999, at the U.S. National Archives and Records Administration in College Park, Maryland, I came across the following report from the "Survey of Foreign Experts" files of the Organization for Strategic Services (OSS), the World War II–era precursor of the Central Intelligence Agency (CIA). The files are interviews of Americans who had the misfortune to be in Poland when the Germans invaded that country, but who had the good fortune to possess U.S. passports that allowed them, in the end, to escape death. For those who wonder what they might have done (or what might have been done to them) as American citizens if they had suddenly found themselves living under the Nazi flag, this account might provide some answers.

"Survey of Foreign Experts" No. N8890, June 19, 1944

COUNTRY: Poland

SUBJECT. Pole, 50, antique dealer in Łódź until 1939, when he fled to Warsaw. He was forced to live there in the ghetto until his arrest in July 1942. After spending three months in prison in Warsaw as the husband of a U.S. citizen, he was interned first in Tittmoning, Germany and then in Vittel, France. He arrived in the U.S. on the [Swedish ship] *Gripsholm* in March 1944. Subject speaks English, Polish, German and Russian and seems entirely reliable and cooperative.

CONTENTS. Conditions in Warsaw (Up to October 1942): Polish-German collaboration; underground; treatment of Poles in Oswiecim [Auschwitz] Concentration Camp; conditions in the ghetto; liquidation of the Warsaw Ghetto.

CONDITIONS IN WARSAW (Up to October 1942):

Polish-German Collaboration. A considerable part of the middle class Polish population collaborated with the Germans in their anti-Semitic measures. In particular this collaboration consisted of refusing to hide Jews, turning them over to German authorities or denouncing them if they were able to obtain false papers. It was from this group of the population also that the Gestapo was able to recruit some agents provocateurs and other helpers.

Underground. Underground [news]papers, printed both in Polish and Jewish, appeared regularly and brought the latest news.

The most active participants in the underground movement were workers formerly organized in the PPS (Polish Socialist Party) and army officers.

Treatment of Poles in Oswiecim [Auschwitz] Concentration Camp. All Poles potentially dangerous to the Germans because of their education or political background were taken to the Oswiecim concentration camp. Releases from this camp were extremely rare. The average life expectancy of inmates there was 2–3 weeks.

Conditions in the Ghetto. A section of the city, which before the war housed 70,000 persons, was walled off and 600,000 Jews from Warsaw and other cities were concentrated there. This overcrowding caused such unsanitary conditions that an average of 500 persons died daily from typhoid or typhus. Burying facilities were frequently so overburdened, that corpses, stripped by the population of their clothing, lay in the streets for several days.

Jewish food rations consisted of small quantities of bread, potatoes, sauerkraut, sugar and occasionally some vegetables. In the winter, small quantities of firewood were allotted. Meat, milk, fats and clothing rations were not given to Jews. Everything, however, could be bought on the black market, which was operated by German soldiers. These German soldiers would drive trucks loaded with supplies to certain dealers in the ghetto and then sell the contents at exorbitant prices. On leaving the ghetto, they frequently smuggled persons out.

Many Jews apprehensive of their fate, especially after reports of the liquidation of the Lublin ghetto reached Warsaw, used these German soldiers as a means of smuggling their children out of the ghetto to be sheltered either by the underground or by Polish families. To counteract this, the Germans instituted the death penalty for families sheltering Jewish children, but in spite of this, a number of Jewish children should be safe.

Liquidation of the Warsaw Ghetto. In July 1942, the report reached the Ghetto that the SS Vernichtungskommando (extermination commando) made up of special German SS [Schutzstaffel] troops and Ukrainian, Latvian and Lithuanian volunteers returned to Warsaw after having been active in other towns. It was commanded by SS officer Nikelaus, who also was in charge of the dreaded Pawiak prison in Warsaw. His assistant was SS officer Buerkel, said to have since been liquidated by the Polish underground.

On July 16th, all Jews with foreign papers were ordered to report to the nearest police station. There they were arrested and taken to Pawiak prison. (Subject and his family were among those imprisoned as his wife was a U.S. citizen.)

On July 19th, Subject was awakened by considerable shooting coming from the direction of the ghetto, only a short distance from Pawiak prison. Of the events taking place there, Subject received the following report from Polish policemen on duty in Pawiak prison.

At 5 A.M. on July 19th, the SS Vernichtungskommando was sent into the ghetto. These SS troops cleared the inhabitants from building after building. Wherever Jews were slow to open doors, they were shot on the spot. The Jews then were herded to Warsaw's freight station.

Once in the station, part of them were driven into freight cars whose floors were covered with quick lime. Between 100 [and] 150 persons were forced into one freight car. Its doors were then sealed and the car remained on a siding for 1–2 weeks. After that period, the suffocated corpses were removed and new groups forced into the cars.

Other groups were shipped from the Warsaw freight station to Tremblinka [Treblinka]. There they were led into a large factory and ordered to disrobe supposedly to be bathed before starting work in the factory. The nude Jews were then led into a large hall whose doors and windows were hermetically sealed. There they were suffocated by poison gas.

The furniture, clothes and other belongings of the exterminated Jews were turned over to bombed-out Germans.

Ronald Carroll, Interviewer

7. The Hongkew Ghetto in Shanghai

From Escape to Shanghai

JAMES R. ROSS

They were eating stew and millet again for lunch, but Eva [Kantorowsky] thought the millet tasted musty. Bob's mother had worked hard to cook the meal over their stove—it was actually more like an upside-down flowerpot—heated by the weak embers of small, round briquettes made mostly of mud and straw. She had fashioned the stew from a cow's spleen and covered it with lots of onion gravy to overcome the taste. But there wasn't much she could do with the millet her husband had bought on sale at the Chusan Road market. It apparently had been stored in a damp warehouse and was discolored from mildew. Neither Eva nor her in-laws could afford to let food go to waste, however, so they ate without complaining. Whatever bargains Bob's father brought home—moldy millet, cracked wheat, half-frozen sweet potatoes, even the nearly inedible free food from the Kitchen Fund—they would eat, as the Germans would say, until it grew from their throats.

Most of the Jewish refugees in Hongkew had similar diets in the summer of 1943, and, as usual, they found humor in their misfortune. They liked to say that the Jews have a blessing before eating food that grows from the ground and another blessing before eating food that grows from a tree. But what, they would ask, is the blessing for food that grows from the throat?

(The dark humor sometimes got refugees in trouble. Comedian Herbert Zernik was nearly arrested after a performance at the Chaoufoong camp that spring for parroting the way Japanese soldiers searched pedestrians and for announcing that Adolf Hitler Square in Berlin had been renamed Stalin Square.)

Eva and her new husband walked to his parents' house every afternoon for tiffin, their big meal of the day. As bad as the food was, it was better than anything they had at home. For breakfast, they usually ate gruel, a mixture of water, flour, and sugar stirred in their small electric cooker. They washed it down with green tea; coffee was too expensive on Bob's small salary. If they ate in the evening, it would be a piece of bread, often dry and moldy, spread with lard Bob's mother had cooked or some of the strange-tasting margarine manufactured in Hongkew. A piece of cheese, or a slice of one of the shriveled salamis hanging over the door, was an occasional treat.

Bob and Eva lived in his aunt's lane house on Kinchow Road, similar to the houses in which most of the refugees now lived in the alleys of Hongkew. Most of the lane houses had thin wooden doors on the outside, leading to an alcove. A second door led to the living quarters, a cramped series of small rooms joined by narrow staircases. The housing conditions in Hongkew were so crowded that many refugees—including Bob and Eva—lived in the tiny concrete rooms that housed the electric meters.

The lanes veered off nearly every street in Hongkew—Chusan, Ward, Tongshan, Alcock, Dalny, and others—and many of them connected to other lanes. They were like little communities of their own, where there were few secrets and almost no privacy. Some lanes were occupied entirely by Chinese, others by the refugees. The Chinese and refugees lived in a few of the lanes together (some of the refugee children became fluent in Shanghai-dialect curses), but the Chinese and foreigners mostly maintained the tradition of polite separation.

In the oppressive summer heat and humidity, it seemed impossible to breathe inside the houses, where mold and mildew grew on food, clothes, linens, and shoes and inside closets and chests. Few people could use fans because electricity was strictly rationed. The ubiquitous insects and mosquitoes added to the discomfort. In the evenings, nearly everyone moved outside into the lanes, where they played cards, gossiped, cooked, ate, and even slept. Men walked around in boxer shorts with sweat towels around their necks; most women wore only bras and panties, a few of them arousing sexual fantasies among some of the boys. The children seemed oblivious to the heat, running wildly through the lanes.

Bob and Eva's tiny concrete meter room was halfway up the stairs from the first floor. It normally was used as a bathroom or kitchen and had two small windows. There was barely enough space for their small brass bed, a portable wardrobe closet, a washbasin attached to the wall, a tiny table, and two stools. For privacy, they usually closed the window to Bob's aunt's room when they made love. They washed and bathed from the cold water tap over the basin and used a bucket in the room downstairs as a toilet. Every day Eva carried their thermos to the water shop down the lane, where she used bamboo tokens to purchase hot water for drinking. (The water sellers used bamboo sticks as currency.)

The conditions were depressing, particularly for Germans used to cleanliness and hearty foods. Eva suffered from intestinal problems caused by the recurring dysentery she first contracted on the train ride across Russia; it was aggravated by parasites and her poor diet. Twice, upset when she feared she might be pregnant, she went to see a doctor she had known from Berlin, who put her on a regimen of vodka and quinine to abort the pregnancy. It made her terribly weak and sick, but Eva and Bob knew they couldn't raise a child under these conditions.

They had only to walk down Ward or Alcock or Seward roads to see others, living in the camps, who were worse off. Refugees who had once been distinguished lawyers and academics now held out tin cups to beg for money or food. They had sold all their possessions and burned their lice-infested clothes. Some wore outfits made from jute flour bags. Women who had worked as bar girls now openly solicited customers as prostitutes. Some twenty mothers even sold their newborn babies to raise money for food. Several babies froze to death that winter in the refugee hospital's maternity ward.

The year after Pearl Harbor had been difficult, but conditions this year were much worse. Since the Japanese proclamation in February 1943 that required all the refugees to live in a designated area in Hongkew, nearly everyone suffered under poor living conditions and malnutrition. But Bob and Eva, young and in love, were rarely depressed. They lived to enjoy each new day with each other. . . .

Eva and Bob found a nice, small room in a lane house on Dent Road, in a fairly new complex of buildings where Eva's parents also lived. Two weeks after they moved in, they heard an announcement over their radio. They were stunned to hear the Japanese army and navy commanders proclaiming restrictions for the "stateless refugees":

> Due to military necessity, places of residence and business of the stateless refugees in the Shanghai area shall hereafter be restricted to the undermentioned area in the International Settlement. East of the line connecting Chaoufoong Road, Muirhead Road, and Dent Road; west of Yangtzepoo Creek; north of the line connecting East Seward Road and Wayside Road; and south of the boundary of the International Settlement.
>
> The stateless refugees at present residing and/or carrying on business in the district other than the above area shall remove their places of residence and/or business into the area designated above by May 18, 1943. . . . [Ross's ellipsis]
>
> Persons who will have violated this proclamation or obstructed its reenforcement shall be liable to severe punishment.

Their new apartment was on the border of the designated area, but on the wrong side of Dent Road. With almost no money, the newlyweds would have to find another place to live.

An article in the *Shanghai Herald* defined the terms of the proclamation. "Stateless refugee" meant people who had arrived in Shanghai "since 1937 from Germany (including former Austria, Czecho-Slovakia), Hungary, former Poland, Latvia, Lithuania, and Estonia, etc. who have no nationality at present." That definition covered almost all of the twenty thousand refugees, the last of whom had arrived from Japan just before Pearl Harbor. It excluded most of the Russian and Polish Ashkenazi Jews who had preceded them to Shanghai.

Refugees with jobs outside the designated area could be granted temporary permission to leave during working hours. Chinese who lived inside the area were encouraged to move outside to make room for the refugees.

The Japanese claimed the proclamation was "motivated by military necessity" and was not intended as a form of oppression. "It is even contemplated to safeguard, so far as possible, their place of residence as well as their livelihood in the designated area," the military leaders announced. They were careful not to use either the word *Jew* or the word *ghetto* in their statement.

The Japanese security concerns may have been affected by reports of black marketeering and other suspicious activities. Their main source of information was the Shanghai Municipal Police special branch, a unit dominated by anti-Semitic White Russians after all the British detectives had been interned. The police records report on a riot at a public meeting of refugees to discuss relief programs and on nuisances created by Jewish beggars. In addition, Japanese naval intelligence relied on reports from Pick Hovans, the White Russian former convict who had tried to extort money from Boris Topaz (a Russian Jewish member of the Japanese-controlled relief committee) and others for information on the refugees. Hovans strongly advocated more controls over the Jews in Shanghai. Local newspapers also fed Japanese fears. Just two days before the proclamation, the *Shanghai Times* published a major story headlined: "Shanghai, Hunting Ground of Thriving Jewish Racketeers: Prominent but Shady Part Played by Unscrupulous Jews in City's Economic Life and Development."

Most refugees were shocked by the proclamation and not comforted by Japanese assurances. It meant an end to the relative freedom they had enjoyed and raised horrifying memories of centuries of oppression against the Jews and of enforced segregation, from Venice in 1515 to Łódź and Warsaw in 1940. There was added terror for the thousands of refugees who had been imprisoned in Dachau, Sachsenhausen, and Buchenwald and those whose families had been resettled in Poland. Was the proclamation to be only the first step? Many refugees saw the influence of Josef Meisinger (chief representative of the Gestapo in the Far East) and the Gestapo in the proclamation, although there is little evidence of this.

Beyond the psychological impact, the proclamation meant that about half of about sixteen thousand refugees who had registered with the Japanese would have to move within three months from their houses and apartments in the French Concession, International Settlement, Western District, and parts of Hongkew outside the designated area. The biggest adjustment came for the three thousand refugees who lived in the French Concession and International Settlement, most of whom lived in nice apartments and some of whom had tried to hide the fact that they were refugees.

The exchange of apartments proved costly. Agents charged excessive rents for apartments and demanded large sums of key money, an illegal payment to a landlord for transferring a lease. Few refugees could afford such sums. The proclamation also divided some families. Several non-Jewish German women who had come to Shanghai with their Jewish husbands registered at the German consulate so that they were exempt from the segregation order and eligible for German relief assistance, which they shared with their husbands. . . .

Eva tried to remain cheerful. But just after they moved to Kinchow Road in the spring of 1943, she received a brief letter from her brother Hans via the Red Cross. It was the first time she had heard from him in months and the last letter she would receive. He had been back in Berlin, he wrote, and now was probably on his way to their father's old *heimat* (neighborhood). Eva understood the message—Hans was being deported to Poland. But he was going even farther east than his father's native town of Loslau, to the Polish village of Oswiecim. The Germans called it Auschwitz.

Other refugees in Shanghai were receiving similar messages. By the summer, nearly all of them had lost contact with their relatives in eastern Europe. In July 1943, the Far Eastern Jewish Information Bureau in Shanghai sent an appeal to a Jewish refugee agency in Portugal:

> Dear Sirs,
>
> During the last time we have begun receiving for our numerous applicants here replies of the International Red Cross Committee from various parts of occupied Poland—mostly from the regions of Lublin, Radom, Kielce, Warsaw, also from the Baltic countries and occupied Soviet Poland. The replies are all the same, vis. that the relatives (respectively, parents, children, brothers, sisters, wives, etc.) are no longer under the given addresses and [have] left for unknown destinations. As to Litz-

mannstadt, formerly Łódź, replies are received that there is no mail connection with the ghetto, i.e. enquiries are sent back to us.

Such replies naturally cause acute mental anguish to the enquirers, and they constantly appeal to us asking to take further steps in order to trace their near of kin. Unfortunately, being so far away from European centres and for that reason not [aware] of the true state of affairs in East European ghettos, we do not know what to undertake. Generally, we ask the applicants to give us several addresses of relatives in the same place and direct an enquiry to the I.R.O. Geneva for further investigation. But it is doubtful whether the relatives are still there and whether they would be able to give to the I.R.O. the information desired. Tracers are also directed by us to our affiliated organization in Stockholm, Zurich, Geneva, etc.

By the present we beg to apply to your esteemed organization with a request to inform us of the following—should you find it possible and convenient for you, naturally:

1. Whether Jewish residents were deported from the small cities of Lublin, Radom, Kielce, and other regions of Poland, and if so where? We mean the constant residents of these places as well as those who in its time were deported there from Central Europe.

2. Do "Jüdenrats" exist (or similar Jewish organizations) in the occupied regions, and if so, is it possible to get in touch with them through neutral countries, i.e., whether tracers could be addressed to them?

3. Is there any possibility of sending any individual assistance there through neutral countries?

We are well aware that all the questions raised by us are extremely complicated at the present moment, and are not very hopeful, therefore. But the desire to know whether there is a possibility of helping our applicants at present, as well as the desire to know more about the situation in Europe, has prompted us to apply to you on the matter. . . .

. . . The Japanese proclamation ordering the refugees to move into the ghetto had not worked as planned. By the deadline of May 18, 1943, more than fifteen hundred refugees remained outside the designated area. Physicians and relief workers were granted three-month extensions; eleven hundred others were put on a waiting list for housing. SACRA [Shanghai Ashkenazi Collaborating Relief Association], the Japanese-controlled organization of Russian Jews that supervised the relocation, had taken over and renovated only a handful of houses and apartment buildings. There were few private apartments available in the overcrowded ghetto, and real-estate agents demanded excessive rents. A Japanese named Kano, who served as secretary to SACRA, had bought a number of buildings in Hongkew and collected huge sums for reselling them.

As late as the winter of 1943–44, there were still hundreds of refugees living outside Hongkew. Some of them, including many of the Polish Jews and yeshiva students, had declined to comply with the proclamation and actively resisted the Japanese order. The Poles, with the help of the Russian Jews, had rented some of the best housing when they first arrived in Shanghai, mostly in the French Concession. Most of them were well clothed and fed and had been receiving support from the local Russians and from abroad, even after Pearl Harbor.

The Polish Jews had refused to recognize SACRA or to name representatives to its board. They claimed they were Polish citizens of the Polish government-in-exile rather than stateless refugees and therefore were exempt from the proclamation. The Poles generated little sympathy from SACRA and even less from the Hongkew refugees, who resented the Poles' comfortable living conditions and their refusal to assist, or even acknowledge, the non-Orthodox German and Austrian Jews, many of whom were suffering from poverty and malnutrition. The Japanese rejected the Polish appeals.

But the Polish Jews continued to resist. Mir Yeshiva students staged a riot in the SACRA office when they were ordered to move to a Salvation Army compound owned by SACRA, smashing furniture and throwing it out the window. The police arrested thirty-three of them until Rabbi Meir Ashkenazi (head of the Russian Jewish community) intervened, rescuing them from jail sentences. The Japanese eventually agreed to let them rent their own private housing.

Other Poles simply refused to move. By the end of 1943, Japanese officials had begun to lose patience. They had established the Stateless Refugees Affairs Bureau, headed by T. Kubota, to oversee the relocation and threatened to arrest anyone violating the order. The arrests began the following March.

Three refugees, two Poles and a German, were arrested on March 3, one for being outside the ghetto without a pass and two others for living outside the designated area. They were sentenced to one or two days in the Wayside Police Station and held in a cell that had been used to detain Chinese beggars. Over the next two months, eighty-seven more refugees were arrested, most of them Poles. The sentences were normally one or two days, but several were held for as long as thirty days.

Subinspector Okura was in charge of enforcing the order. He often beat prisoners before throwing them into the cell. The cell was filled with typhus-infected lice. In April, one of the Polish refugees who had been held in the police station contracted typhus and died.

Word spread that a sentence in the Wayside Police Station meant almost certain death. Okura continued to send violators to the so-called death cell. Seven more refugees who had been jailed there died in May; eight others contracted typhus but survived. The Japanese had accomplished their goal. By the spring of 1944, only about 250 refugees were living outside the ghetto.

The Stateless Refugees Affairs Bureau had another function. As of August 10, 1943, any refugee who wished to leave the ghetto had to apply for a pass. Those with jobs or businesses outside the designated area could ask the bureau for authorization to leave Hongkew during the day. The passes were limited to specified areas outside the district; signs were posted on the border reading: "STATELESS REFUGEES ARE PROHIBITED TO PASS HERE WITHOUT PERMISSION."

The man in charge of issuing most of the passes was less vicious but far more unpredictable than Okura. He was a short, schizophrenic Japanese named Kanoh Ghoya, who liked to call himself the King of the Jews. The refugees called him the Monkey.

Few refugees knew much about Kanoh Ghoya's past. He had been a police chief in a district of Kyushu before coming to Shanghai. He was an aficionado of Western culture, in particular classical music, and spoke English well. Before the proclamation, he had lived on Chaoufoong Road in Hongkew with his wife and two children. They had shared the house with the Simons, Jewish refugees from Germany who arrived in Shanghai in March 1939. Ghoya often would visit the Simons when young Ruth practiced her violin or when he heard Beethoven on their radio. They considered him a kind and friendly neighbor.

Ghoya's wife had been quite ill and died before the Pacific war started. He later remarried and moved with his new wife to 810 East Seward Road, just outside the ghetto. When the Japanese appointed him to supervise the pass system in August 1943, he gradually became a different man.

At first, Ghoya granted most requests for passes from the refugees who lined up daily at the Stateless Refugees Affairs Bureau at 171 Muirhead Road. (Ghoya had the authority to issue passes valid for one to three months. Okura was responsible for issuing daily passes, valid for less than two weeks.) Most passes were restricted to the International Settlement, French Concession, Western District, or Hongkew and Yangtzepoo. All pass holders were required to wear a round blue-and-white badge, inscribed with the Chinese character for "pass," on their right lapel when they were outside the ghetto area.

But after a few months, Ghoya appeared to grow increasingly suspicious and even paranoid. He screamed at some of the refugees and accused them of being spies or liars. Often he demanded that applicants bring him proof of their employment. "Bring me a list of customers," he would say. (Refugees joked that he once demanded such a list from an undertaker.) He accused some women applicants of being prostitutes. Ghoya, only four feet tall, particularly hated tall men and would sometimes jump up on his desk and beat a taller refugee who applied for a pass. During some of his fits of rage, Ghoya would drag a refugee to an office window and threaten to throw him off the second-floor balcony. Several Jewish refugees worked in the outer office and tried to warn applicants if Ghoya was in a particularly bad mood. "Does he beat today?" people in line would ask.

Ghoya made some refugees wait in line all day and then come back each day for two or three weeks before making a decision. His moods swung wildly—on rare occasions he granted nearly every request for a pass. He used his power to abuse and intimidate the refugees, many of whom were dependent on the passes for their daily survival.

He was equally unpredictable outside of his office. Ghoya would occasionally disappear for an entire day, and no one was able to get a pass.

Sometimes he beat refugees on the street or in cafés if they were not wearing their badges. (The regulations required only that they wear badges outside the ghetto). On other days, he played with refugee children and posed for pictures in front of the line of people waiting for passes. He often showed up at refugee soccer matches and concerts and plays performed by the refugees, yet he sometimes prohibited a performance for no apparent reason. He loved to talk with refugees about classical music and often visited a refugee doctor's home to play violin while the doctor's wife accompanied him on the piano. Yet once, when his harmony clashed with the playing of one of the refugees, virtuoso violinist Alfred Wittenberg, Ghoya yelled at him: "You play as I direct, or I kill you."

Ghoya was not the most brutal of the Japanese, but, for many refugees, he was their most visible oppressor. Refugee artists, such as Fritz Melchior, drew caricatures of him and comedians told jokes about him. Ghoya became a symbol of the refugees' oppression, a tyrant whose deeds were compared to the evil Haman of the Book of Esther.

There were other forms of oppression as well. The Japanese used both paid informers and a self-policing force to control the ghetto. The best-known—and most obvious—refugee informer was Ewald Drucker, who was believed to be working for the *kempetai,* the refugee bureau, and possibly the Nazis. Robert Peritz continued to work as an informer and advised the Japanese to jail refugees who complained about the quality of bread or other relief services of the Kitchen Fund he headed. . . .

The ghetto years were the low point for the Hongkew refugees. Malnutrition and disease were widespread as more families lost their sources of income and sold off what remaining valuables and household goods they still owned. Theft became more common, too—refugees would sometimes return home to find nearly everything they owned had been stolen. Rampant inflation magnified the problems. Prices sometimes doubled in a matter of hours.

By the spring of 1944, eggs cost more than $1.00 (U.S.) apiece, pork, nearly $20.00 a pound, a loaf of bread, $2.50, and milk, nearly $10.00 a quart. Refugees adapted to the inflation by hoarding commodities, such as flints and kerosene, because cash had become almost worthless. The commodities themselves sometimes proved to have little value. One refugee bought several tins of kerosene from a Chinese friend as a hedge against inflation, but decided to splurge during a cold winter week and use one tin as fuel. He opened it to find it filled with water. The refugee returned the tin to his friend and demanded an explanation. "I thought you wanted this as a commodity, not to use," his friend said. "If you wanted kerosene for heating, you should have told me."

An increasing number of refugees depended on the limited resources of the Kitchen Fund—little was left from the funds that Laura M. Margolis and Manny Siegel, representatives of the American Jewish Joint Distribution Committee (JDC), had arranged to borrow before they were interned—and on the reluctant assistance of SACRA, which had taken control of the Kitchen Fund in September 1943. The quality and quantity of the food deteriorated steadily as funds ran out. After the JDC had cut off funds in May 1942, no outside money—except those funds sent to the yeshivas—had reached the Shanghai refugees. . . .

In the summer and fall of 1944, Shanghai was only a secondary target for American bombers based in Burma and Chengtu. The first attacks came in June; the bombing grew heavier and more frequent in the fall and winter. The planes bombed docks, warehouses, and shipping. By the beginning of 1945, most of the bombing raids came during the day.

Thousands of Chinese moved from Shanghai into the countryside to escape the attacks, and many of the Japanese still living in Hongkew moved into the French Concession, where they believed they would be safe from the bombing. The Japanese had located munitions depots and communications equipment throughout Hongkew. They also had placed a radio station near one of the SACRA apartment buildings—also the site of a refugee kindergarten—at 826 East Yuhang Road.

By the end of June, U.S. forces had conquered Okinawa and were rapidly constructing air bases there. Shanghai was now an easily accessible target. The Seventh Air Force began to launch daily attacks. On July 17, 1945, twenty-five new twin-engine A-26 bombers from the 319th Bomb Group took off from the Kadena airfield on Okinawa, a little more than five hundred miles from Shanghai, at 9:49 A.M. (Shanghai time), carrying one-hundred-pound bombs. Their mission was to attack the Chiangwan Airdrome, just north of Shanghai. The 319th had just been redeployed from Italy and had flown its first mission in the Pacific, an attack on an airfield on Kyushu, a day earlier. Twenty-three bombers (two had returned after losing contact with the formation) reached Shanghai at 12:09 P.M., flying between 9,600 and 10,600 feet. There was a solid overcast at 6,000 feet, and it was impossible to see the Chiangwan field. Bombardier Robert C. Roberts, flying in the lead plane, could only estimate the site of the target based on their flying time from Okinawa; the other planes released their bombs by following his lead. They dropped 263 bombs.

A few of the bombs had been dropped too early; Hongkew had been hit. Dozens of buildings had collapsed, some solely from the air pressure of the explosions. Refugees and Chinese were wandering in the streets with bloody ears and noses, disoriented by the blast. At the Chinese market on Chusan Road, just past the intersection of Ward Road, dozens of limbs and bodies were scattered in the street. Bloodied corpses had been tossed awkwardly against the walls and atop the stalls of fish and fruit. A few blocks east the SACRA building on East Yuhang Road apparently had taken a direct hit. (Some refugees mistakenly assumed the bombers had targeted the Japanese radio station.) Refugees were beginning to dig bodies out of the rubble. Mothers who had children in the kindergarten in the same building had run to the site, but the *pao chia* [Chinese system-cooperative (group) neighborhood association] held them back. A few mothers climbed to the roof of a nearby building and began to cry and scream; they could see that the roof had collapsed and most of the building was leveled.

[Dr. Sam] Didner had joined a team of refugee doctors. Prison guards had opened the gates of the Ward Road jail, and the refugee doctors set up a makeshift operating room in the yard. The hospital in the Ward Road camp already was filled to capacity. First-aid trucks and refugees with stretchers were collecting the wounded Chinese and fellow refugees and delivering them to the prison yard.

The nurses and doctors quickly organized a triage system. Most of the victims were in shock. Doctors first sutured the wounds and amputated the limbs of victims with the most serious injuries. Didner saw one fourteen-year-old Chinese boy covered with blood; his wounded intestines and liver were dangling outside his stomach. Didner couldn't stand the sight; he knew the boy couldn't be saved. He quickly filled a syringe with morphine and injected it in the boy's arm. He died peacefully from the fatal dose.

The doctors had only a limited amount of ether for anesthesia and quickly ran out of bandages and dressing. Camp residents brought linens and clothing to the yard and ripped them up for use as bandages. Women refugees prepared tea and coffee for the wounded and brought blankets and pillows for them to rest on. The refugees organized a guard service to prevent looting.

By sundown, all of the wounded had been treated. Didner's clothes were covered in blood as he headed back to his office. More than two hundred Chinese and thirty-one refugees had been killed, including Felix Kardegg, the head of the Jüdische Gemeinde and organizer of the refugee *pao chia*. There were more than five hundred wounded, half of them refugees, and hundreds more were homeless. But the kindergarten students had been saved. Their teacher had decided to let the children out early that day, and they had left the SACRA building just minutes before it was hit.

The next day the Chinese residents of Hongkew came to show their gratitude to the refugees. They wheeled dozens of rickshaws loaded with food for the homeless, donated money to the camps, and brought cakes for everyone. The tragedy had momentarily bridged the gulf that had long separated the Chinese from the foreigners.

8. Smuggling in the Ghettos

Survivor Accounts from the Warsaw, Łódź, and Kraków Ghettos

DIANE PLOTKIN

The Nurenberg decrees exclude, expel.
New ghettos rise, essential rights disowned.
Beside the furnace Jews are marked for hell;
where death is forged, despair and madness dwell.
—Jenny Robertson, "Medieval Ghettos"

When German troops invaded Poland on September 1, 1939, Jewish soldiers fought alongside the Polish troops. Powerless to halt the advance of the German army, however, they were destined for destruction. Following the occupation of every town and village, the Jews were singled out for special abuse and massacre.[1] In village after village, Jews were forced to desecrate and destroy sacred Jewish objects while Nazi soldiers burned synagogues as well as Torahs piled on fiery pillars. Lucy Dawidowicz notes that observant Jews were forced to dance around the burning blazes while singing, "We rejoice that the shit is burning." She says that "refinements of cruelty were reserved especially for pious Jews and rabbis, whose traditional Jewish garb—hat and long coat—and whose beard and sidelocks identified them as quintessentially Jewish." Furthermore, "Germans seized bearded Jews and beat them. A more sophisticated entertainment involved plucking beards, hair by hair or in clumps."[2]

On September 21, 1939, Reinhard Heydrich, chief of the Reich Central Security Office, outlined the stages of what would become the ultimate aim of the Nazi forces: the elimination of the Jewish population. As a first step, the Jews were to be concentrated "in cities situated at railway junctions, or along a railway, 'so that future measures may be accomplished more easily.' "[3]

In order to identify the Jews more easily, on November 23, 1939, Hans Frank, governor general of German-occupied Poland, ordered all Jews older than ten years of age to wear white arm bands "at least ten centimeters wide" and to show the Star of David on the right sleeves of both their inner and outer garments. Five days later, on November 28, 1939, he ordered each Jewish community to form a Judenrat, or Jewish Council, a leadership organization composed of rabbis and other persons of influence, who would carry out the orders of the Nazi invaders—the membership of which was to be approved by German officials.[4]

The Warsaw Ghetto

On November 4, 1939, the Schutzstaffel, or security echelon, in Warsaw ordered a special session of the Judenrat, headed by Adam Czerniakow. Facing those who were forced to attend, although it was the Sabbath, Standartenführer Dr. Rudolph Batz read an order in the name of General Karl Ulrich von Neumann-Neurode, which stated that the Jews of Warsaw—approximately 150,000—had three days to move into the area designated by the Germans for a ghetto. Shocked by this demand, the members of the Judenrat decided to bypass the SS and the Gestapo and to appeal directly to General von Neumann-Neurode. When the general received them, it turned out that he knew nothing about the order, even though it had been issued in his name. He promised to look into the matter and told the delegation to await his decision. According to Yisrael Gutman, the general's attitude "was undoubtedly a product of the discord that existed between the SS and the Wehrmacht" within the Generalgouvernement.[5] Consequently, at this time, orders for the formation of a ghetto were withdrawn. The Germans, however, had begun to establish ghettos throughout Poland and had ordered the construction of ghetto walls in Warsaw as well. By mid-November 1940, nearly 500,000 Jews from Warsaw and the surrounding smaller communities were imprisoned within those walls.

There was much haggling over which streets were to be included in the ghetto, or "Jewish section," as the Nazis preferred to call it. When the Jews were finally contained within the walls, the ghetto consisted of 425 acres, 325 of which were utilized for living quarters. The entire ghetto was contained within a boundary of eighteen kilometers (eleven miles). The ghetto possessed 73 streets out of the 1,800 streets in Warsaw, and only a few were full-length streets. The ghetto walls stood three meters (ten feet) high. Initially, 30 percent of the population of Warsaw was enclosed within that space. Later, when evacuees from surrounding towns were forced to move into the ghetto, the population reached 128,000 persons per square kilometer, or 200,000 per square mile. There were approximately 6 to 7 persons per room.[6] Enclosure within the ghetto effectively cut the Jews off from their livelihoods if their places of work were located outside the ghetto walls. Consequently, thousands of Jews milled about the streets. Chaim Kaplan described the scene in his diary: "Jewish Warsaw has changed for the worse, in the direction of ugliness, tastelessness, and lack of beauty. Here too it is a graveyard, only here the skeletons of the dead walk about in the streets."[7]

The inhabitants were forced to live in appalling conditions, crowded into small apartments. Many of these apartments lacked such basic necessities as indoor plumbing. The greatest concerns were disease and shortage of food. Although food had not been in great supply even before the ghetto was established, enclosure within its walls created not only a greater barrier between the Jews and their sources of food, but significantly increased the price of whatever food they could obtain. Regarding the caloric value of the foods available to the people in Warsaw, Gutman writes: "According to a Polish source, the daily caloric content of food distributed to the various national groups in 1941 was as follows: Germans—2,613 calories; Poles—699 calories; Jews—184 calories."[8] Consequently, many resorted to begging. In his diary, Kaplan observed, "The inescapable beggars and paupers have gathered in Warsaw from all parts of the country. And they are the types the like of which you have never seen before. By the thousands they beg for food and sustenance in the streets of the Jewish quarter. They surround you and tug at your sleeve wherever you turn."[9]

On November 27, 1940, he wrote of the lack of food:

A destitute young boy lies on the pavement in the Warsaw ghetto holding a cup in his hand. Photo and caption courtesy of the United States Holocaust Memorial Museum.

> Our constant song—potatoes! This word is repeated a hundred and one times at every moment. It is our whole life. . . . Even in my dreams it visits me. . . . Whoever has potatoes stored in his cellar is considered fortunate, and everyone envies him. In the ghetto we have nothing besides this food, which serves the same function as the manna in the wilderness. It should thus come as no surprise that the price of potatoes has risen from hour to hour. . . . A man who could not afford to buy potatoes with ready cash sold some article of clothing to a Gentile . . . , got the money from him, and at once gave it back to the Gentile for potatoes. All aspirations are gone except for the drive to store up potatoes for the hard and bitter days ahead.[10]

Because existence was nearly impossible with the little food allotted to them, many inhabitants, especially children, resorted to panhandling, while others began to smuggle. Although the Germans attempted to prevent this activity, smuggling continued unabated throughout the existence of the ghetto. Both children and adults smuggled not only food, but also manufactured goods over the ghetto walls, through the gates and cellars, and in any other conceivable hiding place. Some of the smuggling was carried out by organized rings, who smuggled in large amounts of food that would be sold on the black market. Other smuggling was carried out by children, who were able to sneak through cracks in the ghetto walls. The foodstuffs these children brought in, however, were mainly for themselves and their relatives. Thus, although their rations might have been insignificant, every day these smugglers succeeded in bringing in a large amount of food. According to Warsaw ghetto leader Adam Czerniakow, "80 percent of the food entering the ghetto came by means of smuggling."[11]

Two German policemen, two Polish policemen, and two Jewish sentries guarded the gates of the ghetto. The Nazis were initially lax, allowing smugglers to escape and reenter, but later they received orders to guard the gates more diligently. Still, several guards accepted bribes, and the smuggling continued almost unabated. In fact, professional smugglers often worked in cooperation with bribed German, Polish, and Jewish guards. Smuggling was nevertheless dangerous, and many risked their lives to obtain the most basic necessities for existence.

Max Glauben was a child of eleven or twelve when the ghetto was first established. Because he had lived in the Jewish quarter before the Germans occupied Poland, his family was not forced to move. He recalls taking many risks, both on the Jewish and the Aryan side, in his attempts to smuggle food and other necessities. His activities also included carrying messages, which he now feels probably concerned the Underground. Blond and blue-eyed, he could pass as an Aryan outside of the ghetto, which he believes might have saved his life. Although he was constantly afraid, he smuggled until the ghetto uprising in April 1943, after which he and his family were transported to Majdanek.

Max Glauben

I was a young man, about eleven or twelve years old, when the ghetto started.[12] As a twelve-year-old, I wasn't a professional smuggler, but in order to maintain some kind of a food supply in the ghetto other than the rations the Germans gave us, we had to do whatever was possible. I lived on Mila 38, apartment 43. There were two Milas. One was a narrow Mila, where my grandparents lived and where some of the uprising planning started, and the other was the wide Mila, where we lived. It was a more modern street. We were fortunate that our apartment was in the part of the town that was designated for the ghetto. I don't know if it was in the nicest part of Warsaw, but it was close to the railroad yards and to some industry. It was congested but ethnically a Jewish area.

We were in a moderate house. We had all the facilities: water, gas, electricity, and radios. The radio was the first thing the Nazis took away from us. There was a death penalty if you got caught with a radio. But we had a lot of little bitty satellite crystal radios that you could attach to a water pipe and zero in on the little needle that went into the crystal and get some news over it. After that we could easily hide or destroy it.

I only had a brother, but there were other families living in our apartment building. I'd say there were about three or four hundred people living on Mila 38. Our apartment building was five or six stories high and built in a square with a play yard in the middle. There were three and one-half sides to this apartment building with eight stairways going up into one apartment building and six stairways going up into the two apartments on either side. Our apartment was on the second floor, near the third stairway. The coal yard was in another square to the right of us.

We were fortunate that we had a modest-size family. My aunt and my grandparents lived in a different part of town. In my apartment lived one of my aunts. She found me after forty-five years and now lives in Philadelphia. There was my dad, my mom, my brother, my aunt, and two German Jewish people who were related to somebody that my dad knew in the newspaper business. They had been thrown out of Germany and came to Warsaw because they didn't want to go to France. They could also communicate better with the Jewish people in Warsaw because Yiddish is so close to German.

My parents had to go to work, but the children were left behind. We hid during the daytime. In the afternoon, we sometimes cooked whatever we could, and when our parents came home from work, we set the table. Our favorite things were baked potatoes. We just threw them in the coal stove and cooked them. We also made potato latkes, which we cooked on the top of the stove, but we didn't have any grease to fry them in.

We were issued passes for going out of the ghetto in the coal yard. These were for bringing in coal and supplies to be converted into finished products, such as shoes. The fabric for the leather was brought into the ghetto by a Jewish man who drove a wagon with a beautiful horse named Lalka, which means "doll." The wagon had a double bottom and double sides. Even the box the man sat on had a double bottom in which somebody my size could hide.

There was also some lumber in the coal yard. On the corner, on the right hand side by the end, there was a stall where the horse was fed. This was where they took the finished products out of the ghetto. The products that they took out were from the area of the apartments that were close to the coal yard.

Everybody in the ghetto had to work. During the day, when we hid, some of the teachers who could not find professional jobs stayed with us and taught us English, arithmetic, or anything else that they could. Then, either at night or at other designated times, the [smuggled] materials were taken out of the ghetto or brought into the ghetto through gates where the German SS guards were paid off. Not everybody was honorable, and many people did things for money. People usually knew who might let somebody through and who might not. Sometimes we had to go out of one gate and come back through another because they had changed guards between the time we had left and the time we came back. Because communication was very difficult, people sent messages through messengers at different spots or through entrances where they knew a certain guard would be. This was for smuggling in food directly and was done when there were false loads with false passes for going over.

There were also times that we smuggled or rode in the wagon when there was actual merchandise to be brought in or taken out to be utilized by the Germans. As youngsters, we never knew our mission. We carried either a box, a letter, or some kind of package containing information, not for the load that we were riding with, but for a future load. This way, if I were stopped at the gate and caught, I could never tell them what I was doing. All I'd say was that I have this package. If they had opened the package, I don't know what the consequences would have been. I was told to put the package into a spot that had been designated to me prior to my being hidden in the wagon.

I don't know whether this was the only wagon used for smuggling. The way these wagons were built, the food or the objects being transported or smuggled into the ghetto had to be packaged so that they would fit into the crevices. The easiest thing to load were Dutch hams. Even though they weren't kosher, we smuggled them into the ghetto, and many people ate them. I lived in a kosher home, and when we smuggled in the hams, we kept them on our veranda in order to keep them fresh, even though they didn't have to be refrigerated. Then we would cover them up with linens and other things.

Sometimes, when the guard was paid off or would allow us to go out and back in for one reason or another, I sat right next to the coachman and went through the Warsaw ghetto gate without any problem. Most of the time, the guards were paid off. Other times, when I had a package to deliver, I hid under the coachman's seat or even on the bottom of the wagon that was going empty out of the ghetto. Sometimes I had to deliver something to a caboose with a certain number on it that was parked in the railway yard. I would climb up to the caboose, leave the package there, and sometimes pick up information to be given to the people who had sent me out of the ghetto. Sometimes it was to my father, sometimes to the owner of a business or to his partner who had sent me. When I delivered the message or a package to them, I didn't know what they did with it. We never knew. We were never told in order not to endanger our lives. From what I understood, some of these packages contained money for a load for the next trip.

At the beginning, meat was available. Later, when we didn't have any meat, we had to eat nonkosher meat. Kosher beef is from the front part of the cow, but when we got a cow into the ghetto, somehow they had the rabbis kosher other parts of them. When they cut out the unclean veins and certain other parts, there would be a way of making the hind quarter edible for those who ate only kosher food. Later they became more permissive and even slaughtered some horses. Some of them had belonged to the undertaker who drove the wagons that carried the dead bodies to the Jewish cemetery during peacetime. After that, when there were too many corpses in the ghetto and the people had slaughtered the horses, the dead bodies were taken out on handmade wagons with large wheels and flat beds.

After these horses disappeared, we couldn't get any more meat. When we came in one night, even my mother took one of the cans of ham, opened it up, and said, "God will have to forgive us. Starvation is worse than eating something that's nonkosher." And we had some ham. That was the first time I was introduced to nonkosher food, but then after that, whenever we could get something, we would eat it.

I didn't smuggle until about the second year of the ghetto, about 1941 or 1942. There was some smuggling at the beginning, but it was done by other people because at the beginning the Nazis had yet to impose all their rules, so there was still some food available. Maybe the Germans even brought a little bit more food for the ghetto. Later, when they started cutting down, they gave us coupons for rations that weren't obtainable in some of the distribution centers. They also brought less flour into the ghetto for the bakeries. Sometimes we had to wait in line for bread for two or three days. So during those later years, when there was more need for food, we started to smuggle.

In the coal yard, there was a metal grating that you could walk on to cross over to a bakery or to an apartment on the next street from Mila, where they had another bakery. Other kids and I used to climb over that fence and go inside of the apartment where the bakery was located. When people were waiting in line on the outside, we used to cross over, go inside, buy or take some bread and then come back. That's also where we hid later on—after they started burning the ghetto.

There was another type of smuggling into the ghetto. Little kids wore coats with hundreds of pockets sewn into the inside. The coats were made so that they didn't look too suspicious until you opened them up. On the corner, on the left side of the coal yard, there was a wall. On top of it was an entrance or opening where the buildings didn't quite meet. There was barbed wire, but it had been put up by the owners of the building, not by the Nazis. Fifteen or twenty of us would run through a gate that one of the SS men was guarding. Somehow we knew which SS man would shoot us and which SS man would just let us run across. Maybe he would catch or shoot one or two. This was the most dangerous type of smuggling. Most of these kids had blue eyes and blond hair, and when we got to the other side, we would not always be recognized as Jews.

When we smuggled, we just went and took whatever we could organize. When we went out, we'd gather together and start running across. We'd give ourselves a certain time, knowing how long a certain guard would be at a particular gate. We usually went to the marketplace, where we might have to steal apples, oranges, bread, or whatever else we could get. We weren't allowed to speak to the Polish people unless they spoke to us, but after a while we could see that they weren't all bad. Some of them realized what was happening, and they often put some of the rotten fruit in a corner where they knew that the kids would come, pick them up, put them into the[ir] garments, and transport them back to the ghetto. Then, after we finished, we gathered together again.

We went on raids for sugar, beans, and other things in the middle of the night. It might not have been honorable, but we did that in order to save many lives inside the ghetto. I had a lot of ingenuity in doing this. When we went on these raids, we usually went to the railroad yards, where they sometimes had trains with sugar and beans. We would take oil cans that had a sharp edge and a nozzle that narrows at the end, where there's a small opening. When we hit the bottom of the can, the oil poured out. We took larger cans and unscrewed the pointed end. Then we made an opening in one of the ends. It had to be thin, like a sharpened pencil or the thin end of a pen, so it would penetrate a jute bag without tearing it. These big jute sugar bags were in railroad cars parked in the railroad yards. We stuck the smaller end through the jute so the tiny hole wouldn't be noticeable, and the sugar poured out. We had a container for it, and we let as much sugar out of each bag as we wanted. Then we put it in a sewn bag, like a bag that flour used to come in here in the States, but with a strap attached to it. My mom and some of the other women prepared these. We also tied aprons, like those that carry tools, to our bodies. We could put some sugar in them, or sometimes flour, but it was very hard for the flour to flow out. Then we would see what else was in these cars. Sometimes there were beans, and sometimes there were potatoes. For the beans, we had a pipe that had sharp edges on the end. We transported the potatoes loose. In order to do that, we opened our coats and put the potatoes in the pockets that were sewn inside. We didn't do it daily because it would endanger our lives.

I was not too mischievous, but maybe I was too smart, and I was very mechanically inclined. I built a rickshaw from an abandoned bicycle. I would drive people on this rickshaw to make some money either by bartering or trading rides for food. I was able to steal electricity by taking a stone and wire, wrapping it around the trolley tracks, and using it as one conductor to the electricity, then taking another piece of wire and wrapping it around a water pipe. Then, by using the two wires, I could make the electricity. I also made carbide lights by taking two tin cans, one on top of the other, and having water in the upper can dripping into the second can on the bottom. The two were welded, or soldered, together because one can't weld tin. Then I had a wick coming out of it, and the gas escaping to the top would be lit.

Sometimes smuggling like that was done for profit, and people sold things on the black market. But in the later days, it was done mostly for self-survival. There were fewer people in the ghetto, and the needs were greater for families than they were for profit. By then, you couldn't buy anything. You had to barter something in exchange for food.

During the later days, I was involved with some other kids, I don't know how many, in trying to find the gold, furs, and some of the other valuables left by the other Jews in the ghetto. We knew exactly where to look. We also knew how to knock on the walls to find hiding places in the abandoned apartments. One could always knock on a wall and see if it was hollow or whether it was made of brick. There were also certain doors that were camouflaged, and we knocked on them to see if they were hollow. Sometimes drapery hooks were made out of gold or silver. The real hooks had been taken out and those put in. Then they would put plaster around them. The hooks made out of gold and silver were softer than the other metals. When you lived under these conditions for a number of years, you knew all the tricks.

We either bartered these hooks or gave them to our parents, and they either sold them on the black market or traded them for food. Later, in about 1942, I imagine some of the weapons carried into the Warsaw ghetto might have been bought with these things. We kids were doing many things but were never told what they were for. Nowadays I can figure out what was eventually going to be done with them, but at that time we weren't supposed to know so that if we got caught, we couldn't reveal any secrets or tell the Germans what was happening.

I never was caught by the Germans, but during one incident I was almost captured by the Poles. I was riding on the back of a wagon with a load of coal, which was usually unprotected. We would pick the coal up on the non-Jewish side, where there were Polish kids holding sticks with hooks on them. When they saw a wagon with coal on it, they would want some, too, because it was scarce, so they would try to hook onto it and pull it off. This time we were going back into the ghetto, and I was exposed on the Polish side, but I had blue eyes and wasn't wearing my Jewish star. The driver said, "Get the horse whip and don't let them get the coal." So I stood on the back of the wagon and tried to prevent the kids from hooking off the coal. In the meantime, all the kids, whom I was beating with the whip while trying not to let them take the coals, kept following us. They said that sooner or later one of them was going to get some coal. They started ganging up on me and tried to beat me up. When the driver saw that the kids were there, he told me to get out of there. He stopped the wagon in enough time to get some of the kids away from me and sat there waiting for me to get in while the horse ate from the feeding bag that was on an extra horse blanket, on top of a slab of wood. Had the driver not come down and helped me, those kids would have gotten hold of me, and I don't know what they would have done. Perhaps they would have turned me over to the Nazis. As we rode pretty close to the gate, I had very little time to get into the back seat, but I had time to get into the coach's seat. It had a double bottom, so I climbed down to this bottom and placed the flat piece of wood over me. That was the closest I came to being caught. As a result of my narrow escape, I'm here.

There were many close calls, but when you do something like that, you have no fear. There is one objective: to accomplish what you went to do, and you just do crazy things. But every time you go, it is a close call. I also had a close call in the ghetto when I went to get some bread without standing in line. Some people stood in line for two or three days, and sometimes by the time they got to the bread bakery, the bakery had run out of bread. People realized what I was doing, and six or seven bullies got hold of me and didn't let me go back home with all the bread. They wanted to take away from me the bread that I had obtained. I wasn't taking too much, only enough for my family—maybe two or three loaves. After they got hold of me that day, we had only one loaf of bread.

One time I was told to get to the other side and deliver something to a caboose still attached to a train. When I put that stuff in the caboose, I thought I heard a firecracker or something, but it was a shot that had been fired. I don't know who fired it or why, but that was another close call. Sometimes when I rode with a coachman, he decided to leave before I was ready to climb in and go back, so I would be left behind. Luckily, either somebody told me to go to a different gate, or I just found another gate. It sounds like a story, but when you got left in a situation like that, you didn't even think, and you didn't even realize what was happening. Instead of going through the same gate that we went out of, I just took a chance and went to another gate.

Another time, some people had just taken a cart carrying some dead people out to the cemetery. It was a rule to wear a white armband with a Jewish star sewn to it, but it was forbidden to wear one that just snapped on. Because I sometimes went out of the ghetto, I wore the Jewish star that snapped on, so I could take it off on the other side. Someone saw me without the armband. When I saw that cart, I said, "Maybe two or three guys are pushing that cart," and I went ahead and put my armband on and started pushing the wagon in, and that's how I got back in. But this was an unplanned situation. When you went on missions like that, you didn't know who was your friend, and you couldn't talk to the Poles.

I was frightened most of the time. I don't think I ever felt like a hero. None of us did. I felt like I was being a provider, like I was defying the Nazis, like I was keeping some Jewish people alive and not allowing the Nazis to get the best of me. Later I worked in airplane factories. I was a pattern maker for the outer bodies of the planes. On one hand, I felt that I might be helping the Germans, but it prevented me and some other prisoners from being killed, so I was saving a life doing something that might be good for the enemy. But I felt that sooner or later the Germans were going to lose.

The only difference between being a prisoner in the ghetto and one in the camp was that I lived with my family. In the ghetto, I was doing things for my family, but later on I was doing them for self-survival. Sometimes I felt like somebody who doesn't know how to swim but is thrown into the middle of the ocean and told to survive. And that's what I did.

Smuggling was part of my life from when the ghetto started in 1941 until the uprising in 1943. After that, we all went into hiding, and luckily that prevented us from being burned to death. My parents had been moved from one factory to another, and we had moved to an apartment on Platz Muranowsky. During the evening before Passover in 1943, my mom and my aunt lived with some neighbors. My mother was making the utensils kosher. There used to be people who brought a big hot-water bucket—it was larger than I was—to the inside square of the apartment building. They had a stick through the handle of the bucket, and two people would carry it. When they got to the middle of the apartment square, where the play yard was, they would start screaming, "Come and get your things kosher." They would do the pots and some of the utensils, and the women would do the dishes and the rest of the utensils.

Suddenly there was a knock on the door, and about six to eight men walked in with rifles. One wore a German helmet, and the others dressed in plain uniforms. They said, "We are the Underground, and we want you all to go to the shelter," and they stood by the window. They didn't explain to me what they were going to do, but that's when the uprising started. Before that, my mom and I had been at the apartment where she was making all the utensils kosher for Passover, but when the shots started, we went to the shelter. I don't think I realized what was going on until I was there. They must have started in other parts of the ghetto, too, because the uprising started simultaneously in more than one spot. There must have been a designated time. We had to run to the shelter quickly because the Germans returned the fire, but it was just rifle fire. There was a lot of panic because it was at night—two or three hours before dawn. When we started running, some of the people didn't make it to the shelter. They had to hide in empty apartments.

At first, we hid under the public toilet on the bottom of the apartment, but it wasn't our designated shelter. It was the stinkiest place I've ever been in. Water was dripping from the pipes. The following day we were able to move to the shelter. Some of us kids stood guard, waiting to hear whether the Germans were coming to raid the ghetto. The following day, artillery and tanks came in and started bombing the front of the building.

I was not able to smuggle any food in during the uprising. It was a matter of getting what we had already smuggled from the apartments and the living quarters into the shelters where we were hiding. The stairways were wooden and were nailed or attached to wooden beams with brick. When the tanks and the heavy artillery came in, they attacked; they burned the stairways. Two or three days later I went crawling on my stomach, trying to get to the second floor to get some food and some fifty- or one-hundred-pound sugar bags down to the basement. I crawled up through the rubbish, then I pulled some of the food down and got it into the shelter. It was all we could do at that time because we couldn't even be seen. Some of the women and men fought the Nazis from the verandas, but most of the kids and the people other than the fighters had to hide.

At first, my father had to go into a different shelter. Three nights later I was standing guard, armed with a pistol and watching for strangers, when I said to somebody, "Halt, who's going there?" I was ready to see who it was or to shoot, but it was my father returning to the shelter.

There were many instances when kids from other apartments came to our apartment, looking for the wealth that I was looking for, and we confronted each other like cowboys with guns—you go to your territory, and I go to my territory. Sometimes we turned night into day because the Nazis would try to find us in the daytime. At night, we could go outside and enter some apartments, trying to get some of the food left there by the people who went into the shelters and cooking it in an open fire. When they started burning the ghetto, people would just stay in their hiding places, get blistered, and run out of the oxygen. Then they and the children would just smother.

There were many traumatic stories. One involved my aunt. My mom's sister was taken out and supposedly raped and killed. Another incident concerned my mother's father. My grandfather had been an umbrella maker. My mom prepared some food that we had obtained through smuggling. Once I went to take some food to my grandfather. When I started pushing on the door, I couldn't open it. Finally some adult helped me push it in. When I went in, I found my grandfather hanging from the door. He had committed suicide. That was in 1942. Something traumatic occurred after the burning of the ghetto. We all had been in the same shelter in Muranowsky Square. About six weeks later, at the end of the uprising, sometime in May, we were arrested. They rounded us up in Muranowsky Square and disrobed everybody, including my mother and my aunts, and looked in the women's body crevices. I was about thirteen years old, and next to the death of my grandfather, this was the most embarrassing and humiliating thing, more than the shooting and more than the hunger. It might have had something to do with the upbringing that we Jewish kids had. Then we were loaded onto boxcars and taken to Majdanek, where they killed my family. What bothered me almost more was that the Poles would stand by the windows in the tall buildings outside of the ghetto wall and look into Muranowsky Square. They could see everything that was happening. We saw some faces that were smiling and laughing, but we also saw some sad faces.

There were many more things that had an impact on my life. As a thirteen-year-old, I really couldn't understand how I could look up to the sky, and the sky was blue like it always was, yet I had that little knot in my stomach because I was treated cruelly for no reason at all. I might smuggle food into the ghetto in order to save my life, but I hadn't done anything wrong before that. It mostly felt like you would be caught by the police and told that you had committed a crime or done something wrong, but you knew that you hadn't done it. Or perhaps once you had done something wrong in class and the teacher saw it, so you got that lousy feeling. But during the war, people committed horrible crimes for absolutely no reason other than trying to destroy us or kill us. When you live a life like we lived in the ghetto, and then you go into concentration camps and are treated like we were, it affects you forever.

I matured early. I didn't have a childhood, but I always did the best I could with what I had.

To this day, I say that not only I but other Jews, even the ones who perished, did the best they could with what they had. I think we did anything necessary to survive. Afterward, I had some guilt about the others—Why did I survive while they didn't?

The Łódź Ghetto

On December 10, 1939, Regierungspräsident Friedrich Übelhör appointed a staff to plan the formation of a ghetto in Łódź. On February 8, 1940, Łódź (renamed Litzmannstadt in honor of the German general Karl Litzmann),[13] home of the second-largest Jewish community in Poland, became the first major city where Jews were forced into ghettos. Although Łódź was governed by Gauleiter Arthur Greiser, the commander of ghetto operations was Hans Biebow. Mordechai Chaim Rumkowski, an elderly and distinguished lawyer, was appointed Eldest of the Jews. Emanuel Ringelblum, the historian of the Warsaw ghetto, wrote of him in 1940: "Today, the 6th of September, there arrived from Łódź, Chaim, or, as he is called, 'King Chaim,' Rumkowski, an old man of seventy, extraordinarily ambitious and pretty nutty. . . . He considers himself God's anointed."[14]

The site of the Łódź ghetto was the Baluty section, a slum possessing a population of 62,000 Jews. There were, however, more than 100,000 Jews in the vicinity who also were forced into the ghetto, leaving behind most of their personal belongings.[15] In preparation, on February 8, 1940, Brigadeführer Johannes Schäfer, the *Polizeiprasident* of Łódź, ordered all Poles and ethnic Germans to move out of the ghetto site by February 29. The Jews were then to move into the ghetto.

Jews moved into the ghetto not only from other parts of Łódź, but from Germany, Austria, and Czechoslovakia as well. Fifty thousand were deported from greater Germany to Łódź and Riga. Possessing good clothing and more personal property than was owned by most Polish Jews, Jews from these countries increased whatever social differentiation had existed in the area prior to their arrival. Lucy Dawidowicz comments that, short of

A child vendor carries her wares in a tray slung around her neck in the outdoor market in the Łódź ghetto in Poland. Photo and caption courtesy of the United States Holocaust Memorial Museum.

food, "they cornered the black-market supply of bread, thus exacerbating their already tense relations in the ghetto with the resident Polish Jews."[16]

In addition to bringing in western and central European Jews, the Nazis sent to Łódź ethnic Germans, *Volksdeutsch,* offspring of German settlers in Poland in the eighteenth and nineteenth centuries who, according to Martin Gilbert, "felt themselves a deprived minority," demarcated by tongue and customs, isolated from their homeland. These people, says Gilbert, felt that under German rule they enjoyed the chance not only to flourish, but to seek vengeance against Poles under whose authority they had lived. In areas where there were large numbers of them, the German troops considered them collaborators. Of their numbers Gilbert states, "In Łódź, a city with 350,000 Poles and 250,000 Jews, there were 75,000 Ethnic Germans living on the eve of war."[17] This figure doubled by 1941, as the Nazi command continued to send them from Volhynia to western Poland. Thus, as the population of a German element loyal to Berlin increased, it hindered opportunities for armed rebellion and escape, for Jews and Poles alike.[18] With the movement of so many into a small, dilapidated area that was soon to be completely enclosed, tremendous overcrowding existed. Raul Hilberg writes that by September 1941, the population of the Łódź ghetto, an area of 1.6 square miles, was 144,000. There were 25,000 rooms with an average of 5.8 persons per room.[19] According to Lucjan Dobroszycki, of the 31,721 ghetto apartments, most containing only a single room, only 725 possessed running water. The Jews in the ghetto were prohibited from using electricity from eight in the evening to six in the morning. On May 1, 1940, 163,177 Jews lived inside the now closed-up ghetto.[20]

Because of poor sewage and sanitation facilities, the ghettos soon became filthy, the air fetid, the streets congested and lined with beggars. Noted Ringelblum, "Horrible conditions in Łódź. Long lines at the toilets, crowding, no packages are allowed in, only letters."[21] Thus, it was difficult to prevent disease. Dawidowicz notes that although typhus, caused by lice, was the most prevalent result of the existing unsanitary situations, it was not the most deadly. On a scale of thirteen, it ranked eleventh or twelfth. Instead, 30 percent of ghetto inhabitants died of heart disease, the result of the overwhelming pressure and suffering of ghetto life. This was followed by dysentery, then by tuberculosis, hunger, and diseases of the gastrointestinal tract.[22] Ringelblum observed, "Sixty Jews die every day." In March 1941, he added, "During the last ten months, the Jewish populace of Łódź has been diminished by the death of 23,000 individuals."[23]

Mass unemployment spread throughout Poland because of the war. Nonetheless, ghetto inhabitants, although becoming weak and being cut off from their means of employment, were not allowed to remain idle. Hilberg writes:

> at the beginning of the occupation 2,150,000 people were out of work, while 6,420,000 (comprising the unemployed and their dependents) were directly affected by the upheaval. There was no need for a forced labor system during this period, but, to the Germans, the sight of thousands of Jews "milling around" *(herumlungernde Juden)* was a challenge that had to be met right away. Even during the first few weeks of the occupa-

> tion, military and civilian personnel seized the Jews in the streets and forced them to clear rubble, fill antitank ditches, shovel snow, and perform other emergency tasks.[24]

Hilberg notes that forced labor for Jews was established by the Generalgouvernement in 1939. Jews were accosted randomly and ordered to work whenever a specific organization required them. Although the Jews were freed as the day concluded, the procedure occurred continuously,[25] and the practice was the precursor to the labor camps.

The second form of labor existed within the ghetto itself. In Łódź, Rumkowski established workshops, believing that survival depended on productivity. Thus, by February 1941, more than 10,000 Jews were working as carpenters, tailors, and shoemakers.[26] States Hilberg:

> The largest workshop ghetto, in Łódź, maintained its own railroad station at Radegast, from which seventy to ninety loaded cars were dispatched every day. Cheap fabrication of every sort *(billige Fertigung jeder Art)* was being obtained there in exchange for a prison diet and the simplest conceivable life style *(denkbar einfachsten Lebensführung)*. On this basis the ghetto was earning its keep and returning to the city a profit that was "not to be underestimated" *(einen nicht zu unterschätzenden wirtschaftlichen Gewinn)* by the end of 1941.[27]

As early as May 18, 1940, Ringelblum recorded, "Heard very sad news about Łódź, where they're living on a diet of bread and water."[28] Although Jews were forced to work, they were gradually and continually weakened by the lack of food. Hilberg notes that by controlling the amount of food allowed into the ghetto, "the Germans were able to turn the ghettos into death traps. And that is what they did."[29] Noted Ringelblum early in 1941, "Heard today, 5th of January, from someone who visited the Łódź Ghetto. The people there all look like beggars, hunchbacked, starving."[30] No longer able to buy in the open markets, the Jews could obtain only small amounts of food of the poorest quality. Considered prisoners by their captors, the Jews in the ghetto did, nevertheless, require some nourishment. Hilberg states that Dr. Moser, chair of a group of local Łódź officials,

> pointed out that the ghetto, "that is, the Jew community," was a most unwelcome institution but a necessary evil. The Jews, most of whom were living a useless life at the expense of the German people, had to be fed; that in this connection they could not be considered normal consumers in the framework of the food economy required no comment. The quantities, Moser continued, would have to be determined by the Gettoverwaltung after consultations with food experts. As for the quality of the food, Moser explained that "preferably the most inferior merchandise" should be diverted from normal trade channels and delivered to the ghetto. The prices charged by the food growers would have to be controlled very closely, for it seemed natural that the price level would have to be brought into harmony with the quality of the "more or less dubious merchandise."[31]

As the starvation level increased, daily deaths ensued. In fact, Dawidowicz comments that as early as September 24, 1940, "a JDC [American Jewish Joint Distribution Committee] official declared that it was imperative to set up soup kitchens to provide 100,000 warm midday meals, to prevent a complete catastrophe. The cost, estimated at 8 pfennig per person, would come to 8,000 Reichsmarks per day, or 240,000 Reichsmarks per month, which he said was then equivalent to $100,000 at the official rate of exchange."[32]

Actually, some soup kitchens did exist; they were governed by the organizational parties. Both the Germans and the Judenrat controlled the food rations. Dishonesty, nepotism, and theft hindered the fair disbursement of food. Some food stores marketed food at established prices but unloaded the remainder surreptitiously to ghetto inhabitants at outrageous rates. Some ghetto inhabitants received larger rations than others because of their occupations and because of favoritism, thus creating a two-tier society with regard to food—a significant disparity in a place where many people were starving to death. Consequently, some Jews, hungry and demoralized, turned to smuggling food into the ghetto. Dawidowicz writes: "Only the illegal importation of food into the ghettos kept most Jews from dying of hunger. . . . Children were the most numerous class of smugglers, small, spry, and, if caught, an object of pity for the policeman." She adds that all of the inhabitants of the ghetto would have starved to death if not for the smugglers' guile and persistence: "The ghetto's ingenuity and daring, the toughness of its brawling wagoners staved off massive hunger deaths."[33]

When Jews in the Łódź ghetto defied the Nazis and were caught, some were sent to labor camps, and others were killed. According to Alan Adelson, "Sixty thousand people died in the ghetto, whether from starvation, freezing, disease, hanging, or suicide. From the ghetto, 130,000 who were deported died either in the exhaust vans at Chelmno or the gas chambers of Auschwitz."[34] Of the approximately 10,000 Jews who survived, largely those who had been sent to work camps late in the war, many showed incredible ingenuity and tenacity.[35]

Leo Laufer lived in the Baluty area of Łódź. The son of an Orthodox-Hasidic father and an overworked but loving mother, his childhood was typical of the life of the impoverished Jews of Poland in the early twentieth century. Somehow, however, Leo was different from the rest, a factor that helped him to survive the Holocaust.

Leo Laufer

After the Germans took over, they used to come into the part of the city where the Jewish people lived and drag the youngsters and the elderly for work.[36] They used to run them from the house and line them up, maybe twenty to thirty to a group. They had bayonets, and they used to take them to ditches and all other kinds of work. It was horrible. My father was scared to go out of the house.

I was a young fellow, about sixteen, and my friend was my age. I never realized my good friend from across the street, with whom I used to play ball, was of German descent. Suddenly he became a *Volksdeutsch,* and he pointed to the windows where Jews lived. I don't know if it was Wehrmacht, but they had a special type of green uniform. They knocked on the door, came in, slapped me, and dragged me out. They took my younger brother, too, and we went to work. My father wasn't there at the time.

The work was mainly on the outskirts of the city—digging ditches, doing repair work, cleaning, and so on. This is when I really felt that I had lost my dignity. My father was always hiding because he was scared that somebody was going to cut his beard off. He felt so badly because it was so undignified for him. I remember when they actually pulled his beard out. He was almost crying, as old a man as he was. And he put his handkerchief around the part of the beard that was still left across his face, tied in a knot at the top. He wore it like when you have a toothache. It was degrading, and this kept on for a long time. It was tragic; it was very, very bad.

The problems started with food rationing. Immediately, the Germans set up some sort of ration, an allotment of food, such as bread. I remember across the street from our house (we lived on Doina 4), on Doina 5, on the other side of a narrow little street, there was a bakery. Since they started giving out ration cards, so much per family, we used to wait in line. You felt so degraded because you were Jewish. Some of the Polish people waiting in line with us dragged us out: "Jew, you don't have to stay in line; you don't need to eat," they said. It was getting so bad that you could feel that not only did the Poles lose the war, but in addition to their misery, they showed us how much more miserable they could make it for us. We got it from both sides, the Germans and the Poles, the fortunate and the unfortunate. Sometimes you had to stay in line four, five, six, or seven hours. So we used to switch between my brothers and my sisters.

In 1939, my brother from my father's first marriage was already married. He lived across the hall from us. He had a wife and one child. My immediate brother from my family had died in 1938, so I was almost the head of the house. Everyone relied on me because after me, there was a sister two years younger, then another sister, then a brother (Berish), then another little sister. I became the man of the house, for my father was scared, and my mother had her own problems with all the children to raise.

I saw how poor we were in the beginning, but I saw an opportunity to get some food on the other side, so possibly my family would have a better life while we were in the ghetto. I worked out a strategy. I slipped out of the ghetto—of course, this was very dangerous; you were not allowed to. Our house stood at the end of the ghetto. It was a four-story building with a courtyard in the back. The courtyard contained the water. We pumped water because we didn't have any facilities; all the toilet facilities were in the courtyard. There were little sheds in which two or three neighbors stored some wood or coal. And this stood against the fence, which faced the end of the ghetto. Then there was a sidewalk, then a barbed wire, and across the street was where the Gentiles lived.

I feel like I was a manipulator. I worked inside this little shed. I cut out some pieces of wood and made a small door with a little hook, so I could pull it inside. As you looked outside, you could see the Gentile area. The guard was on the corner of Zgierska and Goplanska, a block away. And I opened this door and looked out. Then I had the idea to go across, but before I did it, I consulted with a friend. (I remember that before the war ended, this friend told me that his father went into the Polish army.) This friend had a sister a few years older than he. I used to come over to their house. They couldn't come over to us; my father didn't like me to associate with anyone but Jewish people, but I was a different type of kid.

I wrapped a note around a little stone with a string. On the top of the four-story building [where we lived] was what we used to call the *boyden,* the top level where nobody lived, and everybody who washed laundry used to bring it up. They hung it up there because the wind and air dried it out. So I walked up, and when I saw him, I hollered, "Jan, I'm going to throw something." So I went downstairs, and I took this stone, with the note written in Polish wrapped around it, and I threw him the stone and told him that I would like to come over and talk to his mother. This was the first conversation.

Of course, this little thing was already built in this hut, and I could watch the guard walking from the corner of Goplanska, back and forth, every two hundred to three hundred feet. When he went to the corner, sometimes he made a little turn to the left, and I slipped across. It wasn't too far, maybe fifty feet or less. So I went to Jan's house, and I talked to his mother—Stanislova Grabowska. I sat down and said, "Listen, I have a plan for you. If you would go along with me, I will reward you very handsomely if you would take the risk. The value of food in the ghetto is indescribable because now we have so much money of no value to us that we even throw it away."

In the beginning of May, people were already starving. Some people were hoarding, trying to keep every little thing they had. But still there was nothing available. We couldn't buy anything. People were buying bread and paying ten to twenty times what it was worth, so the ghetto started something like a black market. I felt Mrs. Grabowska might help me smuggle food into the ghetto, not on a large scale. I said to her, "We can work out some places on a prearranged basis where you would come to the street, or even at the place where I have this little door. It doesn't have to be big packages, say a loaf of bread, a pound of butter, some potatoes, a pound of sugar, or whatever, on a small scale." I told her that this would be enough for my family to survive. I added, "I will pay you whatever you want. If it's five or ten times as much, don't worry." Money was no object; you could get money abundantly.

When we first started, if she brought a pound of butter, I used to keep a little for us; the rest of it I would sell. And with this selling, I could get a loaf of bread; I could get marmalade; I could get anything, plus having five to ten times as much money to pay her. On the Christian side, for money Mrs. Grabowska could get almost what she wanted; she could go to the farm. Of course, this started on a very, very small scale, with a little package. Then we got a bigger package. We couldn't get it through this door. I told her, "Why don't you take a *droshka* [a horse and buggy]?" She used to wear a big stole and carried the food underneath. She used to watch, and if I was there when the guard happened to be there, she took off, made the rounds, and came back again. When she came back, she threw it across the barbed wire; I caught it and went home. Then I started my business selling it and keeping some. To tell you the honest truth, from May until October 1940 in the ghetto, my family had more food and more clothes than I had had all my life. And it worked out beautifully, but it didn't last for long.

Several times during this period, probably in September, I had a confrontation with a young man. Any time I took a package from Mrs. Grabowska, he was right in front of me, telling me he wanted to be my partner. I hate to say it, but he was a Jewish fellow. I told him, "I don't need a partner. Why do I need a partner? I'm doing all the risking, and I'm doing all the selling." One time I pacified him by giving him something, and he walked off. Then, he came back again and watched me every time I took a package across. One time he told me, "If I'm not going to be a partner, if you're not going to give me half, I will turn you over to the Gestapo." Of course, I became very upset. I said, "You go wherever you have to go and go ahead." I knew and had heard about *mutches.* A *mutche* is somebody who spies on somebody else; it is a Jewish expression. I wasn't smart enough at the time to realize that maybe the man would really do it. I never suspected that a Jewish person would go to the Gestapo and tell them what I was doing.

Everything was going so beautifully. But one time when I took a package across, he told me, "I am going to the Gestapo." He knew exactly where I lived. The following day, at midnight or maybe 2:00 A.M., civilian Gestapo men, Germans, came to my house. I did not know what was happening. My father opened up the door because there was knocking. Immediately, the Gestapo man hit my father so hard that my father fell down. All the Gestapo man wanted to know was where Leo was. They called me Leibeck or Leibl.

I got up. I went out almost naked in my underwear, and they said, "Put your pants on and your jacket." And they took me; they beat me up even before I got to the Gestapo. I did get to the Gestapo. I remember there was a big church, and right behind the church was a small red brick building. And when I came there, they started beating me so unmercifully that I didn't even know what to say. They wanted to know who gave me the package. They didn't want to know anything else—how many packages, whatever. And immediately it dawned on me that I was not going to tell them. I felt that if I did, I was already beaten. They wanted to find Mrs. Grabowska. I felt that if they beat me a little more, they would still send me home.

They brought in this fellow who squealed on me. They asked him in front of me, "Is this the guy?" And he said, "Yes." You can imagine my feelings. He was an informer for the Gestapo, but he was Jewish. After the war, somebody told me there was such a man. There was a German in the Gestapo who spoke the most fluent Yiddish that I ever heard. He was not a youngster—probably fifty or so. I believe his name was Beeber or something [*Gettoverwaltung* Litzmannstadt chief: Diplom Kaufman Hans Biebow]. He was the head of the Gestapo, and he spoke perfect Yiddish. I don't know how, but he did.

This ordeal lasted for quite a while. They took me to an isolation cell in the basement, and they beat me. One time they pushed me against a light switch. It was a big switch that you turned on. It hit the back of my head.

Every day I got a lecture. All they wanted to know was who gave the food to me. I was, in Yiddish, *aingeschpardt* [stubborn]. I didn't want to tell them, and I didn't. I think I was there almost two weeks. Finally, I wound up in the hospital not far away from home because they beat me so much that I had to have two operations on my behind. It was very, very bad. When my mother came to see me, she told me that at the hallway door a Jewish policeman was watching me. The Gestapo told him to watch me so that I didn't run away. I was there until they operated on me. I was there more than a week. Finally, they let me out.

I had accumulated cigarettes, coffee, and all kinds of things that I was trading with Mrs. Grabowska in order to obtain the things we needed. I didn't know when my mother came to see me that the Gestapo had taken everything I had accumulated, plus anything we had ourselves, and they were beating my mother, father, and the children. It was horrible. When I saw what was going on, I was more determined than ever to start all over again because the poverty was so great. My father was scared to stand in line for bread. I saw that we were going to die like the rest of them that I saw in the street, so I said, "I'm not going to let it happen."

I started with the same little store. I threw another little stone across, and I said, "Mrs. Grabowska, we are going to start all over. I didn't tell anyone about you. Nobody knows because you know that they didn't arrest you." And we started smuggling again. It lasted maybe two or three weeks, not too long. One day a Jewish policeman came. He said I should report for transportation to the labor camp. Then I realized that because I was smuggling, the Gestapo probably got my name, and they wanted me. They wanted to punish me; they didn't take anybody this age. Usually they took boys in their twenties, but I felt that there was nothing I could do about it. You get clothes and a little suitcase, and you report. In these days, there was a transport of about two hundred of us going to what we thought was a labor camp.

The Kraków Ghetto

By March 20, 1941, all "Aryans" had to move out of the area in Kraków known as Podgorze. Janina Fischler-Martinho recalls that although the area was small, the Germans built a brick fence to encircle it. The top was designed to resemble tombstones. Situated on the right bank of the Vistula River, Podgorze was barren of trees and greenery. The Germans had chosen it with an eye to the future, as it lay close to two Jewish cemeteries, which eventually were leveled out, as well as within walking distance of the railroad station, which would transport Jews to the East.[37] On March 3, orders concerning the formation of a "Jewish Living Quarter" emanated from Otto Wachter, governor of Kraków, and appeared in the *Krakauer Zietung.* Of the eighty thousand Jews living in Kraków, fifteen thousand were left to inhabit the apartments formerly populated by Christians in the designated ghetto area.[38]

Despite the formation of the ghetto, it seemed initially that the Jews had a choice as to where to move. Although those from inner Kraków and the Jewish poor moved into what was designated as "the inner ghetto," those living in other areas were free to "escape" to what was called "outer Kraków"—in other words, the country. After the ghetto was sealed, it was guarded day and night by policemen wearing blue uniforms.[39]

Jews living in the ghetto were forced to wear white arm bands bearing the Jewish star on their right sleeve. The Labor Department, or Arbeitsamt, issued identity cards or *Kennkarten,* which permitted the holders to exit the ghetto in order to go to their jobs. Thousands passed through the gates in the morning and returned by the 9:00 P.M. curfew. According to Tadeusz Pankiewicz, the only ones who did not have jobs were "the old, the sick and the children."[40]

The Judenrat possessed twenty-four persons, with Dr. Arthur Rosenzweig, a lawyer, serving as its president. Their duties, conducted under the rule of the Gestapo, concerned "general administration, preparation of the statistical data, lists of residents, registration of stores, distribution of food and fuel for the inhabitants, editing and publishing regulations of the occupying authorities and their execution."[41] They eventually were assigned more difficult and distressing tasks. The Judenrat was located in the police station at the main gate. In this building, there were hearings against the Jews, often accompanied by severe and cruel physical abuse.[42]

Symcha Spira, a glazier, organized a Jewish police unit called the Ordnungsdienst (OD), or Service for Keeping Order. Members wore blue jackets with lapels, neckties, and patches on their sleeves bearing the word *Ordnungsdienst* in Hebrew letters. Spira's job was to create a Jewish police unit loyal to the Gestapo. The OD carried out Gestapo orders, implemented regulations decreed by the Judenrat, kept order within the ghetto, and captured Jews who committed crimes.[43]

One of the first regulations in the ghetto called for the removal of all Polish inscriptions in the area and replacing them with Hebrew, even though many of the ghetto dwellers did not know the language or the Hebrew alphabet. Hence, many felt that they were living in a strange and foreign environment. Nonetheless, at first there was some economic development, for Jews opened new stores, restaurants, patisseries, and dairies. Slowly, however, the quality of life in the ghetto deteriorated. Jews were beaten coming home from work; men's beards were torn from their faces or burned by SS officers and soldiers; rations were severely limited; and Jews began to be transported to the labor and death camps. According to Yehuda Bauer, conditions in the Kraków ghetto were more desperate than in other ghettos.[44]

Pankiewicz recalls that in the fall of 1941 all surrounding communities were included in the district of Kraków. Thus, all Jews living in the small towns were now required to move into the inner Kraków ghetto. Already overcrowded, its population now swelled to 17,000. To decrease the population, the Germans began to evacuate the elderly and the jobless. Symcha Spira, devoted to following the Germans' commands, organized these evacuations directly under orders from Gestapo agent Szymon Szpic.[45] Then on June 1, 1942, Spira was ordered to bring all those who did not have a work card to Plac Zgody, the main entrance and exit gate for those who regularly left the ghetto on foot.[46] A second *Aktion* took place on June 8; those who were selected were transported to Belzec for extermination. During this *Aktion,* many of the sick and invalids were taken from the hospitals as well. By this time, word had filtered through of the mass murders taking place, and there were several suicides. A third *Aktion* occurred on June 27. Seven thousand people were expelled during the June deportations.[47]

In November 1942, the Plaszow concentration camp, governed by Amon Goeth, was constructed near Kraków; thousands of Jews transported from the Kraków ghetto were taken there for hard labor. In December 1942, the ghetto was split into Ghetto A and Ghetto B. All workers living in Ghetto B were required to move to Ghetto A, and vice versa. In Ghetto B, the population decreased daily; the remaining Jews from the surrounding towns, by now tattered and poor, were forced to move there. Starving and desperate, they begged for food from those in Ghetto A.[48]

The final liquidation of the Kraków ghetto took place on March 13, 14, and 15, 1943. About two weeks later, all members of the Judenrat, all members of the OD, and anyone else who had been in the service of the Gestapo, such as Jewish informers, were also arrested and taken to Plaszow.

William Schiff was a young man living in Kraków. With his family, he moved into the inner ghetto. When the Germans withheld rations and the situation became desperate, he began to smuggle food into the ghetto for his family and his girlfriend's family.

William Schiff

At the beginning of the war, I was exactly twenty years old.[49] There were five people in my family: my mother, father, sister, brother, and myself. There were about one and one-half years difference in age between the siblings. I was the eldest. My sister was the only girl. She was a smart girl but spoiled. My younger brother was just an average guy but scared like everyone else. All three of us were practically grown up when the war began.

After the Germans occupied the country, the Polish police took over in Kraków. They were just like the Germans; they did exactly what the Germans told them and were happy to do it. The ghetto was formed in 1941. It was a small ghetto. From north to south, it contained about seven streets; from east to west there were about four or five. They built brick walls around it so we couldn't escape. There were three main gates with Polish police guarding them. Unless you had a pass, there was no way out. I had one, but no one else in my family did.

My family was living in Kazimiercz, the Jewish section of town, but the Germans took a section of Kraków called Podgorze, which was not near the downtown, and started moving Jews there. I was the one who found an apartment in the ghetto for my family. I don't remember the size, but there were two rooms: a kitchen and a bedroom. The kitchen was used for cooking, dining, and everything else.

When they moved us to the ghetto, I was dating Rosalie, who was sixteen at the time. At first, they also allowed some of the Jews from Kraków to move to small towns nearby. She had been living in a nice apartment near the Vistula River and moved to one of these small towns with her mother, brother, and sister in 1941. Her father had run away in 1931 and was never allowed to return to his family. I helped Rosalie's family move out of Kraków. After that, I used to buy off the policeman and leave the ghetto to visit her once or twice a week. My parents didn't know because usually if you were found leaving the ghetto, you could be killed. A Polish policeman or a German would just take you away and shoot you.

There was no work in the ghetto, no way to make a living. My daddy had been a barber and a beautician before the war, but when we moved into the ghetto, he had to sign his shop over to the employee who had worked for him the longest. Now it seemed like my daddy was my child, and I was the father. He just cried all day.

The Germans didn't give us any rations, so we had nothing to eat at all. People were dying on the streets, so somebody was going to have to provide for the family, and I was the guy. We were also concerned about Rosalie's family. Her mother had two sisters, but they had their own problems. When I would see a person lying on the street, I wanted to pick him up and help him, but I had a family of five to feed. I had to worry about my parents. If I didn't take care of my family, no one else would. Human beings are not selfish, just concerned with their own self-preservation.

Many people used to smuggle different things into the ghetto. For instance, there was a baker making bread, and somebody smuggled flour into the ghetto for it. I didn't know how they did it, but some of us had connections with the Poles outside, so I started to buy my way out, too. The second week after I started, I noticed that there was a market close to where Rosalie lived. When I came home, I told my mother about it, and when I told her how I was buying my way out of the ghetto, she got hysterical. I also told her about Rosalie's family, and she said we had to do something to help them or they would die. Then she went with me to visit them and also look at the market. We decided that when I went to visit Rosalie, I would stop at the market and try to buy something. You couldn't buy anything for money because Polish money didn't have any value, so I would take whatever was of value in the house and trade it for food. Rosalie's mother gave me some valuables, too, so I could buy them some food, but they didn't have much left.

My mother and I talked about the best way to smuggle. Subsequently, I would go to the market wearing a ragged jacket and ragged pants with holes in them. On top of this, I wore a heavy coat that was too big for me. It wasn't exactly black but was very dark. I didn't put my arms in it but wore it like a cape, draped over my hands and arms. Then, like an old man, I covered my head with it. I could wear this all summer, too, because it didn't get too hot, only seventy-eight or eighty degrees. I also put a large belt around my waist.

I would go to the market and trade whatever valuables we had for chickens, but I had no idea of what kind of chickens to buy. Because the Jewish people wouldn't eat chickens if they weren't kosher, I had to bring them into the ghetto alive. For me to do that, my mother sewed a little sack of white cloth, like a pillowcase with holes in it. There was enough space inside each one for me to put a live chicken, hang the bag over my belt, and clip it on with two pins. I would buy four chickens at a time and put two on each side and two in back, under my coat. What was considered good at that time was the chicken fat, so fat chickens were very expensive. If they weren't fat, nobody would touch them, and no woman could sell them. My mother also sewed pockets inside my coat so I could smuggle some fruit and sometimes a little bit of butter.

Sometimes I took my brother with me. He was scared and couldn't make decisions, but he followed me blindly. I used to bring him to the gate, find a spot in some Gentile person's house, and leave him there. Then I took the clothes I used for smuggling and went to make sure there was a policeman I knew at the gate. Before I left the ghetto, the first thing I had to do was hand the policeman money to buy him off. I would give him as much money as he asked for and tell him what time I would be back. Sometimes when I came, the policeman wasn't there, so I just took a chance and walked out. I would go out two or three times a week, and I always got away with it.

I went out like this for seven months. Going to the market took, on the average, about two and one-half or three hours to walk there, then four or five hours heading back. I usually got there by about noon. One day I left about seven or eight o'clock in the morning. When I got there, the market hadn't opened yet. It wasn't until about one or two o'clock before I could start my buying, so by the time I came back to the ghetto, it was almost five o'clock. While I was gone for so long, my mother had cried and was eating her heart out because she had let me go. Almost every time I left and came back, Rosalie was waiting at the gate with my mother, and she was there that day, too.

People started to notice that I had connections and was bringing food into the ghetto. I began to need some help and found some other people. This way I didn't have to go out three times a week, maybe once or twice. Almost every morning somebody came to my house and wanted me to go out, but they didn't have the money to buy enough to eat. My mother was soft-hearted. If somebody was a good Jew, she would give the food to them for less than what I had paid for it, and I would get mad. She said to me, "You have to have a heart. You must understand how things are for people." I used to argue with her because when I had a bad day, nobody had mercy on me. I also had arguments with my sister about it. Because she was the only girl, my mother said she was right and always agreed with her. One time I got mad at my mother and told her that I was the one who risked my life, but she was the one who told me what to do. The next time I started to go out, she didn't say a word, so I just left. But I gave in later because I loved my mother, and the smuggling went on.

At the beginning of 1942, all Jews outside Kraków were ordered to move into the ghetto; they had two or three days to do it. When Rosalie moved, I went to the same gate to find the policeman I knew because he was the one who let me out. Each time you did this, you took a chance. You had to pick the right one, and I was lucky each time. When my family had to come into the ghetto, we had been living close to the apartment we moved into, but Rosalie's family had to move several miles away. It was a long distance because we didn't even have bicycles. After the war broke out, the police had confiscated them for the Polish army. We also had no means of communication.

I found them one big room because everything else was taken. I don't think the room even had a window, just a door with a window in it. I don't remember exactly where it was, but it was not far from me, just four or five blocks. I went to their apartment in the small town and moved the whole family to the ghetto, although legally I wasn't allowed to. They brought bags with all their clothes and whatever else was left from their home, such as a few dishes. I gave her mother money to get settled in, but she refused. She was wondering where I got it. After Rosalie came to the ghetto, we were together all day.

The Germans started to reduce the ghetto population, and on June 1, 1942, they evacuated my family. My parents didn't have identity papers, but I did. I didn't want my mother to go because I loved her dearly. She was the smart one in the family. After that, my sister and I were the only ones left. On June 8, 1942, they arrested Rosalie's mother, sister, and brother. If Rosalie hadn't known me, she would have been arrested, too. Her mother trusted me and gave me an ultimatum. She said, "First, you have to marry her. I trust you, and don't touch her until you marry." She [Rosalie] was just nineteen. Her mother had sewn gold coins into Rosalie's coat, but I wouldn't take them. I said, "Don't worry about it." After that, it was hard to get out of the ghetto.

We had few witnesses at our wedding because they had taken our parents. We were first married by a rabbi and then through the Polish court. I think an official came to the ghetto and gave us legal papers. Many Jews at this time refused to be married by government officials. They didn't recognize court marriages, so according to Jewish law we weren't legally married. The Polish court didn't recognize rabbinical marriages because according to them a rabbi was just like any other person. But the majority of Jews, like my parents, were more modern and open-minded.

After my parents and Rosalie's family were taken, my sister, Rosalie, and I were left in two rooms. Before we were married, I had moved Rosalie into the bedroom with my sister while I slept in the kitchen. After I married Rosalie, I moved into the bedroom with her, and my sister slept in the kitchen.

After I married Rosalie, I found another way to smuggle. The Germans sent me to work in a nail factory. They would pick me up every morning and take me there. In charge was a Pole who worked for the Wehrmacht. Our labor group consisted of about twenty or twenty-two boys. The oldest one was twenty-seven, and the youngest was nineteen. The oldest was in charge. I was second oldest, so I was next. Anytime there was trouble, I could get out of it because I was close to him.

I noticed that there were stacks of aluminum in a warehouse, just like pieces of aluminum pipe. The Germans kept them in this storage shed; they had stolen them from the Jews. One of the boys who worked in the factory was stealing these, but I couldn't because I worked outside with the other boys. I decided I could be his partner; I could smuggle them out. Because he was good at stealing, he brought me four or five pieces every day. They were about a half or a full foot wide and about two feet long. I had six or seven at one time and tied them together with my jacket. Then I would give them to my partner, and he would sell them. I don't know who he sold them to. He wouldn't tell me because he was afraid that I would take his business away from him. He had some connections with Jews in the ghetto who had associations with Poles who made a living selling these on the black market. I watched how much money he was selling them for, and he paid me out of that.

I started taking them to sell in the ghetto, too. If I could sell them, I could buy clothes for my sister and Rosalie and get some food. One day the guard suspected me of bringing them into the ghetto and arrested me. He checked me over from top to bottom. I had put the pieces in my right back pocket. Although he checked me from my feet up and in my left back side, he never checked me on the right and let me go. Amon Goeth, the commandant of Plaszow, was there but didn't say anything. I wonder how I got away with it. Just plain luck!

We were forced to leave the ghetto and walk to Plaszow in October 1942. On September 19, 1943, when I came back from work, I found out that they had taken Rosalie to Skarzsysko. My whole world collapsed. I jumped on everybody; I didn't care who. I even jumped on two Germans in uniform, but they didn't shoot me. Two boys tried to help me, but the Nazis shot them. Me, they just hit on the head with a gun. If they didn't shoot me then, they would never shoot me. After that, I jumped on a train, thinking it was going in the same direction, but I wound up in Auschwitz and continued my smuggling there. I never got caught for it, either in the ghetto or in Auschwitz.

9. Facilitating Genocide

Nazi Ghettoization Practices in Occupied Ukraine, 1941–1942

WENDY LOWER

Introduction

The personal chauffeur of the general commissar of Zhytomyr, Ukraine, who had driven throughout the region in 1942, observed that in central Ukraine there were no "closed ghettos like that in Kraków or Warsaw."[1] This chauffeur's observation actually points to a hitherto unknown and extremely significant aspect of Ukraine's Holocaust history.[2] The Polish "model" of urban and transit ghettos—the predominant representation of Nazi ghettoization then and now—does not apply to Ukraine. There the urban Jewish population was much smaller than in Poland, and the ghettos were quite short-lived. Indeed, most of the ghettos in east-central Ukraine, which were haphazardly erected in the summer and fall of 1941, existed for less than three months. These ghettos disappeared so rapidly because in Ukraine Nazi ghettoization was not a prelude to genocide, but rather coincided with it.[3]

For regional German officials who began arriving in Ukraine in late June 1941, it became increasingly clear that the Nazi leadership desired the

The opinions expressed in this essay are solely those of the author and are not to be construed as constituting the opinion of the United States Holocaust Memorial Museum. The author gratefully acknowledges the insightful input and assistance of Richard Breitman, Dieter Pohl, Alexander Rossino, Eric Sterling, and scholars at the museum's Center for Advanced Holocaust Studies in supporting the research and writing of this essay.

complete destruction of the Jewish population, but the implementation of this aim remained subject to conditions in the field that were changing rapidly. Local chiefs in the military, Schutzstaffel (SS) police, and civilian administration received little guidance from central authorities about ghettoization policies, so they improvised. For example, in the Jewish centers of Zhytomyr and Berdychiv, the Germans established ghettos but did not bother with a Jewish self-administration, for the ghetto served mainly as a temporary staging area while Nazi killing units were mustered for the killing *Aktion.* In the smaller communities, army village commanders and SS police personnel "ghettoized" Jews by herding them into bombed-out buildings, freight cars, and barns. Other regional chiefs avoided ghettoization altogether because they considered ghettos to be unnecessary or not useful in their local campaigns of persecution and annihilation. In retrospect, the lack of any uniform policy for ghettoization and the German ad hoc approach indicate that from the start of the occupation of Ukraine (and of the Soviet territories), Nazi leaders foresaw a more radical approach to resolving the "Jewish question"—one that might not require the "problematic" maintenance of ghettos.[4]

To be sure, the ephemerality of Ukrainian ghetto structures, the lack of written traces about them, and the extremely low survival rate of Ukrainian Jews in the Holocaust (less than 5 percent) have made the historian's task of reconstructing Ukraine's wartime ghetto history and Nazi intentions vis-à-vis ghettoization seemingly impossible. Jewish memorial books, which historian Shmuel Spector brilliantly synthesized into a regional study of Volhynia, *The Holocaust of Vohynian Jews, 1941–1944* (1990), offer the most detailed accounts of ghetto life. Yet Spector's pioneering work left many questions unexplored. In particular, why was there such a variation in Nazi ghettoization practices? What role did ghettos play in the evolving implementation of the "Final Solution" in Ukraine? Recent accessibility to former Soviet archival collections of captured Nazi documents and the increase in published survivor accounts from Ukraine have given scholars much more material to work with from both the victims' and perpetrators' perspectives. Drawing from these new and older sources, this essay charts the history of Nazi ghettoization in Ukraine to shed more light on the relatively obscure history of Ukrainian Jews in the

Holocaust and to analyze the various Nazi approaches to ghettoization in Ukraine.

The First Stage of Nazi Ghettoization under the Military Administration, 1941–1942

During the summer of 1941, approximately one-third of the Jewish population just west of the Dnieper River was able to escape the Nazi onslaught. A greater number, perhaps two-thirds, left from the eastern bank regions around Kiev and Kharkiv, where they benefited from the added advantages of more time to flee from the Nazis and information about Nazi atrocities against Jews. By contrast, the swift Nazi advance from Lviv to the outskirts of Kiev between late June and late August 1941 paralyzed much of the Jewish population of Volhynia-Podolia, where about 300,000 remained trapped. Not counting the 530,000 Ukrainian Jews of Galicia (attached to the Generalgouvernement) and the 200,000 Jews in Romanian-controlled Transnistria, in total approximately 650,000 Jews remained in the Nazi-occupied parts of Ukraine known as the Reichskommissariat Ukraine.[5]

In the pre-Barbarossa guidelines for ruling conquered territory, German leaders concerned themselves more with the destruction of segments of the population, such as the Jewish intelligentsia, than with the actual care and feeding of the "defeated" populations of the East. As a "security precaution," Hitler and Wehrmacht leaders instructed the advancing Wehrmacht and SS police forces to eliminate quickly the leading Jewish figures of the Communist state and party apparatus under the "cover of war" (e.g., the "Commissar Order").[6] Because Nazi leaders also predicted that the Soviet Union would be defeated in about six weeks, they assumed that the first wave of military and SS police forces would have little time and manpower to establish ghettos. Ghettoization as a policy was not spelled out clearly, but was to be left in the hands of the civil administration.[7]

It is, therefore, not surprising that one of the few preinvasion references to ghettos did not emerge in the military's administrative guidelines, but rather in a May 1941 memorandum by civilian leader and Nazi Party chief Alfred Rosenberg, the future Reich minister for the occupied eastern territories. Rosenberg advised the Reich commissar for Ukraine (who had not yet been named) that "after the customary removal of Jews from all public offices, the 'Jewish question' must undergo a decisive solution through the establishment of ghettos or labor battalions. Forced labor is to be introduced."[8] In these instructions, Rosenberg anticipated that a more "decisive" solution would materialize after the "customary" preliminary measures had been undertaken, one that involved ghettoization and the use of Jewish labor.

German leaders structured the newly conquered areas under military administration into three zones that extended from the front line westward to the rear areas. The SS and police played a leading role in so-called security measures in the rear areas of the Army Groups by independently carrying out killing actions against "enemies" of the Reich. But the governing power over the entire civilian population was in the hands of the military administration, first in the army staff headquarters (e.g., Armeeoberkommando [AOK] 6) and then under the commander of the Rear Occupied Army Area South, General Karl von Roques. Within von Roques's administration, the leading regional offices in charge of anti-Jewish measures were the field, city, and town command posts, known as *Kommandanturen.*

The field commanders prioritized four tasks related to the "Jewish question":

1. Handling of Jewish property
2. Marking of Jews
3. Exploitation of Jewish labor
4. Registration and listing of the Jewish population[9]

According to this "official checklist," ghettoization was not supposed to be an immediate anti-Jewish measure.[10] Indeed, it demanded precious personnel and material resources and was subject to a number of unpredictable situational factors, such as the size and geographic distribution of the local Jewish population, local housing needs, the influence of the SS police, availability of native auxiliaries, and the length of time stationed in a given place.[11]

Yet despite these complications and limitations, local military and SS police leaders in Ukraine formed ghettos in the summer and fall of 1941. In several outstanding cases, this ghettoization precipitated the Nazi implementation of the Final Solution during its initial stage. Across various towns and cities of Ukraine, local army commanders forced the Jews into the nearest slums to acquire better housing for German personnel, to isolate the Jews as a "security precaution," and to better organize the population for forced labor. They also drove the Jews into makeshift internment sites, or "wild ghettos." These first ghettos derived from decisions made on the spot. The ghetto structures varied widely, but, more important, they all were pursued with the intent of creating unlivable conditions for the Jews.

For example, in Kamianets'-Podil's'kyi, the field commander (FK 183) confined more than 25,000 native and refugee Jews to the old section of the city, which was accessible mainly by one easily guarded bridge. As he explained in a mid-August 1941 report, the Jews were ordered to abandon the newer sections of the city and to move into the old town, which served as the "ghetto." They were allowed to bring only fifty kilograms of luggage per person.[12] Meanwhile, the Ukrainians were pushed out of the *Altstadt* to make space for the Jews. When these native and refugee Jews arrived, they found 3,000 Hungarian Jewish refugees living there, and during the next weeks many more flowed into the area. This same field commander urged his superiors to make a final decision about how to handle the refugees. Supplying food for these refugees, he stressed, created an undesirable burden for the city.[13] On August 25, 1941, this commander's dilemma was resolved during a central meeting of civilian and military officials in Vinnytsia, where it was decided that senior SS and police leader for Ukraine Friedrich Jeckeln would "take care of" the Jewish problem in Kamianets'-Podil's'kyi.[14]

Between August 27 and 29, Jeckeln's units (mainly Order Police Battalion 320), along with allied Hungarian forces, shot two-thirds of the Jewish population of Kamianets'-Podil's'kyi, plus 14,000 Hungarian Jewish refugees (for a total of 23,600 men, women, and children). This was the largest massacre in the Barbarossa campaign thus far.[15] They placed the remaining 4,800 Jews in labor camps in the newer section of the city, where they remained for another year.[16] In this example, the field commander created the ghetto to fulfill two short-term objectives: to secure more housing and to contain the local Jewish and refugee population. Then the commander's superiors (in the army and the Foreign Office) simply handed off the "problem" of maintaining the Jewish ghetto to the SS and police, whose "solution" was to murder most of the Jewish population.

Jeckeln also personally commanded the destruction of the Jews of Berdychiv, a centuries-old center of Jewish culture and scholarship in Ukraine. Here Jeckeln, and not the military commander, initiated ghettoization. On August 26, 1941, Lieutenant General Jeckeln arrived in Berdychiv and immediately ordered the establishment of a ghetto. By this time, local military authorities and members of Sonderkommando (Sk) 4a and Ek5 had tortured and shot Berdychiv's leading Jews. A local volunteer from the military (2. Feld-Ferspruch Kompanie/643) who participated in the ghetto *Aktion* recalled that it was common local knowledge that all the Jews of Berdychiv were to be shot, with or without ghettoization.[17] Following Jeckeln's arrival on August 26, Nazi SS police forces and local volunteers from the military drove approximately 28,000 Jews of Berdychiv into the "ancient shacks, tiny single storied houses and a crumbling brick building" that lay in the poorest section of the city.[18] Units of Jeckeln's Police Regiment South and Ukrainian police auxiliaries killed any Jews who could not walk to the ghetto or who refused to leave their homes. This act of "ghetto formation" raised the local Jewish death toll by another 4,200.[19] A few days later Jeckeln's units in Berdychiv struck at the ghetto again, killing 1,303 Jews, among them 875 female Jews older than twelve years of age. Finally, on the night of September 14–15, SS police units (including Order Police Battalion 45) surrounded the ghetto and drove the Jews from their homes to the nearby air field, where they shot more than 18,000 Jewish men, women, and children. The surviving 2,500 Jews, including 400 workers, were taken to another site—the walled fortress above the city.[20] Most of them were killed in the spring and summer of 1942.

In the rural areas where the military and SS police commanders found that the Jewish communities could not be easily moved into the nearest urban slums, they pursued two alternatives. First, they issued a series of anti-Jewish measures that amounted to, in Spector's words, "ghettoization de facto."[21] The Nazi administration of the towns and villages across Ukraine began with the registration of the population. Within a matter of days, Nazi leaders had at their disposal surveys and lists that showed how many Jews lived on what streets. Jews were ordered to move away from the

Jews from the Ciechanów ghetto in Poland are marched into a fortress. Photo and caption courtesy of the United States Holocaust Memorial Museum.

main streets to the back streets. They could not relocate to another residence or leave the village without permission. They were not allowed on the streets except when going to and from the workplace. Unlike the rest of the native population, the Jews were banned from the marketplace for most of the day. They had to register their property, businesses, and financial assets. They were forced to wear the Star of David as a prominent, humiliating label of their reduced social status, which also exacerbated tense Jewish-Ukrainian relations. As a rule, the military employed the Jews in the most gruesome, hazardous labor, from clearing corpses off the streets to digging up land mines. In effect, local Nazi restrictions and anti-Semitic violence created a life-threatening atmosphere that discouraged most Jews from leaving their homes at all.[22]

The other approach taken by regional leaders was to cram the Jewish population into convenient "holding areas" known euphemistically as ghettos. There was no need to place these sites near railway routes, as were the rural Polish ghettos, because there were no plans to deport Ukrainian Jews. Shortly before the killing squads attached to Einsatzgruppe C and to

Jeckeln's forces arrived in Radomyshyl, Cherniakhiv, Dzerzhyns'k, Koziatyn, and other towns around Zhytomyr, advance subunits of Sk4a, local military commanders, and Ukrainian militiamen registered and then forced the Jews into bombed-out buildings, barracks, collective farms, freight cars, schools, old synagogues, the local stadiums, and other places. For example, in Cherniakhiv the Germans had already killed the Jewish men, so the remaining women and children were forced into a freight car with little air, water, and light. On paper, German military and SS police leaders argued that they lacked the food and medical personnel to care for the Jews under these harsh conditions and therefore had little choice but to kill them.[23] Yet in the well-known incident at Bila Tserkva, where ninety Jewish orphans had been locked up and abandoned in a school-type building, Field Commander Oberst Riedl, who was confronted with the problem of caring for these children, revealed his ideological motives more explicitly, stating that "this brood must be exterminated." His superior, Sixth Army general Walter von Reichenau, was of the same opinion. On August 22, 1941, a Waffen SS platoon, Sonderkommando 4a, and Ukrainian auxiliaries massacred these infants and children.[24]

Thus, German officials found a number of ways to control, exploit, and "reduce" the Jewish population. Confining the Jews was a central part of this local pattern, but creating ghettos was not the main objective.[25] For example, in the city of Zhytomyr (home to 5,000 Jews who remained in July 1941), Einsatzgruppe C leader Dr. Otto Rasch revealed how Nazi leaders differentiated between formal ghettoization and the ad hoc concentration of Jews. In early September 1941, the army field commander and SS officers from Einsatzgruppe C decided to concentrate the Jewish population into the historic Jewish quarter on Tschudnovskaya Street. During the previous month, Sk4a, Waffen SS, Order Police Battalion 82, and individual soldiers (e.g., Infantry Regiment 375) had carried out several killing actions in and around the city, mainly against male Jews. The rest of the population, approximately 3,500 Jewish men, women, and children, were squeezed into a few buildings on Tschudnovskaya Street and placed under the guard of Ukrainian militiamen. As Dr. Rasch later explained it to his superiors in Berlin, in Zhytomyr "the concentration of the Jews without building a ghetto did not suffice." Rasch complained of Jewish resistance activities, which he claimed "had their origin in the Jewish quarter." On September 10, 1941, members of Sk4a met with officials from the local military headquarters to plan for the ghetto liquidation and massacre of Zhytomyr's Jews. This occurred on September 19.[26]

The implementation of the Final Solution occurred in stages, and the period of August–September 1941 was one of the most critical in the history of the Holocaust. During this time, the Nazi intent to commit genocide was manifested by the rapid destruction of the largest Jewish communities of eastern-central Ukraine, centered in Kamianets'-Podil's'kyi, Berdychiv, Vinnytsia, Zhytomyr, and Kiev (claiming the lives of as many as 100,000 Jewish men, women, and children). The escalation in killing stemmed from a confluence of factors and conditions, such as the military slowdown that allowed for an accumulation of killing forces, regional leaders' greater willingness to kill women and children, and increased pressure from SS police and military leaders to act more aggressively against the Jews. In each of these major Jewish "urban" centers, Nazi leaders avoided the "Polish" ghetto model and instead pursued the more radical "solution" of genocide.

This initial phase of the Final Solution was also one of flux. The first wave of mass shootings was by no means spontaneous, for the entire Nazi approach to the murder was evolving toward more systematic methods. Local killing campaigns were somewhat haphazard; the methods of killing were experimental; and from the Nazi perspective, they were too "messy." To a large degree, the inconsistent, regional practices of ghettoization reflect this transitional period when the Nazi aim of genocide was first realized on the ground. In August 1941, German military and civilian leaders, who were responding in part to events in the field, sought to define ghettoization as a matter of policy by issuing the first guidelines on ghettos in Ukraine. On August 28, 1941, the army commander for the Rear Occupied Army Area South, General Karl von Roques, wrote: "They [ghettos] are not to be established in the first place, if according to the local conditions at hand in the operations area the material and administrative resources are not sufficient or if other more urgent tasks must be neglected."[27] As this terse order reflects, senior officials remained uncommitted to specific, detailed instructions about ghettoization, choosing instead to leave local im-

Jews at the killing site outside of Kamianets'-Podil's'kyi, Ukraine. Photo and caption courtesy of the United States Holocaust Memorial Museum.

plementation matters in the hands of their subordinates. However, von Roques insisted on a more pragmatic and orderly approach to anti-Jewish measures in the field.[28] Echoing von Roques's order, Field Commander Markul of Vinnytsia warned his subordinates not to force the Jews into ghettos in a hasty manner.[29] Village commanders who had confined the Jews into "wild ghettos" on their own initiative had not considered, as von Roques advised, the usefulness of this measure. According to Einsatzgruppe C chief Dr. Otto Rasch, once the Jews were forced into these makeshift sites, certain "problems" arose, such as the supply of food, threat of epidemics, and resistance movements. At this stage, ghettos were not to be abandoned entirely in the killing process, but to be viewed as one of several vehicles for bringing about the destruction of Jewish communities. Local leaders found that in one town ghettoization facilitated the Final Solution, whereas in another place ghettos were "unnecessary" or "not useful."

For example in Kiev, Nazi leaders determined that they could destroy the population rapidly without resorting to temporary ghettoization. On September 27–28, 1941, the army *Stadtkommandantur* ordered all the Jews of Kiev to "appear by 7:00 A.M. with your possessions, money, documents, valuables, and warm clothing at Dorogozhitskaya Street, next to the Jewish cemetery."[30] The official rumor was that the Jews were to be "deported," not ghettoized. On September 29–30, members of Paul Blobel's Sk4a and Friedrich Jeckeln's Police Regiment South (mainly Order Police Battalion 45) gunned down 33,700 Jewish men, women, and children in the ravine of Babi Yar at the edge of the city.[31] In contrast, not far from Kiev at Pervomaisk, the SS police deliberately prolonged the "life" of the ghetto because it became a useful way to "trap" Jewish refugees. In mid-September, several thousand Jews, including those who had initially fled to surrounding villages but then returned to the ghetto, were massacred in one rapid, thorough SS police killing spree. In this case, the army field commander had not given his consent to liquidate the ghetto and later complained that local industries had to be closed because the needed Jewish laborers were gone.[32]

Many Jews east of Kiev were able to flee into Russian territory, but thousands (especially the elderly, women, children, and the infirm) were left behind to contend with the Nazis. Advance units of Einsatzgruppe C found 15,000 Jews in Dnipropetrovsk and another 20,000 Jews in Kharkiv. From August to November 1941, Jeckeln's units (members of Ek5, Ek6, and Order Police Battalion 314) killed more than 22,000 Jews in Dnipropetrovsk, 13,000 on October 13 and 14 alone.[33] They did not ghettoize the Jews; rather, they worked from registration lists, targeting districts, apartment buildings, and other Jewish residences. They forced the Jews from their homes in the early morning hours, amassing groups of 1,500–2,000 Jews for the killing actions.[34]

When the Germans arrived in Kharkiv in late October 1941, they immediately began to search out and kill Jewish leaders. More than a month later, in early December, members of Sk4a met with the military city commander (along with the city's housing department chief) to plan for an action against the entire Jewish population. A week or so later, on December 14, the city's military commanders announced that all the Jews of Kharkiv had to move to the barracks of the Lathe tractor factory located at the edge of the city. According to the local leader of the Order Police, these barracks constituted, as he termed it, a "ghetto." Local Order Police and military personnel forced Kharkiv's Jews to march fourteen kilometers along Moscow streets to the Lathe factory, where they crammed the population into wooden barracks with narrow slits instead of windows, no plumbing, and no heating. Although some of the barrack guards were bribable, most of the Jews were unable to leave the barracks to get water and food. Those who tried to flee were shot on the spot. Others died from the combination of hunger, cold, and illness. German SS police units made surprise attacks on the "ghetto," bursting into the barracks to plunder Jewish valuables and to seize groups of about fifty persons, whom they dragged to a nearby execution site.[35] Then on December 26, 1941, the Germans announced that Jews were to be deported to Poland, Romny, and Kremenchung. The next day members of Sk4a and Order Police Battalion 314 brought them by car to the death valley of Drobitzki Yar, where mass shootings and gassings by mobile vans occurred throughout January 1942. To this day, publications and testimonies about the Holocaust in Ukraine persist in using the Nazi euphemism *ghetto* to describe the barracks of the Lathe tractor factory.[36] But as this atrocity and others in eastern Ukraine demonstrate, by the end of 1941 the Nazis had redefined the term *ghetto* altogether, from Jewish quarters with some form of self-administration and life-sustaining conditions to makeshift death traps and staging areas for genocide.

During the first stage of the military occupation, the army, Einsatzgruppen, units of the Senior SS, and Lieutenant General Jeckeln (succeeded by Hans-Adolf Prützmann in November) killed nearly 300,000 Jews in Ukraine. The August–September escalation in the genocide, from groups of male Jews to entire Jewish communities, continued as the Wehrmacht pushed farther east. Very few ghettos emerged as the larger Jewish communities of east-central Ukraine were disappearing from the map in a matter of days and weeks. Meanwhile, in the western regions of Volhynia-Podolia, many Jewish towns survived intact. Rumors circulated about Nazi atrocities against the Jews, and in many places, such as Lutsk, groups of Jewish men had been killed during the summer of 1941 sweep of mass shootings and pogroms. However, the full intent of the Nazi genocide had not revealed itself in all the shtetl communities of Volhynia-Podolia. Some informed and prescient Jews fled to the forests or escaped over Ukraine's borders into Romania and Hungary. There were also cases of suicide among the Jewish Council leaders, who refused to comply with German demands. But the majority clung to the hope that life might improve, that the worst had passed them by. Furthermore, there seemed to be no safe place to go in face of the growing number of German officials and native collaborators who at any moment could reveal one's Jewish identity to the Germans. The early frost that ushered in one of the coldest winters on record also discouraged many Jews from taking flight. Many did not want to abandon family members or risk a life in hiding with few prospects for food and shelter. Unbeknownst to these Jewish survivors, the arriving commissars of the civil administration were committed to making "their fiefdoms" totally "free of Jews."[37]

Jewish Labor and Ghettoization in the Reichskommissariat Ukraine, 1942

By the end of 1941, a clear pattern of ghettoization had emerged in which makeshift ghettos served as holding pens for the Jews shortly before they were killed in the mass shootings. Beyond Ukraine's borders, the genocidal approach to ghettoization expanded to accommodate western European Jewry. At the Riga ghetto, for example, German Jewish deportees were temporarily detained before being shot at the nearby Bikernieki Forest.[38] The Reich commissar for Ukraine, Erich Koch, and Senior SS and police leader Hans-Adolf Prützmann (Jeckeln's successor) explored such an approach in Ukraine. On January 12, 1942, they asked district civilian leaders (commissars and SS policemen) to identify possible future ghettos near railway links where Reich Jews could be brought. This plan did not materialize, but it demonstrates that the formation of ghettos in Ukraine was linked not only to local killing actions, but also to Nazi plans for western European Jewry.[39]

During 1942, German leaders in Ukraine continued to use ghettos to facilitate the killing, but the pace of the killing slowed somewhat after the Germans realized that they needed Jewish laborers. They modified the Final Solution policy to include a new approach known as *"Vernichtung durch Arbeit,"* or extermination through labor. Since the 1941 invasion, local army commanders had relied on Jewish workers, and in September 1941 Einsatzgruppe chief Dr. Rasch had suggested that Jews be worked to death as a more "practical" alternative to mass shootings.[40] As of mid-September 1941, male Jewish laborers were routinely spared from the mass shootings in Ukraine (e.g., at Berdychiv, Zhytomyr, and Vinnytsia). The role of ghettoization in the *"Vernichtung durch Arbeit"* modification to the Final Solution was twofold. First, Jewish laborers remained housed in the ghettos, and, second, as of late 1941 and early 1942 the Nazi process of ghettoization merged with the *Selektion* process. Jewish workers struggled in the "ghettos of life" while the rest of the population was condemned to "ghettos of death."

In the Reichskommissariat Ukraine, ghettoization was a regional development centered in Volhynia-Podolia, where the largest concentration of 270,000 Jews remained. In the Zhytomyr Commissariat, where approximately 80,000 Jews had survived the first killing waves of 1941, very few ghettos were formed in 1942.[41] As one eyewitness recalled, "already in early 1942 actions against Zhytomyr's Jews commenced and continued until the summer of 1942."[42] For example, the rural ghetto of Samgorodok with 500 Jews appeared in early 1942. Its formation, brief existence, and final liquidation represented basically one continuous series of massacres. Here the Nazis allowed little time for the development of any ghetto life such as a self-administration. In Zhytomyr's southern districts along the Romanian border, some "half-empty" ghetto sites from 1941, such as at Khmil'nyk, were transformed into labor camps where Jews from Transnistria were worked to death on the autobahn construction.[43] The continuous Nazi assault against Zhytomyr's Jews during the first half of 1942 stemmed largely from the presence of Hitler's and Heinrich Himmler's headquarters there. To prepare for the Führer's arrival in July

1942, Nazi security forces wiped out the region's Jewish population as a "security precaution."[44] The Jews who survived were either in hiding or in labor camps, not in ghettos.

By contrast, in the neighboring district of Volhynia-Podolia, approximately one-third of the ghettos formed were allowed to remain standing for six months to one year. The individual histories of these scattered ghettos were shaped by local labor needs, district-level initiatives and conditions, and Himmler and Erich Koch's direct influence. In September 1941, Reich Commissar Koch issued guidelines on ghettoization to the commissars of Volhynia-Podolia, stating that "in cities with a noteworthy percentage of Jews, the Jews should be strictly enclosed in a ghetto where no Aryans will be allowed to live." Jewish Councils should be formed to assure "peace, order, and security in the ghetto, and each day to provide the needed Jewish labor. The Jewish Council will be punished for each undesirable act within the Jewish population. A Jewish order service [ghetto police] can be formed to assist the council." But, according to Koch's order, "in villages with less than 200 Jewish inhabitants, no ghettos should be formed."[45] In Volhynia-Podolia, home to the largest Jewish population in the Reichskommissariat Ukraine, Koch relied on ghettos as a short-term measure to concentrate and control the population. The immediate fate of the smaller Jewish populations was left in the hands of local district leaders.

For the administration of anti-Jewish measures, Koch's minions, known as *Gebietskommissare* (district commissars) were given free reign to issue regulations, as long as their local dictates were consistent with Nazi aims and policy guidelines. Empowered with full policing and judicial authority over the Jewish population, the district commissars exerted their direct influence over the formation of ghettos, the composition of Jewish Councils, the use of Jewish labor, and ultimately the fate of the ghettos' inhabitants. All Jews between the ages of fourteen and sixty were subject to slave labor; food rations, when available, were not to exceed the amount normally allotted to a youth under fourteen years of age. According to local commissar "law," any Jews found outside the ghetto were treated as saboteurs (i.e., killed), and any non-Jews who assisted the Jews were also subject to the death penalty.[46]

Like the 1941 phase of ghettoization during the military invasion, German leaders in Volhynia-Podolia did not enforce a uniform policy concerning the structure of the ghettos. They created Jewish quarters in the Ukrainian cities of Lutsk and Rivne as well as in the Belorussian and Polish centers of Pinsk and Brest, which fell within the Nazi administrative borders of the Reichskommissariat Ukraine. In the rural towns and villages across the region, there emerged a mixture of open rural ghettos (allowing for significant Jewish-Ukrainian interaction) and closed ghettos (usually sealed with barbed wire and wooden fencing).

In the "open" rural ghettos of Volhynia-Podolia, interaction between Jews and non-Jewish locals (mainly Ukrainians) was common. In early 1942, an SS leader from Einsatzgruppe C summed up the situation from the Nazi perspective. He wrote that in Volhynia-Podolia

> So far 40,000 have been "resettled" [killed]. The Jews in the towns are at present concentrated in the so-called Jewish quarters which are, however, not completely isolated. Therefore a very active black market flourished in the Jewish quarters; peasants who come to town exchange clothing and household articles [which they needed urgently] for agricultural products. This nuisance was eliminated through strict police measures. The Jews . . . are, for the time being, indispensable as skilled workers and craftsmen.[47]

Despite severe German threats and regulations about Jewish-Ukrainian interaction, Jews and Ukrainians continued to trade goods and foodstuffs in and around the ghettos. For Jews, it was a matter of survival, and for Ukrainians it was a risky but profitable venture. In Olyka, for example, a Jew was willing to trade his house for sixteen kilograms of rye.[48] To curtail the local "nuisance" of illegal bartering, the general commissar for Volhynia-Podolia ordered in March 1942 that all open ghettos be "hermetically" sealed.[49] But as long as the Germans were forced to rely on Ukrainian guards around the ghettos, little could be done to control the black market, which continued to thrive in most ghettos, such as at Dubrovytsia. The punishments meted out to offenders depended on the whim, mood, and impulsive behavior of local Ukrainian auxiliaries and their German superiors. Hence, at the Kremenets ghetto, Jews who were caught smuggling food were beaten mercilessly on one day and then on the next day left unharmed.[50]

There was, however, one area in which the Nazis formally encouraged interaction between Ukrainians and Jews. In April and March 1942, Reich Commissar Koch introduced his remedy for resolving the local labor shortages by establishing apprentice programs for Ukrainians. In the Ukrainian newspaper *Volyn,* Koch declared that in the near future the Jews would no longer control the labor force of craftsmen and that new opportunities for Ukrainians lay on the horizon. When the German commissars established Jewish workshops for Ukrainian apprentices in the ghetto of Letychiv (Podolia) and at Brest (Lutsk), they were in effect removing the Jews' last chance to survive under the Nazis. They trained Ukrainians (and *Volksdeutsche*) to replace the previously "indispensable" Jewish craftsman.

The provisional use of Jewish labor was also a source of conflict among Nazi civilian and military leaders. Historian Christopher Browning has recently illuminated this development through his extensive research on the Brest ghetto. At Brest, the city commissar Franz Burat enforced the complete ghettoization of the city's Jews in December 1941.[51] The Brest ghetto was enclosed within barbed wire and fences, but approximately 4,000 Jews with special work permits were allowed to leave the ghetto (under guard) to labor in local industries. In the ghetto, the nonworking Jews could hardly find food to supplement the meager German daily ration of 150 grams of artificial bread. The future of Brest's Jewish community seemed even more hopeless when the Germans banned Jewish marriages and pregnancies, which were punishable with death.[52] While the conditions for sustaining Jewish life in the ghetto declined, the German demand for labor increased. Burat established workshops where Jewish artisans produced much-needed consumer goods and trained non-Jews in their crafts.[53]

During the summer of 1942, the situation for the Jews of Brest changed from bad to worse. Food for nonworking Jews was extremely scarce. The partisan movement had intensified around the region, inciting more Nazi brutalities against civilians. The Jews in the surrounding rural ghettos had already been placed in labor camps, and the "unfit" Jews were being killed. Rumors of mass shootings and ghetto clearings in Lublin and nearby towns seeped into the ghetto. Fearful of an imminent Brest *Aktion,* many Jews stopped appearing for work, and others pinned their hopes on their value as laborers and so worked even more diligently. Meanwhile, Hitler, Himmler, and other leading Nazis met in Ukraine in August 1942 and determined that the impending food shortages in the Reich could be best avoided through supplies of Ukrainian wheat, produce, and livestock. Feeding the local population in Ukraine was of little concern to them. The first "useless eaters" to be destroyed were the Jews, in particular those in the ghettos, where many women, children, and elderly people remained. Prima facie, this was the catalyst and even served as a rational explanation for pushing through the final extermination of all Ukrainian, if not all eastern European Jews in the following months, but Himmler had already settled on a similar time line for Polish Jewry previous to the August 1942 meeting at the Führer's headquarters.[54]

Brest's local commissar Burat and SS police station leader Friedrich Rohde were not as eager to liquidate the ghetto, which would reduce the remaining Jewish labor force. They argued that Jewish workers were more valuable than the meager food rations that they consumed. But these complaints fell on deaf ears, and the Brest ghetto was attacked by SS police killing forces in mid-October 1942. After several days of mass shootings and intensive "Jew hunts" in and near the ghetto, local German SS police forces along with the mobile Order Police Battalion 310 and the Forty-eighth Motorized Police Company had annihilated 20,000 Jews.

The German need for Jewish labor shaped ghettoization practices into another local pattern of destruction. In Podolia, Nazi commissars and SS policemen divided the Jewish communities into "ghettos of life" and "ghettos of death." For example, in the district of Bar, a notice for ghettoization appeared on December 15, 1941, ordering all Jews to move into one of three "ghettos" by December 20.[55] One ghetto was located in a building near the old synagogue; the second ghetto was on a street near the Komsomol building; and the third ghetto, where only craftsmen were allowed to live, was situated near the town stadium. These designated "ghettos" were clearly meant to serve as preexecution staging areas and future labor camps, distinctions that the Jews themselves referred to as "ghettos of life" and "ghettos of death."[56]

A survivor's recent account of the ghetto at Letychiv (Podolia) provides an outstanding case study of Jewish ghetto life as well as the history of Nazi ghettoization policy in the Reichskommissariat Ukraine. According to Vladimir Goykher, a young craftsman there, the Letychiv ghetto was formed by Commissar Frieber on Rosh Hashana, September 21, 1941. It contained 7,000 inhabitants, who were crammed into huts along the Volk River. At first, a fence was immediately placed around the area, but the front gate was left open. Jews left and reentered the ghetto freely, but they were also required to wear the Star of David and thus were immediately recognizable outside the ghetto. Commissar Frieber personally visited the ghetto, accompanied by guards, and ordered that no one leave the ghetto without a special work permit. Ukrainian peasants were allowed to enter the ghetto with their produce to trade with the Jewish craftsmen, tailors, shoemakers, and so on.

At Letychiv, a ghetto *starosta* (elder) named Mendel Zidulka knew most of the Jews and what they possessed, so, as Goykher described it, when Commissar Frieber demanded valuables from the ghetto, Zidulka knew where to go. Most did not have the valuables or requested skills to trade with the local Ukrainians for food, and, as a result, the poorer Jews of the Letychiv began to starve. Zidulka urged the skilled laborers with higher rations to share their food with the children, sick, and elderly. The local military commanders pulled Jews out of the ghetto to clear snow from nearby roads or for skilled labor assignments such as metal engraving. Goykher recalled after the war, "I don't remember too much about life in the Ghetto. This was because I was too busy and too tired." The shortage of food, Goykher stressed, not only weakened the Jews physically, causing the spread of diseases, but also brought them into more depressed states spiritually and psychologically. (A typical daily diet for a worker was approximately 120 grams of bread, or 260–390 calories.) In Goykher's words, every day the Jews "dreaded starvation and the loss of their lives."[57]

In spring 1942, the Wehrmacht's main labor and construction agency, the Organization Todt, forced Jews from Letychiv to work on the nearby road construction (autobahn) project, whereas the skilled Jews of the Letychiv ghetto were brought to workshops where they trained Ukrainian apprentices. The situation for nonlaboring Jews continued to deteriorate. Commissar Frieber quarantined the ghetto in August 1942 and, together with the SS police, planned its liquidation. Ukrainians took over the skilled and unskilled labor previously held by Jews, and toward the end of September 1942 the Germans and their police auxiliaries divided the ghetto in half. They created "Ghetto Number 1," which was an old, fortified Catholic church and served as a prison. It held mainly the children, the elderly, and the sick, a total of approximately 5,000 persons. These Jews were shot over two days in the nearby ravine at Zaletichevka. In "Ghetto Number 2," the skilled Jews and Jewish laborers continued their work, training Ukrainians, doing odd jobs, and constructing the autobahn. The Germans liquidated the ghetto a few months later, as Goykher dated it, just after the first snowfall in late 1942.

As Letychiv's history illustrates, throughout 1941–42 the Germans stuck to the local killing system of open-air shootings near the ghettos and labor camps. Ukrainian Jews in the Reichskommissariat Ukraine and the military zones in eastern Ukraine were not sent to the death camps of Poland. In Letychiv, as elsewhere along the German-Romanian border, the use of Jewish ghetto labor was connected to the biggest construction project in Ukraine, the building of the autobahn.[58] Jews would continue to work on this project in 1943, but they were placed in a series of roadside forced labor camps under the control of the SS police and Organization Todt. In effect, by 1943 the commissars had lost in the German struggle over who controlled and profited from the dwindling supply of Jewish labor.

The modified Nazi Final Solution policy of "death through work," which the Jews understood conversely as life through work, did not apply to most of the Jewish population of women, the elderly, children, and the infirm.[59] Thus, in spring 1942, the commissars and local SS police leaders began to plan for renewed killing actions against the ghettoized Jewish populations of Volhynia-Podolia. Jews deemed "unfit to work" fell victim to the first renewed wave of killings that began in April and intensified in late May 1942, when the Volhynian ghettos of Dubno, Kovel, Radzivilov, Hoscha, Korets, Meshirische, and Kozin were liquidated. Hundreds of small open rural ghettos were also abolished and their populations moved to the larger closed ghettos. More than 18,800 Jews (primarily women, children, and the elderly) died in these ghetto liquidations in Volhynia.[60] The next and final wave of ghetto liquidations began in August 1942, with the massacres at Mikasewitschi, Kremianez, Wischnowitz, Potschaejef, Katrinburg, and Schumsk, claiming the lives of 3,816 men, 5,454 women, and 3,119 children. In Podolia, German Security Service (SD) Sipo forces from Kamianets'-Podil's'kyi swept through the ghettos of the Bar district, destroying approximately 4,304 Jews over three days (August 19–21, 1942).[61]

The largest of the August liquidations and massacres occurred at Lutsk. Shortly before the Convention of District Commissars was held at Lutsk, the local SS commander there organized the final massacre of the city's 14,700 Jews, who were murdered between August 19 and August 23, 1942. A week later at the convention (August 29–31), the commissars were informed of Reich Commissar Koch's "personal wish" for the Final Solution to be carried out "one hundred percent."[62] As the general commissar for Volhynia-Podolia elucidated in his orders to the SD outposts of the region, actions against the Jews had to be accelerated so that the Jews of Ukraine's ghettos would be destroyed within five weeks. From each killing action, the number of excluded workers was not to exceed 500 men, but these "vital workers" were also to perish within two months. Working with the experienced SS police mobile killing squad leaders, the commissars coordinated the forces of the local SD men, order policemen, and Ukrainian *Schutzmänner* (rural auxiliaries) to carry out these final ghetto liquidations of autumn 1942.[63]

The *Reichsführer* of the SS police, Heinrich Himmler, personally intervened when he ordered the destruction of the last remaining ghetto in Pinsk on October 27. Between October 30 and November 2, Police Regiment 15, local German SS police, and native auxiliaries annihilated approximately 15,000 Jews in Pinsk. Here the commissars took a strong lead in urging that "all the Jews had to go." Armed with axes, picks, and shovels, the local police pulled up planks and demolished parts of the ghetto in a furious search for every last Jew hiding in the ghetto.[64]

In the two months leading up to the Pinsk massacre, the Germans and their native auxiliaries waged a relentless, bloody assault against every Jewish person left in the Volhynian ghettos. During and shortly after the massacres, Ukrainian *Schutzmänner* and the local population often pillaged and plundered former Jewish homes. The commissars obtained the most valuable booty, and the locals snatched up articles of clothing, cookware, bedding, and other household items.[65] As many as 150,000 Jews were murdered in the autumn 1942 ghetto liquidations, which consisted of 80 percent of the entire Volhynian ghetto population of 1942. All the workshops and industries where Jews had clung to the everyday hope of survival and liberation from the Nazis stood empty. In addition to the enormous loss of Jewish life, the region became an industrial wasteland.[66]

Concluding Observations

Throughout Nazi-occupied Europe, the basic German motivation behind ghettoization was to concentrate and isolate the Jewish population from the non-Jewish. According to Raul Hilberg's definition, the process of ghettoization involved five steps: "(1) the severance of social contacts between the Jews and Germans, (2) housing restrictions, (3) movement regulations, (4) identification measures, and (5) the establishment of a Jewish administrative apparatus."[67] Nearly all Jews who fell victim to the Final Solution experienced the first four of these steps. However, in areas such as eastern-central Ukraine, the Germans acted so swiftly and aggressively against the Jews that the last step of Hilberg's model never materialized. Except for the fleeting presence of the Judenrat, Jewish elders who wielded little authority, no Jewish administrative machinery was instituted in the ghettos of Vinnytsia, Berdychiv, Zhytomyr, Kharkiv, and even parts of Volhynia-Podolia.

The history of Nazi ghettoization practices across Europe is one of significant regional variations. In Ukraine, as in other parts of the occupied East, local German leaders and situational factors played a major part in determining whether a ghetto was formed and what form it took.[68] The ghettos of Ukraine (abandoned factories, barracks, and other sites) compared structurally with the rural ghettos found in Nazi-occupied Byelorussia.[69] Yet the rapid formation and liquidation of ghettos in Ukraine during

1941 and 1942 differed chronologically from the relative longevity of the larger ghettos in Poland and the Baltics.

During the summer and fall of 1941, when the implementation methods of the Final Solution were taking shape, ghettoization became a Nazi vehicle for carrying out the genocide. Local authorities in Ukraine did not initiate ghettos with the expectation that these Jews would be deported. No evidence has emerged suggesting that local leaders believed that Ukrainian Jews would be sent to a far off "dumping ground" farther east. The improvised locations that authorities chose for the ghettos reveal a haphazard approach and the lack of a grand blueprint for the resettlement of Ukrainian Jews. Here the "Jewish question" was subjected to local methods and conditions. The initial pattern of ghettoization in 1941 shows that officials intended from the start to create unlivable conditions for the Jews. Moreover, large numbers of male Jews and then increasingly of Jews "unfit to labor" (women, children, and the elderly) were killed during the ghettoization. Thus, the Nazi view of ghettos had evolved to a new stage by the end of 1941, one that was inextricably linked to the policy of genocide.

Holocaust scholar Christopher Browning has analyzed the relationship between Nazi ghettoization practices and the onset of the Final Solution in his work on Poland. Based on events surrounding the formation of the Łódź and Warsaw ghettos (1939–41), Browning has determined that "ghettoization was not a conscious preparatory step planned by the central authorities to facilitate the mass murder nor did it have the 'set task' of decimating the Jewish population." Rather, "ghettoization was in fact carried out at different times in different ways for different reasons on the initiative of local authorities." Browning characterizes these "local authorities" in Poland not as radical anti-Semites bent on annihilation, but rather as cold-hearted pragmatists, or "ghetto managers," who sought to exploit the Jews economically. As Browning writes, "left to themselves, most local authorities followed a course of normalization, not radicalization."[70] It was the direct intervention of central authorities that turned these ghetto managers in Poland into mass murderers. In Ukraine, by contrast, local authorities did not perceive themselves as "ghetto managers" whose challenge it was to "maintain ghetto life under great constraints."[71] They arrived in Ukraine with a license to kill Jews.

In the summer and autumn of 1941, when the overall murder of the Jews began in earnest, there was no uniform policy for ghettoization. Instead, as General von Roques's guidelines revealed, it was up to local leaders to determine whether ghettos might be useful or necessary. Consequently, the regional variations in Nazi ghettoization practices were rather extreme, which makes any comparative analysis of ghettos from the Baltic to the Black Sea a difficult undertaking. In the case of Ukraine, several factors shaped the history of ghettoization: administrative structures, stages in the military campaign, the implementation stages of the Final Solution policy, local demographic conditions and resources, and leading individuals at the senior and regional levels of Nazi rule. During the military advance of 1941, military leaders and SS police commando chiefs from Einsatzgruppe C took the initiative to create makeshift ghettos in rural towns such as Radomyshyl and in major centers such as Kamianets'-Podil's'kyi. If Jewish urban districts could not be easily established, then local German authorities found other ways to concentrate and isolate the Jews—for example, by cramming them into freight cars, bombed-out buildings, schools, and other locales. Here they were kept under guard, tortured, and denied food and water while local Nazi leaders worked out the logistics of the imminent killing *Aktion.* In the larger urban districts, food supplies to the ghettos were also cut off or kept at starvation levels. The Sipo-SD first killed the Jewish intelligentsia, leaving the community without any strong leadership. Mass shootings usually accompanied each ghetto's formation and occurred throughout its brief existence.

As of September 1941, the civilian caste of Nazi rulers, or commissars, began to ghettoize the remaining Jewish populations west of the Dnieper. Now a clear distinction emerged between, as Jewish observers described it, "ghettos of life" and "ghettos of death." In Poland, first the nonworking Jews, women, children, and the elderly were deported from the ghettos to the extermination centers. Primarily male Jewish laborers were allowed for some time to work in the ghettos or camps before they, too, were sent to the gas chambers. In contrast, in Ukraine the Nazi *Selek-*

tion of family members into categories of life and death occurred during the ghettoization, hence the creation in Bar of multiple ghettos.

When the war dragged on longer than planned, Nazi leaders found that they had to depend on Jewish labor and therefore had to prolong the existence of the ghettos. However, the German's short-term reliance on Jewish workers did not protect the Jews who were deemed "unfit," nor did it ultimately save all of the workers. The economic rationale for keeping ghettos intact was not strong enough to reverse Nazi anti-Jewish policy from its most radical point of mass murder. The local authorities who, as Browning depicts them, might have otherwise followed a course of normalization, not radicalization, were clearly outnumbered and outranked by Nazi leaders who were determined to remove the Jews, region by region, once and for all. The final liquidation of the Volhynian ghettos manifests just how irrational, impractical, and criminal Nazi anti-Jewish policy had become. As many as 1.4 million Jews perished in the Holocaust in Ukraine, and most of these Jewish men, women, and children were forced into the Nazi death traps known as ghettos shortly before they were gunned down in the ravines, fields, and forests across Ukraine. In sum, the history of Nazi ghettoization in Ukraine demonstrates that over time the ghetto had evolved from a haphazard yet precedented form of anti-Semitic persecution into a deliberate Nazi facilitator of genocide.

10. Multiple and Changing Experiences of Ghettoization

Budapest, 1944

TIM COLE

Our understanding of the Holocaust as a common experience shared by the majority of European Jews[1] owes much to the pioneering research of Raul Hilberg.[2] In *The Destruction of the European Jews,* first published in 1961, Hilberg identified a fourfold destruction process—definition, expropriation, concentration, and annihilation—experienced by Europe's Jews.[3] This model offers a compelling framework within which to understand the complex events of World War II Europe. The stories of individual ghettos can be examined within the broader narrative of "concentration," which in turn can be examined in terms of the overarching (meta)narrative of "destruction."

Yet although Hilberg was engaged in constructing a model that pointed to a common destruction process, he was also sensitive to differences between national and regional experiences of the Holocaust. Thus, for example, under the heading of "concentration," Hilberg drew a distinction between nations such as Germany, where closed ghettos were not set up, and those such as Poland, where they were.[4] In short, academics have long recognized—and more recently have stressed increasingly—that both the implementation of Holocaust ghettoization and Jewish experiences of Holocaust ghettoization varied across World War II Europe.[5]

The implication of this distinction is that although the theoretical models offered by a political scientist such as Hilberg are useful in providing a broader explanatory framework, the realities of specific histories and geographies challenge as much as they support such attempts at generalization. Thus, writing of "life in the ghettos during the Holocaust" is to write of different as well as shared experiences.

Although the ghettoization of Hungarian Jews in 1944 can be seen as the implementation of policies of "concentration," there are significant differences in experiences of ghettoization *between* Hungary and other nations in central-eastern Europe as well as *within* Hungary and *within* individual cities in Hungary. In this essay, I aim to examine very briefly Jewish experiences of ghettoization in Hungary in general, before turning to look at greater length at multiple and changing Jewish experiences of ghettoization in Budapest in 1944.

Jewish Experiences of Ghettoization in Hungary, 1944

Given the unusual nature of the Holocaust in Hungary, it is perhaps to be expected that life in the ghettos there differed from life in the ghettos in, for example, Poland. Coming so late on in the war, the timescale of the implementation of the "Final Solution of the Jewish Question" was telescoped in the case of Hungary. Although Hungary, as ally of Nazi Germany, had introduced increasingly restrictive anti-Semitic legislation in the late 1930s and early 1940s,[6] the Hungarian Jewish community was still largely intact at the beginning of 1944.[7] It was only after the Nazi German occupation of Hungary in March 1944 that Hungary's Jews were marked with a yellow star, placed into ghettos, and deported to Auschwitz-Birkenau within a period of four months.[8] As Randolph Braham reflects, "in no other country was the Final Solution program . . . carried out with as much barbarity and speed as in Hungary."[9]

Because of the rapidity of the implementation of the Holocaust, ghettos within provincial Hungary were short-lived places of Jewish residence. Whereas in Poland Holocaust ghettos were in existence for a number of years, in provincial Hungary they were in existence for only a number of weeks. The result was that the development of communal institutions and the flowering of cultural life that has been pointed to in other countries did not take place within Hungarian ghettos to anything like the same extent.[10]

Another significant difference between ghettos in Hungary and elsewhere was that in Hungary the short-lived Holocaust ghettos were effectively the places of Jewish women, children, and the elderly because Jewish men of military age had been placed into labor battalions under the auspices of the Hungarian army.[11] Although these labor battalions had been the cause of the majority of Jewish deaths prior to the German occupation,[12] they ironically became a major means by which Jewish males were spared from the mass deportations to Auschwitz-Birkenau.

If ghettoization in Hungary can be seen as in many ways unusual, then ghettoization in Budapest should perhaps be seen as exceptional. Unlike the remainder of Hungary's Jews, the Jews in Budapest were not deported en masse to Auschwitz-Birkenau in the early summer of 1944, following the decision by Hungarian regent Miklós Horthy in July 1944 to halt the deportations. Although deportations—on foot this time, in the so-called death marches of winter 1944—did commence again from Budapest after the Arrow Cross (Hungarian fascist party) rise to power in October 1944, the majority of Budapest's Jewish community lived in a number of ghettos for a little more than six months. In Budapest, unlike elsewhere in Hungary and much of Nazi-occupied Europe, the Budapest ghettos were ultimately "liberated" rather than liquidated. In the country that has been characterized as the place of "the Nazi's last victims,"[13] the solution did not prove to be "final" in the case of the capital city.

But there is more to the unusual nature of the ghettoization in Budapest than simply a story of liberation. During the course of 1944, Budapest saw the establishment of not one, but many ghettos. Thus, Jewish experiences of ghettoization in Budapest in 1944 were both changing and multiple. It is that sense of diverse experiences that I hope to develop further in this essay.

Jewish Experiences of Ghettoization in Budapest, 1944

A form of ghettoization can first be seen in Budapest in early April 1944. After two nights of heavy bombing by Allied planes, Hungarian officials demanded on April 4, 1944, that the recently established Jewish Council in Budapest provide five hundred apartments for use by non-Jews whose own apartments had suffered bomb damage. On the following day, an additional one thousand apartments were demanded after another night of bombing raids. By 6:30 P.M. on April 5, the Jewish Council had requisitioned the required fifteen hundred apartments and deposited the keys at the City Hall.[14] This relatively large-scale request for Jewish apartments came on the back of smaller-scale ad hoc requisitions of Jewish apartments for the use of Nazi German officials.

The Jewish families removed from their apartments in the Eighth and Ninth Districts—where the bomb damage was particularly significant—were relocated by the Jewish Council into apartments principally in the Sixth and Seventh Districts. For Bernard Klein, this process was "actually the beginning of a ghetto, since the Jews were evicted from certain sections of the town."[15] It certainly—at least in the eyes of the rightist press—looked like the Jewish Council was establishing a form of Jewish quarter through these relocations in the Sixth and Seventh Districts.[16] Within a little more than a week, the rightist press was drawing attention to what they perceived to be potential geostrategic dangers in the city's Jews being concentrated into this one area of the city, which would, so it was argued, open the remainder of the city up to bombing.[17] In what became an increasingly important discourse within the rightist press, the city's Jews were highlighted as a potential "human shield" against the Allied bombers. This discourse—along with others—influenced the later decision of June 1944 to place all of Budapest's Jews into designated apartment blocks spread throughout the city.

However, at this stage, in April 1944, ghettoization was not a shared experience for all of Budapest's Jews. Rather, it was an experience restricted to those fifteen hundred families in the Eighth and Ninth Districts of the city and the families whom they moved in with in the Sixth and Seventh Districts. Not only was the entire Jewish community of Buda effectively excluded from ghettoization, but so were Jews living in districts in Pest outside of these four central districts. Thus, rather than being a shared experience, ghettoization in April 1944 in Hungary was a divided—and divisive—one.

Something of that divisiveness emerged in Jewish Council president Samu Stern's postwar testimony. Describing the requisition of apartments by Jewish Council representatives (accompanied by a Hungarian policeman and teacher), Stern acknowledged that the end result was that the Jewish Council Housing Office "swiftly became incredibly unpopular with the suffering Jews" and that "it was only natural that those banned from their dwellings found fault in the first place with the Council's new office."[18] That reaction comes through in the oral history interview of a survivor, who commented on the Budapest Jewish Council: "I think they took the German side. To take away such a flat from me in such a way, that I had to leave just that flat in two hours. And then at least twenty flats of that kind were reserved in that house."[19]

For Stern, such reactions were the result of what he perceived to be an entirely self-conscious attempt by the Hungarian authorities to institute a policy of "divide and rule." Thus, he shifted the blame away from the Jewish Council—which "only did what it could not help doing: carrying out the authorities' orders"—to the Hungarian authorities, whom he claimed aimed to "inflict suffering in the most wretched manner, to stir up quarrels among the Jews, and thus to divert their attention from the imminent deportation."[20] Stern's postwar explanation is problematic given the pressure to justify his own and the council's actions, yet it is significant that even he acknowledges the divisive nature of the April 1944 relocations.

Although ghettoization affected only a restricted number of Budapest's Jews in April 1944, mass ghettoization was enacted later, in June. Rather than being placed into a single closed ghetto, Budapest's Jews were placed into apartment buildings spread throughout the city. It was a policy of "concentration within dispersion" that was adopted on a smaller scale in a number of other Hungarian cities for a mixture of geostrategic, socioeconomic, and pragmatic reasons.[21]

Under the terms of the mayoral decrees issued on June 16, 1944, 2,637 apartment buildings were designated for Jewish use—each to be marked with a large yellow star.[22] It is clear that the primary determinant of whether a building was designated Jewish or not was majority occupation. Broadly speaking, a building that had a majority of Jewish residents was made into a "yellow-star house," although the cost of rents and the condition of the building were also taken into account.[23]

Given the importance of majority occupation in determining the shape of the ghetto, ghettoization in June 1944 was built on the prewar residential patterns of the city's Jews, rather than being enacted within a vacuum. The end result was that ghettoization on June 16 meant staying put as well as relocating. For the relatively large number of Jews whose apartment buildings were designated as yellow-star houses, ghettoization in June meant something rather different than for those who were forced to move from their apartments. Although it did mean relocating to one room within their apartment, it is clear from the petitions sent to the city mayor by Jews requesting yellow-star status for their apartment block that this was seen to be far preferable to relocating to another building.[24]

This view can also be seen in some oral history accounts, where the June ghettoization emerges rather differently in the memory of those for whom it meant staying put and of those for whom it meant the trauma of leaving their apartments. In broad terms, for those forced to move from their homes, ghettoization was experienced as a break with the past, whereas for those who stayed in their homes ghettoization was experienced far more in terms of continuity. Thus, when two survivors remember how their houses were designated yellow-star houses in June 1944, for one that designation meant, "my grandparents and we didn't have to move out of her[e], instead other people moved into the apartment,"[25] and for the other it meant, "my cousins came. And we were forty in the house [apartment] where we were only six [before] . . . so we were forty and that was absolutely . . . we had just one bathroom, so . . . there was some conflicts. But you wouldn't believe how delightful was the warmth of bodies around. There was always company, always discussion, always this and that."[26]

In contrast, two survivors forced to move from their homes remember ghettoization in June 1944 as a far more traumatic event. One remembers, "the most terrible thing was that I had to leave the flat in Fillér Street, the flat that had been so wonderfully furnished and that I liked so much,"[27] and another remembers, "my mother did not want to move from our home. Our neighbor and me together held her back from the windowpane. And looking back, she was right! Because only afterwards came the real sufferings and tribulations."[28] Attempted—and actual—suicide was not restricted simply to this survivor's experience of ghettoization in June 1944.

In other families, it is clear that suicide was the preferred option of those forced to move from their homes.[29]

For those Jews forced to change their apartment, relocation into the apartment of a relative or close friend appears to have been fairly common. Otherwise, Jews were encouraged to move into houses on the same street or at least within the same district, thus limiting the extent of relocations. Thus, although there were mass relocations in Budapest in June 1944, they tended to be *within* a district, rather than being across the city.

Intended to be limited in terms of scope, relocations were in reality far from being so. This increase resulted from the decision to replace the June 16 list of 2,637 buildings designated for Jewish use with a second—"definitive"—list of 1,948 buildings less than a week later, on June 22.[30] The reduction in the number of properties was most marked in Buda and in the outlying districts of Pest (Ninth, Tenth, Thirteenth, and Fourteenth Districts), after Jewish majority occupation had been reinvestigated and the decision made to exclude all villa properties.[31]

For some Jews in these districts who had already moved into the June 16 designated houses, the reduction in the number of properties meant the need to move yet again after a matter of only a few days. Thus, in Buda's Eleventh District, eighty-three Jewish families who had already moved into yellow-star houses were now forced to move out of these buildings after their yellow-star status was canceled.[32] Less than a week after moving for the first time, they had to move again into the remaining eighteen yellow-star houses in the district. Such an experience was not confined solely to the Jews in the Eleventh District, but was a shared experience for other Jews living in Buda and the outlying districts of Pest in particular.

The corollary of the relocation of the eighty-three Jewish families who had moved into buildings in the Eleventh District after their yellow-star designations were canceled was that the twelve non-Jewish families who had moved out of these properties after June 16 were now free to return.[33] As city officials were well aware, ghettoization impacted the non-Jewish inhabitants of houses designated as part of the ghetto as well as the Jewish inhabitants of the city. Yet, although all Jews were required to move into the 1,948 apartment blocks designated for Jewish use on June 22, the non-Jewish residents of those buildings were permitted to stay, and it is clear that a large number did.[34] Those who did stay accentuated the problem of overcrowding, although also in some cases, Braham suggests, they aided the Jewish residents who were subjected to increasingly restrictive legislation.[35]

The 1,948 apartment blocks designated on June 22 remained in essence the "Budapest ghetto" until the winter of 1944, although there continued to be minor changes. On September 15, 14 yellow-star houses in the Second, Fourth, Fifth, Seventh, and Eighth Districts were requested for use by German soldiers.[36] The Jews living there had to move into already overcrowded properties, where they were clearly not welcome.[37] On October 27, a further 8 yellow star-houses in the Second, Fourth, and Sixth Districts were requested, again it would seem for the use of German soldiers.[38] Thus, for a small number of the city's Jews, there was the experience of further relocations in the fall of 1944.

After the Arrow Cross rise to power, the situation for Budapest's approximately 150,000–160,000 Jews changed dramatically. In the days following the October 15 coup, a number of yellow-star houses were attacked by Arrow Cross gangs in a situation of near anarchy.[39] From early November, deportations were restarted, this time on foot. In the so-called death marches in the winter of 1944, thousands of Budapest Jews were marched westward into Austria. The majority of the city's Jews were spared from these deportations, however, and subjected instead to new forms of ghettoization.

In the winter of 1944, two ghettos were established in Budapest. Thus, the "dispersed ghettoization" that had characterized the Jewish experience of ghettoization from mid-June onward was replaced by what is usefully called "hyphenated ghettoization." The context to this multiple ghettoization is the division of the remaining Jews in the city into a number of distinct categories. Far from being a single category in winter 1944, the social construct "Jew" became a multiple—and hyphenated—category.

In their "final plan" for Hungary's Jews issued on November 17, 1944, Ferenc Szálasi's Arrow Cross government divided the remaining Jews in the country into six categories: Jews holding foreign protective passes, Jews to be lent to the German government, Jews awaiting departure from Hungary, Jews holding exemption certificates, clerics of Jewish origin, and

Jews of foreign citizenship.[40] For three of these groups—Jews holding foreign protective passes, Jews awaiting departure from Hungary, and clerics of Jewish origin—separate forms of ghettoization were envisioned. In reality, the critical division was between the so-called protected and unprotected Jews, who were placed into two distinct ghettos in the winter of 1944.

This process of hyphenated ghettoization had been discussed prior to the issuing of Szálasi's "final plan" in mid-November. As early as the summer of 1944, plans had been discussed to house "Christian Jews" (Jewish converts to Christianity) and "protected Jews" separately from the mass of Budapest's Jews, although it is clear that these plans were unacceptable to some members of the Jewish Council.[41] Although these early plans did not come to fruition, in November 1944 "protected Jews"—Jews protected by the neutral powers—were housed separately from "unprotected Jews." On November 12, 1944, Deputy Chief of Police János Solymossy informed the caretakers and air-raid wardens of the yellow-star houses, where Budapest's Jews had been housed for a little less than six months, that Jews "in possession of provisional passports, safe-conduct passes, or protective certificates issued by the various neutral states" were to be relocated to yellow-star houses in the Fifth District of the city by November 15, a date later extended to November 17.[42]

With the establishing of the so-called International Ghetto, between fifteen and seventeen thousand "protected Jews" moved into approximately 120 modern apartment buildings centered around Pozsonyi Street in the largely Jewish middle-class Fifth District of Pest.[43] For the "unprotected Jews" and non-Jews living there, the establishing of the International Ghetto meant forced relocations. "Unprotected" Jewish males between the ages of sixteen and sixty and females between the ages of eighteen and forty were taken to join the death marches westward. "Unprotected" Jewish children and the elderly were relocated to other yellow-star houses, prior to being relocated again within a matter of weeks into the Pest ghetto.

Interestingly, in the oral history testimony of one survivor of the International Ghetto, that history of forced relocations is remembered rather differently. She comments that the area "was only available because it was very Jewish and the Jews were all taken and they were empty houses. That's where Wallenberg was able . . . to acquire those houses. Because about 95 percent they were Jewish and they were already deported."[44] Yet in reality it was the other way round. The yellow-star houses were not available because the Jews living there had already been deported. Rather, the "unprotected Jews" living there were deported or relocated to make way for the "protected Jews," who were to occupy what was now to be the International Ghetto. In the winter of 1944, hyphenated ghettoization meant very different things for "protected Jews" and "unprotected Jews" living in Fifth District yellow-star houses.

A little more than two weeks after the International Ghetto was created in the Fifth District for the city's "protected Jews," the so-called Pest ghetto was created in the largely Jewish working-class Sixth District for the city's "unprotected Jews." Of the approximately 240 apartment buildings in the area designated for the ghetto, approximately 140 had been designated yellow-star houses in June 1944.[45] Thus, for the relatively large number of Jews already living in the area, ghettoization did not mean mass relocation, but rather a farther retreat into less and less living space. However, for the majority of the city's Jews, ghettoization at the end of November 1944 meant mass relocations on a scale even greater than that in June 1944. Although in June 1944 there had been an attempt to encourage relocations within districts, the establishment of a single ghetto in the Sixth District in November 1944 meant mass relocations across districts. Jews were forced to move from yellow-star houses spread throughout the city into the closed Pest ghetto in the Fifth District, effectively making Buda and outlying Pest *judenfrei*—"Jew free."

The corollary of this was that the ghetto area was effectively made "Christian*frei*." Although non-Jews had been tolerated within the yellow-star houses that characterized earlier ghettoization policies, they were forced to relocate from the area designated for the Pest—and international—ghettos. Former yellow-star houses in Pest were made available for non-Jews affected by the new ghettoization policies, although vacated Jewish properties in Buda appear to have been reserved for German, Arrow Cross, and military personnel seeking to "escape" westward across the river away from the rapidly approaching Red Army.[46]

Soviet troops reached and liberated the Pest ghetto in mid-January 1945. A few days later they liberated what remained of the International Ghetto. This ghetto had been reduced in size during the course of December and early January, as "protected Jews" were increasingly being relocated into the Pest ghetto, whose population reached approximately seventy thousand in January 1945.[47] Ironically, the wall of the closed Pest ghetto came to be seen as offering greater protection than the papers held by the "protected Jews" in the International Ghetto. In January 1945, for a large part of Budapest's "protected Jews" and "unprotected Jews," more than nine months of ghettoization ended not in liquidation, but in liberation.

Conclusions

Not only was the ghettoization experience of Budapest's Jews quite different from that of Jews elsewhere in Hungary or elsewhere in occupied Europe, but it also differed from Jew to Jew within the city. With the quite exceptional adoption of policies of hyphenated ghettoization at the end of 1944, there were quite literally two different ghettos for two very different groups of Jews in Budapest.

But right from its inception, ghettoization in Budapest needs to be seen as a divided as well as a shared experience. The relocations of April 1944 were shared by some fifteen hundred Jewish families in the Eighth and Ninth Districts—and also by the families in the Sixth and Seventh Districts into whose apartments they moved; they were not shared by the Jews of Buda or outlying areas of Pest. Even when ghettoization was implemented for the entire Jewish community, it meant rather different things, as I have suggested, for those for whom it meant staying put and for those for whom it meant moving. For many of the Jews living in the traditionally Jewish working-class Sixth District of Budapest, the ghetto quite literally came to them (rather than their going to the ghetto) in its many incarnations throughout 1944. Yet for others, ghettoization was characterized by multiple relocations, sometimes, as in June 1944, within less than a week.

The result is that there is no single Jewish experience of ghettoization in Budapest in 1944, but a variety of overlapping experiences. That variation can, perhaps, be best seen by mapping out the recollections of a small number of "protected" Jewish survivors drawn together under the auspices of the Raoul Wallenberg Project Archive. In many ways, the source material is problematic. As one survivor herself admits, "the life of our family was so complicated in those times, I couldn't even tell the number of flats we were staying at in 1944";[48] the frequency and number of moves in 1944 meant that remembering the precise locations and sequence of those moves is a difficult task. Moreover, in using a series of interviews by the Raoul Wallenberg Project Archive, my sample is heavily skewed. Not only are the interviewees all survivors, but they are all survivors of the International Ghetto or of other Swedish "protected" buildings, who tended to experience a far greater number of relocations than, for example, did Jews from the part of the Seventh District that was ultimately to become the Pest ghetto.

Bearing those reservations in mind, I close this essay by mapping out the recollections of ghettoization in Budapest found in three survivors' oral history accounts. In many ways, in doing that I am doing what Martin Gilbert has done in a different context in his *Atlas of the Holocaust*.[49] The attraction of mapping out individual histories (and geographies) of ghettoization is that it fleshes out the multiple and changing experiences of ghettoization in 1944 Budapest, which I have sought to describe in this essay.

Three Histories (and Geographies) of Ghettoization

For Tamás Ungvári, the implementation of ghettoization in June 1944 did not mean forced relocations. His family's apartment was in a Fourth District building designated with a yellow star; therefore, in a sense the ghetto came to him. However, the later appropriation of the apartment building for use by Nazi German officials meant that the family was forced to move to an apartment in the Fifth District. From here, they moved to another apartment close by, before going into hiding in the Eighth District. After gaining Swedish protection, they moved into the International Ghetto in the Fifth District.[50]

Kate Wacz's experience of relocations was in some ways similar. Like

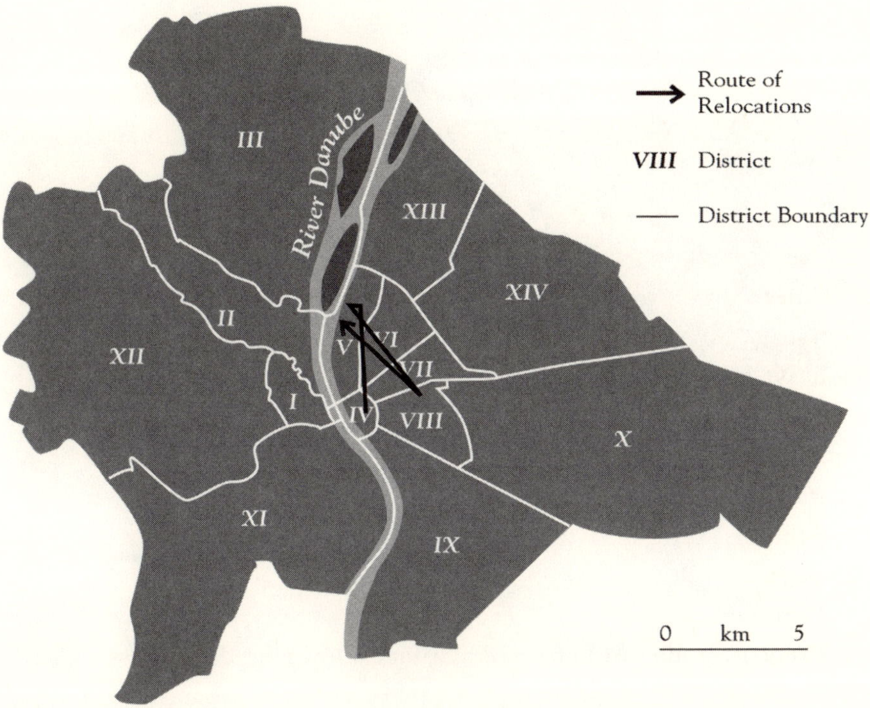

Tamás Ungvári's experience of ghettoization, June–December 1944.

Ungvári, she hid out and also lived in Swedish-protected buildings. However, the implementation of mass ghettoization in June 1944 meant relocation rather than staying put, and she was liberated from the Pest ghetto rather than from the International Ghetto. In June 1944, Wacz moved from her family's apartment in the Fifth District into her grandmother's apartment in the Sixth District, which had been designated as a yellow-star house. In the fall of 1944, she lived in two Swedish buildings—first in the Eighth and then in the Sixth District—as a result of her brother's working for the Swedish embassy. In November 1944, she hid out in Buda for a few days, before returning to Pest and ending up in the Pest ghetto.[51]

Mrs. Pál Kauders lived in a yellow-star house, the International Ghetto, and the Pest ghetto. The creation of yellow-star houses did not mean moving for Kauders, like for Ungvári, but staying put because her apartment building in the Eighth District was designated in June 1944. However, unlike Ungvári and Wacz, Kauders's relocation from the yellow-

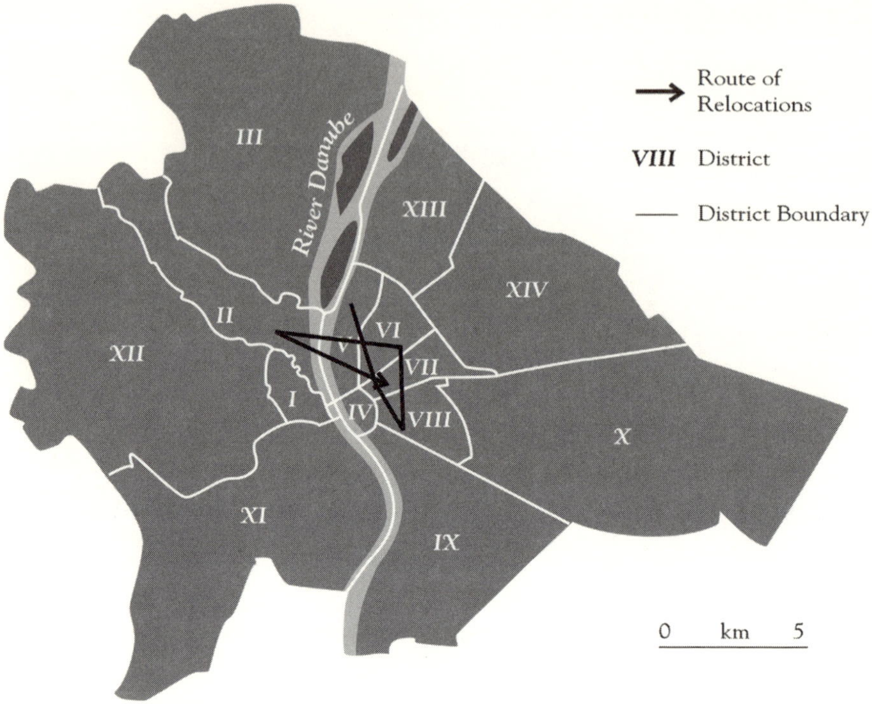

Kate Wacz's experience of ghettoization, June–December 1944.

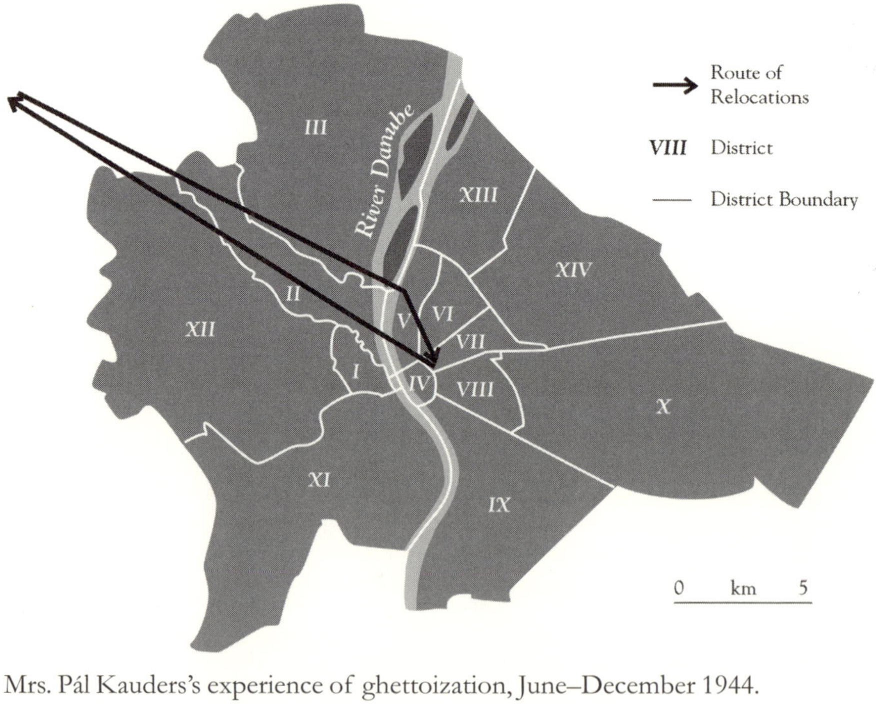

Mrs. Pál Kauders's experience of ghettoization, June–December 1944.

star house was in the form of one of the death marches west in November 1944, from which she was rescued and taken into one of the Swedish-protected houses in the International Ghetto. From here, she returned to her original address—now within the Pest ghetto.[52]

All three of these survivors were placed into the multiple and changing ghettos of Budapest in one form or another during the course of 1944. All three experienced ghettoization. And yet in those experiences we see both overlap and difference. Their overlapping and differing experiences of ghettoization in Budapest in 1944—as I have tried to show in this essay—can be multiplied many times over. In some ways, then, "life in the ghetto" in Budapest was a shared experience of "concentration" for the city's Jews. But in other important ways, ghettoization was an experience that divided as much as it united Budapest's Jews. In our writing of the social histories (and geographies) of life in the ghetto, we do well to attempt to reflect something of that complexity.

11. Death and Ghetto Death

DAVID PATTERSON

When scholars examine life in the ghettos that the Nazis created for the Jews, they often overlook what is most ubiquitous: death. True, they point out, with horror, the pervasiveness of death, but they seldom examine its essence or its significance for a deeper understanding of the Shoah. Perhaps it is left unexamined because it is so pervasive. Many explore starvation, disease, and other forms of murder used against the Jews in the ghettos, but the phenomenon of death in the ghetto is seldom distinguished from the phenomenon of death outside the ghetto. Ghetto life has been thoroughly studied, but ghetto death and what it means to an understanding of the Nazi assault on Jewish life have been all but ignored.

Assuming that the ghetto is indeed an abnormal realm in which death may have an abnormal status, we must begin by asking about the role of death in a normal realm of Jewish life. The eleventh-century sage Rabbi Bachya ibn Paquda explains how death is regarded within the Jewish tradition: "Life and Death are brethren, dwelling together closely to one another, inseparable, holding fast to the two ends of a tottering bridge over which all the world's creatures pass. Life is at its entrance; Death is at its exit. Life builds, Death breaks up. Life sows, Death reaps. Life unites, Death divides. Life strings together, Death scatters what has been strung together."[1] Although the Torah enjoins us to choose life (Deuteronomy 30:19), making this choice does not mean that we no longer pass away from this earth; it does not entail the removal of death from the world. Rather, it means that in choosing life we understand death to be part of the process of sanctifying life through Torah study, religious observance, and deeds of loving kindness. That is why, according to Jewish teaching, kindness can be shown even toward the dead. Thus, like life, death is situated within the contexts of the sacred. It is the culmination, not the negation, of life. Murder is evil; in itself, death is not. Standing by while people die is evil; in itself, dying is not. Taking death to be part of life, Jews begin the Kaddish, the Prayer for the Dead, with a magnification and sanctification of the Name of God, in whom all life originates, and they end by declaring, "Amen." Placed on its proper ground, death in the Jewish tradition becomes an occasion for humanity's affirmation of the dearness of life.

In the Jewish tradition, moreover, "dearness of life" is dearness of the life of the other human being. When we join our voice to the Voice of the Creator to declare creation to be "very good," we affirm the dearness of life. To choose life is to choose this "very good" that distinguishes the living from the inanimate. It inheres in the *nefesh,* or soul, which is life itself. Therefore, choosing this "very good" means realizing that the basis of our ethical relation to another soul—underlying the dearness of our neighbor's life—is our fear for his death. Because the life of the neighbor is *infinitely* dear, our fear for the death of the other person approaches the point of offering up our own life for the other. Such is the basis of martyrdom, which is an assertion that life is "very good" in the very midst of a dying for another that encompasses death. Unless we are able to connect death with this "very good," we shall be entrenched in the proposition that there is no higher good than our own survival. Thus, left with nothing to live for but ourselves, we have nothing for which to die. In the ghetto, however, there is no dying in order that another may live; at best, there is a dying so another might not have to die alone, as when Janusz Korczak accompanies the children from the orphanage in the Warsaw ghetto to Treblinka. Already one can see that ghetto death is problematic.

There is another problem, however, that must be noted as part of this introduction. It is the problem of dying as a human being in a realm where the one dying is not regarded as human. But what does "dying as a human being" mean within Jewish tradition? Quoting Dr. Leo Eitinger, Harry James Cargas explains: "There has been a Jewish religious tradition throughout the centuries, where 'dying as a man' means something quite different from what Western people usually understand by this expression. To die as a man, or as a Jew—for the religious Jew it is the same thing—

means to die with the 'Shema' and with the Holy Name of God on their lips, without resistance, without 'falling into the abyss of the aggressor, namely to kill just as he did.' "[2] Ultimately, to live as a human being is to die as a human being. And to die as a human being is to affirm even in death that life is very good, speaking even in death the Name of the One who is the origin of life in a declaration of "Shema Yisrael!" This utterance of "Hear, O Israel" is itself an offering of life to all who hear it.

Therefore, even as the tide of death is rising all around him, Josef Katz is able to see that, at least in his mother's case, death is not all encompassing but rather is encompassed. For soon after he arrived at the camp in Jungfernhof, he received a message that reads, "My dear Josef, your mother died last night of a stroke in the arms of Chief Rabbi Carlbach. She recited the 'Shema Yisrael.' "[3] What transpires in the Nazis' imposition of death on all of European Jewry, however, is not only the end of Jewish life, but the end of the Jewish affirmation of life that lies in dying as a human being. "[T]he Nazi murder machine," notes Emil Fackenheim, "was systematically designed to stifle this *Shema Yisrael* on Jewish lips before it murdered Jews themselves";[4] public prayer, for example, is forbidden in the ghettos. As will be shown, there is a connection between the assault on the holy at the core of Jewish life and what is here referred to as "ghetto death." Indeed, *this* death belongs to the singularity of the Holocaust itself: casting the Jews into a deluge of death calculated to destroy their humanity, the Nazis deprive the Jews of the death—of the "very good"—that forms the foundation of their lives as human beings.

Because ghetto death is a definitive feature of the Holocaust, it is a significant part of what is addressed in the Holocaust diaries written from the ghetto depths. "We die anonymously," writes Ruth Andreas-Friedrich, for example:[5] stifling the Name of God on the lips of the dying, the Nazis render the Jews themselves not only lifeless, but nameless, literally anonymous. The Jewish dead are not laid to rest in a grave, with their names inscribed on a memorial; they are forced to "live" in a grave that must remain unmarked lest they be murdered, in what Hillel Seidman calls the "underground world" of bunkers and hiding places.[6] Although Helena Dorembus delights in the sight of Schutzstaffel (SS) men being killed during the Warsaw Ghetto Uprising,[7] those German dead retain a certain place in death that connects them to life, a place denied to the Jews: they retain their names. But the Nazis see to it that the Jewish dead have no such link to the living. Each Jew is murdered many times over, in body, in soul, in memory, in name, in substance—and in death.

Perhaps Adam Czerniakow, head of the Warsaw Jewish Council, keeps a model of a Jewish gravestone on his desk to remind himself not only of the ubiquitous death that overwhelms the Jews, but of the calculated obliteration of death that is a distinctive aspect of the Nazi assault on humanity.[8] It is a marker for a people who have no other marker, a sign of their link to life in a realm devoid of all such signs. And as soon as he situates this sign among the signifiers that compose his diary, the diary itself becomes such a sign. Let us consider, then, the ghetto death laid bare in the ghetto diaries by diarists who seek to recover an affirmation of life when the very *idea* of life is under assault—as is the idea of death. Let us see how, transformed into ghetto death, the death that engulfs Jewish life contributes to the murder of death itself. To be sure, ghetto death is precisely the death that is not death, the death that is the murder of death. This murder not only of life but of a sanctified death in life belongs to the singularity of the Holocaust.

Death All Encompassing

If death takes on a sense in which the totality of death is encompassed—that is, when dying is a dying for the sake of another—life is rendered void of all sense and meaning. Just such a totality confronts the Romanian teenager Mirjam Korber when she declares, "Hundreds of people die, and usually it is the best ones who die."[9] The best ones are those who choose life. And yet in choosing life, they are chosen by death. Why? Because, in an overturning of meaning, the very traits of generosity and loving kindness that in the world of humanity engender life are turned against those who possess those traits in the antiworld, until finally the ones who choose life end by succumbing to death. "There are times," writes Korber, "when I might manage to hope for the end of this war and to see once more the beautiful days that used to be. But death is better."[10] In other words, death is more than those days of life. When such words are forced into the mouth of a child—when a girl in the flower of life deems death to be better than life—death is indeed all encompassing. No longer a task to be engaged over the course of three score and ten years, death here becomes the stuff of a life transformed into an antilife before it is lived. That is what the death's head, the symbol set like a frontlet between the eyes of the SS, signifies: the life of the Jew is defined by and confined to an all-encompassing death.

Indeed, for the Jew trapped in the ghetto, the encompassing hand of death reaches even into the womb. "The beginning of November '41," Emanuel Ringelblum records in his Warsaw diary, "news from Łódź that the Łódź Jews had been prohibited from marrying and having children. Women pregnant up to three months had to have an abortion."[11] On February 5, 1942, Vilna ghetto diarist Herman Kruk writes, "Today the Gestapo summoned two members of the Judenrat and notified them: No more Jewish children are to be born. The order came from Berlin."[12] And in his diary from the Kovno ghetto, on July 24, 1942, Avraham Tory writes, "From September on, giving birth is strictly forbidden. Pregnant women will be put to death."[13] Without the secure future of the child, the essence of the mother—of the source of life—is broken: the Nazi assault is targeted not only against mothers but against mother*hood.*

When a pregnant woman is put to death, more than a pregnant woman is murdered, physically and metaphysically, as we see when on February 4, 1943, Tory laments, "It was terrible to watch the women getting on the truck; they held in their arms babies of different ages and wrapped them in more and more sweaters so that they would not catch cold on the way [to their death!]."[14] Exceeding the horror of slaughtering pregnant mothers, the Nazis wait until these mothers hold their babies in their arms before murdering them and their infants with them. This assault on the relation that constitutes the mother as mother entails not only dealing out death, but displacing life with death; it entails a *confusion* of life and death, so that where there should be life, there is only death.

And so in his Warsaw ghetto diary, Hillel Seidman asserts, "The dark wings of the Angel of Death spread over the extinguished sparks of life."[15] So pervasive is death in the Warsaw ghetto that the Angel becomes as seductive as it is dreadful, leading many to spend the days of their lives

Portrait of two young boys wearing Jewish badges in the Kovno ghetto taken shortly before their roundup in the March 1944 "Children's Action." Pictured are Avram Rosenthal (five years) and Emanuel Rosenthal (two years). Emanuel was born in the Kovno ghetto. The children, who were deported in the March 1944 "Children's Action," did not survive. Their uncle, Shraga Wainer, who had asked George Kadish to take this photograph, received a copy of it from the photographer after the war in the Landsberg displaced persons' camp. Photo and caption courtesy of the United States Holocaust Memorial Museum.

seeking death. "The number of suicides among the Jews," Czerniakow records in his diary on October 10, 1940, "has been greatly increasing during the last months."[16] Instilling in the Jews a desire for death, the Nazis achieve just what they set out to achieve: not only will they kill the Jews, but they will force them into a longing for death. And those who do not succumb to suicide will succumb to death nevertheless. "Typhus is raging," says Czerniakow on December 4, 1941. "Friends and acquaintances are dying all around me."[17] A sea of death rises all around the diarist, until death becomes as all encompassing to him as the sea is to a drowning man. The breath of life and the air upon which that breath is drawn—the *neshamah* and *ruach*—are no longer there.

The atmosphere of the Holocaust Kingdom is not one in which a Jew can breathe, and, like the atmosphere surrounding a planet, it extends throughout that kingdom. Hence, in another ghetto, fifteen-year-old Dawid Rubinowicz writes, "Already a lot of Jewish blood has flowed in this Bieliny, in fact a whole Jewish cemetery has already grown up there. When will this terrible bloodshed finally end? If this goes on much longer then people will drop like flies out of sheer horror."[18] The horror arises here not just at the spectacle of death and murder but at the sense that death and murder are the only reality. Indeed, the horror is itself a kind of death that steals over the living before they are dead. Planet Auschwitz, which extends far beyond the confines of the death camps, has an immense field of gravity that tugs on the soul of every Jew, and its deadly, ashen atmosphere fills every Jewish mouth. Unlike other diaries, the Holocaust diary is not the daily record of a life, but the account of a daily struggle against death.

Thus, the Romanian diarist Emil Dorian cries out, "I try to tear myself out of the vortex that is pulling me down. I did manage to complete a translation, it sits ready on my desk, but everything has a taste of ashes and sticks in my throat like a foretaste of death."[19] The lifeline to which the diarist clings as he struggles against the vortex of death is the word that he consigns to the pages of his diary. Returning meaning and life to the word is his one means of resisting the overturning of meaning in the realm of death, for the work of this overturning also arises from words, from words used not to join word to meaning and life to life but to tear the life from the souls of the Jews. The foretaste of death that fouls the mouth of the diarist, then, issues from the mouths of the Nazis and their minions, whose death orders vibrate on their breath and foul the air.

In this connection, Herman Kruk comments on an announcement of death made by the notorious Jacob Gens, head of the Jewish Council in the Vilna ghetto, saying, "A loud weeping breaks out as he begins. A gust of Ponary bursts into the hall, a breath of death, memories of men, women, and children snatched away."[20] Once again, like the atmosphere surrounding Planet Auschwitz, the breath of corruption rises up from Ponary to flood the Vilna ghetto. "The district Ponar," Yitskhok Rudashevski cries out, "is soaked in Jewish blood. Ponar is the same as a nightmare, a nightmare which accompanies the gray strand of our ghetto-days."[21] And the nightmare is as ever present—and ultimately as mundane—as the day itself. The nightmare is a daymare, as banal and diurnal as the setting of the sun. But in the Kingdom of Night, the sun does not set—it turns to darkness. Instead of living in the light of day, the diarist is turned over to the gray of the ghetto day, which swallows up any life that may issue from the earth.

Indeed, the ghetto death that the Nazis spread is so pervasive that the earth itself seems to wither at its touch. "Throughout the summer," laments David Kahane, for example, "I have seen no green vegetation or the shape of a flower. . . . Are there any Jews left in the world? . . . Do Jews still rise to say Selikhoth somewhere?"[22] Here we see a connection between the absence of Jews and the absence of prayer, between the absence of prayer and the absence of life. And so in the ghetto what becomes commonplace is not the beds of flowers seen in the neighborhoods of humanity, but the pools of blood. "Puddles of blood have become an ordinary sight," writes Rivosh from the Riga ghetto. "We walk past them, step in them."[23] Like death itself, the blood of the dead clings to the living: the Jew who walks these streets leaves behind him a trail of death, tracking it everywhere he goes, down the sidewalks where he lives and into his home. This trail of blood is the trace of the death that not only awaits the Jew but is all around him.

Thus established as the condition assigned to Jewish existence, death is not only ontologically all encompassing, but altogether ordinary. "We [have] become quite used to the sight of women walking to their death," Josef Katz comments on the situation at Stutthof, "and the chimney, too, no longer bothers us."[24] The clouds bellowing from the chimney are as mundane as the clouds in the sky. To be sure, they take the place of the clouds in the sky, eclipsing those clouds that God set in the heavens, eclipsing God Himself. For in their assault on God the Nazis have set other clouds on high, clouds of death that bring all things low, to the same level of empty indifference, erasing the difference between life and death. "There is a marked, remarkable indifference to death, which no longer impresses," says Emanuel Ringelblum of the attitude that pervades the Warsaw ghetto. "One walks past corpses with indifference."[25] The Yiddish word used here for "indifference" is *gleikhgiltikeit,*[26] which literally means "having the same value." The same value as what? The same value as life:

there is no qualitative distinction between life and death. Once again we see that the lines of demarcation between life and death have been erased—that is ghetto death.

No longer, then, is one human being joined to another according to an everyday life shared; their only interhuman link, which is not inter*human* at all, is a death endured each day. The most glaring evidence of the erasure of life—the obliteration of the difference between life and death—is the erasure of the word, which is the most fundamental link between one human being and another. What makes the living indistinguishable from the dead and at times indifferent toward the dead is this deathly silence imposed on both. "Death is silence," says André Neher, "silence overtaking life,"[27] and as the Nazis flood the world with death, they deluge the world with silence. Both opposing this silence and transmitting it, the diarist fetches the words from the mouths of the dead and brings them to his diary, where, perhaps, the difference between life and death may be reestablished, even if for only a moment. And the difference is reestablished by making that difference into a nonindifference.

But the diarist cannot take on a stance of nonindifference toward the death of the "other" without being implicated by that death and by the indifference that would collapse the distinction between life and death. In our relation to the other person, we see more than he can see: we see his face, in which are inscribed both his sanctity and his mortality. In the realm of the ghetto, the all-encompassing death blinds us to the face of the other, which is a blindness to life and death, just as it is a blindness to light and dark. Through the words the diarist sets to the page in an act of nonindifference, he sees excessively; that is, he comes to see more than the totality of death that surrounds him. And where does he see the life and death, wherein the all-encompassing death threatens to blind him? In the other person. "Death," says Emmanuel Levinas, "is *present* only in the Other, and only in him does it summon me urgently to my final essence, to my responsibility."[28] Therefore, getting rid of the other, we get rid of death. And if we can get rid of death, then we can get rid of the other.

Only others lie in the cemeteries. During the Holocaust, however, those who lay in their graves in the cemeteries—indeed, as we shall see, the cemeteries themselves, which situate death in the midst of life and place it on its sacred ground—are under attack, for eliminating the "others," the Jews, is the Nazi aim, and this they do, in part, by eliminating the cemeteries. Such is the project that the Nazis undertake in the murder of death that is ghetto death: removing Jewish death from Jewish life, they seek to remove the Jew from life. Let us consider how this process might be understood.

Ghetto Death: The Murder of Death

In the foregoing, we can see that horror is a form of death that steals over the living before they are dead. Here we realize that if horror is a kind of death, it may well be viewed not as a fear of death but as the obliteration of death. "Horror is nowise an anxiety about death," Levinas claims. "In horror a subject is stripped of his subjectivity, of his power to have a private existence. . . . It is a participation in the *there is,* in the *there is* which returns in the heart of every negation, in the *there is* that has 'no exits.' It is, if we may say so, the impossibility of death, the universality of existence even in its annihilation."[29] Stripped of his subjectivity, both the human being and his world are stripped of all significance.

To be a subject who lives and dies is to take up the project of making sense of a world. Bereft of both world and sense, the human being is not alive—he or she is simply there; the world has no inherent meaning or value—it is simply there. The "there is," then, consists of being in the midst of an indifferent being that is merely there, where there is no evaluation of life or death and therefore no distinction between life and death—no human *being*. Bodies are not consigned for burial; like trash, they are collected for disposal. Mourners neither pray nor sit shivah; they simply go about the business of plodding along, so that they are not mourners at all. Here death is not so much impossible as it is meaningless. In the "there is" that descends on the ghetto, death is not a rite of passage; neither a rite nor a passage, it simply is. And one means by which death is thus rendered meaningless is through the removal of the signs, of the gravestones and cemeteries, that would impart to it a significance. Hence, death dies.

Or rather, it is murdered and thus made into ghetto death. For in the ghettos of the Shoah, the conditions and contexts that would make death matter are not just absent; they are annihilated. Emil Fackenheim explains:

> In Ezekiel's image [of the dry bones], the dead have fallen in battle. The dead of the Holocaust were denied battle, its opportunity and its honours. Denied the peace even of the bones, they were denied also the honour of graves, for they, the others, ground their bones to dust and threw the dust into rivers. To apply Ezekiel's image of Jewish death to the Holocaust, then, is impossible. The new enemy, no mere Haman, not only succeeded where Haman failed, for he murdered the Jewish people. He murdered also Ezekiel's image of Jewish death.[30]

Taking note of Fackenheim's reference to the prophet Ezekiel, we realize that sacred texts often address the sanctification of death; as God breathes life into Adam, for instance, so does He claim life in the kiss that He places on the mouth of Moses, the mouth that utters His Holy Word. How is a Jew, then, removed from life? By removing him from the kiss of the Divine that is death. And he is removed from death when he is removed from the signifier and sanctifier of life that is his grave. For God not only kisses Moses, but also lays him in his grave. Thus, usurping God, the Nazis are literally grave robbers: they rob the Jews of their graves. That is why the Hungarian survivor Dr. Miklós Nyiszli describes Auschwitz as a "cemetery of millions, a cemetery without a single grave."[31] It is a cemetery in which the bones of Ezekiel have been ground to dust, in which death itself lies dead and buried beneath the ashes of the dead.

In the ghetto diaries, then, we encounter the chronicle of a calculated onslaught against death that undermines all significance in life. But what exactly does this chronicle contain? First of all, the diarists note that for the Nazis, to whom the Jews are not human beings at all, the Jewish dead are not only objects of contempt, but also sources of curiosity and amusement. In this regard, Michael Zylberberg reports from the Warsaw ghetto that the Germans "gleefully photographed the dead and the accompanying relatives, and even went as far as taking snapshots of the corpses as they were laid out in the mortuary. The Nazis were particularly active in this respect on Sundays, when they would visit the cemeteries with their girlfriends. This, rather than the cinema, was a place of amusement for them."[32] And so the Sunday routine for many Nazis is church, the café, and then the mortuary, where they spend their day of rest admiring the results of their week of labor. Of course, when a mortuary becomes a place of amusement, it is no longer a mortuary, and the dead are no longer the dead. To be sure, once the Jew is robbed of his status as person and is reduced to an object, he cannot die—because he is not alive in any meaningful sense. In their desecration of the dead and their murder of death, however, the Nazis go far beyond such amusements.

Turning to Chaim Kaplan's diary from the Warsaw ghetto, we recognize the stages by which the termination—or the extermination—of death unfolds. On August 6, 1940, for example, he writes, "Every great man or leader of his people who passes on in these evil times is carried to his grave alone, with his death and burial unknown to anyone."[33] The great men and leaders to whom Kaplan refers are those who engendered life in their communities; that is what made them great. What distinguishes these times as evil is precisely the absence of any recognition of the life that these dead fostered. The absence of such recognition belongs to the erasure of life's sanctity, so that the dead, too, lose their sanctity. Hence, says Kaplan on October 9, 1941, "the dead have lost their traditional importance and sanctity. The sanctity of the cemetery is also being profaned; it has been turned into a marketplace." Finally, a month later, he notes, "Henceforward people accompanying their dead for burial will be denied permission to enter the cemetery grounds. They will be permitted to come only as far as the gate and then strangers will accompany the departed to their graves."[34] No stones are to be laid on the gravestones, no measures to be taken against the loss of memory.

Just as the murder of death is linked to the assault on God, so too is it tied to the destruction of the family in this divorce of the family from the dead. Bodies are desecrated as they are torn from the hands of loved ones and turned over to strangers who have lost their human image. Denied entry into the cemetery, the family members are denied their status as family—as mothers and fathers, as sons and daughters, and ultimately as Jews. Because mourning is a form of prayer in the Jewish tradition but prayer is forbidden, the Nazis allow no Jewish mourners. So great is the mitzvah of accompanying the dead to burial, the Talmud tells us that even "the study of Torah may be suspended for escorting a dead body to the burying place" (*Megillah* 29a; also *Ketuvot* 17a). Denied the performance of this mitzvah for the dead, the Jews are denied the mitzvah of choosing life: a Jew cut off from the *mitzvot* pertaining to death is a Jew cut off from life. And so the mitzvah that the diarist performs in bearing witness to this horror is all the more pressing: the diarist becomes the only remaining mourner to accompany the dead to the graves that they are denied. Hence, his or her diary becomes a form of prayer.

Such are the implications of the notation that Czerniakow makes in his diary about a Jew who committed suicide. "The body of a stoker who hanged himself three days ago," he writes, "is still in the boiler room at Jagiellonska Street. He cannot be buried since the workers in the funeral home cannot obtain the passes. To make things more difficult they have forbidden burials at the Praga cemetery."[35] Here death is slain by refusing the living the means of burying the dead and thereby observing the passage of those who in life had borne the image of the Holy One. This point becomes all the more clear when in Czerniakow's diary we read, "Continuous complaints that there is nothing to bury the dead in. They have to be left naked in holes dug in the ground. There isn't even any paper which could be used as a substitute for linen shrouds."[36] Very often the linen burial shroud for a man is the tallith or the *kittel* that he wore in prayer, so once again we have the connection between the assault on prayer and ghetto death. Notice also that in this entry, instead of referring to a grave in the cemetery where a loved one is laid to rest, Czerniakow speaks of a hole in the ground where a corpse is left. But a grave is not a hole. A grave is a tract of ground made sacred through the ritualistic interment of a human body in the earth and the marking of the site with a memorial stone and flowers. When the grave takes on the status of a hole, this marking, too, loses its status. "I looked out my window," says Czerniakow on May 21, 1942, "and saw a hearse full of flowers which were being taken from the cemetery to the ballroom."[37] What transpires in the ballroom decked out with these flowers is neither the dance of life nor the dance of death. It is the dance of ghetto death.

Just as the flowers are among the fixtures that adorn this macabre revelry, so are the bodies of human beings among the fixtures that adorn the Warsaw ghetto. "Not having the money to bury their dead," Ringelblum relates on August 26, 1941, "the poor often throw the corpses into the street. Some houses shut their gates and refuse to permit tenants to leave until they have had the body buried. On the other hand, the police district chiefs, not wanting to bother with the formalities connected with corpses, simply throw the bodies from one streetcar to the next."[38] And so we have the image of the murdered riding around the ghetto alongside the yet to be murdered: the tram is turned into a hearse bound for every stop except the cemetery. Before long, then, not only will the Jews have no money to bury their dead; they will have no place to bury them. In an entry dated May 12, 1942, Ringelblum writes, "The Praga cemetery, which is more than 150 years old, is being leveled. The devils won't even let the dead rest. They've done the same sort of thing elsewhere in Poland and Germany."[39] Thus, the assault on death is taken to the dead themselves in a campaign to destroy Jewish cemeteries.

And the diarists are careful to record this campaign. Walking among the ruins of the Warsaw ghetto, for example, Zylberberg says, "The cemetery wall had been destroyed—it seemed to break down the division between the worlds of life and death. I walked back through the ruins of the ghetto. My footprints were clear in the snow, and they were the only ones."[40] The collapse of the division between life and death is indeed the mark of ghetto death. It signifies the onset of the indifferent "there is" to which Levinas refers, where the impossibility of death lies in the loss of a difference between life and death. And it demonstrates very graphically the point that when death loses its distinction, life loses its meaning.

In a similar vein, David Kahane comments on "the wanton, barbaric profanation of the Jewish cemetery" in Lvov. "The Nazis," he says, "were not content with tormenting the living Jews; they also vented their spleen upon the dead. A special labor battalion of Jewish workers from the camp was ordered to uproot and smash all the tombstones in the cemetery."[41] And in yet another example, Leon Wells writes from Stojanov, "The so-called *Friedhofskolonne* (cemetery brigade) works at the Jewish cemetery, bringing the gravestones that are used here for road construction."[42] Not only, then, do the Nazis undertake the task of desecrating the dead and removing death from Jewish life; they force Jewish hands to engage this task of destroying the graves where they once said the Kaddish over their mothers and fathers. Here an important connection between death and the death of death comes to light. All-encompassing death is coupled with the murder of death when death becomes so pervasive as to undermine the rites of prayer associated with the burial of the dead. For the Jews who have no cemeteries, the world is itself a cemetery—which is to say, it is not a world at all, for the world is a place in which the living define a realm where people are laid to rest and prayers are said at their graves. When the graves and the prayers over them are obliterated, the world and the life that constitutes it are also obliterated.

"During the last few days," Josef Katz says as he observes the rising tide of death at Jungfernhof, "we have had twenty to twenty-five deaths in our barracks every day. It is strange how quickly people die."[43] And, as we have seen, this tidal wave of death soon leads to the elimination of the rites and rituals of death. "In the beginning," says Katz, "when we did not have so many casualties yet, we had a *minyan* for everybody and recited the *Kaddish*. While the dead were carried from the barracks we chanted, *'El molei rachamim.'* But now that has stopped. There are too many deaths."[44] Or, more accurately, there are too many murders. Even the word *death* here becomes a euphemism that threatens to veil the truth of the Nazi project. "Natural death no longer exists," declares Emil Dorian,[45] a point that Yitzhak Katznelson makes more powerfully still in his *Vittel Diary* when he cries out, "Throughout the era of Hitler, the agent of the whole non-Jewish world, not a single Jew died, they were just murdered, murdered."[46] That is why the Nazis target the old and the ailing for murder, as they flood the earth with death: refusing simply to wait for them to expire, they are determined to see to it that no Jew will die, to see to it that Jewish death itself will be eliminated from the world. This erasure of Jewish death from existence is a key to the elimination of the significance of Jewish existence itself.

Concluding Reflection: The Opposite of Ghetto Death

What, then, do we learn about the singular significance of the Holocaust from the diarists' testimonies on death and ghetto death? Written along the edge of this annihilation, the pages of the ghetto diaries are akin to a grave from which the voices of the dead reverberate; to be sure, most of these diarists are themselves fated to lie in unmarked trenches or to ascend to the clouds on fading columns of smoke. Much of what goes into their diaries is like a prayer said for those who were robbed of prayers, a memorial inscription consecrated to take the place of the desecrated memorials that once marked the lives and the deaths of European Jews. Witnesses of the annihilation of Jewish death, the ghetto diarists face the overwhelming task of transforming ghetto death into a moment of witnessing. And so we return to the issue of martyrdom breached at the beginning of this essay.

In one of his most famous statements, Albert Camus opens *The Myth of Sisyphus* by saying, "There is but one truly serious philosophical problem, and that is suicide."[47] To this remark, Rabbi Abraham Joshua Heschel replies, "There is only one really serious problem: and that is martyrdom."[48] Why? Because suicide negates the sanctity of life, whereas martyrdom affirms it. "In martyrdom," Leo Baeck asserts, "death is no longer a mere end of life, a mere fate. It becomes a deed of freedom and of love for God,"[49] and, we may add, of love for humanity. For martyrdom is "an ethical affirmation of the soul," as Baeck states it,[50] and ethical affirmation entails both the relation to God and the relation to humanity. In the Sanctification of the Name, the Jew's conduct of his or her life carries him or her even unto death, to the point where life and death intersect in the testimony of martyrdom. "In martyrdom," André Neher maintains, "human history receives a meaning. Martyrdom is the negation of the absurd. Everything receives a meaning through the ultimate testimony of the man who accepts that meaning to the very limit. Everything is oriented in relation to that testimony. Everything becomes *sanctified* through it."[51] Therefore, every Holocaust diarist, no matter how inarticulate, offers up his or her testimony to the sanctity of human life. Thus, he or she becomes a messenger who is a martyr to Jewish martyrdom. And Jewish martyrdom is precisely the opposite of ghetto death.

But that is just where the difficulty arises: obliterating the signs of sanctity surrounding both Jewish life and Jewish death, the Nazis undertake an assault on Jewish martyrdom itself. "In making the teaching of the Jewish book a capital crime," Fackenheim explains, "Hadrian had created the possibility of Jewish martyrdom for Jewish believers. In making Jewish existence a capital crime, Hitler murdered Jewish martyrdom itself."[52] Confronted with the erasure of every visible sign of Jewish existence, both in life and in death, the ghetto diarist confronts the task of reestablishing martyrdom in Jewish life and death through an affirmation of the invisible. What underlies the ghetto diary, then, is a desire for the invisible—or for the Invisible One, a metaphysical desire for the metaphysical—that arises precisely where, by all that meets the eye, it should not arise. It is the desire that Levinas invokes when he says, "The very dimension of height is opened up by metaphysical Desire. That this height is no longer the heavens but the Invisible is the very elevation of height and its nobility. To die for the invisible—that is metaphysics."[53] And that is martyrdom.

Dying for the invisible—dying in the midst of a living that, from every visible indication, should not be there—is what characterizes the Holocaust diarists' affirmation of life in the midst of this assault on death. That is how they restore Jewish death to its proper, sacred ground. And that is how they cling to life.

12. Attitudes Toward Death During the Holocaust

Writings from the Ghettos

DEIRDRE BURKE

General Attitudes Toward Death

John Hick's *Death and Eternal Life* explores changing attitudes toward death brought about by the experiences people had of death in the late twentieth century. He raises a number of questions that seem current in relation to this study on attitudes regarding death during the Holocaust. First, he states: "We naturally grieve much more for a death that is unexpected than for one that is to be anticipated in the ordinary course of nature."[1] Did Jews during the Holocaust develop such a "philosophical attitude" toward death, which made death easier to accept? This essay explores attitudes concerning death and suffering from Jewish sources during the Holocaust to ascertain whether this was the case. Second, Hick illustrates the "cultural taboos" that have built up around death and claims that institutionalization results in death being "averted and concealed." Was there ever a more vivid example of the institutionalization of death than in the death factory Auschwitz? This institutionalization led to constant daily exposure to death, which forced people into contact with those who were dying and made them more aware of their own mortality. Did such cultural taboos continue to distance people from death during the Holocaust? In addition, Hick states that modern attitudes toward death are influenced by overexposure through the media, which has led to "boredom" when confronted by death: "For those 18,000 deaths on the screen simply trivialize death and make it unreal to the viewer."[2] Hick compares such "unreal" death to the "real corpses" of those slain in wars and disasters, but he points out: "This makes death visible; and yet only death in exceptional forms, for this is not the end which the ordinary person may expect."[3]

What happens if we draw together the overexposure to death on a daily basis and the realization that death in its "exceptional" form is to be the reality? Does such daily exposure lead to trivialization or an acceptance of death as part of daily life? Does the immediacy of death, owing to the threat of starvation, disease, or deportation to death camps, lead to a change in thinking—to an acceptance that one is likely to die?

Attitudes Concerning Death in the Warsaw and Łódź Ghettos

How Was Death Recorded?

There are a number of contemporary accounts of life in ghettos. They provide the perspective of the time because for some chroniclers the aim was to provide an objective historical record: "I deem it my duty to report them [details of the Łódź ghetto], if not in a finished, systematically researched work of history, then at least as source material for the objective historians who will come later," wrote Jakub Szulman.[4] This objective stance was not possible for all. The biblical allusions in the following extract suggest the impossibility of simply recording deaths. The act of writing about what happened took its toll on the writer. Jozef Zelkowicz wrote: "Son of man, go out into the streets. Soak in the unconscious terror of the newborn babies about to be slaughtered. Be strong. Keep your heart from breaking, so you'll be able to describe, carefully and clearly, what happened in the ghetto during the first days of September in the year one thousand, nine hundred and forty-two."[5]

Accounts of death in the Warsaw and Łódź ghettos range between these poles—the objective and the prophetic. First, there exist straightforward accounts, such as that of Władysław Bartoszewski, of what happened: "As a result of the conditions in the ghetto, hunger, and the typhoid epidemic, 1,700 men, women, and children died in the first two weeks of

May."[6] Bartoszewski showed the clear link between those still living and the dead. What the latter were, the former could easily become. Avraham Milgram attempts to indicate the process and show those not present what actually happened: "The numbers of starving were far beyond counting. Scores had already fallen from fatigue, while others dragged their feet, about to collapse at any moment. They were too weak to utter a word and expired in silence. People would cover the bodies with paper, and in the morning the wagons of the Burial Society would collect them like so much trash. It was indeed a city of the dead."[7]

This account reveals the struggle in attempting to provide a matter-of-fact account of the mechanics of dealing with dead bodies in the cemetery, showing that objective, nonemotional words are difficult to find to describe the experience. Oskar Rosenfeld's account of the cemetery struggles in the same way in the extract "Life is narrow":

> The corpses are carried in endless procession from the hall of the dead to various parts of the cemetery. The kind of activity that goes on here resembles that at the market. Every day there are a dozen interments, all at the same time. . . . The body rests between two wooden planks and is wrapped in shreds of old paper. Biers are likewise nonexistent. Like dead fish, the bodies are carried in a net attached to two poles (slats), which is emptied of the dead at the graveside. Here and there sobbing and lamenting. Again and again the tin carts carrying the dead arrive at the hall, and again and again they are carried out in a net. The earth fills with the dead. These are the people condemned to the ghetto of Łódź, that is, to a quick death. The starved, the frozen, the condemned, and those who commit suicide. Like the sand at the sea, like the stars in the heavens—this is how numerous the dying are.[8]

We note the attempt to present what had become an everyday occurrence in as objective a way as possible, but through this veneer we can identify the second feature of such accounts, the prophetic. In such accounts, biblical images and phrases escape, as do contemporary images of death.

Another extract indicates a struggle to provide a reverse indication of the impact that the dead can have on the living, as the living attempt to "adapt to circumstances." The words used to comment on the impact of death suggest that the daily toil of coping with death leads to the death of emotion and ultimately to the death of human values and the breakdown of society. Rosenfeld recorded in his notebook: "Where is X? Dead. Where is Y? Dead.—Dead. Buried. No longer any feelings. Robbers next to the dead begging: soup bowl, bread, shoes, pocket knife—especially when there are no surviving relatives."[9]

These accounts present a view of the struggles to record what was happening in the everyday language of the community, even if this meant the inclusion of some biblical images. In his "Sketches," Oskar Singer takes us beyond description in his analysis of "Litzmannstadt death" ("Litzmannstadt" was the German name for Łódź):

> Litzmannstadt Death has been unknown in Europe. Perhaps our early ancestors experienced similar events, but human beings have not known death like this. In this very brief span of time, life has veered off its usual course, and death has changed its face. This has taken place with a speed not even the wildest imagination could have predicted. Life has become strange, and death, therefore, has also. The surviving world will have only the barest idea of what it was like here. Repeatedly, one hears the muted question: Will there be anyone able to tell the world how we lived and died here? . . . We can no longer die as other people do. We no longer have the possibility of a noble end. Litzmannstadt Death is an alien, ugly death.[10]

The description of death suggests that the "times" had changed, that normal expectations no longer applied. Singer's analogy is that normal death is something to be welcomed—something noble—whereas the death faced in the ghetto was something quite different—alien and ugly.

Evidence of Death Rituals in the Łódź Ghetto

Kaddish

Many challenges to religious belief arose in the situation facing Jews in the ghettos. For many Jews, however, religious beliefs and practices were the main source of inspiration and support. From the works of the chroniclers, it is possible to see the prevalence of religious rituals in dealing with death during the Holocaust.

Jerakhmil Bryman recorded how prayer continued in the Łódź ghetto despite the atmosphere of panic and anxiety. The primary function of the prayer gatherings was congregational prayer, which required a minyan (a quorum of ten men). Such gatherings met for the purpose of Kaddish, the memorial prayer for the dead. Bryman stated: "Kaddish is the most important prayer today."[11] His account suggests that people had lost the impetus for communal prayer for themselves or feared for their safety in such gatherings. However, prayers for the dead were different, and his account shows the ways in which such prayers were maintained. First, minyamin were established at the mourners' homes for the first year, and notices were posted to show whom to contact if one needed a minyan. Second, communal minyamin would say Kaddish for those who died without surviving relatives, using set formulas, to enable congregations to remember those who died or were deported: " 'In memory of ____________, son of ____________, who was taken from the ghetto on ____________. May G_d have mercy upon him wherever he may be.' "[12] The spiritual needs of all residents of the ghettos were met; deportees into the ghetto from other countries required translations of the Kaddish prayer in their own languages, which were sold in the Łódź ghetto. The whole community involved themselves in this important religious ritual of saying Kaddish: "Many children, lined up in rows, come from their schools to say Kaddish."[13]

Scholarly debates on rituals often range between the stress on mechanics and the meanings they embody. In the example of the Kaddish prayer, it is possible to suggest retention for both reasons. The opportunity to act according to tradition in undertaking ritual actions provided a measure of solace and security in following tried and tested means. The use of ritual actions that had stood the test of time linked the living people to their ancestors, many of whom had also faced suffering and death by persecution. Community observance of banned rituals can also be seen as a form of spiritual resistance, which allowed the ghetto inhabitants to maintain Jewish beliefs and identity in the very face of death. It was not possible to complete ritual obligations alone, thus ensuring that at times of mourning individuals had the support of a minyan. Ellen Levine argues that rituals for the bereaved are important in helping them to face the reality of death and to acknowledge their own grief: "These customs and rituals enable the bereaved to grieve, to recover emotionally, to continue their lives, [to] pay respect to the dead and to honour the dead by perpetuating their memory."[14] This focus on the mourner also indicates that following ritual actions might have added an element of normality to the situation and assisted in the return to daily living.

Other Rituals

The ritual of prayer is present in an anonymous "father's lament" for his five-year-old daughter, who was deported. He expresses anguish over his own complicity, for he obeyed the order to bring children for deportation, which he interprets as killing her. His plea turns to God, whom he questions to find out why this tragedy has happened. Then the father concludes with the traditional Yizkor prayer:

> Merciful God in Heaven, grant perfect repose to the soul of my daughter Miriam, who was slaughtered in the deportation of September 8, 1942, and who has passed to her eternal resting place. May she be under thy divine wings among the holy and pure who shine as brightly as the sky. May her place of rest be in paradise. O Merciful One, keep her soul forever alive under Thy protective wings. As the Lord is her heritage, may she rest in peace, and let us say Amen.[15]

The ritual of prayer provides a means of communication and relates to traditional religious beliefs about the nature of God and the efficacy of prayer—beliefs that absolve the father from his guilt and preserve the hope of a future and better existence for his daughter.

Further evidence on the importance of ritual action in giving people something specific to do at times of utmost trauma is provided in Jozef Zelkowicz's sketches: "God Did Not Abandon Us" is an account of a family ravaged by death, which is presented from the perspective of the mother and her daughter-in-law, the only surviving members of the family. This account provides an insight into the centrality of ritual action, which shows that any costs incurred in such obligations were of secondary concern. The focus of the account is the potatoes the women were weighing: "God must know very well how I suffer over my children being buried in others' shrouds. So He sent me these potatoes. Now I am going to sell them and give the money back to the house committee. They can use the money for a good purpose. Lots of people die nowadays in the ghetto."[16] The report contains the mother's words, which indicate her overriding concern to provide for her family at the time of death. Her recollection of the first death to hit the family demonstrates this concern: "The oldest son, the one who was married, was the first to die. He passed away on the Saturday before last Passover. 'He was too gentle to endure this rotten life. His heart gave up . . .' He at least had a decent burial: a new shroud and a coffin made of good boards."[17] The account deals in a matter-of-fact way with death, and her recollection of his loss is set alongside her ability to meet the ritual obligations. Her husband's death is not as traumatic as the deaths of her two other sons because she is able to provide a shroud for him. But she is forced to ask others to help with the rituals for her sons: " 'It vexed my mind that I could not afford to bury my two sons as decently as the others, in their own shrouds.' "[18] In this account, the ritual actions undertaken seem to invest a life, which is in a spiral of descent, with a meaning it would otherwise lack. The heart may have been torn out of the women's lives, but their tradition required them to undertake certain actions, which enabled them to pay their own respects to their loved ones. They may have undertaken this activity in a mechanical way, but it ensured movement at a time when events may have paralyzed the mourners.

Yaffa Eliach, in *Hasidic Tales of the Holocaust,* draws on survivor testimony to recount the last request made by a Jewish woman for the ritual bath to be reopened for their use before death. The conversation that followed the granting of this request reveals the importance of ritual in maintaining faith in the face of Nazi propaganda, which depicted the Jews as a "filthy race": " 'Cleanliness and purity of body and mind are part of our tradition and way of life. God has brought our pure souls into this world in the pure homes of our parents, and we wish to return in purity to our Father in Heaven.' "[19] Such accounts present the power of the tradition in upholding traditional beliefs and practices—a power that invested individuals with the responsibility to maintain their Jewish identity and humanity in the face of the perpetrator.

These matter-of-fact accounts show how religious practices were retained in relation to both the deceased and the mourners. The accounts are perhaps outstanding for the lack of emotion, the unquestioning acceptance of death, and the continuation of religious practices and beliefs in spite of, or because of, what was happening. Religion in this instance does truly seem to be the "sigh of the oppressed," a way of accepting what is happening. Louis Jacobs stresses the psychological benefit to the bereaved through the observance of ritual actions: "Where grief is shared and where it is not kept bottled up but given expression in concrete forms, the burden becomes a little lighter and utter despair is overcome."[20]

But many of the questions we may want to ask as scholars of religion are absent from such accounts. How could people continue to believe in a God whom they believed controlled history and required such sacrifices? There were relatively very few suicides in the ghettos and camps. Chaim A. Kaplan, a chronicler in the Warsaw ghetto, recorded his admiration for "this will to live" and stated that it was the "outward manifestation" of a hidden power: "It is a wondrous, superlative power with which only the most established communities among our people have been blessed."[21] Most "blessed" among the "blessed" are the Hasidic Jews, and it is to the thinking of two communities we now turn to explore how the experiences for Jews crowded into Warsaw and Budapest challenged their beliefs about God.

Theological Responses to Events in Warsaw and Budapest

The final source of theological literature to be explored provides an insight into the world of the ultra-Orthodox Jews, who sought to understand every moment of their existence through the prism of faith. David Roskies found their literature of destruction to include the same components as the literature of earlier generations who sought to reconcile beliefs with a life of suffering.[22] They made use of the Bible and historical archetypes in questioning what was happening and in engaging in ritual action. They did not meekly accept what was happening but sought to understand events against the backdrop of five thousand years of history and key beliefs about God that had been revealed. From such views of history, they had at least three ways of understanding what was happening; first, they could see the Holocaust as another chapter in a long history of suffering, for it was continuous with the experience of history; second, they could view the suffering in the present as part of the birth pangs of the Messiah, as the culmination of the historical process; third, the challenge to belief posed by events could lead even a believer to reject belief in a God of history.

The work of Pesach Schindler on Hasidic teachings is invaluable, particularly in the translations and explorations of the writings of two rebbes: Rabbi Shapiro's *Esh Kodesh* (The holy fire) from the Warsaw ghetto and Rabbi Teichthal's *Em Habanim Semecha* (The mother of children is happy) from Budapest.[23] The writings of both rebbes show the impact of suffering and death upon their communities. Their sermons and other writings attempt to answer questions about the purpose of suffering within the divine plan. In both cases, the rebbes show that the Holocaust challenged their faith and required an exploration of beliefs in order to discern the divine purpose and respond to it.

Rabbi Kalunimus Kalmish Shapiro

Rabbi Kalunimus Kalmish Shapiro (the Piazesner rebbe), writing in the Warsaw ghetto between September 1939 and his deportation to death in Treblinka in July 1942, provides an example of a "quietistic" *galut*-oriented (exile-oriented) view. His theology established the belief that humans had to accept what was happening as God's will and taught that humans could do little to change events. A chronological survey of Shapiro's work reveals the way key ideas relate to specific events and changing understandings of those events. In September 1939, he explained the initial move to the ghetto and the deaths during the German occupation within the context of traditional theodicy. Shapiro saw events as divine punishment for sin, accepting that the deaths of his own son and daughter-in-law resulted from their own sins. The parable of the "abandoned" prince expresses the understanding of the current suffering as a test of faith, as a theological opportunity to get close to God. Like the prince, the Jews were temporarily in the dungeon, where they were better able to appreciate the life they used to lead. The Jews should have been hopeful that they, like the prince, would be rescued by their father. When the situation in the ghetto became worse with overcrowding, the parable of the prince that explained temporary suffering no longer adequately covered a more permanent situation. The realization that release from the dungeon was not likely now was understood in relation to the biblical motif of "sacrifice" as found in the binding of Isaac. The only difference was that Jews were being asked to go further than Abraham: they were being asked to carry out the sacrifice, which was understood as martyrdom, suffering with God for Kiddush Hashem (sanctification of God's name).

During late 1940 and early 1941, in the context of mass deportations from Warsaw to the death camp Treblinka, the next component of the "literature of destruction" came into play. Rabbi Shapiro protested to God that too much was expected from the people. He drew on themes from the midrash to express this protest—that God should not test them too much, or they, like Sarah, would be unable to survive. His prayer called upon God: "Listen to the voice of our cries and to the sighs of our hearts. See our sorrow and oppression, and rescue us from our great distress."[24]

By 1941–42, the willingness to sanctify God's name was taken further with another dimension, termed by Rabbi Nissenbaum as Kiddush Ha-Hayim, sanctification of life. In the situation in which the perpetrators sought to dehumanize the Jews, it was necessary, stated Rabbi Shapiro, to retain human dignity, to remember that they are princes, sons of God. There was severe criticism of those who despaired of life and were ungrateful for their existence. Rabbi Shapiro said:

> Suffering, however, may be a two-edged sword. For the Jew who cannot grasp its positive manifestations, suffering is a physically and spiritually depressing force. To such a person, suffering is partial death. . . . He is unable to find strength in the observance of Torah. Suffering triggers a vicious cycle which inhibits feelings of righteous inspiration and experi-

> ence. Thus suffering prevents man from exploiting the very resources which would make it tolerable.[25]

The resources of the tradition made it possible to sanctify life in the present and to maintain belief in God. Perhaps there was also an echo of the Kaddish prayer, which is recited by mourners and involves an exaltation of the divine in the face of death, showing that belief in God covers both "day," when things go well, and "night," when things do not seem to go according to plan. Pesach Schindler writes of the Hasidic belief in "serving God not only with love, enthusiasm, and joy, implied by the term 'by day,' but also with suffering implied by the term 'by night.' "[26] When Kiddush HaHayim was placed in this context, it empowered the victim to select the way of death. Meir Dvorzeski referred to this replacement as a "new option," for one could either go "to one's death degraded and dejected [or go] confronting [death] with an inner peace, nobility, upright stance, without lament and cringing to the enemy."[27] Rabbi Shapiro's teachings prepared his followers not merely to accept, but also to welcome death. If Kiddush HaHayim became impossible, Shapiro stated, he who is murdered in Kiddush Hashem does "not suffer at all. . . . Therefore, he feels nothing but pleasure."[28]

Rabbi Yissachar Shlomo Teichthal

Rabbi Yissachar Shlomo Teichthal was killed on a death march from Auschwitz in 1945; however, his writings from the period he spent in Budapest from January 1943 to December 1943 survived. The Jewish community in Hungary, although affected by restrictive legislation, did not face concentration into ghettos and deportation to death camps until the German occupation of Hungary in 1944. However, news of the "Final Solution" had reached Jews in Hungary by 1943. Teichthal's work is important, for it reveals the transition from a "quietistic" view to an "activistic" view, in which human action can help to redirect or change events. His transition was accompanied by a shift from an anti- to a pro-Zionist position, in which he took the ultra-Orthodox leaders to task for leading their communities astray by making peace with exile and by rejecting initiatives for self-redemption. He stated that it was necessary to return to *tikkun* (healing or mending) as a prerequisite for survival. The move from destruction to redemption can take place only with human participation within a unified community.

Rabbi Teichthal came to question traditional views. He had been an anti-Zionist before the war, referring to Zionists as "you who disturb God's will." But in the ghetto, his questions concerned the understanding of exile. He felt that the deaths of Jews in Europe had been owing to the teachings of rebbes who kept people in a false exile: "Who shall accept the responsibility for the innocent blood shed in our days . . . but the leaders who prevented Jews from participating with the builders [of Eretz Yisrael]."[29] Teichthal challenged the traditional view, held by some of his contemporaries, that extreme suffering could be the birth pangs of the Messiah (Hevle Mashiah). Rabbi Shapiro described the suffering as the "process that gives birth to the light of the Messiah."[30] Rabbi Teichthal questioned this view: "If only the suffering which has come upon us in recent years were indeed the Messiah pains, so that our righteous Messiah could come and redeem us from them."[31]

Rabbi Teichthal regarded the development of a Jewish state as essential to the process of redemption and regarded the secular Zionists as fellow workers. He believed that links with secular Jews, although "irregular and unexpected means," could unify the community and provide an escape from exile. Pesach Schindler summarizes this view of the Holocaust as the "nadir of this state of abnormality, which should force the Jew to turn his back, once and for all, on his Galut existence."[32]

Conclusions

Records of Death

This essay demonstrates that attempts to chronicle events of the Holocaust developed from of an objective mode into prophetic forms of expression. Such expression made it possible to link contemporary events to historical archetypes and thus to link a present that could not be understood to a past that was understood.

The Observance and Purpose of Rituals

There is clear evidence that many in the Łódź ghetto sought to maintain traditional death rituals. The level of ritual observance depended on a number of factors: how long communities could maintain traditional organizations such as the Chevra Kaddisha (Holy Brotherhood) and how long individuals had the means for full and correct observance—often this would seem to be a matter of financial resources. Also, the faith resources of the individual were crucial; many Jews lacked a traditional religious upbringing and were unable to draw upon beliefs and practices at this time. The final factor was an individual's or family's religious standpoint: clearly for secular or socialist Jews or both, such rituals would have been inappropriate.

The evidence from the chronicles shows that death rituals had a double importance to the community—in retaining a semblance of order, as the Chevra Kaddisha continued to function, and in providing communal support to individuals at the time of bereavement and throughout the mourning period of a year (the saying of Kaddish). Norman Lamm says: "Thus, a semblance of normality was restored to the inmates of the vicious madhouses, as the norms of the Halakhah provided a minimal psychic structure of human dignity and morale. This was infinitely more than 'foxhole faith' and empty consolation."[33]

Rituals unquestionably helped to bring meaning to life, enabling individuals and communities to continue in age-old traditions at this time of crisis. Studies on the purpose of rituals stress their importance, stating that they enable individuals to "feel" their way into handling a situation. Robert Bocock states, "Ritual action which can articulate for people ways of finding resolutions to the problem of meaning and evil, which may be permanent, long-term or temporary solutions, is a highly valuable possession of human cultures."[34]

Theological Responses to Events

Zygmunt Bauman includes belief in God as one of the survival policies used "to channel the horror of death."[35] Many religious Jews clearly interpreted what was happening to them as part of the divine plan for humanity; this interpretation meant that they did not fear death. Rabbi Haim Rabinowitz said to his followers during the long journey to the death camp: "Fellow Jews, do not fear death. To die for *Kiddush Hashem* is a great privilege."[36] Schindler shows how other practices, such as purification and confession, were evident to ensure that Kiddush Hashem would be effective. Prior to death in Treblinka, Rabbi Mendele Alter, brother of the Gerer rebbe, asked for water, which he used for purification. Schindler reports on this incident: "The privilege of *Kiddush Hashem* enabled the Hasid to anticipate his tragic fate with some comfort and dignity . . . [and] to transcend the uneven battle of material forces."[37] The work of the two rebbes shows how the Holocaust challenged faith and how the tradition itself and the existing "literature of destruction" offered ways to interpret events. The traditional understanding of such literature allowed questioning and debate, which enabled communities to move between the "quietistic" and "activistic" poles: "In addition to providing the Hasid with a general frame of faith and some guidelines for response to radical crisis, the research suggested that traditional Hasidic thought offered various 'pegs' upon which the Hasid might hang interpretations of the unfolding horror."[38]

Schindler's research into Hasidic responses during the Holocaust demonstrates the importance of theological and social frameworks. Hasidic leaders drew on concepts within their faith to interpret events and then to utilize their leadership roles within the community to disseminate their teachings. Thus, in the face of intense suffering and almost certain death, many Hasidic Jews utilized their tradition as a type of shock absorber.

13. Art and Imagery of the Ghetto—During and After the Holocaust

STEPHEN C. FEINSTEIN

In a remarkable way, amid the pessimism and desperation associated with the system of ghettos established by the German occupation of eastern Europe during the Holocaust, the role of artists, art as a memoir, and design issues stand out in a unique way. The existence of such civilization-affirming elements does not make for any revisionism of the meaning of ghettos such as Theresienstadt or Łódź, but it does establish the concept that art can be created even in conditions of extreme brutality. This essay surveys aspects of the artistic creativity in several ghettos and the art that was later inspired by those ghettos. The level of artistic creativity is evaluated according to subject matter and place.

Artistic Design and the Ghetto from the Nazi Perspective

There was a paradoxical "official" use of art and design in several of the ghettos, which may be considered atypical. In both Łódź and Theresienstadt, the camp officials issued both special currencies and postage stamps for the Jewish population. The existence of such items reflects perhaps less on art than on design principles, but is important to verify the level of segregation of the Jews. Special currencies, well designed from an artistic point of view, were printed in Theresienstadt, Łódź, Cremona, Westerbork, and a host of other camps. Joel Forman has noted that the special numismatic program at these camps had a threefold purpose: creating a special currency to make use of the currency, and hence escape, difficult on the outside; using inmates' property to maintain the camp by confiscating that property and issuing script; and creating what he correctly observes as "a propaganda device, forcing humiliation and isolation on the internees who had no access to 'real money,' and thereby isolating them from a financial relationship to the outside world."[1] There were some ironies in the design and printing of camp currency. Some had no design at all, just numerical notations at first, indicating the camp and value. Oranienburg was apparently the first camp to introduce some design by artists. Horst-Willi Lippert, prisoner entry number 33 in the camp registry, designed the camp currency. The fifty-pfennig note depicted guards on either side, the Nazi eagle and swastika, and an image of barbed wire running through the center. The inscription read *"Lagergeld des konzentrationslagers Oranienburg"* and was printed in black on white. The five-mark note showed a watchtower, and the one-mark note depicted a man performing manual labor. The design assigned to an inmate artist allowed him to subvert the system in an interesting way, and Lippert succeeded. Forman notes, "In the word 'Konzentrationslager,' he scratched away the top of the letter 'g' and, as the letter opened, the word changed to read 'Konzentrationslayer.' "[2] The money in Oranienburg was employed by factories using slave labor: A. Hausmann Helldunkelmuster Company, the Ernst Heinkel (Ernst Heinkel Aktiengesellschaft Company Werk, Oranienburg Plant). The camp currency was shown to the Red Cross to provide the illusion that workers were not slaves, and the merit of such arguments has cynically been maintained in some recent restitution cases.[3]

In the ghettos, there appears to have been an absence of uniform rules for the printing of currency. However, the two main specimens most available now, from Łódź and Theresienstadt, indicate a fine sense of graphic design and artistic thought in the design of the currency. The Warsaw ghetto did not issue currency as a general feature of administration, although in the spring of 1941 "a script was issued to relieve a critical shortage of small change that occurred when ghetto residents purchased postage stamps." Forman notes:

> These notes were illegal and were crudely printed from hand-cut linoleum or woodplates. The design graphically showed the SS guarding

> Jews imprisoned behind barbed wire. The money was valid only inside the Warsaw ghetto and had no value outside its walls. There was only one issue of this money; i.e., the date and denominations never changed regardless of the actual printing date of the money. It is important to remember that each camp or ghetto currency was unique in design and format.[4]

The best-known example of ghetto money and artistically the best designed is from Theresienstadt. The Prague portrait artist Peter Kien, who arrived in the ghetto in December 1941 and eventually died at Auschwitz, designed this currency. Forman's interesting work on numismatics describes how this money was used:

> On 21 April 1943, the so-called Bank of Jewish Autonomy (located in the former Terezin town hall) received 53 million Theresienstadt crowns (Kronen). The first distribution of this money took place on 12 May 1943. Since there was nothing to purchase, the monetary system resulted in artificial bookkeeping, whereby inmates kept worthless passbooks and accounts for payrolls, goods, and imaginary salaries and savings. The only place where the money was actually used or "spent" was the camp library, where the loan of each book required a deposit of 50 Kronen. By 1944, the Theresienstadt library bank account contained 120,000 Kronen on deposit.[5]

From an artistic point of view, the Theresienstadt notes were distinctive. On the left front of each denomination, inscribed in an oval, was an engraved portrait of Moses holding the Ten Commandments in Hebrew. Forman has noted some of the politics of having the design conform to Nazi artistic aesthetics:

> When Kien initially submitted his designs to Reinhard Heydrich, they were rejected. Because Heydrich objected to the fact that Moses looked too Aryan, the notes were modified to show Moses with more strongly stereotyped Semitic features; the design had to conform to the Nazi vision of Jewish appearance. The final design shows Moses with a long hooked nose and curly hair. Heydrich also demanded that the hand of Moses cover the commandment that stated "Thou shalt not kill."[6]

Peter Kien's Theresienstadt ghetto currency. Lagergeld was issued at a number of ghettos and concentration camps. The ghetto money from Theresienstadt was designed by artist Peter Kien, with an image of Moses holding the Ten Commandments, but with the Sixth Commandment—about murder—obscured. For other examples of numismatic items from camps and ghettos, see http://www.chgs.umn.edu/Histories__Narratives_Documen/Philatelic_Nazi_Philatelic_1_/philatelic_nazi_philatelic_1_.html. Caption courtesy of Stephen Feinstein.

On the far right of the note's face was a Star of David, designed as two intersecting triangles, maintaining, in a certain way, the uniformity of the use of triangles for identification of inmates (the Buchenwald prisoners' chart has thirty-two variations of the triangle in colors). The denomination for each note is listed, for example, "Quitttung uber Zwanzig Kronon," with a warning against counterfeiting at the bottom, and a minutely designed background in color (each note a different size and color) that provides an illusionary image of multiple Stars of David. The reverse side of the notes bears the signature of Jacob Edelstein, *"Der Alteste der Juden,"* and the date of issue, January 1, 1943.

The city of Łódź was renamed Litzmannstadt on April 11, 1940, in honor of World War I German general Karl Litzmann. For the Jews, the Litzmannstadt ghetto became the second largest after Warsaw and was captured on film by Fritz Hippler for the production of *Ewige der Jude,* sometimes dubbed the "most anti-Semitic film ever made." Because Jews were not allowed to use German currency, Jewish money was issued on May 15, 1940, as indicated on the front of the currency. Unlike the Theresienstadt currency, Moses did not appear on the money in Litzmannstadt. Only a small and circular Star of David appeared on the front with the denomination on a field of very distinctive Stars of David woven together. Mordechai Chaim Rumkowski's signature appeared at the bottom right as *"Der Alteste der Juden in Litzmannstadt."* The reverse side included another Star of David that varied in size according to denomination and a seven-branched menorah, the eternal religious symbol of the Jews, at the bottom left. This side was also set against a field of woven Stars of David, which metaphorically has the appearance of a barbed-wire fence. Litzmannstadt was the only ghetto to issue coins, which presented a Star of David on one side with the denomination, the issuing authority repeated in a circular fashion around the coin on the reverse: *"Der Alteste der Juden in Litzmannstadt."* The coins, made of aluminum or a magnesium-aluminum alloy, were minted in denominations of ten-pfennig, and five-, ten-, and twenty-mark coins.

Postage stamps were also issued in two ghettos. They, too, are interesting from an artistic as well as bureaucratic point of view. In Theresienstadt, parcel admission stamps were initiated in 1943 and intended for parcels from Czechoslovakia to the camp. The stamps portrayed the lyrical landscape of Bohemia, perhaps a scene visible from the ghetto itself. They were, however, not used in a typical fashion. If an inmate wished to receive parcels of food and clothing, he could fill out a request every two months. These requests would be forwarded to the Jewish Council in Prague. After processing the requests, the council would send a notice to the proposed sender of the parcel, if living in Prague, to come to the office and pick up the stamp. If the proposed sender were outside of Prague, the stamp would be attached to the notice. The stamp then had to be attached to the parcel itself. When the parcel arrived, it was inspected, and the wrapping paper to which the stamp was affixed was either destroyed or removed, but rarely was the stamp kept. The same stamps were also used in a souvenir sheet format, which were given to representatives of the International Red Cross during their infamous inspections of the camp.[7]

In the Litzmannstadt ghetto, post offices were established, and the first stamps were issued on March 9, 1944. However, this project appears not to have gotten off the ground. Soon after printing, the German military authority renounced the idea of postal autonomy, and the existing stamps, bearing the likeness of Mordechai Chaim Rumkowski on the left side of three denominations, were confiscated. The story of both the ghetto currencies and the postal issue suggests that a "motif" of art was present in the prisoners' lives, certainly used in an untypical way for subversive purposes. Ultimately, the design question in the currency and postage stamps can be related to other questions of design in ghettos, in particular the Theresienstadt and Kovno ghettos.

Art Schools in the Ghettos

It would probably be safe to say that some level of artistic representation existed in all ghettos. However, the greatest production of art came from Theresienstadt, as that camp became a particular enclave for artists and intellectuals. The artistic tradition of this camp has been subject to the greatest level of archival investigation, analysis, and exhibition, for much, but hardly all, of the works produced there by artists survived. Nevertheless, a typology of what was produced, representing the "unofficial" side of artistic endeavors, may serve to put all that is known, at least currently, into a sensible order.

Friedl Dicker-Brandeis and the Art School

One of the most talented artists who was deported to Theresienstadt, and who ultimately died at Auschwitz, was Friedl Dicker-Brandeis. Friedl Dicker was born in 1898 and studied in Vienna with Johannes Itten as a private student and then with him again at the Bauhaus course in Weimar. She lived principally in Vienna from 1924 to 1934, with occasional stays in Berlin, and left for Prague in 1934 after being arrested for Communist activities. She became an established figure in the arts, known for her work in composition, theater design, and sculpture. Dicker became a Czechoslovak citizen in 1936 after marrying Pavel Brandeis, continued working on art projects, and possessed an exceptional interest in developing the artistic sensibilities of children. Her last major public exhibition was at the Royal Arcade Gallery in London during 1940, at a time when Dicker-Brandeis and her husband had moved to the town of Hronov, before being deported from there to Theresienstadt on December 16, 1942.

At Theresienstadt, Dicker-Brandeis established several art schools for girls and at the children's home in the ghetto. It is estimated that six hundred children received art lessons while in the camp. Many were in the age range of ten to twelve when they began their studies in the ghetto. The surviving art works of sixty of these children, only four of whom survived the Holocaust, were exhibited at Yad Vashem, the Israeli Martyrs' and Heroes' Remembrance Authority, in 1990. More than five thousand children's drawings survived. Most of the child artists perished at Auschwitz. The teaching of handicrafts and music was permitted for children in the ghetto. Dicker-Brandeis implemented a teaching plan derived from her earlier association with Itten. It involved free and creative drawing (including the use of fantasy), strengthening observational techniques, avoidance of a rigid curriculum that destroys the artistic personality, and repetition of "rhythmic exercise" to increase suppleness of the hand and to unite the children in "a common purpose."[8]

The common purpose of the art school under Dicker-Brandeis was to establish a sense of normalcy under horrific conditions. Dicker-Brandeis introduced what might be called a rigid method to keep students focused on artistic matters and away from the chaos of the camp. Because many of these works survived, we have a sense of the methodology as well as the results. The artist developed a practice on color field exercises, where students used watercolors (many of the supplies were brought by Dicker-Brandeis herself when she was deported) to test the strength and effect of color mixing. Often, they composed abstract works or landscapes, but each product had to contain an example, set to the side, of the colors used in the work. Thus, examples of this method can be seen in the surviving paintings of Jozef Novak, Jindrich Seiner, Hana Fischerova, Hana Lustigova, Helena Weisova-Hoskova, and others.[9]

Dicker-Brandeis also insisted on rhythmical exercises, which involved repetition of specific patterns and even copying illustrations of standard master paintings. For example, one series of reproductions done by her class involves variations on Jan Vermeer's painting *The Glass of Wine,* and another reproduced Lucas Cranac's *Portrait of a Young Lady.* Dicker-Brandeis later taught principles relating to collage techniques. Erna Furman, one of the child artists who survived, spoke of this period and method:

> We did a lot of "freeing up" exercises, drawing circles and squiggles and letting our hands go, as well as using scissors freely. But what I enjoyed most was drawing special things: portraits (I still have a number of portraits of "my" children), self-portraits, some life-drawing, lots of still-life sketches (I shall never forget the comer with the stove, chair and shelf where Friedl helped me figure out the underlying pattern), and there was a little yard with a few trees of which I made a water colour.[10]

The children's art at Theresienstadt was more than simple class time. Dicker-Brandeis attempted to create an all-around sophisticated environment. An exhibition was arranged in the home for boys, L-417 (the block address because the camp authority had renumbered all the streets in the ghetto). Dicker-Brandeis on this occasion gave a lecture on the aesthetics of children's drawings, a specific analysis of the works, as if in a "real" and competitive artistic school, and some discussion of the "therapeutic importance" of the artistic process for children in such circumstances.[11]

Art exhibits in ghettos may seem strange, but they were apparently conducted repeatedly. Scholars have yet to accomplish a full compendium of such events. But we know, for example, that a document survives from the art jury committee in the Vilna ghetto from March 16, 1943, that indicates approval for exhibiting *Portrait of a Man* plus three Vilna landscapes and six water colors by Rokhl Sutzkever; an amalgam of works in clay, papier-mâché, and oil paint by Yudl Nut; seven paintings of the Vilna ghetto by Yankev Sher; twelve caricatures by N. Drezin; twenty-seven sketches by S. Bak (nine years old); and two sketches by S. Walmark, age fourteen.[12]

Samuel Bak survived and has become one of the most significant painters of Holocaust themes, both surrealist and midrashic. Many of his current paintings contain vignettes and the motif of the ghetto as a central aspect, framed within the larger theme "Landscapes of Jewish History." What is most interesting about the Vilna ghetto exhibition, however, is the high level of organization. The participants for the exhibition's jury were "F. Rom, N. Oklienicke and N. Borowski in the presence of the Chief of the Cultural Division, G. Jaszunski."[13]

Art in the Kovno Ghetto

The Kovno ghetto in Lithuania also had a cultural and artistic life. The Altestenrat, the Jewish Council, actually commissioned artists to draw and paint aspects of daily life in the ghetto. Although there was no art school in Kovno for the Jews, Peter Gadiel, an established German-born graphic artist who ended up in the ghetto after fleeing the Germans, established a paint and design workshop there. The workshop employed fine artists, graphic designers, and others with artistic and design sense. This workshop produced high-level aesthetics in the design of documents, ghetto workshop logos, calendars, and even a logo for the Altestenrat: a Star of David formed by two triangles, one black and one white, surrounded by a *G* that intersected the star, symbolizing "ghetto." This type of design work may be compared to the "official" designs for currency and postage stamps in Theresienstadt and Litzmannstadt. In Theresienstadt, Peter Loewenstein developed a similar type of design in his posters and production charts used in the ghetto.[14]

The most famous visual record of the Kovno ghetto was collected by Avraham Tory into a secret archive known as Slobodka Ghetto 1942. It included detailed architectural drawings of the Kovno ghetto and each of its reductions, rendered by Gadiel, plus compilations of German laws prefaced by artistic collages and drawings, and well-designed graphics depicting various numbers and methods of death in the ghetto. Tory is of absolute importance in understanding events in the Kovno ghetto and the importance of visual representation. In his diary entry of July 25, 1943, he wrote: "We are obligated first of all to remember and note events, people and forms, images and moments, in words and in writing, in clay and in painting, in every place and in every manner that one can."[15]

Art as Witness to Atrocity

As Theresienstadt possessed a *Zeichenstube* (technical drawing office), a number of artists who came to the camp were assigned there to do official work. The best-known artists from this group were Leo Haas, Bedrich Fritta, Karel Fleischmann, Otto Ungar, and Felix Bloch. Haas became head of the *Zeichenstube.* The unofficial paintings of this group, which portrayed the realities of camp life, were created in dark studios. Haas described this process of witnessing to Mary Constanza:

> We were so oppressed by the horrible surrounding that we devoted ourselves to our office duties in the day, and then night after night, gathered in our darkened workroom, we drew our works telling what the Nazis were really doing and they matured as a cycle. This is how Fritta did his great cycle of 150 drawings and how Ungar, Bloch and I did ours. Then we hid them and when I went back after liberation, I found all the works intact. We would take turns standing watch in case Keidl, the SS official in charge of us, would check on us. We always dreaded his visits to our workroom.[16]

A group of paintings was eventually smuggled out of the ghetto to Switzerland. The Reich labeled these works *Greuel-propaganda* ("atrocity propaganda") and punished and deported the artists. Only Leo Haas survived the war.

The artists were forced to work in terrible conditions in the camps and ghettos. In addition to lack of art supplies and the need to develop and use ersatz materials, any artist who attempted to depict the realities of the camp might find himself or herself faced with a death sentence.[17] As with children's art, the art produced by professional artists was not always concerned with atrocity. Often it contained landscapes, portraits, and other views, sometimes invented.[18] In order to interpret these works, one must use almost a postmodern analysis of presence and absence, for these elements are found in almost all paintings. Thus, the simplest painting may contain elements of documentation that need a detective's eye. Malvina Schalkova's *Forced Labor,* a watercolor from Theresienstadt, depicts women working in a handicraft-like environment sitting at tables, each wearing a kerchief and looking down at her work. There is no hint of atrocity in the painting, but there are elements of absence: the world outside the windows is simply white; the women's faces are uniform in their seriousness; the colors, muddied hues of maroon, green, gold, and brown, seem to convey the sense of the environment.[19] Charlotte Buresova's *Child Prisoner,* also from Theresienstadt, suggests the obvious from the title: Why a child prisoner? Otto Karas-Kaufman's *Faraway Landscape,* undoubtedly drawn from memory, is of a different time and place, not the world of Theresienstadt.[20] One of the most subversive drawings is by Bedrich Fritta, *The Café.* The work shows a three-piece band playing to a crowd of café-goers. All have blank stares on their faces or have an emaciated and depressed look. All wear the yellow star. The café tables lack refreshments. On the wall clock, the minute and hour hands are the same length, suggesting the timelessness of the experience. Outside the window of the café is a guard and a fence topped with three rows of barbed wire. By contrast, many of Adolf Aussenberg's drawings, which possess a very high level of artistic excellence, do not portray the drama of camp life or the horror there.[21] However, a unique and intriguing series of portraits by Max Placek that has survived from Theresienstadt provides not only the physical memory of the people there, but also some psychological insights into their personalities.[22]

Fritta and Haas were probably the most important artists in Theresienstadt, although it certainly seems unfair to compare these artists. Born Fritz Taussig in 1907, Bedrich Fritta was a graphic artist deported to Theresienstadt on December 4, 1941. Fritta's drawings, created with free strokes of pen and ink, reveal some of the darker and cynical sides of ghetto life. *Fortune Teller,* for example, suggests the religious problem that developed in many ghettos, that of God's absence. Fortune-telling and seances often replaced the normative forms of Jewish ritual, especially after deportations or raids. *The Shops in Theresienstadt* shows the false facades of stores that were constructed to fool outsiders. Behind the facade marked "Parfumerie" and "Lebensmittel" are a pile of corpses. In the left foreground, a male inmate and female inmate embrace under the eyes of another face behind bars. *Film and Reality* attempts to suggest the artificiality of the documentary films made about the camp. A Jewish woman is shown in front of a camera, serving as a makeup person, attempting to improve the physical appearance of a bearded inmate, while a skeleton lies behind the curtain. *In the Attic* depicts the horrendous conditions of overcrowding in the ghetto, especially the inconveniences imposed on the elderly. *Life of a Ghetto Prominent* indicts those who were able to achieve some higher standard of living in the ghetto because of their affiliation with the Jewish Council or simply because of bribery. A theater set of sorts shows the "prominents" dressed in rich attire, drinking wine in a salonlike environment. The set is supported by thin wooden poles, revealing how most inmates of the ghetto live.

Fritta also drew a complete children's book called *Tomickovi,* dedicated to his son Tomas on his third birthday, which he celebrated in the ghetto on January 22, 1944. The drawings depict the life of a three-year-old in the camp. The first illustration shows Tomas standing on a suitcase, looking out of a Theresienstadt window toward the ramparts of the town and a dead tree. The book later depicts Tommy praying, Tommy imagining a bright future in a garden, Tommy contemplating a future in any of the following careers: an engineer, a painter, a boxer, a general, "but not a big businessman, I beg you!" or "possibly a detective?"[23] Tomas survived, although his father did not. Gerald Green has described the simple drawing and text as "evidence of the capabilities of the human heart and hand under the vilest conditions."[24]

Leo Haas was born in 1901 and grew up in Opava, Moravia. He attended art school at the Karlsruhe Art Academy, moved to Berlin in 1922 but returned to Opava in 1926. He was arrested in 1939 for his Communist affiliations and deported to the camp at Nisko, then to Ostrava. He arrived in Theresienstadt in 1942. He was one of the few artists to survive 1944 deportations from Theresienstadt to Auschwitz. Haas's works from the camp demonstrate his excellence in drawing, as his drawing of lines quickly became an artistic memory of camp life. This is seen in the pencil drawing

Prayer (1939), which depicts a group of men praying in the barracks. It is a direct and unsentimentalized drawing. *Laundry Room* (1939) and *Living Quarters* (1939) show the tight living conditions in the camp. Yet the former suggests the urge for creativity under adverse conditions, as the artist is shown working at his desk in the midst of a room of drying laundry. *Hunger* (1943) is an ink drawing that shows an endless line of Jews moving through a mystically drawn arch at Theresienstadt, each holding his own empty bowl.[25] *Life in the Ghetto* is a series of pen-and-ink drawings that provides a sense of the overcrowdedness, starvation, hopelessness, and cynical symbolism, such as the smoke coming from a chimney with a Schutzstaffel (SS) "lightning bolt" emblem in the center or an outdoor concert in the camp while a funeral cortege with mourners walks past in profound grief.[26]

Alfred Kantor's *The Book of Alfred Kantor* has been in print since 1971 and probably represents one of the most familiar visions of Theresienstadt, Auschwitz, and Schwarzheide. Interestingly, he did not do these works while in any of these camps, but immediately after liberation. Done in watercolor and pen and ink, with descriptive notations, Kantor's diary begins with his deportation from Prague and forms one of the most coherent visual narratives available. By page 3, Kantor has arrived in Theresienstadt. The next twenty-five pages provide a colorful and artistically intriguing visual documentation of camp life. The diary might be compared to the propaganda film made by the Germans about the same camp, *Der Führer Schenkt den Juden eine Stadt* (The Führer gives the Jews a state). Kantor's work is not horrifying, like the work of the French member of the Sondercommando, David Olere, or sarcastic like the work of Bedrich Fritta. It is, rather, precise in detailing the ghetto's dehumanization, overcrowdedness, attempts at maintaining culture, and false pretenses. Particularly interesting are his paintings of how Theresienstadt was improved in appearance as a "Potemkin Village" before the visit of the International Red Cross Commission.[27] Interestingly, in Kantor's diary and paintings, the only specific dates that appear are those that stand out in his memory as significant rites of passage—the days of his initial transport and his liberation. As in Primo Levi's writings, chronology disappears within the world of the ghetto and death camps.

The best-known artist from the Kovno ghetto was Esther Lurie. Lurie was born and educated in Latvia, and she received her higher education in art in Brussels and Antwerp. She moved to Tel Aviv in 1934 but returned to Europe for additional education and went to Kovno to join her sister. She was caught by the war and because of her artistic skills was asked by the chairman of the Jewish Council, Elkhanan Elkes, to document events in the ghetto. The intensity of her work has been described in the following fashion:

> The very act of drawing was Lurie's first sustained response to the confusion that occurred in the ghetto's early days. She first depicted displaced families trying desperately to set up living quarters in a former school of handicrafts among heavy machinery and industrial equipment. Other renderings during this period, including one of a girl and another of a group of individuals—each wearing the yellow star—capture disconsolate moods. It was her portrait of inmates frantically raiding the potato field that aroused the Altestenrat's interest in her work.[28]

Lurie's works, like those of other ghetto artists such as Jacob Lipschitz, Joseph Schlesinger, Nolik Schmidt, and Ilya Gerber, provide visual evidence of daily life in the Kovno ghetto as well as the horror of deportations, hangings, gradual starvation, and death of its population. These works are important because they can be distinguished from other art works by the typical architecture of Lithuania, whether newer urban apartments built during the 1930s or the older wooden buildings common to the Baltic states. Lurie survived the ghetto, Stutthof, and other camps, although many of her watercolors were lost. Schlesinger also survived. Schmidt and Lipschitz died in the ghetto. Gerber's fate is unknown, his last diary entry and drawing appearing on January 23, 1943.[29] By noting the activity of the few artists in places such as Vilna and Kovno, especially as compared to Theresienstadt, one can see that the latter was a special place because of the density of artists there. Thus, its destiny was to leave a huge artistic legacy that almost dwarfs the important achievements of artists in other ghettos. But overall, all of this art is important in an essential way for providing witness to the Holocaust. According to Mary Constanza's beautiful analysis of it,

> The selective eye and the touch of the artists, the feeling and spirit so essential to humanistic art, are ever present in these works. Foreboding, discomforting, heart-rending yet elegiac and majestic, one is hushed when viewing this art, feeling oneself to be on sacred ground. It is a revelation of the life and death struggle in the last moments and we are the uncomfortable witnesses of these elegies in form and shape. Even the most sparing of designs reveals much in the little rendered. Looking at this art is not comfortable; it is meant to arouse the conscience and inflame some decent human outrage and indignation.[30]

Still another area of the arts that can be noted, but is too broad to consider in this context, is art and theater design in the Theresienstadt ghetto. Most of these designs for plays, musical events, and other theatrically based cultural activities were under the direction of the Czech artist and architect Frantisek Zelenka.

Eli Leskley represents one of the several artists of Theresienstadt who took a reverse course in his imagery. Instead of the elegiac, Leskley used biting satire and humor as well as a visual form similar to editorial cartoons. Leskley was born Eric Lichthau in 1911 in the Czech lands of the Austro-Hungarian Empire. He and his wife, Else, were sent to Theresienstadt, where he worked as a sign painter. Leskley survived Theresienstadt, as did some of his art. He and Else immigrated to Israel, where, immediately after the war, he repainted all his works from memory. Many have a sharp edge, critical of both Germans and Jews. *Senior Inmates* shows a detainee making off with three slices of bread from a table filled with full loaves. *Doctors Are Hungry Too* depicts a camp medical doctor welcoming a patient dressed as a chef. *Three Kings of the Ghetto* is a commentary on whose work is important: it shows cooks and bakers at work, each wearing a crown with a cook's hat topped by a Jewish star and holding a metaphorical orb in the form of the baked goods they produce; their symbolic swords are wooden utensils used in the ovens. The inscription across this work, which makes the artistic content something between a broadside and poster, reads, "One can look into the stomachs!" *Stealing and Schleussing* shows an inmate stealing coal on one side and coins from the cup of a blind inmate on the other. The text reads: "If two people in the Ghetto are equal, nevertheless

Eli Leskley's *Jewish Antisemitism in the Ghetto.* Image courtesy of the Los Angeles Museum of the Holocaust, used with permission. One of seventy satiric watercolors produced by the artist while interned at Theresienstadt. Many of the original works deteriorated, which led the artist to repaint all of them immediately after the war. This image suggests the struggle for survival that pitted Jews against Jews in some cases. For more images, see http://www.chgs.umn.edu/Visual_Artistic_Resources/Eli_Leskley/eli_leskley.html. Caption courtesy of Stephen Feinstein.

they are not equal: one smuggles and the other steals. EVERYONE LOSES." *Jewish Antisemitism in the Ghetto* depicts a bird in a cage with facial characteristics of a member of the Jewish Council. The bird is marked with a Jewish star and is hatching chicks from eggs marked the same way. A text reads: "Leisure activity, work, everything else is arranging leisure time. The 'bird' *Gelbstern* [literally, Yellow Star] makes its own suitable nest in the Jewish Estates of Theresienstadt." The metaphor criticizes privilege and collaboration by Jewish elders with the SS camp administration. All are commentaries on the system of *protektsiia* (obtaining favors through influence) in the camp, which is only occasionally written about and rarely discussed by survivors. The brutality of the ghetto dehumanized the best people, and hunger, as has been the testimony in many memoirs, pushed ethical people to do unethical things to survive.

Leskley also dealt with disease and starvation in the camp. *Terezinka: The Ghetto Disease* shows an inmate running for a toilet, and *Impetigo in the Ghetto* is a colorful depiction of a nude male inmate covered with bandages, standing in front of the official seal of the town of Theresienstadt with a black Star of David scribbled across the gate. Both works comment on the diseases that caused diarrhea. *Return after Disinfection* depicts an encounter in the barracks between an inmate and a Jewish policeman. The policeman extorts a twenty-Kronen bribe apparently for allowing the inmate to go to delousing. The text reads: "Payback for the delousing, only a 'Gvok' [naïve newcomer] pays with the Ghetto money." The currency shown is precise and accurate: the viewer can discern it is Theresienstadt currency, with the correct green color of the twenty-crown note and the engraving of Moses holding the commandments. In *Honeymoon Cottage,* a man's head peeks out of an upper bunk with a wink and a bright light shining from inside, while curtains tied with red ribbons suggest the most privacy one might obtain in the ghetto on such a special occasion.

Unlike most artists, Leskley portrayed his affinity for Zionism as a solution to the Jews' problems. *Beit Halutz—The Zionist Ghetto Home* shows a man dressed in blue with the Jewish star walking a tightrope. As he walks, he dreams of Eretz Yisrael. In one hand, he carries a book with the inscription "learning" both in Hebrew and German. In the other is a ration of sugar and margarine "for other *chaverim* [comrades]." Another watercolor, which may be considered minimally optimistic about the future, warns in its title, *Do Not Build in the Diaspora,* and shows one ghetto Jew repairing a rafter with an axe, while the other takes his bags and departs both the camp and presumably Europe. *A Home for Tired Halutzim* shows the artist himself, an old man, sleeping in the ghetto bunk and dreaming of an eventual home in Palestine.

The Ghetto as Artistic Memory: Some Contemporary Examples

A number of post-Holocaust images of the ghettos should be mentioned, as memory itself is something that cannot be counted on to recall a group of images produced in a wartime ghetto and seen only infrequently in museums or elsewhere by those who were not actually there. During the war, the Lithuanian-born American artist Ben Shahn produced a number of posters dealing with Nazi crimes, such as the famous colored work that tersely details the destruction of Lidice (*This Is Nazi Brutality,* 1942) and the fate of its population. However, this work was a venture in commercial design to fit the needs of the American position in the war and contained no direct references to the Holocaust. Shahn later mentioned that the war left him with "the sense of emptiness and waste," and "the sense of littleness of people trying to live on through the enormity of war." The result of these feelings was his creation of a "symbolism which [he] might once have considered cryptic."[31]

Over a long period (1944–66), Shahn chose to deal with the events in the Warsaw ghetto. When working for the U.S. Office of War Information, he saw a series of photographs taken in Warsaw and other places from 1939 onward. They inspired him to paint children and other scenes:

> During the war I worked in the Office of War Information. We were supplied with a constant stream of material, photographic and other kinds of documentation of the decimation within enemy territory. There were the secret confidential horrible facts of the cartloads of dead; Greece, India, Poland. There were the blurred pictures of bombed-out places, so many of which I knew well and cherished. There were the churches destroyed, the villages, the monasteries—Monte Cassino d Ravenna. At that time, I painted only one theme, "Europa," you might call it. Particularly I painted Italy as I lamented it, or feared it might have become.[32]

These tendencies became symbolic points of departure for a number of paintings: *Boy* (1944), *Hunger* (1946), *Cherubs and Children* (1944), and *Italian Landscape II* (1944) are inspired by wartime photographs. In many of these paintings, Shahn employed symbolic references to the suffering of children in the Warsaw ghetto. *Cherubs and Children* depicts children lying on the ground in an urban landscape, apparently sleeping. *Italian Landscape II* depicts a mother and child climbing over rubble toward a Hotel Europa, which actually stood in Warsaw. In 1963, Shahn produced a serigraph in black with brown Hebrew calligraphy entitled *Warsaw, 1943*. Another work, *Alphabet and Warsaw,* appeared in 1966 as a serigraph in black with watercolor and conte crayon rubbing.

To understand Shahn's approach to the subject of Warsaw, we should know a bit of his own background. First, Shahn seems to have always been aware of his eastern European roots. Like many Jews not in Europe, he hypothesized about being a potential victim. Second, Shahn was well schooled in the Bible from time spent in a Jewish school in Russia, although he came away with a sense of some unfairness of the Old Testament Lord. Third, he thought at least once, in 1927, of the importance of being alive at an important time in history, "when something big was going on, like the Crucifixion. And suddenly I realized I was!"[33] His reference here was to the Sacco-Vanzetti case, which incited him to create twenty-seven representational works about the event in seven months. Many original drawings possess references to Sacco and Vanzetti with Jewish symbols, as if they might have been Jews.[34] In 1939, Shahn did a sarcastic portrait of Father Coughlin, the infamous American anti-Semitic priest.

Shahn returned to the theme of Warsaw in the 1960s through an artistic evolution. Previously, in 1951, Shahn had produced *Composition for Clarinets and Horn,* which shows five vertically standing clarinets in the foreground and a musician with his head in hands, as if exhausted, in the background. This work is not at all related to the Shoah, but the representation of the musician would return in other forms. In 1962, Shahn produced a black serigraph entitled *Martyrology*. With a background in calligraphy from his days in printing and lithography, he had become interested in Hebrew calligraphy during the late 1940s, and use of Hebrew inscriptions became a trademark of his work thereafter as symbols of life and creation, against the backdrop of death and despair. However, he apparently did not read Hebrew, at least fluently. The inscription in *Martyrology,* taken from the Musaf Service for Yom Kippur (the Day of Atonement), deals with the legend of the execution of ten Jewish sages by the Roman emperor Hadrian. The work is double printed, with the second printing deliberately off center so as to create the impression of tears. The prayer translates as follows: "These martyrs I well remember, and my soul is melting with secret sorrow. Evil men have devoured us and eagerly consumed us. In the days of the tyrant there was no reprieve for the ten who were put to death by the Roman Government."[35] A year later (1963), Shahn used the same inscription on a serigraph entitled *Warsaw.* This work shows the upper torso of a man, a replica of the man in *Composition for Clarinets and Horn,* with the head obscured by massive fists bent upward from his elbows in front of him. The drawing at first coveys an aura of despair, relating to Shahn's memorialization of the destruction of the Warsaw ghetto. However, the hands also appear disfigured, perhaps inflamed, even with wounds as if the victim had been crucified. There is also power in those hands. So there is also a sense of enigma in the drawing, which is perhaps elucidated by the quotation from *Martyrology,* which clarifies the sense of the destruction of the Warsaw Jews.

In 1966, Shahn again used the motif of Warsaw in another serigraph, *Alphabet and Warsaw.* He began this work with the printing of the same figure from *Warsaw,* of 1951 and 1963. Over it, he printed the Hebrew letters from *The Alphabet of Creation,* from 1957. The letters obliterate most of the emotion-charged figure, except the fists, which now emerge with defiance. The predominance of the letters is perhaps a vindication of the survival of the Jewish people and their culture, despite the Nazi attempt to destroy both.[36] The importance of Shahn's visual works about Warsaw involves the absence of a distinct narrative. He relied on fragments of memory to produce memory of the affliction in the Warsaw ghetto.

Jozef Kaliszan, a Polish (non-Jewish) artist raised during the Nazi occupation of Poland, viewed the events that overtook his country. In 1966, he undertook a massive project in which he described the Warsaw ghetto visually. Kaliszan was born in 1927 in Wilchin, Poznan Province, and his education was interrupted by the war. He apprenticed with a German blacksmith in 1940, then became a locksmith for the Poznan Opera in 1942. After the war, he attended and graduated from the State Higher School of Plastic Arts, was very active in the Poznan region, and became involved with unofficial art groups in 1956. He was best known for his sculptural constructions of the late 1950s and early 1960s, abstract compositions exhibited in Germany, and set designs for Polish theater and television. As of 1995, he still lived in Poznan.

Kaliszan's decision in 1966 to create a large series of forty paintings entitled *The Warsaw Ghetto* was triggered, undoubtedly, by his own memory of events in the ghetto; the antifascist theme of the narrative made it acceptable to the cultural authorities in Communist Poland. The works are done in pen and ink with an occasional wash of dry point color. The series is divided into four sections, each with ten works: *Exodus, Ghetto, Ghetto Fighting,* and *Massacre.* The visual narrative of these works is exceptionally detailed and appears to be one of the few artistic renderings of the Jewish Holocaust story that has appeared in Poland. Although the series attempts a realistic rendering of the Warsaw ghetto, it does not have the strong impact of some of the works created in the camps or some of the less direct works realized by other Polish artists. This is probably because Kaliszan was more in line with the precepts of socialist realism in Poland during the period in which he created the series. In the printed edition that was also released in the United States, the artist accompanied each work with a written text that serves as an explanation, which suggests that the series is an effort to tell the story. But to whom should the story be told? It is unclear if this edition was only for foreigners or if it was printed in Poland also at a time when there was still a modest Jewish population.

All of the works include some common characteristics. First, each is distinctively framed with a border, with color variants on each work in white, blue, black, and red. The border creates a sense of the ghetto and its closed, claustrophobic environment. In addition, inner divisions of the painted surface are created as extensions of the borders, thus providing a sense of the actual physical divisions and barriers in the ghetto: overcrowded apartments, closed quarters, and lack of individual space. Aesthetically, the divisions provide space for multiple narratives on the same surface, in the tradition of hagiographical icons. However, here nothing can be said to be idealized. Although interesting visually, the drawings are caught in time, much like Nathan Rapoport's *Warsaw Ghetto Monument.*

In the first series, *Exodus,* Kaliszan artistically defines the Polish Jewish dilemma with the Nazis' lightning-like victory in Poland. The first group deals with the enigmatic aspects of Jewish identity, as all Jews are branded with a Star of David or even with graffiti-like stars on the heads of bald men. Above, a synagogue has been destroyed, indicated by broken windows, doors, and swastika and Star of David markings on the outside. The menorah, upright as a symbol of unity in the first painting, is now relegated to the bottom left of the frame, knocked over with other debris.

The second part of Kaliszan's series, *Ghetto,* is a visual narrative of daily life in the Warsaw ghetto and is the most interesting part of the series. Because the artist was in Poznan during the war, the presumption with regard to these paintings is that they represent a mixture of some things he saw himself and placed into the historical setting of the Warsaw ghetto. However, Kaliszan also appears to have been a keen student of the films and photographs that documented daily life in Warsaw. One of the works in this group, *I Will Follow My Way and You Take Yours,* shows the infamous bridges that crossed sections of free streets to maintain the ghetto, with an endless line of people crossing. To the right are a forlorn couple, perhaps contemplating escape but looking in despair at fellow Jews hanging near the ghetto wall after a failed attempt at escape.

Kaliszan's *Nearer to God* and *The Interrupted Passover* continue the impression of the ghetto, emphasizing Jewish attempts to maintain faith. In the former, five men are set in the center, reading a Torah. Kaliszan's commentary suggests that those exposed to the inhumanity of the ghetto were "fortified" by the verses of the Talmud and that faith intensified: "All of those imprisoned need[ed] faith that God did exist, in spite of all the evil that surrounded them."[37] In reality, the survivors' testimony seems to be unclear on the matter of faith during and after the Holocaust.

The Poorest of the Poor focuses on the plight of children, in particular the Polish Jewish story of Janusz Korczak and the children in his orphanage, along with his acceptance of death on a deportation to Treblinka. Although children appear in many of Kaliszan's series, the narrative in this particular work is simple rather than complex. The remainder of the *Ghetto* series dramatizes aspects of daily survival: fuel shortages (*Coal More Precious Than Gold*), work routines, and those people who did not survive, dying on the ghetto's streets and pavements. The series ends with visual discourses on the great deportations of 1942 to Treblinka, titled *Transportation Towards the Unknown,* and on the Warsaw Ghetto Uprising of 1943, titled *Ghetto Fighting,* beginning its chronicle with the events of September 6, 1942, when the ghetto was decreased in size both in amount of space and in population through deportation. Mordecai Anielewicz appears in a portrait in one of these works, and Kaliszan emphasizes the equal role played by women in the battle. The visual texts of these works carry the battle through the events of May 8, 1943, when SS Brigadeführer Jürgen Stroop's troops captured Anielewicz's bunker. Much of this sequence probably derived from the testimony of Marek Edelman, last surviving member of the Warsaw ghetto command structure, who continued to live in Łódź, Poland, after the war, one of the few Jewish leaders who did not emigrate. *Massacre,* the last part of Kaliszan's work, focuses on the destruction of the Warsaw ghetto and its last survivors. Here, for the first time, there is an attempt to focus on the perpetrators as well as the victims. Much of this work is based on the photo-imagery of *The Stroop Report.*

Kaliszan's *The Warsaw Ghetto* series stands in the realm of visual history and is very close to an acceptable official type of socialist realism found in conservative circles during the mid-1960s. It is not the vision of a survivor, but derivative. There is a literal quality to the work, but it is very poignant in its focus on victims and human suffering. Kaliszan did succeed in producing an interesting commentary on the human drama played out in Warsaw, despite its hopelessness. In terms of durability, the series may remain what it appears to be, a series of book illustrations that serves as a means of visually telling the story, which may grow pale, as the Rapoport monument (Nathan Rapaport's monument in Warsaw commemorating the Warsaw ghetto) has in maintaining memory.

One of the strongest examples of a post-Holocaust vision of the ghetto comes from the work of Samuel Bak, born in 1933, who survived the Vilna ghetto and now lives in the United States. At first, Bak's approach to art was through abstraction. However, by 1963, after he turned thirty, the artist began to question the direction of his modernist canvases. The reason for the shift, Bak now understands, was the suppression of Holocaust memory immediately after World War II. Later came his own realization of the importance of this past in his painting: the inner traumas of his life experience, "elements of my inner self[,] . . . were asking to be communicated through art."[38]

His painting style eventually matured into a form of surrealism mixed with complex theological questions that related to the artist's own feeling of estrangement. Bak does not describe this process as a long intellectual journey, but rather as a "responding to something that was pushing out from the inside, something visceral, something that takes a long time for the mind to comprehend."[39] The result was a large body of painted work on canvas dealing with the themes of absence, the post-Holocaust landscape of Jewish existence, and technologies and people of the modern age who do not function. Metaphorical uses of specific objects such as chess pieces or pears for a midrash offer comments about the post-Holocaust world. Bak has described this particular vision in this manner:

> These representational paintings of mine depicted devastated landscapes of ancient cities, urban constructions that seemed to be made of a child's building blocks. In painted figures that were half-alive, and half-contrived of bizarre prostheses, I imagined helpless and abused angels. Chess pieces were involved in games without rules. Huge fruit, mostly pears in various stages of re-invention—pears giving birth to other pears, pears made of stone, pears in the form of hovering planets—metaphors of a world without explanations. My painting carried no answers, only questions.[40]

A great deal of Bak's work has a spiritual connection. Much of it questions God's absence during the Holocaust and what humankind is to make of this absence. The physical place for his discourse about God, however, is the ghetto.

Bak's oeuvre is extensive. However, the ghetto appears and reappears in all of his work, interspersed most frequently with images of the shattered Ten Commandments. Several exhibitions have been entitled "Landscapes of the Jewish Experience" (for example, in 1993 and 1997), and one of the most common themes is the ghetto. For Bak, the ghetto was also his home, and the elements of the destruction of that home and the community it represented are seen in his paintings. *Shema Israel* (1992), for example, depicts a destroyed ghetto whose buildings often have no interiors, while running through the scene of destruction, in strong, not somber colors, are the words of the most important prayer in Judaism ("Hear, O Israel, the Lord our God, the Lord is One"). This conjunction serves not to affirm the presence of God during the Holocaust, but to question his ab-

Samuel Bak's *Ghetto,* 1996. Oil on canvas, 160 x 200 cm. Image courtesy of the artist and the Pucker Gallery. Bak's most recent works reflect his return to Vilnius in the year 2000 and his memories of the Vilna ghetto. For more of Bak's images, see http://www.chgs.umn.edu/Visual_Artistic_Resources/Samuel_Bak/samuel_bak.html. Caption courtesy of Stephen Feinstein.

sence and the uses of prayer after the Shoah. *Wilner Ghetto* (1992) shows a destroyed ghetto whose buildings are colored in the stripes of the ritual prayer shawl, the tallith. However, people are absent, and a virtually blank stone Ten Commandments appears in the background. The Commandments show only God's name and nothing else.

In *Behind the Line* (1992) and *Voyage* (1992), Bak depicts the ghetto as part of the structure of a stone ship whose mass renders movement impossible. Nevertheless, it appears to ply through water, which could also be other rock formations in the shape of water. The ship's funnel resembles the chimney at a crematorium, and a rainbow in the upper part of the first painting is held up by wooden braces and suggests unconvincing expectations of redemption and hope. *Shtetl, Near the Wall, In Flight, Memory, Tefilah,*

Study of Stars, and *Gele Lates,* all from 1992, contain images of the shtetl or the shtetl that became the ghetto. In every canvas, there is a sense of mourning, of flight that did not succeed, of the absence of both God and humans.

Terminus from 1995 shows a series of gondola-like train cars, each with wooden wheels moving uniformly together toward a chimney. Each car contains the remnants of the ghetto, several lit by candles that evoke memorial candles as well as the memory of the Sabbath and, cynically, God's creation. There is no track, and the chimney spouts no smoke. However, the level of destruction is clear, and it is difficult to see any redemption from the events of the Shoah. *Camp* shows the ghetto/camp/shtetl in the form of a Jewish star in the middle of a rocky wilderness. A star is propped up as if it is an advertising sign, and behind it are two lit candles. The buildings evoke the images of the Lithuanian small towns, but, again, hope is slim as no human forms appear in the painting.

A strong and repeated theme found in Bak's work is that of "Pardes," which comes from a Cabalistic story of four rabbis who entered the Garden of Eden seeking truth. In the Cabalistic story, each meets a different fate, with only Rabbi Akiva finding the source of truth and knowledge. In Bak's images, the word PARDES (four letters in Hebrew–"peh," "raish," "dalet," and "sommet") is spelled out across the front of an enclosed garden in the form of the Ten Commandments, isolated in the wilderness. One letter appears over each of the four possible entry doors. Three doors are open or partially open, but the fourth door, on the extreme left, under the S in PARDES, is nailed closed with two boards in the shape of a cross or a Roman X, signifying the number 10. Like the forbidden area, outside human entry, knowledge, and comprehension, this zone shows a fire burning from an oven that looks like a crematorium, with the smoke rising and flowing through the air. Inside, however, are images of the ghetto and mazes, as well as a burning fire. Bak suggests that paradise was the world of eastern European Jewry, and it was destroyed. The danger, for the artist, survivor, and even outsider who tries to study the Holocaust and to understand it, is the potential for both an obsession for understanding and the frustration of never being able to go back.[41]

A fourth variant of artistic remembrances of the ghetto was done by Eleanor Antin, a well-known southern California filmmaker, who has long focused on causes of social justice in her films, performance pieces, and installation work. Her works have been shown in New York's Whitney Museum and the Museum of Modern Art. A 1999 retrospective of her work at the Los Angeles County Museum of Art, "Now Showing: Eleanor Antin," suggested the expanse of her artistic abilities. Her cultural Judaism led her to focus on the Holocaust as an important subject in two of her works: a silent movie, *The Man Without a World* (1991) and the installation *Vilna Nights* (1993), which was shown at the Jewish Museum in New York in the multiartist show, "From the Inside Out."

The focus of both artistic works is the shtetl and an attempt to recapture some of the energized and mystical life of eastern Europe's lost Jewish world. This is especially true in *The Man Without a World,* a silent movie. Through her use of film, the artist recalls the extensive breadth of Yiddish filmmaking in the prewar period, which can never be repeated because of the devastation to Yiddish culture.

In 1993, Antin created a major installation dedicated to the memory of the Holocaust, called *Vilna Nights,* which is currently on permanent exhibition at the Jewish Museum of New York. The installation gives the first impression of a white, plastered ghetto wall, partially destroyed by artillery shells. The viewer is enticed to look into the space, which provides the impression of the streets, apartments, and store fronts of Vilna, once called the "Jerusalem of Lithuania," an active center of Jewish life and Yiddish culture. Within this dark setting, three videos play simultaneously, with muted sound effects to make the viewer a voyeur of sorts. On the immediate right, upon visual entry into the space, is a film about an elderly Jewish tailor. This man, who symbolizes an old and destroyed eastern European Judaism, is repairing articles of clothing when he glances at some small photos and begins to weep. He kisses the photos. The viewer cannot identify the specificity of the mourning process. However, according to Vicky Goldberg, this repetitive action suggests the tailor's attempt to mend the clothing of dead children.[42]

The center vignette portrays an apartment-like atmosphere. Two children are playing games. In a mystical darkness, a candelabra appears, frightening the kids. Immediately following this is the appearance of a dining table, glasses, a challah, and all the ornaments of a Shabbat dinner. The children play the game of Shabbat. Then, everything suddenly disappears. The viewer is left with the image of absence, an absence of Jewish children, Jewish traditions, and Jewish life. On the viewer's immediate left, a third film depicts a young woman in front of a hearth or open stove. She tries to warm herself, then begins to cry. She then initiates a process of opening packages and throwing the contents, apparently letters, into the fire. At one point, she tries to pull a thin scarf or chord around her neck, perhaps a silly attempt at suicide.

Simultaneously, grim events occur in each of the three vignettes. Church bells ring in the background. A strong sound of wind blows through the ghetto, for it is a ghetto. The napkins from the Shabbat table float away. The sound of a departing train is heard. The woman burning the letters holds her hair. All of the color disappears, and the films turn to a cold, blue-gray color. The woman closes the firebox door, and the story is over.

But what exactly is the story? This is not so difficult. It comes across as an elegant deconstruction of a Holocaust narrative, plus a reminder that Holocaust-related art belongs in an art museum, just as it belongs in history books or novels. In addition to a story line with odd twists, the viewer is forced to confront several important questions about the Jewish past, present, and future. The old man represents an almost mythic view of the Orthodox, eastern European Jew, who weeps for his own disappearance as well as for the fate of his fellow Jews. The children represent the newer generation, perhaps even contemporary Jewry, with a "fear" of tradition, as represented by their reactions to the appearance of the candelabra and then its sudden disappearance. The woman burning the letters symbolizes the Nazi crime, the death and burning of the Jews of Europe, and the question of how contemporary Jews choose to remember, or forget, this period as well as their own identities. The young woman knows her fate but tries to burn the letters, nevertheless, as if she can affect her own destiny. Her closing of the firebox door symbolizes the fate of Europe's Jews.

Conclusion

In the study of the Holocaust, the archetypal symbol is Auschwitz. The ghetto is hardly forgotten, but it is frequently not remembered because in its structural form it was a variant of the concentration camp. From the artistic point of view, ghettos, during the period when they were viewed as a partial answer to the slave labor question, had the unique ability to produce elements of culture, especially art and music, amidst atrocity. The ghettos' cultural achievements do not discount the fact that similar artistic forms were found in concentration and even death camps. But the amount of art produced in the Theresienstadt, Vilna, Kovno, and other ghettos is a testament to the artists' life-driven forces and their attempts to provide evidence of the atrocities that surrounded them. Many, such as the Theresienstadt artists who smuggled their work out of the camp, paid dearly for making the truth known.

The post-Holocaust interest in the ghettos continues. Undoubtedly, contemporary artists will continue to examine more aspects of ghetto life in their art work. However, like other aspects of the Holocaust experience, those who were not there will have a difficult time understanding and depicting the event. Jozef Kaliszan, using a narrative form to describe the Warsaw ghetto, provides us with a book illustrator's version. But this approach hardly gets the viewer "there." Shahn does a better job in a metaphorical sense, and Antin combines modern artistic installation and film techniques to provide a unique understanding. One senses that Bak, an exceptional painter, is condemned to paint about the ghetto and God for the rest of his career, as it is part of the past that does not go away, a perpetual "unchosen hour," to use Primo Levi's phrase.

In 1964, Dr. Rudolph Iltis wrote, "We believe that neither film artists, nor writers, poets, sculptors, painters and composers have yet said their last word on the subject that offers itself with such urgency as the theme of the 'Terezin ghetto.' "[43] The same may be said about every ghetto as more information emerges, more research is conducted, and more of an understanding is reached concerning how Jews under such adverse circumstances managed to indulge in life-enhancing endeavors such as art.

14. The Jewish Resistance Movements in the Ghettos of Eastern Europe

Reflections on the Relationships of Force

DANIEL FEIERSTEIN

STEPHEN A. SADOW, TRANS.

The genocide committed by the Nazis during World War II is an important "laboratory example" of the problems involved in systematic, serial extermination of large population masses. This historical instance inaugurated the possibility of applying industrial practices to collective murder, by its dealing with questions such as the functional use of time and space, as well as the capture and transport of large contingents of human beings or the elimination of the bodies. Diverse political regimes have used these lessons (including the political and military "forms") from this "laboratory" to repeat the experience, often on a smaller scale, in their own countries. The latest Argentine military dictatorship (1976–83) is an example. It is symptomatic that, although the accumulation of knowledge about methods of implementation of genocide has increased rapidly, few studies have undertaken a political analysis of the problems of resisting the social practice of genocide. This study furthers the latter investigation, concentrating on the analysis of the Jewish armed urban resistance.[1] This study focuses on the three most important experiences during the confrontations with the Nazi process of extermination: the resistance movements in the ghettos of Vilna, Lithuania, and of Warsaw and Bialystok, Poland, and the reflections and lessons learned by their participants.

Brief Description of the Historical Process

The Resistance in the Warsaw Ghetto

To undertake this analysis, it is necessary to describe briefly the central elements of the three rebellions to establish this study's dimensions. Warsaw, unlike Vilna and Bialystok, was under Nazi control from the beginning of the war. The German armies easily overwhelmed the Polish resistance. The Molotov-Ribbentrop Treaty (August 13, 1939), which divided Poland, placed Warsaw in the territory to be conquered by Germany. With a Jewish population of 360,000, 30 percent of its total, Warsaw was the city with the largest Jewish population, comparable only to Łódź, with more than 200,000 Jews.

In 1940 and 1941, isolated political groups conducted activities such as strikes and street demonstrations in protest of the German occupation and the measures implemented against Jews. Because of the formation of a unified organization exemplified in Vilna, by March 1942 the Anti-Fascist Bloc was established in Warsaw. Initially, they formed two blocs—one organized by the Socialists-Zionists and Communists, the other by the Bund (Jewish Workers Party) and the Polish Socialist Party (PSP). These groups did not unite until October 1942.

In April 1942, the Germans publicly shot fifty-two members of the resistance in Warsaw. On May 15, the resistance published the first clandestine newspaper. Five-member cells began to function; they took on not only military tasks, but also political ones such as the support of ghetto social organizations (soup kitchens, relief organizations). At the end of May, the Nazis assassinated part of the leadership of the resistance, including Andrei Schmidt, the commander of the Socialist-Communist-Zionist bloc. On July 22, the first massive deportation of Jews began. The Nazis sent nearly 300,000 Jews to the extermination camps within three months. The Socialist-Communist-Zionist bloc fought during the deportations. The other bloc initially considered this a mistaken tactic, though it eventually joined the battle when it understood the magnitude of the "selection" and extermination process carried out by the Germans. Approximately 8,000 Jews (not counted among the 300,000 deportees) died in combat during resistance actions. Among these operations was the attack on the chief of the Jewish police, Josef Szerynski, who conducted the recruitment of Jews sent to the camps. On October 29, 1942, Jacob Lejkin, the new chief of the Jewish police, was assassinated. On November 29, 1942, the Nazis killed Israel Furst, the ghetto's chief of economic services.

On January 18, 1943, two hundred German soldiers, eight hundred Lettish and Lithuanian soldiers, and the Jewish police entered the Warsaw ghetto to initiate a new series of deportations. The resistance's counteroffensive repulsed them, forcing them to abandon the ghetto. From January 19 to January 21, the Germans began a new offensive. Of the quota of 16,000 Jews whom the Nazis had intended to deport, they collected fewer than 7,000. To achieve this objective, the Nazis suffered more than twenty casualties and had to abandon the ghetto again. This fighting was crucial. The population realized that the only way to lower the quotas for deportations (other than respect the German orders and negotiate with them) was armed resistance. This lesson would prove extremely important to the events of April 1943, the most celebrated event of the armed Jewish resistance to Nazism.

On January 29, the resistance confiscated the Judenrat's[2] treasury and purchased arms with the money. Subsequently, the unified resistance organization became the military and political authority in the ghetto. They expropriated all Jewish funds for the construction of shelters and the acquisition of armaments. In February, the Germans created a parallel "resistance movement," consisting of spies who intended to cause dissension in the ghetto and, because of the provocation, separate the ghetto population from the armed organizations. The Jewish resistance discovered and foiled this organization, executing many of its members. From another quarter, the Germans offered the Jewish workers the option of transferring from the ghetto to other areas of German production. Not even a tenth of the Jewish workforce responded to this initiative. In February, the focus of resistance actions was the settling of accounts with members of the Gestapo and with Jewish "turncoats."

On March 13, the Germans began another offensive, which also failed. After a day of combat, the Germans were repulsed and forced to leave the ghetto. The German offensive stalled for more than a month, control of the resistance forces being impossible. On April 19, the Germans carried out the final offensive when new troops joined the units stationed in Warsaw. At this point, the resistance organization proposed three modes of combat: street fighting in the first phase, continuing until April 23, when the Germans broke the resistance organization's domination of the streets of the ghetto; defense of fortified bunkers in the second phase (from April 24 to May 11, when the last bunkers on Bonifraterska, Schwienticherska, and Wollowa Streets fell); nocturnal combat in the ruins of the city in the third phase (from May 13 until September, when the last seventeen combatants succeeded in climbing aboard the truck belonging to the Polish Communist resistance, which carried them to the forests, where they joined the partisan brigades). The Germans could not take complete control of the city until October. Trying out various forms of combat, a national army succeeded in defeating a civil and municipal resistance organization only after several months of clashes.

The Resistance in the Vilna Ghetto

Vilna, the capital of Lithuania, was called the "Jerusalem of the North" because of the immense intellectual production of the Jewish community. According to the 1931 census, Vilna was home to more than 55,000 Jews, making up 28 percent of the city's population. The Red Army occupied Vilna at the beginning of the war, as part of the Molotov-Ribbentrop Treaty. With the beginning of "Operation Barbarossa," the German invasion of the Soviet Union, the Einsatzgruppen, commando units of the elite Schutzstaffel (SS) troops, were in action at the rear guard of the front. They were responsible for the first massive executions of Jews. On June 24, 1941, the Germans conquered Vilna. Almost immediately, they established the first Judenrat, directed by Saul Trotsky. As the functioning of the Judenrat did not satisfy the Germans, it was closed down on September 2 and most of its members murdered. Between June 1941, when the Germans invaded, and the end of the same year,

35,000–40,000 Jews were killed in the Ponar forests by the German Einsatzgruppen.

Jacob Gens assumed control of the ghetto on July 19, 1942, after a period of no leaders and a second Judenrat that also lacked substance. By the end of 1941, Jews had already formed the clandestine resistance organization, one of the first of its type. On January 1, 1942, the resistance distributed its first proclamation, beginning with the motto, "We will not allow them to take us like beasts to the slaughter," and culminating in the call for the creation of an armed resistance organization. On January 21, the United Partisan Organization (UPO) was formed, bringing together Socialists-Zionists, right-wing groups, and the Communist Party. A month later, the Bund joined them.[3] Yitzhak Wittenberg (a Communist) was first in command , with Josef Glazman (Betar) and Abba Kovner (Socialist-Zionist) completing the tripartite leadership. Among the proposed activities were the self-defense of the ghetto, the sabotage of the German industrial and military activities, and the joining the partisan and Red Army combat against the Nazis.

However, the organization of the resistance did not match that of the Warsaw experience. By mid-1943, while the last skirmishes were still going on in Warsaw, a resistance agent in the forests fell into Gestapo hands, and, while being tortured, gave the Gestapo the names of the Vilna resistance commanders. The Germans did not act directly but ordered the Vilna Judenrat to turn over Wittenberg to the Gestapo, threatening to search the entire ghetto for arms if the council did not bring in Wittenberg.[4] On July 16, the Judenrat invited the resistance commanders to a meeting and, betraying them, handed Wittenberg over to the Gestapo. The members of the resistance organization, however, were prepared. They intercepted the German patrol and rescued Wittenberg in an armed clash.

That same day the resistance organization abandoned its clandestine operations. It opened its arms depositories, set out mortars at the ghetto entrances, and mobilized its squads to armed positions in strategic ghetto points. However, they neglected the political tasks. Fortified in their positions, the members of the resistance did not pay attention to the city's Central Plaza, where Jacob Gens, the chief of the Judenrat, gave a speech to a large group of people, offering them the Nazi alternative: hand over Wittenberg or perish. The notice spread throughout the ghetto, and the populace, led by the Jewish police, confronted the resistance commandos under the slogan, "Let us turn Wittenberg in. We want to live." Clashes began between the resistance and the ghetto population, without Nazi intervention. An hour later Gens improvised another speech in the plaza, promising that if the resistance turned in Wittenberg, they would then ransom Wittenberg with Judenrat funds. The fighting worsened. Because the squads of the resistance refused to fire on their own people, they were disarmed by the Jewish police and arrested.

The command of the resistance found itself facing a dilemma without a solution: use its limited arms and tactical-strategic abilities in a confrontation with the Jewish masses or turn over their commander. They opted for the latter alternative. Unlike in Warsaw, in Vilna the Jewish resistance did not become the authority of the ghetto. Gens's complicity with the Germans frustrated the plans for collective resistance. After relinquishing Wittenberg, the resistance tried a different tactic: sending some of its younger fighters to the Naruch forests, two hundred kilometers from the city, to join the partisan brigades. This initiative also failed, however, when the Germans detected and annihilated the first contingent.

Early in September 1943, the Germans entered the Vilna ghetto to liquidate it. There they encountered their first resistance on Strashun Street, which possessed fortified bunkers. Gens again negotiated with the Nazis for the pullback of the German troops from the ghetto in exchange for his taking charge, along with the Jewish police, of filling the deportation quotas that the Germans required, more than half the surviving population. Gens fulfilled this quota by penetrating, with the aid of the Jewish police, the "nonfortified" bunkers, places occupied by Jews who were willing to fight but who were not yet enrolled in the resistance and therefore were unarmed. In this operation, Gens deliberately avoided approaching Strashun Street, and the members of the resistance did not leave their bunkers to fight Gens on the streets. Finally, after a great deal of discussion, some contingents of the resistance fled to the forests. The "selections" continued in the ghetto, but the Germans always kept some people alive. On September 15, another large deportation took place. Only 3,000 Jews remained in the ghetto, primarily the members of the Judenrat and their families. The Nazis definitively liquidated the ghetto on July 2–3, 1944, when the last Jews were shot in the Ponar forest, in a fashion similar to the first Jews murdered in Vilna in 1941.

The Resistance in the Bialystok Ghetto

In 1931, Bialystok, Poland, had almost 40,000 Jewish inhabitants, almost half the city's population. Bialystok was among the cities of the world with the highest percentage of Jewish population. The Red Army occupied Bialystock, like Vilna, at the beginning of the war, as part of the Molotov-Ribbentrop Treaty. Bialystok's Jewish population grew as refugees arrived from the Polish cities conquered by the Nazis. The Communist regime prohibited Zionism (left-wing or right-wing), so the Zionists' middle-level cadres became accustomed to working in secret. The leadership cadres were deported to Siberia or left to go on their own to Moscow. The direction of the Jewish political movements was left in the hands of young people from eighteen to twenty years of age.

At the end of June 1941, the Germans entered Bialystok, and, as in Vilna, the Einsatzgruppen carried out large-scale killings. On June 27–28, they murdered more than 6,000 Jews, 1,000 of whom were burned alive. During July, there were massive roundups. From August to October, they deported another 5,000 Jews to concentration camps. In early 1942, the Socialists-Zionists began to provide social welfare in the ghetto and formed two combat groups: one consisted of Communists and Socialists-Zionists, and the other of Zionist groups. The Socialists-Zionists participated in both.

During the second half of 1942, the resistance organizations selected two central goals: finding provisions for the ghetto and sabotaging German industrial establishments in the ghetto. Because of the latter, many "Bialystok boots" used by German soldiers fell apart during the offensive against the Soviet Union. Also, a group of Nazi infiltrators who tried to penetrate the Soviet resistance in the forests was foiled: their berets carried a white tag stating, "Made by the Jewish workers of Bialystok"—a signal to the resistance forces in the forests.

On November 1, 1942, the ghetto was closed to deport 12,000 Jews.

At the start of negotiations with the Bialystok Judenrat, the Germans agreed to replace the Jews from the ghetto with Jews from "the surrounding areas."[5] Sources differ greatly as to the number of deportations, which were not fewer than 15,000 Jews, though some documents speak of 40,000.

On February 15, 1943, the Germans initiated a new "action," the deportation of 6,300 Jews. The two resistance organizations, not yet unified, differed in their response. The Communists and the Socialists-Zionists decided to confront the Germans when they entered the ghetto. The rest of the organizations proposed to fight if the Germans did not keep their word and took 6,301 Jews.[6] Many people confronted the Germans spontaneously, joining the banner of the Communists and Socialists-Zionists' combat groups. More than 1,000 Jews died in the fighting, and the Germans suffered a 20 percent casualty rate. They deported close to 12,000 Jews. Jewish informers sold out the resistance's "fortified bunkers," but a few days later, ghetto inhabitants exacted revenge.

By the middle of 1943, actions like those in Warsaw were carried out in Bialystok. The resistance concentrated its operation on the execution of informers, such as Zvieklish and the Yudkovsky brothers. During this period, the combat organizations became a single movement, with a unified corps and a central command, directed by Mordechai Tenenbaum. In August, they designed the plan for the final resistance against the imminent German invasion, following the plan of the resistance in the Warsaw ghetto: street fighting, defense of the shelters, and a final flight to the forests, aided by their geographic proximity. They sent contacts to the "Aryan" part of the city to guarantee the rebellion survivors' movement to the forests.

However, the Germans had learned from the Warsaw experience and entered the ghetto in a surprise move on August 16 at 2:00 A.M. They placed a division of tanks at the entrance to the ghetto and insisted that the Jews "embark" to be deported. The surprise entrance, supported by the tanks, rendered the first stage of the plan—street fighting—impossible, and the population did not react as it did in Warsaw. Facing the German presence in the streets, the greater part of the ghetto attended the "embarkation," leaving the resistance isolated in its bunkers. The resistance organization changed its plans about the march. It maintained its bunkers in the factory zone but ordered its squads in the central zone to march with the general population, carrying hidden arms, and to initiate combat near the entrance to the ghetto; they planned to break the German siege and create a human bridge that would permit the population to reach the forests and join the partisan brigades. This plan failed also. The ghetto population did not take advantage of the "human chain" and separated from the combatants. The battle lasted more than seven hours. The Germans used the tanks and air power to crush the street fighting rapidly. Very few fled successfully to the forests. The great majority remained, kept together at the embarkation point. The defense of the fortified bunkers in the industrial zone proceeded for a week. Some isolated combatants successfully reached the forest. The combatant's central bunker was sold out to the Germans, who surrounded and liquidated it before the resistance fighters could flee to the forests.

Analysis of the Relationship among Forces

A work concerning the specific characteristics of the Jewish resistance in the ghettos cannot avoid the analysis of the relationship between the forces involved. This analysis cannot limit itself to repeating mechanically, as has been often done, that an enormous distance existed between the strength of the German army and the ability to provision the Jewish population (in the military and technical aspects only). It should consider the population of the ghetto as a social force with its own specific characteristics. It should identify the important moments in the relationship between forces and the possibilities at each stage.

Theorist Antonio Gramsci expresses clearly some basic principles for analysis of "force relationships" that allow us to avoid the superficial treatments that merely discuss the technical disparities. Gramsci says: "In historical narrative, one often reads the generic expression 'relationship of forces, favorable or unfavorable to such and such a tendency.' In the abstract, this explanation explains nothing or almost nothing, because it is limited to repeating the very fact that needs explaining, presenting it once as a fact and then again as an abstract law and as an explication."[7]

Gramsci developed a three-stage model that can be employed to illuminate the situation of the Jewish resistance in the ghettos during their confrontations with the German occupation troops: the relationship of objective forces, the relationship of political forces, and the relationship of military forces. My analysis is based on this model.

The Relationship of Objective Forces

Antonio Gramsci understood the relationships of "objective forces" as: "a relationship among social forces, strictly tied to the structure, independent of human will. . . . This fundamental strategic division allows the study of whether the necessary and sufficient conditions exist in a society of a transformation, that is, it controls the realism and viability of the various ideologies born in its own territory."[8] It is, therefore, worth asking: What was the social position of the Jewish population in the territory of the three cities under study? How many people are we talking about? What was the social structure of that population? What percentage of the general population did it represent? What type of work was done? How did this work fit into the economic structure of each city? What transformations occurred at the beginning of the war? This essay offers a map of some of these questions as "conditions of realism and viability" to the political answers born in this social force.

In September 1939, Poland had approximately 350,000 Jews, overwhelmingly concentrated in urban centers: Warsaw, Łódź, Grodno, Bialystok, Pinsk, Kraków, Lvov, and Lublin. In many of these cities, the Jews oscillated between 30 and 50 percent of the general population yet never surpassed 15 percent of the population in all Polish territory. The Jewish population was socially concentrated in small businesses (shopkeepers, peddlers—between 35 and 50 percent of the Jewish population), artisans and workers (who made up another 25–30 percent), and domestic workers, service workers, and professionals (who made up the final 25–30 percent). Also, the Jewish population possessed an upper middle class, which, though it was never greater than 2 or 3 percent of the population, was basically concentrated in the financial sector. For example, at the middle of the nineteenth century, of the twenty bankers in Warsaw, seventeen were

Jews. By the end of the nineteenth century, the tiny group of Jewish upper middle class (mainly bankers and officers in the Polish army) underwent a notable process of conversion to Christianity.

The three cities contained high concentrations of Jews. In all three, before the war, the Jewish population began to drop proportionately because of a process of "nationalization" in Polish and Lithuanian territories as well as emigration to the United States, South America, South Africa, and Palestine. The population, divided approximately in thirds (traders; artisans; and workers and domestic and other service personnel) began to suffer a large increase in unemployment, particularly among the workers—the result of, among other factors, Polish and Ukrainian nationalism that discriminated against minority groups, especially Jews, not included in the national identity. By 1931, Jewish unemployment in Warsaw had reached 34.4 percent. In the 1930s, the Jews were particularly affected by governmental actions and by public companies, just when financial obligations were imposed on them or they were denied access to credit. Although sharing these difficulties, Vilna had a markedly higher proportion of professionals, which led to its becoming a cultural and artistic center. Vilna had become a transit point and a place of asylum for Jews during World War I, which led to its population being more heterogeneous. Approximately 20 percent of the Jewish population of Poland perished during the first two years in the ghettos—victims of epidemics, malnutrition, and killings. This attrition made the preservation of the social force (the populations of the ghettos) a necessary precondition for any type of resistance.

Vilna and Bialystok geographically shared the proximity to the great forested zones and (depending on the period) to the battlefront between Germany and the Soviet Union. On the contrary, Warsaw was almost three hundred kilometers closer to German territory (in fact, it was annexed to the Reich), and it possessed a dense urban structure that did not allow for access to the forests. Of a highly objective character, this issue played an important role in the design of resistance strategies because the possibility of breaking the German siege to flee to the forests and join the partisan brigades, an important option for the Bialystok and Vilna organizations, was implausible in Warsaw. In sum, the Jewish population in this area was mainly urban, with a large proportion of small businesses, workers, and artisans who were affected gravely by unemployment and thus underwent a process of growing proletarianization and declining social mobility. Simultaneously, this population included proportionally tiny sectors placed in strategic enclaves, such as finance and the army. These sectors continuously felt themselves less involved with their Jewish identity, so they tried to distance themselves from it through assimilation or conversion.

Geography affected the impact of the war on each community. Those who remained in the Soviet sector (Vilna and Bialystok) joyfully received the Red Army and believed that the possibility existed to reverse the process of pauperization. Nonetheless, the Soviet troops prohibited the functioning of the Zionist movements (even the Socialists-Zionists, who reappeared as Marxists-Leninists). The arrival of Jewish refugees from German-held zones did not alleviate the social situation, but rather made it worse. Elsewhere, in the areas occupied by Germans, the Nazi government's legal and economic restrictions polarized the Jewish population between an enormous mass converted into a slave workforce, which would die through illness and malnutrition, and a tiny fraction that would continue enjoying a comfortable life while carrying out administrative functions in the ghetto (the Judenrat, Jewish police) or getting rich by dealing in contraband with the "Aryan" zones of the city.

The creation of the ghettos, in the German-occupied zone at the beginning of the war and in German-occupied areas in 1941 after the invasion of the Soviet Union, consolidated the Jewish population as a social force but in a different sense than previously. It was now a social force defined by an enemy intent on its annihilation. The conditions that defined the Jewish people as a force in these circumstances did not lie only in the cultural, linguistic, religious, and ideological affinities that signified the membership in a group, but mainly in their forming the undesirable entity that the political regime was ready to discriminate against, aggravate, isolate, and exterminate.

Contradictions appear between sectors of the population whose situations were dissimilar but who saw themselves as equally subject to extermination. Nazism ably used these contradictions. Among the subjective problems of the resistance organizations, the identity of this social force was the first question to be resolved. In what terms, in what context, with what possibilities should Jews think about themselves as Jews? How could they redefine this identity after the rise of Nazism? This was the first great problem to be resolved, which is clear in every story told by survivors of the resistance organizations.

The Relationship of Political Forces

According to Gramsci, "The relationship of the political forces is an ulterior motive, that is, the estimate of how much homogeneity, the self-consciousness and organization achieved by various social groups. This moment can be analyzed, in turn, by distinguishing in it the differing levels that correspond to differing moments in the collective political consciousness."[9] At the beginning of the twentieth century, the political structure of the Jewish cities was extremely heterogeneous. The pauperization of the population had led to the formation and consolidation of secular Jewish groups, generally nationalistic in nature. Like the other ethnic minorities in Poland and Lithuania, these groups sought to represent the socioeconomic interests of their sectors. Consequently, from the classic opponents among the diverse religious groups—Hasidim and Mitnagdim, for example—came forth the creation and growth of a wide spectrum of Zionist parties: general Zionists, with five different parties, and Socialists-Zionists, with seven parties to represent them. From another direction, the Russian Revolution had led to increased Jewish participation in left-wing parties—Communists and Socialists–and in the later decades had taken over the enormous force of the Bund, which defined itself as "nationalist, secular, proletarian, Socialist, and non-Zionist." They therefore possessed a strong autonomy from the Communists, Socialists, and Zionists.

During the period between the wars, the rising Jewish secular parties were displacing the Orthodox in the direction the Jewish communities would take in Poland and Lithuania.[10] In 1918, an alliance between the Bund and the Poelei Zion (the Socialist-Worker-Zionist movement, founded in 1906 with Ber Borochov as its principle ideologue) assumed the leadership of the Jews of Warsaw. The same thing happened in Polish Galicia. These parties were popular particularly among the youth, who primarily experienced the discriminatory practices, unemployment, and the lack of vision by a Judaism that was "careful" when facing the general hostility and that closed in upon itself. These youth movements took on not only the political responsibility from the state, but also the development of the forms of production and self-created means for subsistence (schools, banks, cooperatives, orchards).

Before the beginning of the war, the first task of the political forces in the Jewish cities was, therefore, the redefinition of their own identity—how the Jews saw themselves, how they came together, and how they characterized the period in which they would plan appropriate actions: in short, what Gramsci calls "self-consciousness." It should be remembered that most of the political leaders had fled toward the East, so the problem of identity remained, most often in the youth sections of the political organizations of the time. Testimonies of resistance movement survivors make clear a common preoccupation with the issue, although with important variations among the diverse political forces. Three main matters had to be defined: an accurate characterization of German objectives, the construction of a Jewish identity as a social force that would resist its extermination, and the necessity to reserve its own political cadres for any later construction. I now examine how each of these questions looked in each of the political forces.

Marek Edelman, one of the leaders of the Bund in Warsaw, became one of the commandants of the resistance in the ghetto. In his testimonial *The Ghetto Fights,* he analyzes the problem of the "characterization of the situation" as the basis for the development of a social force:

> In February 1941, the first news of the extermination of Jews by gas in Chelmno reaches Warsaw. The news is carried by three fugitives, who had been miraculously saved. . . . The Warsaw ghetto did not believe the news. . . . The youth organizations were the first to accept these events as probable or certain, and they decided to carry out a broad campaign propaganda campaign in order to make the population aware of them. [As a result of the acts of extermination in Warsaw proper, the same situation repeated itself]: The majority insisted that the editors of illegal journals had been illuminated, that the action was directed only toward political activists, and that abandoning this sort of behavior was neces-

> sary so as not to uselessly increase the already large number of victims. [But the Bund's weekly insisted on the ideological struggle]: This is only a step in the extermination of the Jews. The Germans want to assassinate the most active elements of the community so that later the entire population go passively to its death, as occurred in Vilna, Bialystok, Lublin and other cities.[11]

Most of the testimonials of the period square with this evaluation. Tzivia Lubetkin, a member of Dror, the Socialist-Zionist movement, had returned to Warsaw as part of the political necessity to establish clandestine organizations in the zones occupied by Germany.[12] He describes lucidly the consequences of this dispute in the formation of the Jewish combatants' identity: "We knew that alone we were not able to carry out the defense. The first thing that had to be done was to convince the masses. But, for the people to find an understanding of the need to defend themselves, it was necessary for them to know the tragic fate that awaited them."[13] Yisrael Gutman skillfully describes the difficulties of this first stage:

> It should not be surprising that the Jews, who were incessantly shaken by the deceitful maneuvers and false promises of the Germans, did not understand what was happening. . . . At first, they thought that the Nazis' main intention was that the Jews were productive, and in exchange for their labor that would contribute to the Nazi economy, the workers would save their lives. Then, when they realized that even their forced and exhausting work did not constitute a defense, they decided that the Nazis had decided to annihilate a portion of the people and that they had to try to save the largest number possible and the best. . . . From this position, the combatants appeared to be adventurers capable of aggravating the situation and causing a terrible disaster. Knowing the irrepressible Nazi tactic of attributing responsibility in a collective manner, many thought that the young people's battle a worthy effort, but the trouble that they could cause was incalculable.[14]

The work involved in social action was a second issue shared by all these movements but especially developed in the diverse Zionist groups and to a lesser extent by the Communists. An enormous percentage of the Jewish population perished daily because of exhaustion, malnutrition, and exploitation. The opening of school cafeterias, the prevention of infectious diseases, and the maintenance public health, therefore, became extremely important, not only to stop the process of death of their own social force, but to build consensus within it. Active social work by the resistance movements was directed toward the masses of pauperized workers. The prebendary actions of the Judenrat, in contrast, generally involved the distribution of *favors* among chosen factions of the population. The importance of this sort of work cannot be underestimated. In the Warsaw ghetto, only 27,000 worked—out of a population of approximately 550,000. The archives of the period describe the actions of the "housing committees" in Warsaw. Tenant organizations, recognized by the Judenrat, though later persecuted by it, carried out social work, hygiene maintenance, and the resolution of neighborhood disputes. Many of these committees ended by joining, a posteriori, the armed resistance movements.[15]

This political process of building Jewish "self-consciousness" in the resistance movements, however, was undercut by the Germans' actions, with the complicity of the well-off sectors of the Jewish population and, in most cases, of the Judenrat. Jaika Grossman, a member of HaShomer HaTzair and the resistance movement in Bialystok, describes clearly this situation:

> The Germans employed "divide and conquer" tactics: cut off a single member; separate one part from the other. The intent of this was to intensify the desire to survive in those who were still alive, kill their souls, and put their consciences and their feelings to sleep. Destroying the spirit inferred annulling the power for resistance. Meanwhile, the crowd would continue advancing toward the slaughter, and, until the last moment, they would have to believe in a miracle, the miracle of the survivors.[16]

Particularly suggestive is Grossman's analysis concerning the theoretical formation of each of the Jewish political organizations and their expression in dealing with extermination. Grossman describes one of the most important political debates of the moment; there are:

[t]hose who, before the war, believed that achieving socialism peacefully was possible, bringing the workers to power through an indirect route, avoiding confrontations. Some thought that liberating the people without victims was possible, without extreme actions, but through a profound internal revolution. Those were the same who brought equivocation to the people and falsely deluded them with the idea that the Nazi conquest, the murders, and the oppression could be avoided. They oriented their own movements and those of the city toward the evasion and disappearance of reality, in times of such desperate confrontation of two worlds. It was as if an entire nation could slip through the grates of history. A few could slip between the cracks. But a whole people? The leaders and the society? We didn't want to nor could we understand them. We didn't want to increase tensions nor arrive at any kind of agreement with them. These meetings were painful, as much for us as for them. They weren't about differences between young and old, as some have thought. Nor was there discord between pessimists like us, who sensed the proximity of genocide and didn't want to hide it from the people, and the optimists like them who believed that humanity . . . would have to rise up and help them avoid the misfortune. Who ever said that to deny reality was optimistic and to see it clearly was pessimistic? Perhaps the reverse was true. We wanted the news about the massacres at Ponar to be known everywhere, not to create feelings of helplessness and desperation that would cause them to say, "Of course, the Nazis are going to destroy us." That would have been criminal. We wanted to publish the truth about what was awaiting us, show in all their crudeness those terrible events that were beginning to take place so that we could defend ourselves. We sought to organize ourselves, to be in the thick of it, to use armed opposition while there was still time. . . . And our adversaries? It seemed that they no longer had the strength to take on any important project, any great gesture, and therefore, they resisted seeing what was happening. Was it psychological fear? In no way! You couldn't attribute a fear like that to a "Jew of the streets" who doesn't know the reasons for his equivocations and doesn't understand his relationship with the avatars of the world. That is, it was an absolutely private panic without visible social sources. It was the fear of an ideology, a conception of the world and of history that, unfortunately, succeeds in paralyzing many. This fear also became a participant in historical events.[17]

When Marek Edelman writes of the actions of the Jewish police, his testimony is eloquent. Describing the deportations in Warsaw, he says:

> The blockades become ever more terrible for us, because there are fewer people, and the sector is progressively shrunken and difficult for the Germans as the people had already learned to hide. For that reason, they obliged each Jewish police officer to bring in "seven heads" per day. And with this, the Germans make their best play. No one carried out the action with such wildness as the Jew. No one was ever so impious, so inflexible when detaining the victim. To collect the "seven heads," the Jewish police arrested a doctor wearing a lab coat (they later sold the lab coat for a good price), a mother with a child in her arms or a lost child looking for his home. The Jewish police alone write its own history. . . . *At the very end,* they [the Nazis] brought the families of the Jewish police in.[18]

This same issue reappeared in the Jews' analysis of the role of the ghetto in Nazi strategy. Many Jewish sectors saw the isolation as a sort of freedom from the persecutions they were suffering.[19] The resistance movements were clear about this:

> The ghetto was not a way of achieving Jewish autonomy, as many thought, but an instrument with which they would first kill our souls and then our bodies. They [the Nazis] designed the ghetto to destroy our people, to wipe them completely from the face of the earth. I also spoke about the *scheine* [special permits] that the Nazis had implemented in the Vilna ghetto with the intention of creating new social classes, new levels and categories that, in all ways and without exception led to death, but gave the individual Jew the illusion of possessing a special rank. This status, they thought, would make them immune to the Germans, who had given this special and preferential *scheine.* In this way, the Germans were finishing off our people's soul, taking away their essential logic, their common sense. With this system, they were corrupting an organized community's most healthy impulses. I assured them that the same thing was going to happen in Bialystok, because, if it were not so, the Germans would not have set up the ghetto, the police or the Judenrat. The Germans were not trying to help the Jews, but to harm them. They had per-

> mitted them the autonomy and the self-management so that they would fight each other and wish to destroy each other, and to destroy that natural instinct for human solidarity that always ties together those who suffer.[20]

In Short, a Struggle for Identity

Starting with the German occupation of the spheres of Jewish life, an internal dispute erupted in each collective. The battle group was the subjective construction of the identities. The Nazi initiative counted among its objectives the confirmation of "the Jewish prototype" in each Jew. Converting the Jews into what the Germans considered them proved useful to the dominant regime. Before implementing genocidal policies, Nazism worked to convert the Jew into that docile subject, collaborator, and traitor to his or her own survival, to guarantee materially and to justify ideologically his or her extermination. The moral and human degradation of many members of the Jewish police; the position taken by members of the Judenrat, who accepted the responsibility of making up the lists of who would live and die; the profusion of individual Jews who maintained their reproduction and subsistence by informing on members of the group—all exemplify the genocidal initiative's capacity for penetration of the self-consciousness of some factions of the Jewish people.

The resistance organizers, therefore, had to focus on the creation of an opposing Jewish identity—relentless, united, ready to fight, and capable of organizing themselves efficiently so as not to succumb to provocation and be defeated in the first skirmish. Within this creation of a contrahegemonic Jewish subjectivity, the perception of Nazism as a genocidal force and a thorough understanding of its extermination plans played a central role, especially because those plans seemed irrational at the time and could easily be dismissed as "paranoiac exaggerations." The rebuilding of Jewish self-esteem, constantly under attack from Nazism, also played an important role. This self-esteem was indispensable in creating a combatant force. For that reason, the Zionists and Communists could organize most quickly, sustained by ideologies that, through the Jewish national identity or the international proletarian identity, contributed to the recuperation of self-esteem.

The resistance organizations had to move constantly within this paradox. It was difficult to synthesize a propaganda line that publicized the fate awaiting European Judaism and the belief that the knowledge of the final destiny would not demoralize the Jewish populations and strip them of their confidence as a force capable of resisting and confronting such a future.

The Material Preservation of the Force

Superimposed on the necessity to create a combatant subjectivity as a central element of Jewish identity, another question is more elemental, if not less important: the material exigency to protect their own militants against the harassment and annihilation that they faced in their daily lives. Despite correctly understanding the characteristics of a genocidal process, not all the political organizations could conclude from those precepts applying to the general Jewish population the consequences that affected their own organization. Extreme differences occurred: for the Zionist parties, in particular HaShomer HaTzair, it was a very important issue; for the Bundists and the Communists, who lost an enormous number of combatants in the daily deportations, it was essentially ignored. Jaika Grossman describes how they prioritized this issue: "The first danger was that, before we could begin to take any action, they would take away all of our men in those incessant massive roundups. Consequently, first, we had to take care of our people. It was the responsibility of Mordechai and me to find out how much they could expect from the provisional leadership of the Jewish community, the Judenrat."[21]

HaShomer HaTzair established a true "self-protection network" in Vilna. They had a center for the falsification of "Aryan documents" for those who took part in the "Aryan network," members of the movement who lived outside the ghetto, under false identities, as contacts with other antifascist political forces, or for the "contacts" between the ghetto and the city, who possessed a double identity (Aryan and Jewish) and who put on the yellow star or took it off depending on which side of the wall they found themselves. Moreover, they had placed part of their squadron leaders in a convent called Vilna Colony, in which Arie Wilner and Abba Kovner, who would later be members of the resistance command, were billeted. They also worked to obtain work permits for the fighters who remained in the ghetto. For the moment, it was the safest situation, given that, for the most part, the deportations consisted largely of the unemployed. The counterexample was the Bund. Although the largest and most representative group that maintained intense clandestine activity, it saw many of its best fighters disappear permanently. Marek Edelman describes it dramatically: "During that period [of the deportations in Warsaw in 1942], we lost most of our comrades. From more than five hundred members, scarcely a few dozen were left. The already existing Zionist combat organizations are luckier. They can keep, by chance, most of their militance. . . . A small group of us is left. We do what we can. Nevertheless, there is very little we can do."[22]

Edelman refers once to "luck" and once to "chance." From a distance, it is possible to observe that the difference is not random. The Socialist movement's perception of the necessity to preserve its own group left its members in better condition to carry out their struggle. Actively publicizing the Nazis' genocidal objectives, the Bund failed to apply this knowledge to itself, so it did not sufficiently emphasize self-protection. Something similar occurred with the Communists, although their situation differed. With more contacts in the "Aryan zone," they found themselves doubly discriminated against in the ghetto—by the Judenrat, whose members were not disposed to give them jobs in the ghetto, given the risk that the Germans would discover this connection.

The Hegemony Issue

Gramsci analyzes a final stage in the relationship between political forces when, the forms of self-consciousness having been developed, they fight for the hegemony of each social force:

> This is the most strictly political phase, which shows the clear step from the structure to the sphere of the complex superstructures; it is the phase

> in which previously germinated ideologies become "party." They clash and enter the struggle, until only one of them, or, at least, a single combination of them, tends to prevail, to impose itself, to spread itself through the entire social area.[23]

The deportations of 1941–42 brought the political confrontation in the ghetto to this final level. First in Vilna, later in Bialystok and Warsaw, the resistance movements formed unified organizations and contested the hegemony of power inside the ghetto with the Judenrat and the Jewish police. The possibility of armed resistance depended mainly on the results of this confrontation. There was no fundamental technical difference among the three resistance movements: the three lacked arms, had been decimated, and possessed similar political structures. Nonetheless, in Warsaw, the resistance movement won political hegemony in the streets. The resistance contested this situation in Bialystok yet never achieved political hegemony in Vilna. The three processes correspond with these events: the massive insurrection in Warsaw contrasts with the partial successes in Bialystok and with the repeated failures in Vilna that included the turning over of Yitzhak Wittenberg, the commander of the resistance, to the Nazis.

All of the political forces were conscious of this situation, some more quickly than others. It should not be forgotten that the first armed actions of the Warsaw resistance were not against the Germans, but rather against the Jewish police and some "informers" from the Judenrat. Here are some perceptions of these actions:[24] "We proposed to kill Scherinski, the chief of the Jewish police, who was moreover, the director of the expulsions [deportation of the Warsaw Jews to Treblinka]. Although it may seem strange, we could not continue in any other way."[25] Itzhak Zukerman (Antek), a member of Dror and one of the commanders in Warsaw, clarifies the question of hegemony: "And so we defeated the Judenrat. The situation reached a stage where Mark Lichtenbaum didn't know whom to fear more: the Germans or the Jewish Combat Organization. When the Germans came to him and insisted that he appear before the Jewish activists and organize the pacific evacuation of the ghetto, he answered them: I am not the government in the ghetto. There is another government: the Jewish Combat Organization."[26]

Marek Edelman describes the characteristics of the conquered hegemony as a preparatory step to the spread and massiveness of the insurrection:

> The Jewish Combat Organization [JCO] rules the ghetto completely, without fissures. It is the only force and the only power that has authority and to which the population listens. At the end of February 1943, when the Germans call for the deportation of workers of the Halman carpentry factory, only twenty-five out of a total of a thousand workers come forward. At the beginning of March, when the Germans again call for the members of the brush workers to travel, of three thousand five hundred people, nobody comes. The JCO carries out its plans without compromises. The transport of the brush factory machines . . . is burned *en route,* with incendiary bombs. . . . They raise special taxes for the purchase of arms from the better-off inhabitants. The JCO also makes sure that the Kehilah institutions contribute. Anyone who doesn't give voluntarily is required to do so. The Judenrat pays two hundred fifty thousand zlotys. . . . This money is sent to the "Aryan zone" where our representatives organize the purchase of arms and explosives.[27]

Neither Vilna nor Bialystok experienced events of this type—a central factor in the limited nature of their rebellions. Gramsci believes that military confrontation is not likely to succeed if political hegemony has not been established previously. Of these three cases, only the resistance movement in Warsaw won this hegemony from the Judenrat.

In Bialystok, the ambiguous role of Efraim Barasz, the director of the Judenrat, confused the resistance organizations. Jaika Grossman's own testimony expresses this confusion. Grossman says, for example: "Barasz, on a personal level, was a loyal Jew, not an informant of the Nazis. . . . But he was convinced that he would save the ghetto through his own intervention and with bribes. . . . He would end by inevitably betraying us."[28] Nevertheless, this analysis did not lead Grossman to dispute with Barasz's political hegemony of the ghetto. The agreements and disagreements with the Judenrat impeded the development in Bialystok of a resistance front capable of challenging the leadership. At the time of confrontation, Barasz's policies of pacification affected the spirit of the Jewish population more than the calls for armed insurrection.

In Vilna, the German demand for the custody of Yitzhak Wittenberg produced a crucial confrontation over hegemony. The Nazi threat of "collective punishment" permitted Jacob Gens to strengthen his political hegemony by labeling the resistance organization "irresponsible" and by accusing it of provoking the destruction of the ghetto. The resistance movement emphasized the military tasks but did not engage in political confrontation (for instance, none of its political squads appeared in the ghetto's central plaza while Gens harangued the population to find Wittenberg and turn him over to the Nazis). This confrontation strengthened the Judenrat, having gained the support of a large portion of the population by indicating that the resistance sharpshooters would fire on the Jews and by using German threats of collective punishment.[29]

In these three cases, the Judenrat was to some extent the Germans' accomplice. Nonetheless, this problem did not occur in all the ghettos. The ghetto in Lachva, where the Judenrat organized the armed resistance, was one of several counterexamples. In many ghettos, a tactical alliance existed between the two power bases.

The Relationship of Military Forces

"The third moment is that of the relationship of military forces, which, every time, is the immediately decisive stage. . . . But this stage is neither indistinct nor immediately identifiable in a schematic form. In it, too, two stages can be distinguished: the military in the strict sense and the stage that can be called 'politico-military.' "[30]

Material Force and Moral Force

According to Roberto Jacoby, nineteenth-century German military strategist Karl von Clausewitz redefines

> the concept of combat forces, distinguishing the corporal forces, of a mechanical character from the moral forces that put them in movement,

> while he seeks to determine the relationship of the two. Clausewitz points out that the moral forces determine the size of the corporal forces, constituted by valor and audacity, the cohesion and capacity to act according to a joint plan. That is, that takes into account not only the natural quality of the human body—the fact that, in reality. It is not a thing—but also a social character. The driving force of soldiers depends on their belonging to a nation—the national motives that move the mass of the population—, of its organization and leadership, in quality of soldiers-citizens by the state and the military leadership. . . . Lenin takes Clausewitz's position further. . . . He not only assumes what Clausewitz pointed out—that the material force of the bodies depends on their moral and social force—but he subsumes this law into another that points out the specific conditions in which this process takes place: he adds that moral force depends on its class character, whether it be bourgeois or proletarian.[31]

The Jewish forces in the ghetto found themselves at their lowest level, as much in the sense of their "material strength" as in their "moral or social strength." Defeated and decimated by Nazism, they became malnourished, victims of a process of extermination, of infectious diseases, of poor military training, and of disillusionment caused by the flight or the betrayal of their leaders, authorities, and companions. It is difficult to imagine a condition of defeat worse than that of the ghetto Jews. In these conditions, there was no chance of group identity or of resistance without a redevelopment of its own moral strength, which in turn would weaken the enemy's moral strength.

This analysis of the relation of political forces leads me to offer a few lines through which I touch on the process of rebuilding. The struggle for a correct conceptualization of the genocidal objectives of Nazism and, in particular, the struggle to redefine Jewish identity constituted the bases for moral rearmament. As noted earlier, with respect to the reconstitution of social force, Clausewitz's and Lenin's visions are pertinent: the first groups to begin the articulation of a resistance initiative were the various Zionist parties, the Communists, and the Bundists. The national identity in the first group, the proletarian identity in the second, and a complex combination of both in the Bundists and the Socialists-Zionists permitted the rebuilding in terms of an undefeated subject, in terms of a subject ready to undertake the defense of a social collective. Seeing themselves as a people with a right to a land or as a proletariat fighting for social revolution, these groups formed the leadership of the resistance.

As the regeneration of the moral force began, the technical-military problem of "material strength" occurred: how to provision a civil population, isolated in guarded territory, and how to train the unemployed, the merchants, professionals, and adolescents for military combat. Also on this level, the Jewish resistance organizations showed that even in the worst defeat, taking advantage of the resources generated by the objective situations themselves was possible.

As for provisioning, these organizations used diverse and imaginative modes. They took advantage of the existence of a network for smuggling foodstuffs—initiated to relieve the nutritional deficits and tolerated by the Nazis as part of the conditions for maintenance of the ghetto—to bring in some arms, found and dismantled in the city by the "Aryan faction" of the resistance organizations and reassembled in the ghetto by Jewish artisans or workers, who had a greater familiarity with these technical problems. Meanwhile, they opened clandestine workshops in the ghetto itself, where the most skilled Jewish artisans began to make weapons from the most unusual and unexpected materials: bottles, light bulbs, wires, sticks, knives, and more. They produced everything from explosives to imitation armaments. This production was quite important in Warsaw. The distribution of these simple arms sustained the popular rebellion. For example, Grossman says:

> The national armament was an electric light bulb filled with sulphuric acid and some other acids. The cells had the task of collecting burnt out bulbs. . . . We also collected large homemade knives. The people of the cells didn't make them; specialists did who were generally welders. The comrades were in charge of collecting the material: metal bars, ironwork lying around on all the patios. . . . In those days, one of the boys brought the first rifle to the ghetto. It wasn't very modern, but it served, at least for training. As we used it for practice, and passing it from one cell to another was necessary, we took off the wooden gunstock.[32]

In his testimonials, Grossman illustrates with particular poignancy the role of Jewish artisans in supplying the ghetto. He describes the rescue of Kuba Rogozinsky, a craftsman imprisoned in the Volkovysk concentration camp. The resistance organization risked several of its men in Rogozinsky's rescue, who, once in Bialystok, opened an "explosive[s] workshop" in the ghetto.[33]

Ultimately, the Jewish artisans played an important role in the capacity for rebuilding and in the "relative success" of the resistance strategies to break the Nazi moral strength. The Nazis were consolidating their actions around the subjugation of the Jewish population.[34] From the first discriminatory laws through the campaigns of harassment to the internment in the concentration camps, the German actions against the Jewish population drew their strength from the negation of Jewish "humanity." The Jew was seen as a subhuman, as a degenerate being, incapable of acting as a person, not equal to another being of the same species. For that reason, a Jew could be murdered, tortured, denigrated without moral conflicts, as in the treatment of a member of a lower species.

Poor conditions in the ghettos reinforced this image of the Jewish population, as malnutrition and exhaustion, resulting from their forced relocation, continually led to their physical and moral deterioration. Before the extermination, the Germans encountered a Jewish population that was sick, weak, undernourished, sometimes betraying its own members, and living in terrible and unclean conditions. All of this confirmed and supported the Germans' theories of asseveration. It became easier for them to identify this population as a subspecies and to act based on that assumption.

Inside this imaginary construction, the Jewish resistance subverted and broke the model. How is this possible? How can a "subhuman, subspecies" successfully combat the army ravaging Europe? The survivors' testimonies discuss this point. The Germans arrogantly entered the ghetto, often lightly armed, without planning tactically or strategically their meetings with the Jewish population. They were convinced of their adversary's passivity and defeat. Nevertheless, when they encountered resistance, their entire sociomoral construction was subverted, so their first reaction was confusion, which caused them to flee. It is worth remembering that the occupation troops in the ghettos and the camps consisted of the SS and the Gestapo—not an army accustomed to combat, but one prepared to carry out torture, degradation, and the extermination of a defenseless civil population. This "army" of torturers showed its cowardice when faced with armed Jewish resistance. The German casualties were "exaggerated" by the truly slight military power of the Jewish resistance. In turn, the German "retreats" were numerous, and in some cases—the most symptomatic was Warsaw—after the slightest expression of Jewish resistance, they displayed the white flag and awaited the arrival of army troops to reenter the ghetto and engage in combat.[35] This crack in Nazi moral force proved an essential element in the rebuilding of the resistant moral strength and exemplified how the relations of moral forces can overpower technical-military relationships. There is no other way to explain how the resistance seized control of the Warsaw ghetto between January and April 1943.

Genocide as a "Campaign of Siege and Annihilation"

Regarding the theories about the armed confrontation of civilian troops, the fighting of irregular armies, made up of segments of the population, against a regular, compact army, Mao Tse-tung's reflections on the struggle between the Red Army and the imperial forces of Chiang Kai-shek are crucial. Even if the characteristics of the combat are not totally similar, the theoretical reflections are pertinent, especially because Mao saw the struggle from the perspective of the "campaigns of siege and annihilation" that the imperial forces carried out against the revolutionary troops. The trajectory that extended from the creation of the ghettos to the exterminations has the same characteristics. These characteristics include entrapping the Jewish people, isolating them from the non-Jewish world as a pretext for their extermination. Consequently, many problems treated by Mao relate to the understanding of the questions concerning the relationship between military forces: "The enemy suffers a strategic defeat when we break his campaign of 'siege and annihilation' and our defense becomes an offense and when he goes on the defensive and has to reorganize his forces before launching another campaign."[36]

In the ghettos, the campaigns of siege and annihilation took the form of the "selection," the *Aktion*. One main element in reversing the process was the capacity of the armed Jewish resistance to stop the selection process. The frustrated German incursion into the Warsaw ghetto, in January 1943, when only 7,000 of the announced 16,000 Jews were deported, transformed the equilibrium between forces and for the first time put the resistance organization on the offensive. Three months later the enemy regrouped its forces and by July reseized control of the ghetto, but only after having burned it down, house by house. According to Mao,

> Political mobilization is a problem important in the fight against a campaign of "siege and annihilation." This means that we must clearly, emphatically and in detail, tell the combatants and the supporting population that the enemy offensive is inevitable and imminent and that it will cause great harm to the country. At the same time, we have to make them aware of the enemy's weaknesses, the factors favorable to us, our will to win at all costs, the direction that our efforts should follow. To tell the truth, it is easy to lose the initiative while on the defensive. . . . Nevertheless, giving it to the defensive posture is possible, which is passive in form, an active content and move from the passive phase in form to the active phase in form and content. In the strategic counteroffensive, the initiative is manifest not only in the content, but also in th\e form, in the rejection of passivity that accompanies the retreat. For the enemy, our counteroffensive signifies our ability to take away his initiative and convert it into passivity. . . . The concentration of forces is necessary to change the enemy's situation and our own. . . . When we concentrate our troops, and we win a battle, we achieve this objective in the battle; moreover, this influences the entire campaign.[37]

Once a resistance organization guaranteed the minimal conditions for the survival of the central nucleus of militants, it proposed the "concentration of forces." These forces could come together in a "general assembly," where the actions to be taken were decided. This assembly was secret, of course, and took place at the very moment that another 3,000 were being taken from the ghetto. In the assembly, members realized that the only resistance was "active resistance" and that "passive defense" was a "false defense." They developed a plan for action containing four central ways to stop the retreat and initiated the "active defense":

> Abba [Abba Kovner, a resistance leader in Vilna] had prepared a project:
>
> 1. Establish the combat organization and its cells. Each member of the movement, after having been ratified by the secretary, would be mobilized to the combat organization and each of them would know only the members of his or her own group.
>
> 2. Seek allies among the other Zionist movements and among the Communists. The organization should include all the antifascist forces existing in the ghetto.
>
> 3. Improve and extend our network in the "Aryan zone." Its function would be to seek allies outside the ghetto, establish connections with them, and obtain arms. The armament was fundamental and required the elaboration of a well-defined plan, made after examining all the existing possibilities in the German workplaces. We should also involve the Poles with whom we intended to extend our chain of contacts.
>
> 4. Disseminate to all the Jews and especially the young people, the cruel truth about the total annihilation of the Jews that the Germans would impose on Eastern Europe. We ought to excite them to defend their lives with arms, sticks, tools, and when there was no other option, with our own fists.[38]

The four central objectives were: "open political mobilization and agitation," "centralize military mobilization," "organize provisioning," and, a specific and central objective, "break the siege."

Nevertheless, the Vilna resistance organization never succeeded in definitively regaining the initiative. Gens's political sense and the use that the Germans made of it always placed the resistance in a passive position, responding to the Nazi blows and lacking the capacity to initiate its own policies. The experiences in Warsaw and Bialystok differ in this sense. They had greater margins for defining where, when, and how to fight.

The notion of "concentration of forces" also reappears in other forms in the reflections by many resistance militants, with particular richness by Jaika Grossman: "If you're dealing with a war of the few and the weak against the many and the strong whose strategy is ten to one, the tactic should be one to ten; the forces should not be divided, but should 'strike with a single fist.' "[39] Even in the Bialystok ghetto rebellion, when the last resources had been used, the resistance decided to build an "Aryan network" outside the ghetto, forming a cell of women who maintained three or four apartments in the "Aryan zone" of the city, where survivors of the battle sought shelter. Those apartments served as an intermediate stop for the combatants on their way to the forests, where they joined the partisan brigades, with whom they had also carried out respective contacts. Even if there were casualties in the cell that worked in the "Aryan zone," when the German intelligence services discovered them, several combatants broke the siege of the ghetto, arrived at the apartments, and proceeded to the forests. But given the conditions in which they carried out each action, it may be thought that they reached there so that by word of mouth the rebellion of the Bialystok ghetto could be reconstructed historically. If not, the only information about it would come from Nazi documents.

Also suggestive are some reflections about the importance of "recovering the initiative" in combat. There is a constant return to this question, and even if the process of extermination never stops, even if something new occurs every day, one central objective of the organization is to be able to set, by itself, the moment and place of the rebellion. It is interesting how this issue played out in the different uprisings. The Vilna resistance responded to a Nazi offensive, but only succeeded in fragmenting its own forces, despite Grossman's description of Vilna's organization as "the most advanced politically." In the first Bialystok uprising, a small portion of the resistance organization took the initiative, creating panic and causing important casualties in the German forces, in spite of suffering important "denunciations." In Warsaw, the resistance took back the initiative, and the battle went on for months. In Bialystok, the resistance had devised a plan similar to Warsaw's, with an organization perhaps better defended. Nevertheless, the lesson learned by the Nazis at Warsaw, the denunciations of the resistance by the Jewish leadership, and a lack of access to Nazi information took the "initiative" from the resistance, and its members had to change their plans for the march, exposing themselves to a frontal attack in poor conditions, but even then resisting for a week with a "battle of bunkers" in the ghetto.

The Ghetto or the Forest: Some Questions of Strategy

In forming a resistance strategy, the issue arose concerning whether to send contingents to the forests to support the partisan brigades in guerilla warfare against the Nazis or to remain in the ghetto. The option of the forest was tied to the issue of efficacy: in the forests, the preservation of one's own forces was simpler; there were better conditions for the provisioning and training of troops; and sabotage actions against the German army were carried out when a victory by the Allied forces seemed possible. The ghetto option was based on a political understanding: emigrating to the forests would signify the abandonment of the greater part of the ghetto population to its passive extermination. Going to the forests could be considered a break from the destiny of the Jews' identity as a people.

The discussion crossed over all the political groups of the resistance, but each group's orientation was in no way random. Overall, the Communists were inclined toward the forest option. Identified with the resistance of the Red Army at the gates of Moscow, hoping for a possible Soviet counteroffensive, they favored military action as a way of mining the German front itself. On the contrary, the Zionists and the Bundists identified themselves with the popular resistance to move the survivors to the forests, whenever that might be necessary. They saw the urban resistance as the ultimate demonstration of Jewish dignity and their responsibility to the Jewish past and future. The mass insurrection in the ghettos would show the world an image of a Judaism resisting, heeding the call of the desperate Abba Kovner, commander of the resistance in Vilna: "We won't let ourselves be taken like lambs to the slaughter."

Again, Jaika Grossman most skillfully summarizes the debate, transcribing the position of the HaShomer HaTzair, as stated by its commander, Edek Buraks:

> Comrades, I want again to clarify our position for you. It may be that in the forests there are better opportunities for an effective war. But are we

> going to allow the people to be taken like lambs to the slaughter, as happened in Vilna, while we seek more effective warfare in the forests? I'm not opposed to acts of sabotage, bridges destroyed, telegraph cables broken, munitions trains exploded. All of this is of great importance, but it doesn't answer our great question: how to organize a massive reaction that gives expression to the resistance of an entire people, how to make the Jewish masses enclosed in the ghetto rebel against its destiny of being a passive herd? Let us suppose that we go to fight in the forests, and we wash our hands of all responsibility. We will have fulfilled our responsibilities, and that is a good solution for some who seek to take part in the anti-Fascist war. But what is the collective and national solution? Are we going to desert the ghetto still disintegrating with all its elderly, women and children? Then will we say: we have saved our own lives? And where is the vanguard of our movement? I see our comrades at the head of the oppressed majority, not as a sect of the elect that acts according to the dictates of its own conscience, rather than as the leaders of our people. We have educated our comrades for that: the rebellion should be by the masses and take place in the ghetto. . . . If they kill us as Jews, we should fight them as such. Not as individuals, but as an organized community. To him who so acts will be destined a place in history.[40]

Even when they decided on the urban insurrection, the question of the military squads' destiny remained. This problem also appeared in discussions between Communists and Socialists-Zionists, as described by Grossman:

> In fact, we come here to the same conception held among the Communists in Warsaw, with a few differentiating details, because the conditions in Bialystok were different. They postulate the need to defend themselves, but they sent those who knew how to use arms to the forests, to join the general partisan movement. That meant that the defense of sixty thousand Jews of Bialystok, including women, children, old people, and the sick, that resistance that should represent the soul of our people, its national honor, we would leave to others, to the disorganized masses, to the conservative and antipopular parties.[41]

The "ghetto option" implied not only the willingness to fight, but also the political planning that supposed only a slight chance of personal survival for the military squadrons of the resistance. Not many could take on such a commitment to remain in the ghetto for a struggle whose objective was more symbolic than material, whose defeat was anticipated beforehand.

Edek Buraks, commander of the resistance in the Bialystok ghetto (A Front), exemplified the coherence between his political conviction of the importance of a Jewish mass rebellion and his willingness to become a combatant in it, even at the cost of sacrificing his very limited chances for survival. Jaika Grossman writes:

> Wednesday wasn't any better. They discovered Edek's position. He used the revolver, and his men [there were eight] attacked the SS empty-handed. Traitors had also been at work here, for Edek's base, its layout, and structure had been known to the Germans beforehand. . . . That night, a rumor spread in the ghetto: they were organizing the resistance. It wasn't a spontaneous uprising of the masses. And they saw the group that was going to be deported. Gedalya, a member of HaShomer HaTzair, hidden among the Jewish police, moved close to them; he wanted to speak to them, to cheer them up. The Germans pushed him violently, in spite of which he could catch Edek's words: "We are still going to give them what they deserve." . . . Edek, with his face burning and his eyes feverish, led the group. . . . From then on, we never saw Edek again. The transport left the ghetto, and when they were already far away, we could still see how the blows were falling on their heads and how our people responded arrogantly. They were injured, but they returned the blows, they bit, they pierced their fingernails into the flesh of the SS men. . . . And so Edek left. The first commandant and the first organizer of our struggle. And only from afar a few echoes reached us. Jews who had been in the same boxcar with him and had escaped told us of that leader and friend so beloved by his people, who had decided with his comrades not to jump from the train; they only wanted to help others jump. When those who were arriving, barely alive and without any desire to keep on living, were taken from their boxcars near Treblinka, Edek and his companions organized a rebellion, in the portals of the crematoria, so

> that the Jews would not enter voluntarily. Edek and his men were assassinated in front of the crematoria ovens, they wouldn't enter. When they were shot, they were inciting the Jews to flee. This is what the witnesses told us.[42]

Edek Buraks consubstantiated himself with his mission to be the vanguard of the Jewish popular rebellion. He led the first rebellion in the ghetto, directed the escape from the trains, and generated the final powder flash in front of the crematory ovens of Treblinka.

Tactical Planning

The Jewish Combat Organization (JCO) found itself in a state of "informal" war for a year and a half since the German occupation. The final moves of the ghetto uprising had been laid out in a "battle plan." This plan contained three central stages. The first was named the "street fight." This stage was intended to tie up the German occupation of the ghetto. Groups of militants, trained in confronting the Nazis and bringing the Jewish masses into the combat, would take the offensive at four strategic points. In Warsaw, these points were:

1. the "central ghetto" (directed by Mordecai Anielewicz and Rosa Rosenfeld)
2. the Muranow Plaza (directed by Gutkowski)
3. the "brushers" (directed by Grinspan, Marek Edelman, and Berlinski)
4. the "producing ghetto," where the majority of the factories were located (directed by Kawe, Schwartzfus, Nowodworski, and Geller).

In Vilna, the focus of the fighting was on Strashun Street, but street fighting with the Germans was unsuccessful, for Jacob Gens guided the German incursions into the ghetto, avoiding Strashun Street. In Bialystok, there were two central sectors: the central ghetto and the factory area. However, the Nazi surprise attack made street fighting impossible. The resistance moved automatically to the second stage, especially in the factory area; they changed tactics in the central ghetto.

On March 13, the Germans launched their first attack on Warsaw but were repulsed in the streets of the ghetto. They retreated, carrying with them a dozen casualties. Reinforcements did not arrive until April 19, more than a month later, and the Nazis tried again. The fighting went on all day in different areas of the ghetto, but at nightfall the Germans had to retreat again, leaving another dozen casualties on the streets.

The next day, the Germans gained control of the Plaza Muranow and the "brush factories," after bloody fighting that cost them almost one hundred casualties. It took them another day to overtake the position in the central ghetto. The resistance forces, with only several hundred combatants, successfully involved the ghetto in battle and maintained the offensive for four days. On April 23, the resistance organization pleaded with the Polish population of Warsaw to join the battle against Nazism—a last desperate attempt to break the separation from the non-Jewish world. They sought to involve the Polish armies, nationalist and Communist, Armia Krajowa and Armia Ludowa, and the civilian population in the confrontation. The proclamation read:

> Poles! Citizens of liberty! In the midst of the roar of the cannons with which the German army is destroying our houses, the homes of our mothers, wives and children; in the midst of the blasts of the machine guns that we let go in the battle against the cowardly gendarmes and the men of the SS; from the burning remains and the smoke that envelops the massacred Warsaw ghetto, blood and dust. We, the slaves of the ghetto, send you our cordial salute! We know that with the most profound pain and with tears of sympathy, with amazement, fear and anxiety, you await the result of the battle that we have, in the last few days, carried out against the cruel invader; every threshold in the ghetto continues to be a fortress. All of us may perish in combat, but we will never surrender. Like you, we are thirsty for vengeance and desirous of making our common enemy pay for its crimes. This is the battle for our liberty and for yours! For our and your social and human rights and for national honor and dignity! We want vengeance for the crimes of Oswiecim, Treblinka, Belzac, and Maidanik! Long live the fellowship of Poland combatant![43]

When the position on Mila Street, the second stage of the plan, fell, the resistance forces began to defend the fortified bunkers. In his last letter, April 23, 1943, Mordecai Anielewicz, the commander of the Warsaw rebellion, described this change of phases:

> I don't have the words to express my feelings: something has happened that goes beyond our wildest dreams: twice the Germans fled the ghetto. One of our units maintained its positions for forty minutes, and another resisted for six hours. Ichiel fell by his machine gun like a hero. The ghetto has been in flames for three days. We have been fighting a guerilla war since last night. You need to know that the revolver is useless. We need grenades, rockets, machine guns and explosives.[44]

Once the offensive failed, the resistance planned to fortify itself in a series of "key" positions, bunkers prepared before the January combat. The strategy was to remain hidden during the day and harass the occupation forces at night. At this point, the chain of events surprised the JCO itself. Each Jew converted his home into a fortified bunker. Beyond the ten or twelve positions of the organization, the Germans encountered resistance in every street, in each dwelling. On April 24, the Germans began the "clean up," house by house, burning them one by one and finding themselves obligated to fight at any moment.

Vilna and Bialystok differed in this second stage also. Vilna Jews carried out some attacks in front of the bunkers on Strashun Street but avoided the Germans who engaged in combat. Many resistance fighters abandoned the ghetto in groups and fled to the forests. In Bialystok, the bunkers in the factory zone resisted for a week; the resistance forces in the central ghetto left with the bulk of the population for the embarkation station and sought a confrontation with the Nazi army at the station, thus opening a way to flee to the forests. However, the Jewish population of Bialystok did not join the fighting, so the battle ended after seven hours of skirmishes.

On May 8, the Nazis reached the bunker on Mila Street in Warsaw. After a battle, the central command post of the resistance fell, but many other posts remained viable. On May 11, Bonifraterska, Schwienticherska, and Wollowa Streets fell. It then took the Germans twenty days to "cleanse" the ghetto. They could scarcely sweep a block a day. Nevertheless, the plan did not end with the fortified bunkers. The JCO proposed that once they themselves were defeated, the survivors would try to leave to the forests in armed groups to join the partisan brigades. Several contingents left the ghetto with that intention. On April 28, a group passed through the factory zone for "Aryan" territory. On May 10, another contingent left. The survivors hid in the sewers and harassed the German troops at night. This situation continued, in spite of air bombardments, artillery, and the Nazi gassing of the sewers. Some bunkers were still resisting in June. On June 19, the bunkers on Grzybowslta and Prosna Streets fell, at the edge of the ghetto. The fighting continued at least until September, when a group of seventeen partisans escaped to the forests.

Conclusion

Much has been written about the heroism of those who carried out the rebellion during such extreme moral and physical defeat. It is impossible to deny the heroic character of these social and human representations of the Jewish people. Heroism is a necessary, although not sufficient condition for a politics of resistance against social practices such as genocide—a massive extermination of their own social forces. The political squadrons of the resistance learned from their own experiences, at the cost of sacrificing many of their best men. It would be irresponsible not to gather the legacy of their apprenticeships, of their political constructions, to make those constructions available to all the social factions ready to combat the realization of new processes of extermination, wherever they might occur.

15. "Theater in a Graveyard"

The Ghetto Theater in Vilna

ERIC J. STERLING

In Joshua Sobol's Holocaust documentary drama *Ghetto* (1983), Srulik, the elderly one-armed puppeteer and former artistic director, reminisces about the ghetto theater, which existed in Vilna, Lithuania, from 1942 to 1943. Srulik responds to an interview question, just as Sobol has asked interview questions during his exhaustive research in preparation for the writing of the play.[1] Freddie Rokem observes that "[t]he realistic document has been confined to the memory of the individual, and the work of art can thus liberate and communicate it."[2] Srulik's memories (which derive from the actual reminiscences of the theater's artistic director, Israel Segal), along with the diary of Herman Kruk, the ghetto librarian, dramatize the creation and demise of the theater as well as the destruction of the ghetto itself. Kruk initially disapproved of the theater, which the ghetto leader (Jacob Gens) had created; Kruk's leaflets and posters, which actually appeared on the ghetto walls in 1942, condemned the establishment of the Vilna theater, proclaiming, "YOU DON'T PERFORM THEATER IN A GRAVEYARD."[3] The librarian's protest slogan alluded to the creation of a theater near the site of the massacre of approximately 33,500 (out of 57,000) that occurred in the Ponar forest from July to December of 1941,[4] a mere few weeks before the establishment of the theater (January 18, 1942), as well as to the fact that the actors used the clothes of the murder victims as costumes for their plays. Sobol believes, however, that the historical Herman Kruk changed his mind about the ghetto theater "even after the first show—to which he had been opposed. He reviewed the first show in his diary and gave it some positive comments."[5] Kruk later acknowledged in his diary that Gens was justified in creating the theater because in addition to allowing more people to survive, it helped preserve their Yiddish language and their culture. In fact, when the partisan Yitzhak Arad visited the Vilna ghetto in April 1943, he was greatly impressed by the "lively cultural life. On the bulletin board in the Judenrat was the weekly announcement of theatrical performances, music, the Yiddish and Hebrew choirs."[6] In his play, Sobol supports Gens's idea for the theater by demonstrating that it brings vibrancy and hope to the Jews' lives and by manifesting that the theater helps to preserve many families who otherwise would have perished. Kruk eventually realizes, as Gens maintains, that although the creation of a theater shortly after the massacre might appear to show disrespect for the dead, the survivors have an obligation to preserve their culture and their own lives, and, furthermore, the performance of theater serves as an act of defiance against the Nazis.

In *Ghetto,* the Israeli playwright defends Jacob Gens, the leader of the Vilna ghetto, for his creation of the ghetto theater and portrays his attempts to save the lives of many Jews—even when he preserves some people at the expense of others. Gens considers survival essential at all costs, so he willingly makes sacrifices in order to save lives. Although he recognizes that many members of the ghetto have relatives who perished during the massacres at Ponar, he considers the creation of the theater near the mass grave to be an opportunity to save others' lives. When Srulik complains that "fifty thousand Jews were murdered on this spot. The blood's not dry yet and you want us to create theater here?" the ghetto leader dramatically rebuts his complaint by bringing out from hiding the actors whom he has rescued from death (166). Historically, many actors and stagehands died at Ponar, but those who survived hid in the ghetto until the establishment of the theater. Gens hoped that the theater would save their lives (just as the women's orchestra in Auschwitz preserved the lives of Fania Fenelon and other Jewish musicians—which Arthur Miller dramatizes in *Playing for Time*). In Sobol's play, Gens promises Srulik that if the artistic director can "make them into an acting company on this spot, I can get them yellow work permits—and bread. And butter—and potatoes. And soap!" (168). Thus, the theater provides the ghetto inhabitants with an occupation and purpose, which allows them to attain the label "skilled workers." This appellation entitles them to receive food and soap, which will enable them to survive. When pondering the establishment of the theater, the empathetic Srulik and Kruk concern themselves with the feelings of those who have suffered the loss of loved ones, yet the sole concern of the pragmatic Jacob Gens is the preservation of the lives of those who have managed thus far to escape the death pits at Ponar.

Although Gens's idea to create a theater appears more practical than compassionate, one must remember that the ghetto inhabitants unquestionably went to the plays partly as a means of escape from their hardships and mental anguish. Audiences attended the ghetto theater to see plays such as David Pinski's *Shlomo Molcho* (the initial Vilna ghetto production, which premiered April 26, 1942), *The Man under the Bridge* (which opened November 1942), Pinski's *The Treasure* (which premiered March 27, 1943), and Pinski's *Eternal Jew* (which opened June 10, 1943). They went to the theater so that they could spend a few hours of enjoyment without having to think about the deaths of their family members at Ponar, impending selections, or their own sorrowful dilemmas. In a historical speech commemorating the first anniversary of the ghetto theater, Gens remarked: "Last year they said that the theater was just a fad of mine. . . . It was a vital necessity. . . . How did the idea come up? Simply to give people the opportunity to escape from the reality of the ghetto for a few hours. This we achieved. These are dark and hard days. Our body is in the ghetto but our spirit has not been enslaved. . . . Heaven forbid that we should let our spirit collapse. We must be strong in spirit and in body."[7] Gens realized that the Vilna Jews were in the midst of a tragic situation and that moments of pleasure, emotional escape, and defiance were essential if they were to maintain their sanity and fortitude. Judy E. Yordon, who directed Ball State University's production of *Ghetto,* labels the play "a testament to spiritual defiance, the durability of memory, and the saving power of art."[8] Although some might believe that the theater provided the ghetto inhabitants with a foolish diversion and escape when they should have concentrated exclusively on their present dilemma, it actually created a bond among Jews and strengthened their resolve to endure Nazi oppression.

In *Ghetto,* Gens also believes that the Jews can survive by remaining strong psychologically and that the presentation of cultural events such as plays will allow the Jews to bond together emotionally rather than to become fragmented. During times of desperation, people (such as the tailor Weiskopf) can become selfish and preoccupied with only their own welfare rather than concerned about that of the group. Primo Levi, for instance, discusses in *Survival in Auschwitz* how the starving Jews in the concentration camp often could only think of saving themselves—even at the expense of others—and that "everything can be stolen, in fact is automatically stolen as soon as attention is relaxed."[9] Jewish theater, Gens maintains in the play, will cause the people to bond together and behave altruistically because they will take pride in their culture and have a reason to live. The ghetto leader assures Srulik: "As a troop [*sic*] of Jewish actors, you can make a difference! Look around! Our self-esteem is in the sewer. People walk the streets staring at their shoes—if they have shoes to stare at. You can change all that—give them back their self-respect. That's what I want: show them they have a culture—a language, a powerful inheritance: an inner life" (168). The actors and audience members in the Vilna ghetto take pride in their culture, thus providing their lives with meaning, with purpose—and a desire to survive. As Kruk later admits, "Every form of cultural activity is essential here in the ghetto. It's the battle plan in our fight to remain human beings. . . . They can't obliterate our humanity—not as long as we cling to a spiritual life" (208). In 1942, the performance of plays such as *The Eternal Jew* reinforced their identity as Jews, causing them to bond together, which resulted in less fighting among the ghetto inhabitants and the concomitant perspective of the Nazis as their common enemy. According to Rokem, Sobol's play manifests that

> the Jewish community as a collective, the Jewish culture and its traditions, was stronger and more viable than the attempts of the Nazis to bring about the "Final Solution." . . . The ghetto theater functions in Sobol's play as such a form of deception [one that purports to be a form of cooperation]—and theater is in itself a form of deception—which at the same time is based on a form of creativity. Even though all of its members except one are finally executed, the theater in the ghetto is presented as a successful revolt against oppression and thus a form of survival.[10]

Thus, the theater performances in the Vilna ghetto served as a means of defying the Nazis, manifesting that despite the adverse conditions, the Jews would succeed in preserving their culture, dignity, and way of life.

Sobol manifests how the ghetto theater became an integral part of the people's lives by portraying the interactions between the people and the theater. For instance, the playwright includes the ghetto palm reader, who begs for money in order to survive. Elinor Fuchs notes that "*Ghetto* owes a debt to the Yiddish theater. (Even Sobol's wily Hasid, here a rogue palm reader, is a stock comic figure of the Yiddish theater.) These echoes are especially evocative as [V]ilna had been at one time the seat of Europe's greatest Yiddish theater."[11] The Hasid in Sobol's play is an actor who joins the troupe so that he will receive food. His death becomes an important part of the plot because Gens must demonstrate to Gestapo officer Bruno Kittel that he is capable of ruling the ghetto by exacting justice upon the Hasid's killer. The drama includes several other examples of how reality and theater merge in the ghetto. When discussing everyday life in the ghetto, the tailor Weiskopf remarks, "Life is a rehearsal" (173), as if all the ghetto inhabitants play a part. The actors entertain their audiences while the ghetto inhabitants try to please the Nazis so that they may survive. And when the actress Chaja hints that she will work with the partisans to blow up a bridge, she refers to her book on explosives as a play entitled *Beneath the Bridge*—as if her part in the covert action is yet another role she will play. Furthermore, Sobol points out that historically the theater was located in the same building as the Judenrat, so a relationship undoubtedly existed between the theatrical and political aspects of the ghetto; this is apparent in the play when Gens leaves his office to visit the theater.[12]

A bond also emerged historically between the theater troupe and the other ghetto inhabitants because of the playwriting contest that began on July 26, 1942, with a prize awarded for the best drama written about the ghetto. This contest caused many Jews in the Vilna ghetto to employ their artistic skills to create dramas about their experiences and culture, as well as enabling many people to become part of the theater—almost as if the ghetto and the theater merged into one. From this contest, one can assume that Gens believed that the pride his people had in their culture would allow them to remain strong, and the popularity of the performances supported his belief.

Sobol notes in his postscript that during its first year (January 1942–January 1943), the theater sold 34,804 tickets. The theater "was usually packed and the shows were often sold out weeks in advance. By the time the ghetto was liquidated on September 20, 1943 . . . [a] population of twenty thousand people had bought seventy thousand (!) tickets."[13] The fact that the impoverished ghetto inhabitants purchased theater tickets weeks in advance is telling; during a time in which arbitrary and unforeseen selections meant that the Jews could be sent off to a concentration camp any day, they still bought theater tickets weeks in advance, manifesting their hope for survival as well as their need for culture. During the bleakest times of their lives, the theater gave them something to which they could look forward. In the play, Srulik, perhaps voicing the memories of the historical Vilna theater director Israel Segal, claims that "the audience came right up to the last days of the ghetto. People who were loaded up and sent away in trains the next morning, still put on their best clothes the evening before and came to our theater performance" (155). And the fact that these impoverished ghetto dwellers, who barely had sufficient money to purchase bread, spent their money on plays demonstrates unequivocally what a significant role theater played in their lives.

According to the play, the actors, playwrights, and songwriters who create art in the ghetto theater help preserve the culture that anti-Semitic villains such as Dr. Paul, who has come from the Rosenberg Institute to collect Jewish artifacts for his study on Judaism without Jews, wish to destroy. We know that Gens's idea of preserving Jewish culture in the ghetto was successful because songs by writers of the ghetto theater, such as Schmerke Kaczerginski's "Shtiler, Shtiler" (Be still) and "Friling" (Springtime), still exist—and appear in Sobol's play. *Ghetto* contains not only songs from the Vilna theater, but also some actual scenes from dramas performed by the ghetto theater troupe. And the historical Gens astutely correlated the perpetuation of culture with the survival of its people. Sobol concurs, citing the vitality of the cultural activity as a means of survival: he claims that without this vitality and devotion to the culture, "there is no accounting for the ability of the defenseless survivors to cling dauntlessly to life, to retain their joy of life in the face of armed tormentors and murderers."[14]

The clothes that the actors (both the Vilna actors in the ghetto from 1942 to 1943 and the performers in Sobol's play) wear symbolize the strong desire to live, no matter how intense the adversity. As Srulik sits in his apartment and begins to reminisce about the ghetto theater, there is a thunderous crash, and the audience finds "a bare stage. At the rear wall is a tremendous, chaotic mountain of clothing" (156). The clothes, like the ghetto theater and Sobol's play itself, commemorate the lives and honor the memories of the victims of Vilna. Audience members might be shocked that the costumes for the Vilna actors and actresses have originated from the huge pile of clothes that once belonged to Jews killed by the Nazis. Nazi officer Kittel remarks to Chaja, who searches for a pair of shoes, "[i]f you knew where these shoes had been, you'd stay barefoot" (157). When the actors don costumes stained with blood—clothes owned by Jews who lost their lives during the massacre at Ponar—they do not merely portray the Jews who died at the hands of the Nazis and the Lithuanians: they identity with them and even become them, allowing the dead to live on through the people who wear their clothes and who can empathize with their sufferings.

When the actor playing Weiskopf enters the stage as the play begins, the stage direction states that he is *"dressed in rags"* (156). When he puts on clothes that he receives from the huge pile, he becomes the successful but egocentric ghetto entrepreneur who thrives as other ghetto inhabitants die. But the audience recognizes that his rich clothes belonged previously to a murdered Jew. Rokem correctly observes that the clothes represent "an image of loss and absence."[15] An impoverished and starving woman finds a dress and shoes from the pile; when she wears them, she becomes Chaja, the ghetto actress and singer. The tragedies she performs onstage remind the audience of the actual tragedies the Jews in Vilna have experienced. By wearing the clothes of the dead and acting out parts—some of which relate to those who perished at Ponar—the actors remember and portray the dead. *Ghetto* concludes with a "dance of the coats" scene in which the clothing worn, which belonged to "past ghetto victims[,] is animated by current characters who are actors in the [V]ilna ghetto. This gives us a triple vision of the already lost bodies enacted by the invisible but live actors' bodies playing performers-characters whose own loss of bodies will be enacted in the future."[16] The actors in the Vilna ghetto revive the memories of the dead Jews whose clothing they wear, and the actors in modern productions of Sobol's play give life to the actors who were murdered during the liquidation of the ghetto, which began after their last performance.

Judy E. Yordon reports in an article in *Text and Performance Quarterly* that the actors who performed in her Ball State University production of *Ghetto* in October 1991 experienced humiliation and persecution (although obviously not on the same level as the Jewish actors in Vilna during the Holocaust) because they wore yellow Stars of David from the play on their clothes everywhere they went during the five-week rehearsal period. She mentions that because the actors in the production, midwesterners born decades after World War II, found that "an emotional and a psychological distance between cast and characters remained,"[17] they pinned these stars, which were part of their costumes, to their regular street clothes. One of the cast members was victimized and traumatized the first day; he cried as he reported the racial slur and harassment that he endured. Yordon quotes the actor's relation of the incident: "For a brief fraction of a moment, I somewhat got a feeling of what happened to those Jews who had to wear the star. . . . What I couldn't believe was that at this time and location, someone would actually go out of their way to roll down a window and yell a racial slur across the street." Other actors heard remarks such as "See you at the camps" and "Check out the showers"; furthermore, one person feared for his life, and another, an English department faculty member who appeared in the show, was almost run over intentionally by a car driver; he decided subsequently to put his coat on to hide the star.[18] The actors in the ghetto theater in Vilna and the other Jews during the Holocaust regrettably did not have this choice; they had to show their yellow star. The hatred and prejudice that the Ball State actors experienced because of the star they pinned to their clothing manifested how close to the surface anti-Semitism was in their own community and allowed them, as well as many people in this midwestern community, to learn and to empathize with the sufferings of the inhabitants of the Vilna ghetto. The performance, therefore, helped to honor the memories of the victims in Vilna.

The actors in contemporary theater, such as those at Ball State, who perform in Sobol's drama commemorate the dead when they portray the Vilna actors. The character Srulik reminisces about the ghetto theater (the drama, which occurs in his mind, replays actual documented events), thus reviving the memories of the deceased—the Jews who died at Ponar as well as the Jewish actors and actresses who perished two years later during the liquidation of the ghetto. This commemoration is significant because one of the most crucial aspects of Holocaust literature is memory—the remembrance and the honoring of innocent victims. Although the clothes reminded the 1942 Vilna theater participants of others' tragedies, their donning of those clothes manifested their ability to survive while other Holocaust victims did not and symbolized Gens's acquiescence that some Jews had to die so that others could live.

Gens, like Mordechai Rumkowski, the leader of the Łódź ghetto in Poland, enabled thousands of Jews to survive for years by sacrificing the elderly, the children, and the sickly—as well as by employing Jewish workers at factories where they manufactured and repaired uniforms for the German army. Although one may rightfully argue that the Vilna Jews were aiding their Nazi adversaries, "Sobol's *Ghetto* echos [*sic*] the Brechtian slogan 'food before morality' and, as in Brecht's work, the stakes are not just food, but human life."[19] Critics of Gens point out that he saved few lives because the Nazis eventually liquidated the Vilna ghetto, but those Jews who survived the massacre of 1941 lived two years longer than they would have otherwise, and their lives might have been preserved had the Russian soldiers reached Vilna earlier than they did. The partisan Arad mentions that the Jews in the Vilna ghetto were optimistic when he met them: "Despite the daily hardships, everyone felt that the fall of Nazi Germany was imminent, and the goal was to hold out for a few months more until Germany would collapse under pressure from the Allied armies. Approaching victory was the major subject of conversation in the ghetto, although there was an underlying fear that the Germans would try to wipe out the surviving Jews before their retreat."[20] Gens believed that if he sacrificed some lives, he could preserve the rest of the Vilna Jews for several more months—long enough for the Russians to enter from the eastern border and save them from the Nazis; he could not have foreseen that the Russian army would mysteriously stop their offensive and consequently fail to rescue them. Modern critics enjoy the advantage of hindsight not afforded to Gens.

Gens's detractors also fail to discern that the ghetto leader could not act upon his own initiatives, but rather was compelled to follow Nazi rules. Robert Skloot points out that even though the "despair and hope that seized the ghetto could be frequently reversed by the manipulation of the economic, social, or nutritional conditions he [Gens] controlled, in truth the political space Gens operated in was exceedingly small."[21] In Sobol's drama, Kittel, a Schutzstaffel (SS) officer who specializes in the liquidation of ghettos, speaks condescendingly to Gens, ordering him about and making demands. When Kittel threatens Gens because some Jews have escaped the work crews and perhaps the ghetto itself, he plays on the Jewish concept of mutual responsibility: "If anyone disappears, his family will be shot. If a family disappears, everyone who shared a room with them will be shot. . . . All workers will be divided into groups of ten. One runs, the other nine die" (217). Gens merely grunts a reluctant acceptance to the conditions because they are orders, not requests. Kittel's comportment toward Gens signifies the latter man's lack of authority and his status as a figurehead whom the Nazis employ to provide Jews with a false sense of security that they are governing themselves.

Kittel's control over Gens in the play manifests why the historical ghetto leader may have felt compelled to allow the selections of Jews. Historian Leni Yahil claims that although Gens saved some lives, "by deciding who remained and who had to go he now became involved in the murderous activities of the Germans."[22] Vivian Patraka adds that Sobol's play "is about the obscenity of the so-called choices the Nazis imposed on their victims, including these ghettos' Jewish administrators, and the kind of ruination of larger ethical systems these 'choices' produced (this time, should we give up children or old people to death?)."[23] In *Ghetto,* however, Sobol portrays the ghetto leader as a man who believes that he has no alternative. If Gens refuses to conduct selections, the Nazis will storm the ghetto and murder more Jews than they had demanded for their quota. Because only a small number of Jews in the Vilna ghetto possess weapons, they cannot defend themselves adequately;[24] in Gens's opinion, their only hope is to obey Nazi dicta as they wait for the Russian army to destroy the German forces. Isaiah Trunk claims that although the Judenrat

> may have reasoned that, thanks to their "rescue-through-work" strategy, the working segment of the ghetto population, the young men and women, would have a better chance of survival, they understood at the same time that people on welfare or otherwise not working had no chance at all. . . . Beset by the impending ordeal, a sizable number of Councils fearfully came to the conclusion that since not all the Jews could be saved, it was better to deliver to the Nazi Moloch those ghetto dwellers with little or no chance of survival in order to save others.[25]

Thus, Gens allowed some Jews to be taken to their deaths, yet he did save many others, including a few dozen actors and stagehands through his creation of the ghetto theater.

Devoutly religious Jews who criticized Gens for allowing the selections adhered to Maimonides' principle, from the *Mishne Torah Hilkhot Yesoday Hatorah,* which reads, "If pagans should tell them [Jews], 'Give us one of yours and we shall kill him, otherwise we shall kill all of you,' they should all be killed and not a single Jew should be delivered."[26] The enactment of Maimonides' belief, albeit heroic and noble, would clearly result in the murder of thousands more Jews in the ghetto and could be construed as an act of mass suicide. If the commandment "Thou shalt not kill" includes self-murder (suicide), Maimonides' principle perhaps comes into conflict with Old Testament teachings.

A refusal by Gens to allow selections might have provided the Nazis with a reason to liquidate the ghetto even earlier. Zelig Kalmanovich, an inhabitant of the Vilna ghetto and a Yiddish literature and culture archivist, wrote the following diary entry regarding Gens's decision to select who would live and die: "It is horrible, perhaps the worst of all predicaments, still there is no other way. Blessed be the God of Israel, who sent us this man [Gens]. . . . The result: over 400 souls have perished—elderly people, the weak and ill, retarded children. However, 1,500 women and children were saved. If this had been the work of strangers [Nazis], 2,000 people would have perished, God forbid."[27] Kalmanovich accepted Gens's decision to save the lives of the strong by sacrificing the elderly and weak, and his perspective is noteworthy because he provided the aforementioned opinion in the midst of the situation, not years later, as some scholars have. Critics possess the luxury of hindsight, for they know the history of the ghetto, but Gens could not have known the future or the Nazis' ultimate intentions. In fact, during Sobol's play, the character Gens ponders self-consciously how history will portray him and others in the ghetto:

> We have to protect our spirit, our essence in here, in the ghetto. And to do that, we have to save those who are strong. Physically, spiritually strong. Selection! We have no choice. The sick, the weak, the hopeless ones: let them go. They're a sacrifice. . . . What will our children, our grandchildren think? Will they be able to justify our actions in their minds? Can they possibly understand the world we had to survive in? (184)

Scholars who disdain Gens's actions have never had to render painful decisions that the leader of the ghetto had to make. If the Nazis had lost the war before the liquidation of the ghetto, Gens would have been a hero rather than a scapegoat.

The villain of Sobol's play is not Gens, but Weiskopf, the owner of the ghetto's clothing factory. Gens allows some Jews to die so that others will live, yet Weiskopf covets personal gain and self-aggrandizement at the expense of his people. Weiskopf, a historical figure who was murdered in the ghetto, seeks profit and power through his clothing business, but Gens realizes that although the factory benefits the Nazis, it, like the ghetto theater, has the potential to save thousands of Jewish lives. When four hundred carloads of Nazi uniforms arrive for repair, Gens demands that Weiskopf employ five hundred more Jews in his clothing factory, but the ghetto businessman wants to hire only fifty because he wishes to save money. Weiskopf is willing to hire fifty Jews, not five hundred as Gens desires, because he does not want to lose money by hiring extraneous workers—even if he can save lives by doing so. Weiskopf thinks only of himself, which is especially heinous during the Shoah, a time when it is imperative that Jews comport themselves altruistically. The following argument ensues:

> GENS: You think I give a shit about saving money for the German army? Are you crazy? Five hundred more workers means five hundred more families saved. Does that make sense to you?
> WEISKOPF: What am I, a welfare fund now? I run a factory, it's a business. I pay a decent living wage to my employees, and what little is left over I live on. (213)

Gens does not care about Weiskopf's profits or how skillfully the factory workers repair Nazi uniforms; he desires only to save as many Jewish lives as possible. Sobol contrasts Gens's altruism with Weiskopf's self-absorption, the latter of which is evident in the tailor's response to SS officer Kittel's question about the distinction between partial and total liquidation of the ghetto: "If you kill fifty thousand Jews but not me, that's partial liquidation. If you kill me, that's total liquidation" (175).

Weiskopf succeeds financially as a ghetto entrepreneur primarily by focusing on profit rather than on the preservation of Vilna's Jews. Weiskopf declares that his factory is a business, but the ghetto's sole business is to save lives. The factory, like the theater, exists as a microcosm of the ghetto; it is a factory operated by the Nazis, with Gens as foreman until the Nazis close it down permanently. Weiskopf lies to Gens when he declares that he attains only a meager profit. In the factory owner's house, a Jewish police officer discovers cognac, salami, rice, olive oil, sugar, and other foodstuffs that manifest his wealth. As viewers, we must here keep in mind that during the historical Holocaust Jews determined riches by portable and practical goods, not by currency, which often proved worthless to them. Many Jews in Weiskopf's ghetto, furthermore, died of starvation. Those who possessed wealth and influence in Jewish ghettos during World War II sometimes provided themselves with a deluded sense of grandeur. As Harold Lieberman and Edith Lieberman note in their Holocaust play *Throne of Straw,* Mordechai Rumkowski devised currency that included his portrait, insisted that his face appear on postage stamps, and wore a cape as he toured the Łódź ghetto (his kingdom) in a carriage drawn by a horse. In Sobol's play, Weiskopf believes that his own craftiness in business has permitted him to climb to the top of Fortune's wheel and that he owes his prosperity to no one but himself. He refuses to comprehend that his primary responsibility in the ghetto is to save as many Jewish lives as possible. The Talmud says that one who saves another person saves the world.

The concept of mutual responsibility that Kittel and Gens discuss applies as much to Weiskopf as to the ghetto leader, for Weiskopf possesses the ability to save the lives of his fellow Jews by hiring them to work in his factory. Mutual responsibility, which involves altruism and philanthropy, has permitted Jews to endure various persecutions for thousands of years. Unlike in other situations in Jewish history, these desperate times render Jews antagonists rather than humanitarians toward one another. During tragic circumstances, such as when the law decrees that if one person escapes the ghetto, that person's family and a total of nine people will die, money and marketable goods should lose significance; only the preservation of human life carries importance. Weiskopf violates this principle by denying Gens's request to hire five hundred workers in order to acquire more profits—at the expense of Jewish lives. Gens selects some Jews to die so that others may survive, but Weiskopf willingly allows many to perish merely so that he may thrive financially. The tailor's elitist attitude manifests to the audience that Weiskopf is turning into a tyrant and acting like a Nazi. He brags proudly to his fellow Jews that he anticipates a forthcoming business meeting with Nazi field marshall Hermann Göring, as if he is receiving a magnificent honor (199). In fact, one of the reasons that Kittel turns on Weiskopf, calling him a leech (216) and arranging his death, is that he is disturbed by seeing a Jew transform himself into a Nazi.

Weiskopf's factory functions as a means of saving the Nazis money because the Jewish workers repair the German uniforms and the Nazis don't have to ship them all the way back to Germany for mending. In *Ghetto,* Sobol employs the ghetto actors to expose Weiskopf's selfishness. Unlike Weiskopf, who prospers by aiding the Nazi cause, the ghetto actors and stagehands help their fellow Jews by entertaining them and preserving the culture. Weiskopf acts selfishly and egoistically, whereas the actors work together and stress teamwork, which, of course, plays a significant role in theater.

In Sobol's exploration of this juxtaposition between Weiskopf and the actors, Weiskopf brags to the acting troupe about the abundance of clothes with which he can provide them for their plays, and the actors respond by working together to mock his arrogance. In a play-within-a-play, the actors satirize the tailor for his hubris: an actress in the troupe dresses in rags and, in character, approaches another actor mimicking Weiskopf and asks for help, claiming that her husband has been arrested for smuggling food. The impersonated Weiskopf makes an insincere but bombastic promise to help her: "I beg your pardon. Do you know who you're talking to? . . . Why is my name Weiskopf? You can go home now. *It will all work out.* I'll speak to my German before the day is out" (179). In this pretentious speech, the phrase "my German" is telling, for the possessive pronoun manifests Weiskopf's illusion of power, as if he controls the Nazis rather than the reverse. The actor playing Weiskopf is "confronted" by the woman, who says satirically, "We should kiss Weiskopf's shoes! He gives carloads of food to the poor. He gets people out of jail. . . . We should kiss Weiskopf's shoes I say" (179). The actors mock Weiskopf for his arrogance and for his insincere claims that he will aid others. In this skit, Sobol may be drawing from historical accounts of the plight of the theater's renowned singer, Lyuba Levicka, who was arrested and subsequently executed by the Nazis for smuggling food. Sobol may have changed the gender of the victim in his play-within-a-play because he patterned the character Chaja, who also is caught smuggling food, partly on the historical personage Levicka.[28] Levicka was a famous singer in the ghetto who sang "Zamd in Shtern" (Sand in the stars) at the ghetto theater's opening on January 18, 1942.[29] She was arrested and executed at Ponar in January 1943 for "being in possession of 2 pounds of grits (groats) and a little butter."[30] As in the play-within-the-play, this Vilna ghetto inhabitant was captured for smuggling food and was executed because no one helped to win her release.

Through Joshua Sobol's drama, the memories of the Jewish victims of the Vilna ghetto—such as Levicka (Chaja), Gens, and Kruk—survive. The open defiance and the subtle anti-Nazi satire in the plays and songs actually performed by the Vilna acting troupe (scenes and songs written for and performed by members of the Vilna ghetto theater) manifest that Jewish drama performed during World War II did not aim merely to provide audiences and participants with a false sense of comfort. In the play, Gens becomes angry when the plays attack the Nazis, especially because armed German soldiers occasionally attend the performances—the only circumstance in the ghetto in which Nazis and Jews join together. Consequently, Gens interrupts Chaja when she sings "Zog Nit Keinmol" (Never say you can't go on), a famous song written by Vilna ghetto inhabitant Hirsh Glick:

> Some day soon the sun will bless us with its light
> And our foes will be devoured by the night
> But until the sun can burn away the mist
> Then this song shall be our theme as we persist.
>
> Not a song the robin sings throughout the land
> But a song a people sings grenade in hand!
> It was written not with ink but with our blood
> Mid collapsing walls and storms of flying mud! (205)

But defiance and satire in theater can exact political and social change, and they served as an important emotional release available to the Vilna Jews—one of their few methods of venting their anger. As Alvin Rosenfeld correctly notes, "To submit to the finality of silence is to confirm, however unwillingly, the triumphant nihilism of Nazism."[31]

16. Inside the Ghetto

A Teaching Strategy

SUSIE JANS-THOMAS

In the summer of 1995, teachers gathered at Mount Mary College in Milwaukee, Wisconsin, to take a course entitled "Remembering the Holocaust." The course was designed for classroom teachers in elementary and secondary classrooms who wanted to teach Holocaust studies effectively. The purpose of the course was to provide historical background information regarding the events of the Holocaust and to examine the literature available for children and adolescents. The idea was that the use of literature would establish a cohesion between theory and practice, and strengthen the integration of Holocaust studies across content areas. The literature-based approach was chosen to increase students' knowledge base; to improve their critical thinking skills; to increase affective learning; to stimulate effective discussion by using reactions to readings, research, opinions, and others' ideas; to encourage reflective thinking practices; and to establish the importance of literature in the understanding of oppression.

Literature was chosen to reflect the themes of prejudice, anti-Semitism, institutional oppression, the right to coexist, racial hygiene, children of the Holocaust, refugees, life inside the ghettos, heroic women, resistance, happenings in the United States, rescue, survivors, and deniers. Using these themes, the teachers examined methodology for successful implementation of content in elementary and secondary classroom environments. The oppressive nature of Hitler's regime permitted the teachers to examine the persecution of various groups of people based on the victims' religion or their sexual orientation, the censoring of their ethnic heritages and ethnic histories, and racial stereotyping. The course generated a need for the coexistence and acceptance of groups, ideas, philosophies, and beliefs by providing an opportunity for teachers to read works of fiction and nonfiction about the Holocaust.

"Inside the Ghetto" was one of the themes used in the course. Students read *The Cracow Ghetto Pharmacy,* the autobiographical account by Tadeusz Pankiewicz—one of the two "Aryans" allowed to remain inside the Kraków ghetto (see the bibliographies provided at the end of the essay); the other "Aryan" was the jail guard who was removed after the June 1942 resettlements. Pankiewicz begins his autobiography by describing the creation of the Kraków ghetto. His description of how, in a brief period of time, 320 apartments were filled with approximately sixteen thousand Jews creates an urgency in the reader to understand how the conditions were endured as time passed.[1] The overcrowding, the establishment of the Judenrat (Jewish Council), the feeling of imprisonment that existed within the ghetto, the use of the black market, and the fear of people from day to day are critically described through the words of a man who operated a pharmacy named Under the Eagle. Pankiewicz writes, "Time was doing its job. People got used to the new life in such changed conditions" (5). His words carefully describe the systematic methods used by the Hitler regime to implement the "Final Solution."

Pankiewicz's sweeping, introspective eyes took in the activities of the Kraków ghetto over the counter of the pharmacy: the legal and the illegal activities of those who were struggling to live with dignity; the humane and the inhumane treatment of people who once walked proudly through the streets and smiled at their neighbors, friends, and merchants; the religious and the secular ceremonies hidden from the Gestapo's view so that prayers might relieve grief and life might continue; the ghetto inhabitants' suffering and happiness; the oppression and the freedoms predetermined by the government, which often stripped people of their individuality; the fear and the courage demonstrated by those who refused to succumb to the atrocities of the oppressive environment; the realities and the hopes for the future that were protected or denied based on the papers in one's possession; the comfort of friends and the brutality of foes enticed by the propaganda; and the insomnia and the sleep of those who struggled to do good. Pankiewicz says, "The pharmacy was, in the opinion of most of the people, a sort of embassy, a diplomatic station, representing the world, singularly free, within the walled and imprisoned city" (12). The pharmacy was the place where people could go to obtain medicine for their physical well-being and philosophical dialogue for their souls.

Pankiewicz's eyewitness description of the sophisticated system for attaining news is intriguing, for it demonstrates the power of the human spirit to survive. Pankiewicz reflects that so much information was hidden in basements, apartments, and attics that problems could be quickly solved within the confines of the pharmacy's walls. As decisions were made, the solutions quickly traveled out the back door of the pharmacy and were given to those in need. The pharmacist's critical eye saw the deportation of Jews from the Kraków ghetto, and Pankiewicz later describes it in great detail. The process of selecting those who would remain and those who would be taken to camps is carefully told so that no individual can remain ignorant. Pankiewicz admits knowing that many Jews were in hiding throughout the ghetto, and he was amazed to see them come out of hiding: "I saw an old lady about 70, with windblown hair, walking some distance away from a large group of deportees; her eyes were glassy—unmoving—wide with fright—staring ahead. She walked slowly, calmly, wearing only a dress, shod in bedroom slippers; She had no luggage not even a purse. With both hands hugging her old woman's chest, she, [*sic*] clutched something tiny and black. It was a little dog—she took only that which was most precious to her and with which she did not want to part" (46).

In describing the torture conducted by the Gestapo, Pankiewicz admits that he was horrified. He condemned those who conducted the beatings while listening to the victims' screams. Seeing the infirm, the mentally deficient, and the elderly killed on sight was almost too much for him to bear. The pharmacist provided assistance through drugs to silence the cries of children during raids so that hiding places would not be detected and drugs to euthanize terminally ill patients so that death might come with dignity rather than from fear. He explains that all tortures were alike in their ritualistic manner of beating, kicking, and shooting, yet each was different nonetheless: "Each abuse had its own distinctive tragic characteristics" (47). His eyewitness accounts reflect the revulsion of all survivors who remember the horror of individuals suffering the atrocities inflicted by Nazi soldiers.

On the day the class at Mount Mary College covered life inside the ghetto, students were required to read *The Cracow Ghetto Pharmacy* in its entirety. When the students came to class, they drew pieces of paper from an envelope: each paper contained a description of a person, which included the individual's age, occupation, marital status, and the number of people for whom the person was responsible. The students assumed the roles of the following individuals:

Oskar
AGE: sixty-seven
OCCUPATION: cooper
MARITAL STATUS: married, one parent

Leon
AGE: seventy-one
OCCUPATION: writer
MARITAL STATUS: two dogs, two finches

George
AGE: twenty-nine
OCCUPATION: artist
MARITAL STATUS: married, four children

Bernard
AGE: forty-six
MARITAL STATUS: married, five children, two parents

Henry
AGE: thirty-two
OCCUPATION: musician
MARITAL STATUS: widower, three children, one housekeeper, one nanny

Anne
AGE: forty-one
OCCUPATION: professor of physics
MARITAL STATUS: married, four parents, three cats

Saul
AGE: forty-seven
OCCUPATION: jeweler
MARITAL STATUS: married, two children

Simon
AGE: sixty-four
MARITAL STATUS: married, three single children, three married children, five grandchildren

Hannah
AGE: twenty-seven
OCCUPATION: nurse
MARITAL STATUS: married, no children

Victor
AGE: forty-eight
OCCUPATION: barber
MARITAL STATUS: single, both parents

Nora
AGE: fifty-one
OCCUPATION: housewife and mother
MARITAL STATUS: widow, two daughters, three married sons

Daniel
AGE: thirty-eight
OCCUPATION: teacher
MARITAL STATUS: married, three children, one dog, one cat

Hilda
AGE: twenty-seven
OCCUPATION: secretary
MARITAL STATUS: single, one parent, one grandparent

Milton
AGE: thirty-four
OCCUPATION: carpenter
MARITAL STATUS: married, five children, two dogs

Julius
AGE: fifty-six
OCCUPATION: banker
MARITAL STATUS: married, three children, one married son, two grandchildren

Emily
AGE: eighty-eight
OCCUPATION: historian
MARITAL STATUS: widow, two dogs, one housekeeper, one gardener, one secretary

The professor divided the teachers into three small groups and instructed them to design ghettos for the individuals they had been assigned. These ghettos met the people's needs: they reflected the move that many Jews made from their homes into the apartments of the Kraków ghetto about which the students had read. The groups were able to find jobs and housing for all of their people. Everyone had dignity in spite of the conditions because all lives had meaning and purpose.

The first group's ghetto design contained many things that allowed the inhabitants to live life in a humane manner. Remembering that the assignment was to design a ghetto that would meet all the occupants' needs, the group included some extras that had not been found in the reading. For example, a garden plot was incorporated so that the elderly would have a role in helping others. A theater was incorporated so that everyone could appreciate the richness found only in the arts. A school was provided so that children could continue learning because there was no telling when the nightmare brought about by ghetto living—overcrowding, lack of privacy, uprooting from family and friends—would be over and because an education was viewed as the one element that no one can take away from another. This ghetto had plenty of space for everyone. There were many single family houses, stores, markets, a library, parks, and public meeting areas. This group had designed a ghetto that would have been found only in a fantasy land.

The second group designed a ghetto that was a bit more realistic. There were apartment buildings, few outdoor areas for physical activities, and a couple of stores and buildings that reflected the occupations of the people living within the ghetto. This ghetto design had an interesting maze of sewers to serve as escape routes and passageways for black-market trading. Some of the people in the second ghetto were forced to relinquish their jobs in order to perform tasks that would assist the people. For example, if one were an artist, it was deemed that there was no need for such aesthetics, and therefore the artist became a machinist or a sewer sweeper in order to meet the community's needs. This ghetto design included a pharmacy. The designers felt the importance of Pankiewicz's influence and the need for people to be treated with dignity.

The third group's ghetto design manifested a dreary environment. There was barbed wire along the perimeter. A moat surrounded the area, with one bridge so that individuals could cross to go to work on the outside. The buildings held just enough space to allow the residents to sleep. There was a very small area set up for exercise and meetings. This area was located in the center of the entire ghetto so that in crowded conditions trading could take place out in the open where no one would be viewed as conspicuous. There was a hidden school located in the attic of one of the buildings so that children could attend school without the authorities' discovering that Jewish children were being educated. Group three's ghetto was the most realistic. The design reflected the crowded conditions of the ghetto that Pankiewicz describes in his account.

A general discussion was held to share the differences and similarities between the three ghettos. All wanted their children educated. All wanted the conditions to be different than what they had read about. Even the third design, the most realistic one, included the bridge in place so that there was a way for some inhabitants to work on the outside and perhaps to learn news. Doing away with the arts was a difficult decision for one group, but the arts were deemed unnecessary for survival. Each teacher tried to relate to the story of Tadeusz Pankiewicz and how he often felt that he simply could not do enough. After this discussion, the students took a break.

During the break, the discussion continued. Students talked about their assigned identities as if they were real. They told stories of the importance of people having pets and of the need for art and music to rid life briefly of its dark moments. They remembered parts of their reading and discussed the woman who had only her dog when she was forced to leave the ghetto. They discussed why there was only one garden and the importance of food for maintaining life. There was an interesting dialogue about the fact that no group had included a synagogue. A location where groups of Jews could worship had seemingly been stripped away from the Jews. This dialogue lasted for quite some time. They discussed how the ghettos truly restricted their inhabitants to simply existing, not to live a rich life.

When the break was over, the students returned to class and continued to maintain their assigned identities. At this time, the numbers 1, 2, and 3 were written on individual pieces of paper and placed in a paper bag. A student was asked to pull one number from the bag. The number chosen was number 1. Another student was asked to pull another number from the bag. The second number chosen was number 2. Number 1 represented the ghetto into which all of the inhabitants of the second ghetto were now forced to move.

Ghetto one was the most elaborate ghetto, but now the people were forced to find housing and employment for all of the new members of ghetto two, using only the existing design. For one hour, the two groups were to become one. They complained about having to relinquish living space to others. They fought about the need for maintaining individual occupations. They yelled about what to do with so many elderly and children to feed, for many of the former inhabitants of ghetto two were people who could not work and contribute to the overall well-being of the community. Some members were forced to perform lesser jobs than those for which their earned education had prepared them; their frustration was evident as their status was stripped away from them. After all, how was one to be respected as a historian when there was no money to be made in the field?

The bickering continued. And during the arguing, group three simply sat and listened to the other groups. They claimed that they would have no problem figuring out how all of the people would fit into that ghetto design as it truly did have something for everyone. They paid careful attention to the details, and they discussed excess space, which was uninhabited, where others would be able to live. This group realized that there was plenty of space in the theater, under the stage and dressing rooms, where an entire family could live. They were trying to figure out what kind of work they would have to do once they got into the ghetto. This discussion was not prompted by the instructor: the students of ghetto three simply assumed that they were going to move into ghetto one.

Each class period lasted three and one-half hours, so there was the need for a second break, which occurred as soon as the larger group, now made up of groups one and two, finished relocating all of its new members. During this break, the conversation remained lively. The students conversed about how the quality of life was declining as a result of the crowding conditions. They discussed the importance of writers, artists, and musicians in society, but the contributions of these people were weak when they were on the labor market. There was a lively discussion on extended families and how society in the United States has grown away from having many generations living under one roof. This discussion fed the fires of dignity and respect for life as a whole, and the importance of children's accepting intergenerational relationships to carry on tradition and cultural heritage.

At the end of this second break, the students returned to class and automatically began to make room for the third group to move to the large table. Instead, all three numbers were placed back into the bag. This time only one number was drawn—number 3. All of the members of the class were forced to move into ghetto three. All of the groups moaned, for when two groups had become one, they had worked feverishly to include all of the new members into the transformed ghetto. The third group had plotted among themselves as to how they were going to fit into the transformed larger ghetto without imposing on anyone. By the simple drawing of a number, however, these people's lives were changed forever, for now this combined ghetto would have to be depopulated and moved to ghetto three, an unexpected hardship. The process was very simple. Because there were no frills and everyone was required to work, a quick decision was made to move each family into whatever existing space was available. It was decided that all single people were to live together so that families with children could remain together. All of the elderly were to live together so that they would not hinder anyone. They were to remain in the ghetto while others went to work. Some of the elderly would teach the children. It was believed that education was the key to a better future, no matter what the circumstances. Everyone's pets were to be turned loose to fend for themselves. The small open area was now crowded with people struggling to trade with each other in order to find food and medicine. The moat surrounding the ghetto widened the gap between them and the outside world. The barbed wire haunted all of the new members of ghetto three, and having only one way out was a cause of panic for the original group two. But group two no longer existed, for it had been altered and dismembered with the first pull of a number from the bag. It was this realization of eradication that demonstrated the arbitrary and systematic nature of the Third Reich's Master Plan to erase an entire people from the face of the earth.

When the struggle to find housing for all had ended, there was silence. However, it was a pride-filled silence, for the students had worked together to maintain some fraction of dignity for each member of the newly formed ghetto community. The next section of the lesson was perhaps the most difficult for the instructor. Because it was deemed that the ghetto was too crowded, some people had to leave. Each student was asked to write the name of the person he or she had become on a piece of paper and to place it in a bag. Three names were drawn from the bag: George, the artist; Victor, the barber; and Hannah, the nurse. These three members of the ghetto became the Judenrat and were required to expel people from the ghetto so that the overcrowding could be eliminated. The three reviewed the list of people and their occupations to determine their overall worthiness and usefulness concerning the quality of life in the ghetto.

The Judenrat began with Leon.

"How can a writer help us?" one asked.

"He can remember our stories," said another.

"He can teach our children," argued the third.

"We already have a teacher" was the final decision. Leon was forced out of the ghetto. His fate was in an envelope, which one of the Judenrat then opened and read: "Committed suicide."

The Judenrat continued examining ghetto members' occupations to determine individuals' worthiness and usefulness. Gone was Simon, the tailor. "Who needs a tailor when there are no clothes to be had?" asked the Judenrat. Simon, his wife, three single children, three married children, and five grandchildren were to perish at Treblinka. Gone was Nora, the housewife and mother. One of her sons survived, but her daughters and three other sons perished at Treblinka. Gone was Henry. What was the worth of a musician? Everyone with him perished at Treblinka.

The three students continued to complete the task that they had been assigned. They were shaking as they made each decision, and they cried as they read the fate. The three students were being stared at by their peers in a haunting manner. In real life, away from class, one member of the Judenrat was an accountant who was trying to explain to her coworkers why she was taking a course on the Holocaust, and here she was accepting a handkerchief to dry her eyes from a teacher of children with emotional disturbances. When the three members of the Judenrat made the decision to expel the artist, the third member of the group could not believe that he was doing away with the person who reflected his own occupation. He handled George's envelope as if it were on fire. The artist survived Auschwitz, but his wife died, and his children were executed.

Hilda survived, but her parent and grandparent died of starvation.

Oskar, along with his wife and parent, survived.

Anne survived Auschwitz but lost her husband and parents.

Milton and his family became refugees in Switzerland.

Saul, along with his family, perished at Auschwitz.

Emily and her work staff perished.

Bernard and his entire family perished.

Julius and his family did not survive.

Hannah survived Auschwitz.

The last person on their list was Daniel. They saved Daniel until the end, for he was a teacher. Teachers affect the future. They will tell the stories to others. Teachers make certain that people learn. Teachers make sure that students do not forget. Daniel survived, but his wife and children were executed. Daniel was asked if he would teach the stories of the people, and he said he would.

The room was silent. There were still thirty minutes of class remaining, but everyone simply sat there in stunned silence for fifteen minutes before the instructor broke the silence. The students spoke of this ghetto experience and related it to the story of Tadeusz Pankiewicz, who had done his best to help as many people as he could. The solemn discussion focused on the absence of human dignity when individuals are unable to make their own decisions.

After the discussion, the students wrote to the professor in their journals. The journal prompt was, "What is a secret? Why should a secret be kept?" They wrote of the importance of keeping secrets and the damage that can be done when some secrets are told. Many wrote on the importance of keeping secrets in the ghetto as a means of survival. The ghetto conditions incited the creation of secret hiding places for the elderly and children. The conditions forced people to keep secrets about their true occupations, their family status, and their beliefs, for if the secrets were made known, there would be a penalty of death. Many students focused on the fact that secrets imply trust, and trust builds relationships that nurture survival. One student wrote, "Knowing the kind of secret I knew this evening about the roulette wheel of life makes me never want to know a secret again. Tonight's class was probably the most moving class I have ever experienced. It was a lesson I will never forget."[2]

Another student wrote, "A secret is something you don't want anyone else to know, until a later time. A secret should be kept until revealing it won't hurt the people it is about. In the book, Tadeusz knew many secrets from both sides. He kept most of them until after the war, when revealing them would be more of a help than a hurt. This was very hard tonight.

Even though we were role playing, it seemed so real. It made me sad to know fictitious people died. More people should be exposed to this. Even though it is difficult, it is reality. Maybe some people would change if they had to experience this activity. In this book, the process was just as important as the product."

And so the evening ended. The students gathered their belongings and cleared the tables of any garbage. The professor hung the ghetto drawings on the wall in the back of the classroom, and when she turned to go back to the front of the classroom, she saw a student rummaging through the garbage can, looking for his fictional identity. A member of his group had thrown away the slip of paper, and he was frantically looking for it. He found it, smoothed out the paper, and pressed it in the pages of *The Cracow Ghetto Pharmacy*. He seemed to be saying to himself that Oskar would survive.

The course "Remembering the Holocaust" has been offered again at Mount Mary College, but the theme "Inside the Ghetto" has not been taught as effectively. *The Cracow Ghetto Pharmacy* is no longer in print, and the effects from other books have not been deemed as realistic. Students have not connected as well to these other stories as well as they did to the words of Tadeusz Pankiewicz. A longitudinal study was conducted of all of the students who had taken the course since its first offering, and the research showed that the ghetto design was the most memorable topic of the course.

Students felt that "Inside the Ghetto," as a teaching strategy, helped them to understand the crowded conditions, the lack of food and water, and the need to treat all humans with dignity. One student commented on how creating the ghetto forced individuals to create new families. Because of the conditions, people were forced to care for one another, in spite of the poor conditions. Another student commented about the overall feeling he was left with after the course: "I cannot, to this day, believe the depth of despair, horror, grief, and angst that I experienced the night of our ghetto creations. How can one explain this to anyone! That is the most amazing, most inspirational, and most lasting gift of the course." These comments demonstrate the power of the activity, for students became involved in the role playing and supported their beliefs with Tadeusz Pankiewicz's words.

Another student from the class referred to the ghetto activity as "The Night." She continued by writing that being forced into overpopulation demonstrated how life in the ghetto was one horrible event after another, but there was always an element of hope. Her comments, furthermore, reflected the seemingly arbitrary ways in which the Nazis decided who would live and die, then leaving the premises as if the people never existed. "The night of the ghetto activity was the best teaching I have ever experienced," she said. "It will be difficult to find an individual who would even come close to such memorable teaching as was demonstrated that night."

It was perhaps Pankiewicz's words that rang out most in the memories of the students and the instructor who participated in the course. In the final pages of the book, he writes:

> A few days after the liquidation of the OD [Ordnungsdienst, or Service for Keeping Order], all the warehouses on the site of the former Ghetto were transferred to Plaszow. The barbed wire, which was the last remaining symbol of the Ghetto, was torn down and the renovation of the destroyed buildings started. They were to be made available to the Polish people who were evicted from the officers' colony. Weeks later, the demolition of the walls which surrounded the Ghetto began. In this way, all traces (with the exception of two small parts of a wall) were removed from the little town which had experienced such monstrosities.
>
> A new era began. The Ghetto was gone. The war was over. People scattered to all parts of the world, but in spite of all the passing years, our friendships with those with whom we lived together through the tragic times and the all too brief moments of elation did not diminish. (150)

Fifty years after the liberation, a group of graduate students and teachers met to study the events surrounding the Holocaust. They left remembering the pharmacy Under the Eagle, for it had taught them the power found in knowing one's enemies and the need to continue telling the stories of life.

Bibliography for Teaching the Holocaust

Required Course Readings

Atkinson, Linda. *In Kindling Flame: The Story of Hannah Senesh, 1921–1944.* New York: Beech Tree Books, 1985.

Auerbacher, Inge. *I Am a Star: Child of the Holocaust.* New York: Puffin Books, 1986.

Finkelstein, Norman H. *Remember Not to Forget: A Memory of the Holocaust.* New York: Mulberry Books, 1985.

Fry, Varian. *Assignment: Rescue an Autobiography.* New York: Scholastic, 1945.

Greene, Bette. *Summer of My German Soldier.* New York: Dell, 1973.

Jans-Thomas, Susie J. "Beyond Anne Frank: Using Literature to Teach the Holocaust." In *Annual Scholars' Conference on the Holocaust and the Churches, 1985–Present.* Irvine, Calif.: Vista InterMedia Corporation, 2003.

———. "Teachers Remember the Holocaust." In *Annual Scholars' Conference on the Holocaust and the Churches, 1985–Present.* Irvine, Calif.: Vista InterMedia Corporation, 2003.

Kerr, Judith. *When Hitler Stole Pink Rabbit.* New York: Dell Yearling, 1971.

Levi, Primo. *Survival in Auschwitz.* New York: Collier, 1958.

Lowry, Lois. *Number the Stars.* New York: Dell, 1989.

Matas, Carol. *Daniel's Story.* New York: Scholastic, 1993.

Meltzer, Milton. *Rescue: The Story of How Gentiles Saved Jews in the Holocaust.* New York: HarperCollins, 1988.

Pankiewicz, Tadeusz. *The Cracow Ghetto Pharmacy.* Translated by Henry Tilles. 1947. Reprint. New York: Holocaust Library, 1987.

Plant, Richard. *The Pink Triangle: The Nazi War Against Homosexuals.* New York: Henry Holt, 1986.

Proctor, Robert N. *Racial Hygiene: Medicine under the Nazis.* Cambridge, Mass.: Harvard Univ. Press, 1988.

Richter, Hans Peter. *Friedrich.* New York: Puffin Books, 1961.

Roeder, George H., Jr. *The Censored War: American Visual Experience during World War Two.* New Haven, Conn.: Yale University Press, 1993.

Uchida, Yoshiko. *Journey Home.* New York: Aladdin Books, 1978.

Zar, Rose. *In the Mouth of the Wolf.* Philadelphia: Jewish Publication Society, 1983.

Sources to Establish Background Knowledge and Course Framework

Brecher, Elinor J. *Schindler's Legacy: True Stories of the List Survivors.* New York: Plume, 1994.

Cumoletti, Henry V. *Crimes Against Humanity: Reflections on the Nurnberg Trials.* Gouverneur, N.Y.: Henry V. Cumoletti, 1989.

Durlacher, Gerhard. *Drowning: Growing up in the Third Reich.* Translated by Susan Massotty. New York: Serpent's Tail, 1993.

Eckardt, A. Roy, and Alice L. Eckardt. *Long Night's Journey into Day: A Revised Retrospective on the Holocaust.* Detroit: Wayne State Univ. Press, 1988.

Eibeshitz, Jehoshua, and Anna Eibeshitz. *Women in the Holocaust.* 2 vols. Brooklyn: Remember, 1993.

Frankl, Viktor E. *Man's Search for Meaning.* New York: Washington Square Books, 1959.

Grunfeld, Frederic V. *Prophets Without Honor: Freud, Kafka, Einstein, and Their World.* New York: Kodansha America, 1979.

Hillesum, Etty. *An Interrupted Life: The Diaries of Etty Hillesum, 1941–43.* New York: Washington Square Books, 1981.

Klein, G. W. *All about My Life.* New York: HarperCollins, 1957.

Levi, Primo. *Moments of Reprieve: A Memoir of Auschwitz.* New York: Penguin, 1979.

———. *The Reawakening: The Companion Volume to* Survival in Auschwitz. New York: Collier, 1965.

Lifton, Robert J. *The Nazi Doctors: Medical Killing and Psychology of Genocide.* New York: HarperCollins, 1986.

Scholl, Inge. *The White Rose: Munich 1942–1943.* Middletown, Conn.: Wesleyan University Press, 1980.

Taylor, James, and Warren Shaw. *The Third Reich Almanac.* London: Grafton, 1987.

Wyman, David S. *The Abandonment of the Jews: America and the Holocaust 1941–1945.* New York: Pantheon, 1985.

Other Books for Children and Adolescents

Banks, Lynne Reid. *Broken Bride.* New York: Morrow Junior Books, 1994.

Bishop, Claire Huchet. *Twenty and Ten.* New York: Trumpet, 1995.

Frank, Anne. *The Diary of a Young Girl: The Definitive Edition.* New York: Bantam, 1995.

Keneally, Thomas. *Schindler's List.* New York: Touchstone Books, 1982.

Korn, Abram, Richard Voyles, and Joseph Korn. *Abe's Story: A Holocaust Memoir.* Marietta: Longstreet, 1995.

Leitner, Isabella, and Irving A. Leitner. *The Big Lie: A True Story.* New York: Scholastic, 1992.

Levitin, Sonia. *Journey to America.* New York: Atheneum, 1970.

Morpurgo, Michael. *Waiting for Anya.* New York: Viking, 1991.

Sender, Ruth Minsky. *To Life.* New York: Macmillan, 1988.

Van der Rol, Ruud, and Rian Verhoeven. *Anne Frank: Beyond the Diary.* New York: Scholastic, 1992.

Voight, Cynthia. *David and Jonathan.* New York: Scholastic, 1992.

Yolen, Jane. *Briar Rose.* New York: T. Doherty Associates, 1992.

Notes

Bibliography

Index

Notes

Foreword: How to Live in the Interim?

1. Adam Czerniakow, *The Warsaw Diary of Adam Czerniakow: Prelude to Doom,* edited by Raul Hilberg, Stanislaw Staron, and Josef Kermisz; translated by Stanislaw Staron and the staff of Yad Vashem (New York: Stein and Day, 1979), 386. Indebted to introductory material provided by the editors of the Czerniakow diary, my discussion of Czerniakow is drawn from Marilyn Harran, Dieter Kuntz, Russel Lemmons, Robert Ashley Michael, Keith Pickus, and John K. Roth, *The Holocaust Chronicle: A History in Words and Pictures* (Lincolnwood, Ill.: Publications International, 2000).

2. For Ziering's obituary, see Myrna Oliver, "Sigi Ziering; Tycoon Survived Nazi Camps," *Los Angeles Times,* November 14, 2000, B6. The reflections on Ziering and his play about the Riga ghetto are adapted from John K. Roth, *Holocaust Politics* (Louisville, Ky.: Westminster John Knox Press, 2001).

3. Lawrence L. Langer, *Preempting the Holocaust* (New Haven, Conn.: Yale Univ. Press, 1998), 10.

4. James E. Young, *At Memory's Edge: After-Images of the Holocaust in Contemporary Art and Architecture* (New Haven, Conn.: Yale Univ. Press, 2000).

Introduction

1. Ernest G. Heppner, *Shanghai Refuge: A Memoir of the World War II Jewish Ghetto* (Lincoln: Univ. of Nebraska Press, 1993), 114–15.

2. Yitzhak Arad, *Ghetto in Flames: The Struggle and Destruction of the Jews in Vilna in the Holocaust* (New York: Holocaust Library, 1982), 172–79.

3. Otto Dov Kulka, "Theresienstadt," in *Encyclopedia of the Holocaust,* 4 vols., edited by Yisrael Gutman (New York: Simon and Schuster, Macmillan, 1990), 4: 1462.

4. Arad, *Ghetto in Flames,* 320.

5. Yisrael Gutman, "Warsaw: Jews during the Holocaust," in *Encyclopedia of the Holocaust,* 4: 1620.

6. Abraham Foxman, "The Resistance Movement in the Vilna Ghetto," in *They Fought*

Back: The Story of the Jewish Resistance in Nazi Europe, edited by Yuri Suhl (New York: Crown, 1967), 151.

7. Yehuda Bauer, *A History of the Holocaust* (New York: Franklin Watts, 1982), 198.

8. Isaiah Trunk, *Judenrat: The Jewish Councils in Eastern Europe under Nazi Occupation* (New York: Scarborough, 1977; reprint, Lincoln: Univ. of Nebraska Press, 1996), 420.

9. Chaim A. Kaplan, *Scroll of Agony: The Warsaw Diary of Chaim A. Kaplan,* rev. ed., translated and edited by Abraham I. Katsh (New York: Collier, 1973), 384.

10. Rumkowski quoted in Josef Zelkowicz, *In Those Terrible Days: Notes from the Łódź Ghetto,* edited by Michal Unger, translated by Naftali Greenwood (Jerusalem: Yad Vashem, 2002), 280–81.

11. Lucille Eichengreen and Rebecca Camhi Fromer, *Rumkowski and the Orphans of Łódź* (San Francisco: Mercury House, 2000), 45.

12. Quoted in Jacob Robinson, "Introduction: Some Basic Issues That Faced the Jewish Councils," in Trunk, *Judenrat,* xxxi.

13. Calel Perechodnik, *Am I a Murderer? Testament of a Jewish Ghetto Policeman,* translated and edited by Frank Fox (Boulder, Colo.: Westview, 1996), 22.

2. Some Clarifications on the Warsaw Ghetto Uprising: Based on Interviews with Marek Edelman and Simcha Rotem

1. Andrzej Wirth quoted in Lawrence L. Langer, *Versions of Survival: The Holocaust and the Human Spirit* (Albany: State Univ. of New York Press, 1982), 104.

2. Emanuel Ringelblum, *Notes from the Warsaw Ghetto: The Journal of Emmanuel Ringelblum,* translated by Jacob Sloan (1958; reprint, New York: Schocken, 1974), 316.

5. Historical Position of the Hungarian Jewry and Untold Ghetto Accounts

1. László Kársai, ed., *"Befogadok" Writings Against Antisemitism 1882–1993* (Budapest: Aura, 1993), 14.

2. Ibid., 20.

3. Ibid., 16.

4. Randolph L. Braham, *A Magyar Holocaust* (The Hungarian Holocaust) (Budapest: Gondolat, 1990), 34.

5. Sandor Scheiber, ed., *Evkonyv 1970* (Jewish yearbook 1970) (Budapest: Magyarorszagi Izraelitak Orszago Kepviselete, 1970), 5.

6. Braham, *A Magyar Holocaust,* 39.

7. Geza Komoroczy, ed., *A Zsido Budapest* (Jewish Budapest), 2 vols. (Budapest: MTA Judaisztikai Kutatócsoport, 1995), 2: 496.

8. Radnoti quoted in ibid., 2: 499.

9. Braham, *A Magyar Holocaust,* 174.

10. Ibid., 33.

11. Rudolf Vrba, "The Preparations for the Holocaust in Hungary: An Eyewitness Account," in *The Nazis' Last Victims: The Holocaust in Hungary,* edited by Randolph L. Braham and Scott Miller (Detroit: Wayne State Univ. Press, 1998), 55.

12. László Kársai, "The Last Phase of the Hungarian Holocaust: The Szálasi Regime and the Jews," in *The Nazis' Last Victims,* 107.

13. Ibid., 108.

8. Smuggling in the Ghettos: Survivor Accounts from the Warsaw, Łódź, and Kraków Ghettos

1. Chaim Potok, *Wanderings: Chaim Potok's History of the Jews* (New York: Alfred A. Knopf, 1978), 388.

2. Lucy S. Dawidowicz, *The War Against the Jews, 1933–1945* (New York: Holt, Rinehart, and Winston, 1975), 201.

3. Martin Gilbert, *The Holocaust: History of the Jews of Europe during the Second World War* (New York: Henry Holt, 1985), 89, see 838 n. 17 for more information.

4. Dawidowicz, *The War Against the Jews,* 203.

5. Yisrael Gutman, *The Jews of Warsaw, 1939–1943: Ghetto, Underground, Revolt,* translated by Ina R. Friedman (Bloomington: Indiana Univ. Press, 1982), 49.

6. Ibid., 60.

7. Chaim A. Kaplan, *Scroll of Agony: The Warsaw Diary of Chaim A. Kaplan,* rev. ed., translated and edited by Abraham I. Katsh (New York: Collier, 1973), 219.

8. Gutman, *The Jews of Warsaw,* 66. Gutman obtained the information from Czeslaw Madaczyk, *Polityka III Rzeszy w Okupowanej Polsce* (Warsaw: Panstwowe Wydawn Naukowe, 1970), 2: 71.

9. Kaplan, *Scroll of Agony,* 220.

10. Ibid., 226–27.

11. Gutman, *The Jews of Warsaw,* 67. Gutman derived this information from the unpublished diary of Henryk Brysker.

12. Max Glauben, interviewed by Diane Plotkin, Dallas, Texas, November 9, 1999.

13. Lucjan Dobroszycki, ed. *The Chronicle of the Łódź Ghetto, 1941–1944,* translated by Richard Lourie, Joachim Neugroschel, and others (New Haven, Conn.: Yale Univ. Press, 1984), xxiii.

14. Emanuel Ringelblum, *Notes from the Warsaw Ghetto: The Journal of Emmanuel Ringelblum,* translated by Jacob Sloan (1958; New York: Schocken, 1974), 47–48.

15. Raul Hilberg, *The Destruction of the European Jews: Revised and Definitive Edition,* 3 vols. (New York: Holmes and Meier, 1985), 3: 222. Hilberg derived this information from a statistical report by the Jewish Council that exists in the Łódź Ghetto Collection No. 58.

16. Dawidowicz, *The War Against the Jews,* 214. Dawidowicz uses three sources: Isaiah

Trunk, "Mayrev-eyropeishe Yidn in di mizrekh-eyropeishe getos," *Di Goldene Keyt* 15 (1953): 80–102; Danuta Dabrowska and Lucjan Dobroszycki, *Kronika getta lodzkiego,* 2 vols. (Łódź: Wydawnictwo Lodzkie, 1965), 1: 517–20; and Max Kaufmann, *Die Vernichtung der Juden Lettlands: Churbn Lettland* (Munich: Hartun-Gorre, 1947), passim.

17. Gilbert, *The Holocaust,* 141.

18. Ibid., 141–42. Gilbert derived this information from Dobroszycki, ed., *The Chronicle of the Łódź Ghetto.*

19. Hilberg, *The Destruction of the European Jews,* 1: 227. Hilberg derived this information from Isaiah Trunk, "Epidemics in the Warsaw Ghetto," *YIVO Annual of Jewish Social Sciences* 8 (1953), 87.

20. Dobroszycki, ed., *The Chronicle of the Łódź Ghetto,* xxxix (see also p. 27, the reference for the order of the day regarding electricity in the entry for March 3, 1941), xxxix (see M. C. Rumkowski, "Letters," June 16 and 20, 1940, to the German Ghetto Administration [AZIH (AJHI)], Rum. Records, no. 66).

21. Ringelblum, *Notes from the Warsaw Ghetto,* 43.

22. Dawidowicz, *The War Against the Jews,* 215. Dawidowicz derived the information from Isaiah Trunk, *Lodzher geto: A historische un sotziologishe shtudie* (Łódź ghetto: A historical and sociological study) (New York: YIVO/Yad Vashem, 1962), 222–23.

23. Ringelblum, *Notes from the Warsaw Ghetto,* 43, 144.

24. Hilberg, *The Destruction of the European Jews,* 1: 252. Hilberg employed a report by Armament Economy Inspectorate Ober-Ost, October 28, 1939, Federal Records Center, Wirtschaft und Rüstung (hereafter Wi/ID), Wi/ID 1:49, Alexandria, Va. and *Krakauer Zeitung,* February 4–5, 1940, GG page, and May 19–20, 1940, GG page.

25. Hilberg, *The Destruction of the European Jews,* 1: 252. Hilberg derived this information from the report given by Friedrich-Wilhelm Krüger in the Generalgouvernement conference, December 8, 1939, cited in the Hans Frank diary, PS-2233, part of the Nuremberg documents available in Office of United States Counsel for Prosecution of Axis Criminality, *Nazi Conspiracy and Aggression,* 8 vols., 2 suppl. (Washington, D.C.: Government Printing Office, 1946–48).

26. Gilbert, *The Holocaust,* 141.

27. Hilberg, *The Destruction of the European Jews,* 1: 259. Hilberg used a memo from Technischer Kriegsverwaltungsintendant Merkel regarding a conversation with Hans Biebow, March 18, 1941, Wi/ID 1:40, and a report in *Rüstungsinspektion* 21 (October 1, 1940-December 31, 1941), pt. 2, 33–34, Wi/ID 1:20.

28. Ringelblum, *Notes from the Warsaw Ghetto,* 43.

29. Hilberg, *The Destruction of the European Jews,* 1: 263.

30. Ringelblum, *Notes from the Warsaw Ghetto,* 120.

31. Hilberg, *The Destruction of the European Jews,* 1: 264–65. Hilberg uses "Łódź Ghetto Conference," a summary of this October 25, 1940, conference in *Dokumenty i Materialy,* 3: 241–42.

32. Dawidowicz, *The War Against the Jews,* 211.

33. Ibid., 212.

34. "Notes on Rumkowski," in *Łódź Ghetto: Inside a Community under Siege,* compiled and edited by Alan Adelson and Robert Lapides (New York: Penguin, 1991), 494.

35. Ibid., 493.

36. Leo Laufer, interviewed by Diane Plotkin, Dallas, Texas, November-December 1988.

37. Janina Fischler-Martinho, *Have You Seen My Little Sister?* (London: Vallentine Mitchell, 1998), 52–53.

38. Tadeusz Pankiewicz, *The Cracow Ghetto Pharmacy,* translated by Henry Tilles (1947; reprint, New York: Holocaust Library, 1987), 1.

39. Ibid., 4.

40. Ibid., 5.

41. Ibid., 5–6.

42. Ibid.

43. Ibid., 6.

44. Yehuda Bauer, *A History of the Holocaust* (New York: Franklin Watts, 1982), 172.

45. Pankiewicz, *The Cracow Ghetto Pharmacy,* 32–33.

46. Ibid., 40.

47. Ibid., 57–58.

48. Ibid., 95–96.

49. William Schiff, interviewed by Diane Plotkin, Dallas, Texas, November 4, 1999.

9. Facilitating Genocide: Nazi Ghettoization Practices in Occupied Ukraine, 1941–1942

1. Statement of Josef Quante, Central Office for War Crimes Investigations, I 204, AR-Z 8/80, May 24, 1965, p. 71, Ludwigsburg, Germany.

2. "Nazi-occupied Ukraine" refers specifically to the territory encompassing the Reichskommissariat Ukraine and the military's rear occupation zones in eastern Ukraine. The numerous ghettos of the western district of Galicia, including the Lvov ghetto, fell under the administration of the Generalgouvernement, and their history corresponds more closely with events and policies in Nazi-occupied Poland. For ghettoization in Galicia, see Dieter Pohl, *Nationalsozialistische Judenverfolgung in Ostgalizien 1941–1944: Organisation und Durchführung eines staatlichen Massenverbrechens* (Munich: Oldenbourg, 1997), 154–216. The southeastern strip of Ukrainian territory, known as Transnistria, which Hitler gave to Romanian leader Ion Antonescu on August 18, 1941, also remains outside the geographic and administrative borders of this essay. On the Holocaust in Transnistria, see Radu Ioanid, *The Holocaust in Romania: The Destruction of Jews and Gypsies under the Antonescu Regime, 1940–1944* (Chicago: Ivan R. Dee, 2000); and Dalia Ofer, "The Holocaust in Transnistria:

A Special Case of Genocide," in *The Holocaust in the Soviet Union: Studies and Sources on the Destruction of the Jews in the Nazi-Occupied Territories of the USSR, 1941–1945,* edited by L. Dobroszycki and J. Gurock (New York: M. E. Sharpe, 1993), 133–54.

3. In this essay, the current Ukrainian spelling of geographic locations is used as much as possible.

4. The general quartermaster did not issue any guidelines about ghettoization, although planners such as Peter-Heinz Seraphim and officials under Alfred Rosenberg presented ghettos as a possible means of solving "the Jewish question." See Christian Gerlach, *Kalkulierte Morde: Die deutsche Wirtschafts und Vernichtungspolitik in Weissrussland 1941 bis 1944* (Hamburg: Institut für Sozialforschung, 1999), 521–22.

5. Dieter Pohl, "Schauplatz Ukraine: Der Massenmord an den Juden im Militärverwaltungsgebiet und im Reichskommissariat 1941–1943," in *Ausbeutung, Vernichtung, Öffentlichkeit: Studien zur nationalistischen Verfolgungspolitik,* edited by N. Frei, S. Steinbacher, and B. Wagner (Munich: Sauer, 2000), 126–27; Shmuel Spector, "The Holocaust of Ukrainian Jews," in *Bitter Legacy: Confronting the Holocaust in the USSR,* edited by Zvi Y. Gitelman (Bloomington: Indiana Univ. Press, 1997), 49.

6. Also see "Guidelines for the Conduct of the Troops in Russia," which identified the Jews as a racial political threat more specifically than did the Commissar Order, U.S. National Archives and Records Administration (hereafter NARA), NARA RG 242, T-315, roll 2215, frame 000711–13, College Park, Md.

7. On pre-Barbarossa orders, see Jürgen Förster, "The Relation Between Operation Barbarossa as an Ideological War of Extermination and the Final Solution," in *The Final Solution: Origins and Implementation,* edited by David Cesarani (London: Routledge, 1994), 85–102.

8. This translation is of the edited version. The earlier typewritten text, which was crossed out, included this statement: "In so far as the Jews have not been driven out by the Ukrainians themselves, the small communities must be placed in large camps and forced to work, like the practice already being carried out in Łódź." International Military Tribunal at Nuremberg, NARA Doc. No. 1028-PS, 12–13.

9. Field commander (hereafter FK), Pervomaisk records, August 1941, United States Holocaust Memorial Museum (hereafter USHMM), RG 11.001M13, 1275–3–661, reel 92, Washington, D.C. Similar measures (with no mention of ghettos) were outlined in the widely distributed "Merkblatt über Sofortaufgaben der Ortskommandanturen," Kriegstagebuch (KTB) SD 454 Anlage zum Div. Befehl Nr. 59, NARA RG 242 T-315, roll 2216, frame 000091–94.

10. One of the earliest mentions of "separate housing districts" formed by members of Einsatzgruppe C (hereafter EGC) in Lutsk appeared in early August 1941. This ghetto was formed in the wake of mass shootings of leading intelligentsia. See EM no. 43, August 5, 1941, in Yitzhak Arad, Shmuel Krakowski, and Shmuel Spector, *The Einsatzgruppen Reports: Selections from the Dispatches of the Nazi Death Squads' Campaigns Against the Jews, July 1941–January 1943* (New York: Holocaust Library, 1989), 66.

11. The FK in Dnepropetrovsk described his reluctance to undertake administrative tasks that were beyond their personnel resources and would be completed by the civil administration anyway; instead, the military was supposed to focus on *Finanzpläne, Geschäftsverteilung,* and *Stellenpläne* in a somewhat superficial, ad hoc manner. FK 676, report dated November 15, 1941, USHMM RG Osobyi 11.001M13, 1275–3–661, reel 92.

12. See the ghetto announcement "An die jüdische Bevölkerung in Kamenetz-Podolsk," in Khmelnitskiy Oblast Records, USHMM Acc 1996.a.0150, reel 4, 434–1–3.

13. FK 183, August 13, 1941, USHMM RG11.001M13, 1275–3–662.

14. Meeting in Vinnytsia, August 24–25, 1941, summary notes in the Kriegstagbuch (KTB), Army Group South, NARA RG 242, T-501/R5/000773; and meeting notes of September 2, 1941, document of the Nuremberg Military Tribunals (NMT), NARA RG 238, NOKW-1554.

15. See Richard Breitman, *Official Secrets: What the Nazis Planned, What the British and Americans Knew* (New York: Hill and Wang, 1998), 63–65.

16. Vadim Altskan of the USHMM is completing a doctoral thesis on the ghettos of Podolia.

17. Hans Safrian, "Komplizen des Genozids: Zum Anteil der Heeresgruppe Süd an der Verfolgung und Ermordung der Juden in der Ukraine 1941," in *Die Wehrmacht im Rassenkreig,* edited by Walter Manoschek (Vienna: Picus, 1996), 106.

18. "The Murder of the Jews is Berdichev," in *The Black Book: The Ruthless Murder of Jews by German-Fascist Invaders Throughout the Temporarily-Occupied Regions of the Soviet Union and in the Death Camps of Poland during the War, 1941–1945,* edited by Ilya Ehrenburg and Vasily Grossman (New York: Holocaust Library, 1981), 14.

19. German Police Decodes ZIP GPD 335/30, August 1941, NARA RG 457, Box 1386, re: 546 Jews killed by HSSPF staff units and 549 shot by Police Battalion 314 in Berdichev; in NARA RG 457 also see intercept from August 26 regarding Police Battalion 320, which in a *Sonderaktion* killed 4,200 Jews. See Breitman, *Official Secrets,* 65.

20. Abschlussbericht in the case against *Schutzpolizei* chief Friedrich Becker, Central Office for War Crimes Investigations, 204 ARZ 129/67, 1000, Ludwigsburg, Germany; and Pohl, "Schauplatz Ukraine," 136.

21. Shmuel Spector, *The Holocaust of Vohynian Jews, 1941–1944* (Jerusalem: Yad Vashem, 1990), 118.

22. Ibid., 117–19; Leni Yahil, *The Holocaust: The Fate of European Jewry,* translated by Ina Friedman and Haya Galai (1987; reprint, New York: Oxford Univ. Press, 1990), 266–67. Examples of anti-Jewish restrictions in Tulchin without forming a ghetto can be found in Semjon Umanskij, *Jüdisches Glück: Bericht aus der Ukraine 1933–1944* (Frankfurt: Fischer, 1998), 66–67.

23. For the Radomyshyl atrocities and Rasch's report, see EGC, EM on September 19, 1941, and September 25, 1941, NARA RG 242 T-175, roll 233, frame 2722427–9; and Arad, Krakowski, and Spector, *The Einsatzgruppen Reports,* 158. On Cherniakhiv, see the

statement of Friedrich Wilhelm Ebeling, case against Kuno Callsen et al., August 11, 1965, Central Office for War Crimes Investigations, 207 AR-Z 419/62, Ludwigsburg, Germany. On Dzerzhyns'k, see the oral testimony of survivor Micheal Alexeyevich Rosenberg, April 25, 1996, original tape and transcript are with Kira Burova, Office of Jewish Affairs and Emigration, Zhytomyr, Ukraine; and for Koziatyn, see the oral testimony of survivor Nina Borisovna Glozman, interview by Kira Burova, February 2, 1995, Zhytomyr, Ukraine, tape recording in Wendy Lower's possession.

24. See August Häfner, statement of February 8, 1966, Callsen trial, Central Office for War Crimes Investigations, 207 AR-Z 419/1962, Abschlussbericht 204 AR-Z 269/1960, Ludwigsburg, Germany. Also in Hans Safrian and Bernd Boll, "Auf dem Weg nach Stalingrad: Die 6 Armee 1941/1942," in *Vernichtunsgkrieg, Verbrechen der Wehrmacht 1941 bis 1944,* exhibition catalog edited by Hannes Heer and Klaus Naumann (Hamburg: N.p., 1995), 275–76.

25. This pattern of persecution and annihilation occurred in Khmil'nyk, Brailiv, Tulchin, and other rural towns in eastern-central Ukraine during the summer and fall of 1941. FK 675, instructions to the village commanders, according to orders of to SD 444, August 25, 1941, USHMM, RG 11.001M13, reel 92, 1275–3–662, 4; Arad, Krakowski, and Spector, *The Einsatzgruppen Reports,* 102–3; Abschlussbericht for Litin Commissariat case, Central Office for War Crimes Investigations, Case 204a AR-Z 135/67, 565–66, Ludwigsburg, Germany. "In My Hometown (Brailov)," in *The Black Book,* 39–50. Aleksandr Kruglov, *Unichtozhenie evreiskogo naseleniia v Vinnitskoi oblasti v 1941–1944: Khronika sobytii* (Mohyliv-Podil'skyi, Ukraine: A. I. Kruglov, 1997), 9.

26. EGC Ereignismeldung, October 7, 1941, in Arad, Krakowski, and Spector, *The Einsatzgruppen Reports,* 174. In the action, the Germans spared 240 Jewish laborers. September 19 was the same day that 10,000 Jews were shot in Vinnytsia, just ninety-five kilometers south of Zhytomyr. Between August 26 and September 30, the largest mass shootings occurred in Ukraine, at Kamianets'-Podil's'kyi (23,600), Berdychiv (17,500), Zhytomyr (5,000), Vinnytsia (10,000), and Kiev-Babi Yar (33,145). Combined with smaller actions, the total killed for this period was approximately 100,000, mostly women, children, and the elderly. Between the end of June and the end of August, SS and police forces had killed in all of Ukraine approximately 40,000 Jews, mainly men. See Pohl, "Schauplatz Ukraine," 133.

27. These orders were in accordance with earlier Oberkommando des Heeres (OKH), OKH orders of August 19, 1941, NARA RG 242 T-501, roll 5, frame 000805.

28. Armeeoberkommando (AOK), AOK 6 order of August 10, 1941, Anlage Kriegstagebuch (KTB) SD 454, NARA RG 242 T-315, roll 2215, frame 000959; see also Karl von Roques, memo of September 1, 1941, KTB SD 454, NARA RG 242, T-315, roll 2216, frame 000081.

29. FK 675, August 30, 1941, instructions to the village commanders, according to

orders of SD 444 from August 1, 1941, item (d) Juden states ôkeine plötzliche Ghettoisierungö, USHMM RG 11.001M13, reel 92, 1275–3–662.

30. "Kiev, Babi Yar," in *The Black Book,* 5.

31. Christopher Browning, *Ordinary Men: Reserve Police Battalion 101 and the Final Solution in Poland* (New York: Harper Perennial, 1998), 18. "Kiev, Babi Yar," 3–12.

32. FK 676 Pervomaisk, September 21, 1941, USHMM RG 11.001M13, reel 92, 1275–3–661, 4.

33. The FK's city administration counted 7,962 Jews in early to mid-November. FK 676 report dated November 15, 1941, USHMM Osobyi RG 11.001M13, 1275–3–661, reel 92, 5.

34. See Arad, Krakowski, and Spector, *The Einsatzgruppen Reports,* 228, 241–42, 300; Pohl, "Schauplatz Ukraine," 138.

35. See Orpo Battalion 314, about killings and confiscation of Jewish monies, January 24, 1942, Bundesarchiv Berlin-Lichterfelde, R 2104/25, Berlin. I am grateful to Martin Dean for this document.

36. Yuri M. Lyakhovitsky, *Poprannaya Mezuza: Knyga Drobytskoho Yar* (Trampled Mezuzah: The book of Drobitsky Yar: Evidence, facts, documents concerning the Nazi genocide of the Kharkov Jewish population during 1941–1942) (Kharkov, Ukraine: N.p., 1991). Yitzhak Arad, Yisrael Gutman, and Abraham Margaliot, eds., *Documents on the Holocaust: Selected Sources on the Destruction of the Jews of Germany and Austria, Poland and the Soviet Union* (Jerusalem: Yad Vashem, 1981), 421. Arad, Krakowski, and Spector, *The Einsatzgruppen Reports,* 289. Pohl, "Schauplatz Ukraine," 138.

37. Umanskij, *Jüdisches Glück,* 75–78. See also Isaiah Trunk, *Judenrat: The Jewish Council in Eastern Europe under Nazi Occupation* (New York: Macmillan, 1972), 444–46.

38. See the affidavit of survivor Alfred Winter, NARA RG 238, NO-5448. Also see the Soviet interrogations of Friedrich Jeckeln, December 13–14, 1945, USHMM, KGB (FSB) records from Riga, RG 06.025*01.

39. RKU Koch and HSSPF Prützmann to the General Commissars and SS Police, re: *Einrichtung von Ghettos,* January 12, 1942, Zhytomyr State Archives, P1151–1–137, 8, Zhytomyr, Ukraine.

40. EGC event report of September 17, 1941, NARA T175, r233, frame 2722383.

41. Kruglov, *Unichtozhenie evreiskogo naseleniia Ukrainy,* 96. Pohl, "Schauplatz Ukraine," 159. A less-certain number, perhaps one thousand, lived in the General Commissariat Nikolaev, and some of these Jews were killed upon the liquidation of the Zlatopol ghetto in February 1942. Approximately eight hundred remained in the city of Kiev. Some of these Jews were interned in the Syrets camp near Kiev; others were killed in gas vans or by shooting during 1942 (some at the labor camp of Buky); see Kruglov, *Unichtozhenie,* 56, and Martin Dean, *Collaboration in the Holocaust: Crimes of the Local Police in Belorussia and Ukraine, 1941–1944* (New York: St. Martin's, 2000), 61.

42. Josef Quante, statement, May 24, 1965, Central Office for War Crimes Investigations, I 204a, AR-Z 8/80, 71–72, Ludwidsburg, Germany.

43. See Hermann Kaienburg, "Jüdische Arbeitslager an der 'Strasse der SS,' " *Zeitschrift für Sozialgeschichte des 20 Jahrhunderts* 11 (1996): 13–39; and a survivor's diary about the Todt DGIV autobahn camps, Arnold Daghani, *The Grave Is in the Cherry Orchard* (London: Adam International, 1961); also see Abschlussbericht investigation of SS police Vinnytsia, Central Office for War Crimes Investigations, II 204 AR-Z 135/67, Ludwigsburg, Germany.

44. See reports of Hans Rattenhuber, chief of Reich Security Service, Kiev Archives, USHMM RG 31.002M, reel 11, 3676–4–116.

45. "Reichskommissar Koch to Kommissare in Podolia and Volhynia," September 5, 1941, Kiev Archives, USHMM AOR, 3206–1–69.

46. "Verordnung über die polizeiliche Strafgewalt der Gebietskommissare," August 23, 1941, in the Brown File, 56–57, State Archives of the Russian Federation (GARF), 7021–148–183, Moscow; Nicholas Lasovsky, "Practicing Law in Nazi-Occupied Ukraine," *American Slavic and East European Review* 11 (April 1952): 123–37. Umanskij, *Jüdisches Glück,* 69–70. On the Tulchin order dated November 17, 1941, see Vinnytsia State Archives, records, USHMM RG 31.011M, reel 4, P1417–3c-1.

47. Arad, Krakowski, and Spector, *The Einsatzgruppen Reports,* 329.

48. Spector, *The Holocaust of Volhynian Jews,* 133.

49. Dean, *Collaboration,* 81.

50. Spector, *The Holocaust of Volhynian Jews,* 34.

51. Christopher Browning, *Nazi Policy, Jewish Workers, German Killers* (New York: Cambridge Univ. Press, 2000), 129.

52. "Brest," in *The Black Book,* 213–16.

53. Browning, *Nazi Policy,* 131.

54. Himmler-Berger correspondence, July 28, 1942, in Helmut Heiber, ed., *Reichsführer! Briefe an und von Himmler* (Stuttgart: DVA, 1968), 134. Himmler order concerning the Jews of the Generalgouvernement, dated July 19, 1942, Bundesarchiv NS 19/1757.

55. "Nakaz #21," bar poster, Vinnytsia Oblast Archives, USHMM RG 31.011m, P1358–1c-1, reel 3.

56. Yahil, *The Holocaust,* 258.

57. Vladimir Goykher, *The Tragedy of the Letichev Ghetto* (New York: Vladimir Goykher, 1993), 8. Spector determined a similar level of daily caloric intake in his detailed study of the Volhynian ghettos, *The Holocaust of Volhynian Jews,* 130–32.

58. Economic Staff East report on feeding the population of the eastern occupied territories, order no. 44, dated November 4, 1941, NARA RG 238, 1189-PS. Jews in the cities were the last to be fed; see RKU orders of February 20, 1942, Kiev Archives, USHMM RG 31.002M, reel 2, 2206–1–65.

59. On commissars meeting of August 1942, see Dean, *Collaboration,* "Ghetto Liquidations of 1942–43," 93–94.

60. Spector, *The Holocaust of Volhynian Jews,* 184.

61. Polish Main Commission Warsaw, reports of commander of the Sipo SD Volhynia-Podolia 1942, reports dated August 8, 1942, and August 15, 1942. I am grateful to Martin Dean for these documents, which are in his private collection.

62. Pohl, "Schauplatz Ukraine," 150.

63. Spector, *The Holocaust of Volynian Jews,* 172, 184–87; "Brest," 214–16; Dean, *Collaboration,* 96; Raul Hilberg, *The Destruction of the European Jews: Revised and Definitive Edition,* 3 vols. (New York: Holmes and Meier, 1985), 1: 144–47.

64. Dean, *Collaboration,* 96.

65. The role of material greed among perpetrators of the Holocaust can hardly be overestimated. Spector found that some Ukrainian leaders pushed through Jewish ghettoization without German prodding because they wanted the vacated Jewish properties and the personal belongings the Jews had to leave behind. See Spector, *The Holocaust of Volhynian Jews,* 120. On the plundering during the ghetto liquidations, see Dean, *Collaboration,* 95–96.

66. Raul Hilberg, *Die Vernichtun der europäischen Juden,* 3 vols. (Frankfurt am Main: Fischer, 1990), 1: 400.

67. Ibid., 1: 165.

68. Christopher Browning, "Nazi Ghettoization Policy in Poland, 1939–1941," *Central European History* 19, no. 4 (1986): 343–68.

69. For Byelorussia, see Gerlach, *Kalkulierte Morde,* 521–33. On Galicia and the Baltics, see Trunk, *Judenrat,* and Philip Friedman, "Jewish Ghettos of the Nazi Era," in *Roads to Extinction: Essays on the Holocaust* (New York: Jewish Publication Society of America, 1980), 59–87.

70. Browning, "Nazi Ghettoization Policy in Poland," 344–45.

71. Ibid., 368.

10. Multiple and Changing Experiences of Ghettoization: Budapest, 1944

1. Rather than assuming that the category "Jew" is a "commonsense" primordial one, I prefer to use quotation marks to stress that the category is both contested and constructed. On the construction of the category "Jew" in interwar Hungary, see Tim Cole, "Constructing the 'Jew,' Writing the Holocaust: Hungary 1920–45," *Patterns of Prejudice* 33, no. 3 (1999): 19–27.

2. Raul Hilberg, *The Destruction of the European Jews* (Chicago: Quadrangle, 1961).

3. Raul Hilberg, *The Destruction of the European Jews: Revised and Definitive Edition,* 3 vols. (New York: Holmes and Meier, 1985), 1: 53.

4. Ibid., 1: 158.

5. On the question of the differing "Jewish" experiences of ghettoization, see in particular the growing literature on gender and the Holocaust—for example, Leonore J. Weitzman and Dalia Ofer, eds., *Women in the Holocaust* (New Haven, Conn.: Yale Univ. Press, 1998).

6. See Cole, "Constructing the 'Jew,' " for details of the 1938, 1939, and 1941 so-called anti-Jewish laws.

7. As Randolph Braham—the writer of the major work on the Hungarian Holocaust—points out, however, an estimated sixty-three thousand "Jews" were killed prior to the German occupation in March 1944. Randolph L. Braham, *The Politics of Genocide: The Holocaust in Hungary,* 2 vols. (New York: Columbia Univ. Press, 1994), 2: 1298.

8. It is worth noting, however, that the precise relationship between the Nazi occupation and the Hungarian Holocaust is to some extent a point of debate within the historiography.

9. Randolph L. Braham, "The Holocaust in Hungary: A Retrospective Analysis," in *The Nazi's Last Victims: The Holocaust in Hungary,* edited by Randolph L. Braham and Scott Miller (Detroit: Wayne State Univ. Press, 1998), 38.

10. Although communal organizations were of some importance within the Pest ghetto (see László Kársai, "The Last Phase of the Hungarian Holocaust: The Szálasi Regime and the Jews," in *The Nazis' Last Victims,* 103–16)—their role was much less than within longer-established ghettos such as Warsaw, which even boasted a medical faculty (see Yisrael Gutman, *The Jews of Warsaw 1939–1943: Ghetto, Underground, Revolt,* translated by Ina R. Friedman [Bloomington: Indiana Univ. Press, 1982], esp. chap. 3; and Charles G. Roland, *Courage under Siege: Starvation, Disease, and Death in the Warsaw Ghetto* [Oxford: Oxford Univ. Press, 1992]), esp. chaps. 4, 5, and 10).

11. For the history of Jewish labor battalions, see Randolph L. Braham, *The Hungarian Labor System 1939–1945* (New York: Columbia Univ. Press, 1977).

12. Braham estimates a figure of forty-two thousand; see Braham, *The Politics of Genocide,* 2: 1298.

13. See the title of Braham and Miller's 1998 collection of essays, note 9.

14. Braham, *The Politics of Genocide,* 1: 517–20.

15. Bernard Klein, "The Judenrat," *Jewish Social Studies* 22, no. 1 (1960), 32.

16. "A zsidók tágas lakásai és villái alkalmasak a kibombázott Magyar családok betelepítésére" (Large flats and villas belonging to Jews are suitable for resettling bombed Hungarian families), *Függetlenség* 12 (April 7, 1944), 7.

17. "A város különbözõ helyeire tömöritik a zsidókat" (The Jews will be gathered in various places in the city), *Magyarság* 20 (April 16, 1944), 4.

18. Samu Stern, " 'A Race with Time': A Statement," in *Hungarian-Jewish Studies,* 3 vols., edited by Randolph L. Braham (New York: World Federation of Hungarian Jews, 1973), 3: 23.

19. Raoul Wallenberg Project Archive (hereafter RWPA), RWPA F2C/340, Univ. Library, Uppsala, Sweden. The interviewee suggests that this appropriation—mediated by the Jewish Council—took place on March 20 to provide apartments for Nazi German officials. The scale of the appropriations, however, suggest that they may well have been the larger-scale appropriations of early April.

20. Stern, " 'A Race with Time,' " 23.

21. Tim Cole and Graham Smith, "Ghettoization and the Holocaust in Hungary: Budapest 1944," *Journal of Historical Geography* 21, no. 3 (1995), 305.

22. Mayoral Decrees, 147.501–514 (1944), *Budapesti Közlöny* 135 (June 16, 1944).

23. Cole and Smith, "Ghettoization and the Holocaust in Hungary," 306.

24. See petitions in Országos Levéltár (hereafter OL, National Archives), Microfilm I collection, reels 15, 16, 17, and originals in Budapest Fõváros Levéltár (hereafter Bp. FL, Budapest City Archives), IX/2781–2792.1944.

25. RWPA, F2C/344.

26. RWPA, F2C/558.

27. RWPA, F2C/309.

28. RWPA, F2C/335.

29. Bp. FL, "Mayoral Correspondence, 1944," IX/2789.1944—148.381, June 21, 1944.

30. Mayoral Decrees, 148.451–452 (1944), *Budapesti Közlöny* 141 (June 22, 1944).

31. Cole and Smith, "Ghettoization and the Holocaust in Hungary," fig. 1, 307.

32. Bp. FL, "Eleventh District Councilor's Reports," IV/1480, 1944—XI elöljárója 018.325, June 21, 1944, and attached reports.

33. Ibid.

34. It is clear that in the area of the Seventh District, which was to become the Pest ghetto in the winter of 1944, a large number of "non-Jews" remained in yellow-star houses. Uj Magyar Központi Levéltár (hereafter UMKL, New Hungarian Central Archive), "The Jewish Council Diary," XXXIII-5-c-1, XI. 23, Budapest.

35. Braham, *The Politics of Genocide,* 2: 853.

36. Bp. FL, "Mayoral Correspondence," IX/2915.1944—151.929, September 15, 1944.

37. Bp. FL, "Mayoral Correspondence," IX/3354.1944—529.342, September 27, 1944, and IX/3354.1944—152.396, October 5, 1944.

38. Bp. FL, "Mayoral Correspondence," IX/3535.1944—153.346, October 28, 1944, and IX/3535.1944—153.650, November 9, 1944.

39. Braham, *The Politics of Genocide,* 2: 952–53.

40. Ibid., 2: 971–72.

41. See documents in Elek Karsai, ed., *Vádirat a Nácizmus Ellen,* 3 vols. (Budapest: Magyar Izraeliták Országos Képviselete Kiadása, 1967), 3: 305–8, 428–32.

42. See translation in Braham, *The Politics of Genocide,* 2: 973.

43. See József Szekeres, *A Pesti Gettók 1945 Januári Megmentése* (Budapest: Budapest Fõváros Levéltár, 1997), 49, who notes that the Interior Ministry estimated 15,600 "protected Jews" being relocated into 120 houses. A higher figure of 17,000 was given by Swedish ambassador Danielsson; see Péter Bajtay, *Emberirtás, Embermentés: Svéd Követjelentések 1944-bõl. Az Auschwitzi Jegyzõkönyv* (Budapest: Katalizátor Iroda, 1944), doc. 49, 155.

44. RWPA F2C/532.

45. Cf. UMKL, "Report of the Distribution and Number of Inhabitants in the Ghetto Houses," and June 22 list of yellow-star houses, UMKL XXXIII-5-c-2.

46. UMKL, "Announcement Relating to the Jews," UMKL XXXIII-5-c-10, copy of 142/4 Zs. Ü. 1944; and OL, letter dated November 24, 1944, from Third District councilor to the city mayor, Microfilm I collection, reel 18.

47. Braham estimates the figure of seventy thousand to be the peak population of the ghetto; see Braham, *The Politics of Genocide,* 2: 982.

48. RWPA F2C/307.

49. Martin Gilbert, *The Macmillan Atlas of the Holocaust* (New York: Macmillan, 1982), see especially map 306, p. 234 ("The Death of Geza Havas, 5 May 1945"), and map 313, p. 240 ("One Man's Journey, 17 January–24 October, 1945"), where Gilbert maps the journeys taken by two men—one to his death, the other to Palestine.

50. RWPA F2C/558.

51. RWPA F2C/003.

52. RWPA F2C/306.

11. Death and Ghetto Death

1. Bachya ibn Paquda, *Duties of the Heart,* 2 vols., translated by Moses Hyamson (New York: Feldheim, 1970), 2: 389.

2. Harry James Cargas, *Reflections of a Post-Auschwitz Christian* (Detroit: Wayne State Univ. Press, 1989), 25.

3. Josef Katz, *One Who Came Back: The Diary of a Jewish Survivor,* translated by Herzl Reach (New York: Herzl Press and Bergen-Belsen Memorial Press, 1973), 37.

4. Emil L. Fackenheim, *God's Presence in History: Jewish Affirmations and Philosophical Reflections* (New York: Harper, 1970), 74.

5. Ruth Andreas-Friedrich, *Der Schattenmann: Tagebuchaufzeichnungen 1938–1945* (Berlin: Suhrkamp, 1947), 179.

6. Hillel Seidman, *Tog-bukh fon Warshever geto* (New York: Avraham Mitlberg, 1947), 221.

7. Helena Elbaum Dorembus, "Through Helpless Eyes: A Survivor's Diary of the Warsaw Ghetto Uprising," *Moment* (April 1993), 58.

8. Adam Czerniakow, *The Warsaw Ghetto Diary of Adam Czerniakow,* edited by Raul

Hilberg, Stanislaw Staron, and Joseph Kermisz; translated by Stanislaw Staron and staff of Yad Vashem (New York: Stein and Day, 1979), 90.

9. Mirjam Korber, *Deportiert: Jüdische Überlebensschicksale aus Rumänien 1941–1944: Ein Tagebuch,* translated by Andrei Hoisie (Konstanz: Hartung-Garre, 1993), 75.

10. Ibid., 99.

11. Emanuel Ringelblum, *Notes from the Warsaw Ghetto: The Journal of Emmanuel Ringelblum,* edited and translated by Jacob Sloan (1958; reprint, New York: Schocken, 1974), 230.

12. Herman Kruk, "Diary of the Vilna Ghetto," translated by Shlomo Noble, *YIVO Annual of Jewish Social Sciences* 13 (1965), 20.

13. Avraham Tory, *Surviving the Holocaust: The Kovno Ghetto Diary,* edited by Martin Gilbert, translated by Jerzy Michalowicz (Cambridge, Mass.: Harvard Univ. Press, 1990), 114.

14. Ibid., 195.

15. Seidman, *Tog-bukh fon Warshever geto,* 63.

16. Czerniakow, *The Warsaw Ghetto Diary,* 205.

17. Ibid., 305.

18. Dawid Rubinowicz, *The Diary of Dawid Rubinowicz,* translated by Derek Bowman (Edmonds, Wash.: Creative Options, 1982), 55.

19. Emil Dorian, *The Quality of Witness,* edited by Marguerite Dorian, translated by Mara Soceanu Vamos (Philadelphia: Jewish Publication Society, 1982), 167.

20. Kruk, "Diary of the Vilna Ghetto," 41.

21. Yitskhok Rudashevski, *The Diary of the Vilna Ghetto,* translated by Percy Matenko (Tel Aviv: Ghetto Fighters' House and Hakibbutz Hameuchad, 1973), 41.

22. David Kahane, *Lvov Ghetto Diary,* translated by Jerzy Michalowicz (Amherst: Univ. of Massachusetts Press, 1990), 3.

23. "From the Diary of the Sculptor Rivosh (Riga)," translated by John Glad and James S. Levine, in *The Black Book: : The Ruthless Murder of Jews by German-Fascist Invaders Throughout the Temporarily-Occupied Regions of the Soviet Union and in the Death Camps of Poland during the War, 1941–1945,* edited by Ilya Ehrenburg and Vasily Grossman (New York: Holocaust Library, 1980), 340.

24. Katz, *One Who Came Back,* 216.

25. Ringelblum, *Notes from the Warsaw Ghetto,* 194.

26. Ibid., 153.

27. André Neher, *The Exile of the Word: From the Silence of the Bible to the Silence of Auschwitz,* translated by David Maisel (Philadelphia: Jewish Publication Society, 1981), 37.

28. Emmanuel Levinas, *Totality and Infinity,* translated by Alphonso Lingis (Pittsburgh: Duquesne Univ. Press, 1969), 179, emphasis in original.

29. Emmanuel Levinas, *Existence and Existents,* translated by Alphonso Lingis (The Hague: Marinus Nijhoff, 1978), 61, emphasis in original.

30. Emil L. Fackenheim, *The Jewish Bible after the Holocaust* (Bloomington: Indiana Univ. Press, 1990), 67.

31. Miklos Nyiszli, *Auschwitz,* translated by Tibere Kremer and Richard Seaver (New York: Fawcett Crest, 1960), 151.

32. Michael Zylberberg, *A Warsaw Diary* (London: Valentine, Mitchell, 1969), 31.

33. Chaim A. Kaplan, *Scroll of Agony: The Warsaw Diary of Chaim A. Kaplan,* rev. ed., edited and translated by Abraham I. Katsh (New York: Collier, 1973), 176.

34. Ibid., 267, 275–76.

35. Czerniakow, *The Warsaw Ghetto Diary,* 218.

36. Ibid., 300.

37. Ibid., 357.

38. Ringelblum, *Notes from the Warsaw Ghetto,* 196–97.

39. Ibid., 267.

40. Zylberberg, *A Warsaw Diary,* 212.

41. Kahane, *Lvov Ghetto Diary,* 53.

42. Leon Weliczker Wells, *The Death Brigade = The Janowska Road,* translated by Leon Weliczker Wells (New York: Holocaust Library, 1978), 137.

43. Katz, *One Who Came Back,* 46.

44. Ibid., 47.

45. Dorian, *The Quality of Witness,* 322.

46. Yitzhak Katznelson, *Vittel Diary,* 2d ed., translated by Myer Cohn (Tel Aviv: Hakibbutz Hameuchad, 1972), 228.

47. Albert Camus, *The Myth of Sisyphus,* translated by Justin O'Brien (New York: Random House, 1955), 3.

48. Abraham Joshua Heschel, *I Asked for Wonder,* edited by Samuel H. Dresner (New York: Crossroad, 1983), 45.

49. Leo Baeck, *The Essence of Judaism,* rev. ed., translated by Victor Grubenwieser and Leonard Pearl (New York: Schocken, 1948), 174.

50. Ibid., 174.

51. André Neher, *The Prophetic Existence,* translated by William Wolf (New York: A. S. Barnes, 1969), 338–39.

52. Emil L. Fackenheim, *The Jewish Return into History* (New York: Schocken, 1978), 247.

53. Levinas, *Totality and Infinity,* 34–35.

12. Attitudes Toward Death During the Holocaust: Writings from the Ghettos

1. John Hick, *Death and Eternal Life* (London: Harper and Row, 1976), 82.

2. Ibid., 87.

3. Ibid.

4. "Jakub Szulman's Notebook," in *Łódź Ghetto: Inside a Community under Siege,* compiled and edited by Alan Adelson and Robert Lapides (London: Penguin, 1989), 81.

5. "Jozef Zelkowicz, in *These Nightmarish Days,*" in *Łódź Ghetto: Inside a Community under Siege,* 320.

6. WŁadysŁaw Bartoszewski, quoted in Avraham Milgram, Carmit Sagui, and Shulamit Imber, *Everyday Life in the Warsaw Ghetto—1941: A Study Unit for Junior High and High School Students,* 2 vols., translated by Jerzy Michalowicz (Jerusalem: Yad Vashem, 1993), 1: 46.

7. Ibid.

8. Oskar Rosenfeld, *In the Beginning Was the Ghetto: Notebooks from Łódź,* edited by Hanno Loewy, translated by Brigitte M. Goldstein (Evanston, Ill.: Northwestern Univ. Press, 2002), 47–48.

9. Ibid., 174.

10. "Oskar Singer, Sketches," in *Łódź Ghetto: Inside a Community under Siege,* 298–99.

11. "J. B. A. [Jerakhmil Bryman], 'The Nature of Ghetto Prayer Services,' " in *Łódź Ghetto: Inside a Community under Siege,* 404.

12. Ibid., 402.

13. Ibid., 404.

14. Ellen Levine, "Jewish Views and Customs on Death," in *Death and Bereavement across Cultures,* edited by Colin Murray Parkes, Pittu Laungani, and Bill Young (London: Routledge, 1997), 103.

15. "A Father's Lament," in *Łódź Ghetto: Inside a Community under Siege,* 349.

16. "Jozef Zelkowicz, Sketches," in *Łódź Ghetto: Inside a Community under Siege,* 125.

17. Ibid., 124, ellipses in original.

18. Ibid.

19. Yaffa Eliach, *Hasidic Tales of the Holocaust* (New York: Oxford Univ. Press, 1982), 161.

20. Louis Jacobs, *The Jewish Religion: A Companion* (Oxford: Oxford Univ. Press, 1995), 116.

21. Chaim A. Kaplan, *Scroll of Agony: The Warsaw Diary of Chaim A. Kaplan,* rev. ed., translated by Abraham I. Katsh (New York: Collier, 1973), 131.

22. David G. Roskies, *The Literature of Destruction: Jewish Responses to Catastrophe* (Philadelphia: Jewish Publication Society, 1989), 3–4.

23. See Pesach Schindler, "Tikkun as Response to Tragedy: *Em Habanim Semeha* of Rabbi Yissakhar Shlomo Teichthal—Budapest, 1943," *Holocaust and Genocide Studies* 4, no. 4 (1989): 413–33, and Yissachar Teichthal, *Em Habanim Semeha* (The mother of children is happy) (Budapest: Zalman Katz Katzburg, 1943).

24. Rabbi Shapiro quoted in Mark Weitzman, Daniel Landes, and Adaire Klein, *Dig-*

nity and Defiance: The Confrontation of Life and Death in the Warsaw Ghetto (Los Angeles: Simon Wiesenthal Center, 1993), 80.

25. Rabbi Shapiro quoted in Pesach Schindler, *Hasidic Responses to the Holocaust in the Light of Hasidic Thought* (Hoboken, N.J.: KTAV, 1990), 26.

26. Ibid., 27.

27. Meir Dvorzeski, "Ha'amidah Behaye Yom Yom Begeta'ot U'vemahanaot" (Resistance during daily routines in the ghettos and camps), in *Jewish Resistance during the Holocaust: Proceedings of the Conference on Manifestations of Jewish Resistance, Jerusalem, April 7–11, 1968* (Jerusalem: Yad Vashem, 1970), 128.

28. Rabbi Shapiro quoted in Schindler, *Hasidic Responses to the Holocaust,* 63.

29. Teichthal, *Em Habanim Semeha,* 14–15.

30. Rabbi Shapiro quoted in Schindler, *Hasidic Responses to the Holocaust,* 38.

31. Teichthal, *Em Habanim Semeha,* 22–23.

32. Rabbi Teichthal quoted in Schindler, *Hasidic Responses to the Holocaust,* 38, 44.

33. Norman Lamm, "Foreword," in *The Holocaust and the Halakhah,* by Irving J. Rosenbaum (New York: KTAV, 1976), ix.

34. Robert Bocock, *Ritual in Industrial Society: A Sociological Analysis of Ritualism in Modern England* (Edinburgh: George Allen and Unwin, 1974), 51.

35. Zygmunt Bauman, "Survival as a Social Construct," in *Cultural Theory and Cultural Change,* edited by Mike Featherstone (London: Sage, 1992), 13.

36. Y. M. Kersh, "Brief fun Churef-Gevorene Yiddishe Shtet un Shtetlech" (Letters from destroyed cities and towns), *Forvertz,* July 11, 1946, 8.

37. Schindler, *Hasidic Responses to the Holocaust,* 117, see also 62 for the story of Rabbi Alter.

38. Ibid., 119–20.

13. Art and Imagery of the Ghetto—During and After the Holocaust

1. Joel J. Forman, "Holocaust Numismatic," available on the Simon Wiesenthal Center Web site, Annual 2, http://motlc.wiesenthal.com/resources/books/annual2/chap08.html. Forman notes that many aspects of the monetary systems have yet to be understood fully: it is unclear why some of the early camps (e.g., Oranienburg and Lichtenburg) had such camp-specific monetary systems, whereas others (e.g., Papenburg, Sonnenburg, Hohenstein, Sachsenburg, and Dachau) did not. Starting in 1933, Oranienburg and Lichtenburg began issuing *Lagergeld* (camp money).

2. Ibid. Lippert survived the war and confirmed this story in a 1981 interview.

3. A Holocaust survivor from Łódź who now lives in Minneapolis was denied further reparations by the German government in 1998 when he was told that he had perjured himself in a claim from 1954 when he failed to note he had been paid in currency while in the Łódź ghetto.

4. Forman, "Holocaust Numismatic." The list of camps and ghettos using currency or script were:

Parent Camp	*Country*	*Type*
Amersfoort	Netherlands	Transit Camp
Auschwitz	Poland	Concentration Camp
Bielsk	Russia	Concentration Camp
Bohlen	Germany	Concentration Camp
Bozen	Italy	Transit Camp
Brabag	Germany	Concentration Camp
Buchenwald	Germany	Concentration Camp
Cremona	Italy	Transit Camp
Dachau	Germany	Concentration Camp
Flossenburg	Germany	Concentration Camp
Grini	Norway	Transit Camp
Gross-Rosen	Germany	Concentration Camp
Haselhorst	Germany	Concentration Camp
Holysov	Czechoslovakia	Concentration Camp
Lichtenburg	Germany	Concentration Camp
Łódź	Poland	Ghetto
Mauthausen	Austria	Concentration Camp
Mittelbau	Germany	Concentration Camp
Neuengamme	Germany	Concentration Camp
Nordhausen	Germany	Concentration Camp
Orienenburg	Germany	Concentration Camp
Ravensbrück	Germany	Concentration Camp
Sachsenhausen	Germany	Concentration Camp
Sokolka	Russia	Ghetto
Stutthof	Germany	Concentration Camp
Theresienstadt	Czechoslovakia	Ghetto and Transit Camp
Westerbork	Netherlands	Transit Camp
Vught	Netherlands	Concentration Camp

5. Ibid.

6. Ibid.

7. Correspondence between Edward Victor, Los Angeles Judaica Philatelic Resources Page, and Stephen Feinstein, October 2001.

8. Elena Makarova, *From Bauhaus to Terezin: Friedl Dicker-Brandeis and Her Pupils* (Jerusalem: Yad Vashem, 1990), 6, from the chapter "The Bauhaus in Terezin." See also Anton Lehmden, *Theresienstadt: Vystava Meisterschule Lehmden* (Vienna: Projekt Gedenksienst, 1993), and Susan Goldman Rubin, *Fireflies in the Dark: The Story of Friedl Dicker-Brandeis and the Children of Terezin* (New York: Holiday House, 2000).

9. See examples of these paintings in Makarova, *From Bauhaus to Terezin,* 29.

10. Erna Furman (camp artist and later professor at the University of Cleveland), letter from 1989, in ibid., 38.

11. As related by Makarova in ibid., 33.

12. "Minutes of the Exhibition Jury, March 16, 1943, Vilna Ghetto," YIVO Institute for Jewish Research, translation of YIVO document no. 466 by Dina Abramowicz, original document in Yiddish. New York. Also cited in Hermann Kruk, *The Last Days of the Jerusalem of Lithuania: Chronicles from the Vilna Ghetto and the Camps, 1939–1944* (New Haven, Conn.: Yale Univ. Press, 2002), 484.

13. Ibid.

14. Mary S. Constanza, *The Living Witness: Art in the Concentration Camps and Ghettos* (New York: Free Press, 1982), 30–33.

15. Avraham Tory, diary entry quoted in Dennis B. Klein and the United States Holocaust Memorial Museum (USHMM), *Hidden History of the Kovno Ghetto: A Project of the United States Holocaust Memorial Museum* (Washington, D.C., and New York: USHMM; Bullfinch Press; Little, Brown, 1997), 164.

16. Leo Haas quoted in conversation with Mary Constanza in Constanza, *The Living Witness,* 33.

17. Constanza has a chapter devoted to the media in the camps and ghettos. See ibid., chap. 6.

18. For more on this contradiction, see Janet Blatter, "Art from the Whirlwind," in Janet Blatter and Sybil Milton, *Art of the Holocaust,* (New York: Routledge, 1981), 32–33.

19. A copy of this work can be found in Blatter and Milton, *Art of the Holocaust,* 75.

20. Ibid.

21. See Adolf Aussenberg, *Kunstenaar in Theresienstadt* (Haarlem, Netherlands: Uitgeverij Tuindorp, Ab Caransa en Zuidhollans Verzetsmuseurn Gouda, 1993).

22. Max Placek, *Double Signature: Portraits of Personalities from the Terezin Ghetto* (Jerusalem: Yad Vashem, 1994).

23. Copies of the illustrations for *Tomickovi* can be found in Gerald Green, *The Artists of Terezin* (New York: Hawthorne, 1978), 45–55.

24. Ibid., 55.

25. See Blatter and Milton, *Art of the Holocaust,* 59–61 and 90–91.

26. For reproductions of these drawings, see Frantisek Ehrmann, Otta Heitlinger, and Rudolf Iltis, eds., *Terezin* (Prague: Council of Jewish Communities in Czech Lands, 1965), plates 18, 27, 35, 36, 37, 41.

27. See Alfred Kantor, *The Book of Alfred Kantor* (New York: McGraw Hill, 1971).

28. "Artists," in Klein and USHMM, *Hidden History of the Kovno Ghetto,* 168. See also Constanza, *The Living Witness,* 91.

29. Klein and USHMM, *Hidden History of the Kovno Ghetto,* 196.

30. Constanza, *The Living Witness,* 87.

31. Ben Shahn, "The Biography of a Painting" (1957), in *Ben Shahn,* edited by John D. Morse (New York: Praeger, 1972), 84.

32. Ibid., 81

33. Ben Shahn, "Interview" (1944), in ibid., 31.

34. For an extended discussion of Shahn's Jewish symbolism, see Ziva Amishai-Maisels, "Ben Shahn and the Problem of Jewish Identity," *Jewish Art* 12–13 (1986): 304–19.

35. Kenneth W. Prescott, *The Complete Graphic Works of Ben Shahn* (New York: Quadrangle, 1973), 51.

36. All of these prints appear in ibid., 51, 56.

37. Ibid., 56.

38. Samuel Bak, "About Myself," text of talk from the Decordova Museum, Lincoln, Mass., December 14, 1999.

39. Ibid.

40. Ibid.

41. Many works show Bak's long and serious attempt to manage his own past and to convert it into images that convey the issues of the Holocaust to his viewers. Among the many works available that show these images are *Bak: Landscapes of the Jewish Experience* (Boston: Pucker Gallery, 1993), *Bak: Landscapes of the Jewish Experience II* (Boston: Pucker Gallery, 1996), and *Samuel Bak: The Past Continues* (Boston: Pucker Safrai Gallery, 1988). Bak's new series is called *Return to Vilna.*

42. Vicky Goldberg, "As a Feminist, a King; as a Ballerina, a Klutz," *New York Times,* August 8, 1999, sec. 2, 35.

43. Rudolph Iltis, "Terezin—Its Influence on Czechoslovak Literature, Music, Plastic Arts, and Film," in *Terezin,* 316.

14. The Jewish Resistance Movements in the Ghettos of Eastern Europe: Reflections on the Relationships of Force

1. Another type of armed Jewish resistance was the partisan guerrilla experience in the forests, which involved another set of problems, perhaps closer to the classic questions of guerrilla war and therefore studied more at an academic level.

2. The Judenrat was a Jewish council established by the Germans to be a sort of self-government in the Jewish zones. In the first stage, these councils consisted of the relevant political leaders in each community, but it rapidly became clear that the Nazi intention was to create an organized unit capable of collaborating in their plan of "siege and annihilation." The first members of these councils resigned or were assassinated, and, in general terms, the posts on the Judenrat were assumed by sectors unconnected to the community, with a strong predisposition for collaboration with the Germans. However, this majority conduct was not uniform; in some ghettos, Lachwa among others, the Judenrat led the armed resistance. For a detailed analysis of the Judenrat in the Jewish ghettos of Europe,

see Isaiah Trunk, *Judenrat: The Jewish Council in Eastern Europe under Nazi Occupation* (New York: Scarborough, 1977; reprint, Lincoln: Univ. of Nebraska Press, 1996).

3. In Vilna, therefore, the resistance unified its diverse political factions six months before Warsaw, becoming the first example of this type of action, but a series of political errors weakened the will for rebellion.

4. See Daniel Feierstein, *Cinco ensayos sobre el Genocidio* (Buenos Aires: Acervo Cultural, 1997), chap. 5. This book has been revised as *Seis estudios sobre Genocidio: Analísis de las relaciones sociales: Otredad, exclusion y exterminio* (Buenos Aires: Eudeba, 2000).

5. The Germans frequently used this mechanism to fragment the Jewish population, turning one faction into a betrayer of another. The clearest example of this tactic was in the Vilna ghetto.

6. A similar situation had already taken place in Warsaw, showing the failure of the Bundists and Socialists' politics, which led to the delay of the moment of insurrection. In the Warsaw uprising in April, this faction discovered the size of its political error and actively participated in the resistance action from their inception.

7. Antonio Gramsci, "Análisis de las situaciones: Relaciones de fuerzas," in *Escritos políticos (1917–1933),* translated by Raul Crisafio (Mexico City: Siglo XXI, 1990), 346.

8. Ibid.

9. Ibid.

10. The case of the Jewish communities in western Europe, not analyzed in this study, was very different.

11. Marek Edelman, *El gueto lucha,* translated by Israel Laubstein (Buenos Aires: Editorial Milá, 1994), 26–27, 37.

12. Many Socialists-Zionists took this position, which represented an enormous amount of political responsibility and personal risk. This position, however, was expressed in the growth of these groups in the ghetto, with sizes much greater than the proportion that they had represented before the war. Among the important political operatives who returned to the occupied zones were Yitzhak Zuckerman, Frumka Plotnitzk, Ida Drori, Josef Kaplan, Tusia Altman, and Mordejai Anielewicz (from HaShomer HaTzair, the Socialists-Zionists), to name only the best known.

13. Tzvia Lubetkin, "Días de exterminio y rebelión," in *Guetos, martirio y rebelión,* edited by Asociación Mutual Israelita Argentina (AMIA) (Buenos Aires: AMIA, 1969), 80.

14. Yisrael Gutman, "El comienzo de la rebelión en el gueto de Varsovia," in *El Holocausto: Un estudio histórico,* edited by Dan Michman, translated by Gabriel Lerner (Ramat Aviv: Open Univ. of Israel, 1987), 5: 130.

15. See Ber Mark, *La insurrection del gusto de Varsovia* (Buenos Aires: Ediciones Aporte, 1956).

16. Jaika Grossman, *La resistencia clandestina,* translated by Monica Sifrim (Buenos Aires: Editorial Milá, 1990), 107.

17. Ibid., 105–6.

18. Edelman, *El gueto lucha,* 53–54, emphasis in original.

19. The role of the ghetto in the isolation of the Jews is discussed in chapter 2 of Feierstein, *Cinco ensayos sobre el genocidio.*

20. Grossman, *La resistencia clandestina,* 83.

21. Ibid., 28–29.

22. Edelman, *El gueto lucha,* 51–52.

23. Gramsci, "Análisis de las situaciones," 347.

24. During the deportations, the resistance struck in an attempt to kill Scherinski, chief of the Jewish police on August 25, 1942. On October 29, 1942, they killed Jacob Lejkin, Scherinki's successor as chief of the ghetto police and one of those responsible for the "liquidations" from July to September. On September 29, Israel Furst, chief of the ghetto's economic service was executed. Later, there were actions against Jewish "deliverers."

25. Lubetkin, "Días de exterminio y rebelión," 81.

26. Quoted in Gutman, "El comienzo de la rebelión," 31.

27. Edelman, *El gueto lucha,* 61–63.

28. Grossman, *La resistencia clandestina,* 85–86.

29. For an analysis of the role of "collective responsibility" in the construction of Nazi hegemony, see chapter 5 of Feierstein, *Cinco ensayos sobre el genocidio.*

30. Gramsci, "Análisis de las situaciones," 348.

31. Roberto Jacoby, *El asalto al cielo* (Buenos Aires: Cuadernos de CICSO, n.d., mimeo), 128–30.

32. Grossman, *La resistencia clandestina,* 125–26.

33. Ibid., 191–99.

34. For a more detailed analysis of this question, see the first two chapters of Feierstein, *Cinco ensayos sobre el genocidio.*

35. We have an example of the actions of this type of "army" in Argentina. When the Argentinean army, with officers with the worst records of repressive acts, had to confront the British army on the Malvinas-Falkland Islands, Astiz, Rico, and other special "commandos" rapidly unfurled the white flag. They showed the characteristics of an army formed with the objective of repressing the civilian population when it encounters military confrontation.

36. Mao Tse-tung, *Selection de escritos militares* [no translator listed] (Buenos Aires: Editions de la Rosa Blindada, 1972), 108.

37. Ibid., 117, 143–44.

38. Grossman, *La resistencia clandestina,* 46. Aba Kovner was designated leader of the "Jewish" tasks (within the Vilna ghetto) and Jaika Grossman leader of the "Aryan" tasks (those carried out in the zone of the city whose access was prohibited to Jews. Grossman and his group converted themselves into "Aryans." The emotional cost of this identity

change, necessary to the political strategy, is described in detail in Grossman's writings, and although it is not pertinent to this study, it merits further analysis.

39. Ibid., 227.

40. Ibid., 123.

41. Ibid., 130–31.

42. Ibid., 250–51.

43. Mordejai [Mordecai] Anielewicz and the Organización Judía Combate (OJC). "Llamado a la OJC del gueto de Varsovia, el 23 de abril de 1943," in *Guetos, martirio y rebelión,* 47.

44. Mordejai [Mordecai] Anielewicz, "La última carta del comandante de la rebelión, in *Guetos, martirio y rebelión,* 49.

15. "Theater in a Graveyard": The Ghetto Theater in Vilna

1. Freddie Rokem, *Performing History: Theatrical Representations of the Past in Contemporary Theatre* (Iowa City: Univ. of Iowa Press, 2000), 46.

2. Freddie Rokem, "On the Fantastic in Holocaust Performances," in *Staging the Holocaust: The Shoah in Drama and Performance,* edited by Claude Schumacher (Cambridge: Cambridge Univ. Press, 1998), 47.

3. Joshua Sobol, *Ghetto,* translated by Kathleen Komar, adapted by Jack Viertel, in *Plays of the Holocaust: An International Anthology,* edited by Elinor Fuchs (New York: Theatre Communications Group, 1987), 170. All quotations from Sobol's play derive from this edition and are hereafter cited parenthetically by page number in the text.

4. Yitzhak Arad, "Vilna," in *Encyclopedia of the Holocaust,* 4 vols., edited by Yisrael Gutman (New York: Macmillan, 1990), 4: 1573.

5. Joshua Sobol, interviewed by Eric Sterling, Catholic Univ., Washington, D.C., February 22, 1995.

6. Yitzhak Arad, *The Partisan: From the Valley of Death to Mount Zion* (New York: Holocaust Library, 1979), 106.

7. Jacob Gens, "Address by Gens on the First Anniversary of the Establishment of the Jewish Theater in the Vilna Ghetto, January 15, 1943," in *Documents on the Holocaust: Selected Sources on the Destruction of the Jews of Germany and Austria, Poland and the Soviet Union,* edited by Yitzhak Arad, Yisrael Gutman, and Abraham Margaliot; translated by Lea Ben Dor (Jerusalem: Yad Vashem, 1981; reprint, Oxford: Pergamon, 1987), 449–50.

8. Judy E. Yordon, "More Than a Sense of the Other: An Account of the Events Surrounding a Production of Joshua Sobol's *Ghetto,*" *Text and Performance Quarterly* 12 (1992), 372.

9. Primo Levi, *Survival in Auschwitz: The Nazi Assault on Humanity,* translated by Stuart Woolf (1958; reprint, New York: Macmillan, 1993), 33.

10. Rokem, *Performing History,* 40–41.

11. Elinor Fuchs, "Introduction," in *Plays of the Holocaust,* xix.

12. Sobol, interviewed by Eric Sterling.

13. Joshua Sobol, "Postscript: A Theatre in the Wilna Ghetto," translated by Ami Weinberg, in *Plays of the Holocaust,* 228.

14. Ibid., 230.

15. Rokem, *Performing History,* 42.

16. Vivian M. Patraka, *Spectacular Suffering: Theatre, Fascism, and the Holocaust* (Bloomington: Indiana Univ. Press, 1999), 99. It is worth noting that the "dance of the coats" scene occurs in the Jack Viertel adaptation and Kathleen Komar translation of the play. David Lan's translation includes a different scene by Sobol in which the play-within-a-play is done with Nazi uniforms, not the clothing of dead Jews.

17. Yordon, "More Than a Sense of the Other," 373.

18. Ibid., 374.

19. Rachel Shteir, "In Search of Sobol," *Theater* 21, no. 3 (1990), 41.

20. Arad, *The Partisan,* 90.

21. Robert Skloot, *The Darkness We Carry: The Drama of the Holocaust* (Madison: Univ. of Wisconsin Press, 1988), 40.

22. Leni Yahil, *The Holocaust: The Fate of European Jewry, 1932–1945,* translated by Ina Friedman and Haya Galai (1987; reprint, New York: Oxford Univ. Press, 1990), 279.

23. Patraka, *Spectacular Suffering,* 100.

24. For information regarding Jewish resistance in the Vilna ghetto and the weapons the Jews had accumulated, see Eric Sterling, "The Ultimate Sacrifice: The Death of Resistance Hero Yitzhak Wittenberg and the Decline of the United Partisan Organization," in *Resisting the Holocaust,* edited by Ruby Rohrlich (Oxford: Berg, 1998), 59–76.

25. Isaiah Trunk, *Judenrat: The Jewish Councils in Eastern Europe under Nazi Occupation* (New York: Scarborough, 1977; reprint, Lincoln: Univ. of Nebraska Press, 1996), 420.

26. Quoted in ibid., 422.

27. Kalmanovich's diary quoted in ibid.

28. Sobol, interviewed by Eric Sterling.

29. Yitzhak Arad, *Ghetto in Flames: The Struggle and Destruction of the Jews in Vilna in the Holocaust* (New York: Holocaust Library, 1982), 321.

30. Ibid., 306.

31. Alvin H. Rosenfeld, *A Double Dying: Reflections on Holocaust Literature* (Bloomington: Indiana Univ. Press, 1988), 185.

16. Inside the Ghetto: A Teaching Strategy

1. Tadeusz Pankiewicz, *The Cracow Ghetto Pharmacy,* translated by Henry Tilles (1947; reprint, New York: Holocaust Library, 1987), 3. Hereafter cited parenthetically in the text by page number.

2. All students' written comments are from Professor Jans-Thomas's personal files.

Bibliography

Archival Materials

Abschlussbericht for Litin Commissariat case. Central Office for War Crimes Investigations, Case 204a AR-Z 135/67, 565–66. Ludwigsburg, Germany.

Abschlussbericht in the case against *Schutzpolizei* chief Friedrich Becker. Central Office for War Crimes Investigations, 204 AR-Z 129/67, 1000. Ludwigsburg, Germany.

Abschlussbericht investigation of SS Police Vinnytsia. Central Office for War Crimes Investigations, II 204 AR-Z 135/67. Ludwigsburg, Germany.

"An die Jüdische Bevölkerung in Kamenetz-Podolsk." In Khmelnitskiy Oblast records. United States Holocaust Memorial Museum, USHMM Acc 1996.a.0150, reel 4, 434–1–3. Washington, D.C.

Armament Economy Inspectorate Ober-Ost. Report, October 28, 1939. Federal Records Center, Wirtschaft und Rüstung, Wi/ID 1:49. Alexandria, Va.

Armeeoberkommando (AOK). AOK 6 order of August 10, 1941. Anlage Kriegstagebuch (KTB) SD 454. U.S. National Archives and Records Administration, NARA RG 242 T-315, roll 2215, frame 000959. College Park, Md.

Bak, Samuel. "About Myself." Text of talk from the Decordova Museum, Lincoln, Mass., December 14, 1999.

Budapest Fõváros Levéltár (Bp. FL, Budapest City Archives). "Eleventh District Councillor's Reports," IV/1480.1944—XI elöljárója 018.325, June 21, 1944.

———. "Mayoral Correspondence, 1944," IX/2789.1944—148.381, June 21, 1944.

———. "Mayoral Correspondence," IX/2915.1944—151.929, September 15, 1944.

———. "Mayoral Correspondence," IX/3354.1944—529.342, September 27, 1944, and IX/3354.1944—152.396, October 5, 1944.

———. "Mayoral Correspondence," IX/3535.1944—153.346, October 28, 1944, and IX/3535.1944—153.650, November 9, 1944.

Ebeling, Friedrich Wilhelm. Statement, case against Kuno Callsen et al., August 11, 1965. Central Office for War Crimes Investigations, 207 AR-Z 419/62. Ludwigsburg, Germany.

Economic Staff East. Report on feeding the population of the eastern occupied territories, order no. 44, dated November 4, 1941. U.S. National Archives and Records Administration, NARA RG 238, 1189-PS. College Park, Md.

Einsatzgruppe C (EGC). EGC event report of September 17, 1941. U.S. National Archives and Records Administration, NARA T175, r233, frame 2722383. College Park, Md.

———. EM on September 19, 1941, and September 25, 1941. U.S. National Archives and Records Administration, NARA RG 242 T-175, roll 233, frame 2722427–9. College Park, Md.

Field commander (FK). FK 183, August 13, 1941. United States Holocaust Memorial Museum, USHMM RG11.001M13, 1275–3–662. Washington, D.C.

———. FK report, November 15, 1941, United States Holocaust Memorial Museum, USHMM RG 11.001M13, 1275–3–661. Washington, D.C.

———. FK 675 to SD 444, August 25, 1941. United States Holocaust Memorial Museum, USHMM RG 11.001M13 reel 92, 1275–3–662, p. 4. Washington, D.C.

———. FK 675, August 30, 1941. Instructions to the village commanders, according to orders of SD 444 from August 1, 1941, item (d) Juden states ôkeine plötzliche Ghettoisierungö. United States Holocaust Memorial Museum, USHMM RG 11.001M13 reel 92, 1275–3–662. Washington, D.C.

———. FK 676 Pervomaisk, September 21, 1941. United States Holocaust Memorial Museum, USHMM RG 11.001M13, reel 92, 1275–3–661. Washington, D.C.

———. FK 676, report, November 15, 1941. United States Holocaust Memorial Museum, USHMM Osobyi RG 11.001M13, 1275–3–661, reel 92. Washington, D.C.

———. Pervomaisk records, August 1941. United States Holocaust Memorial Museum, USHMM RG 11.001m13, 1275–3–661, reel 92. Washington, D.C.

German Police Decodes ZIP GPD 335/30. August 1941. U.S. National Archives and Records Administration, NARA RG 457, Box 1386. College Park, Md.

Glozman, Nina Borisovna. Interview by Kira Burova, February 2, 1995, Zhytomyr, Ukraine. Tape recording in contributor Wendy Lower's possession.

"Guidelines for the Conduct of the Troops in Russia." U.S. National Archives and Records Administration, NARA RG 242, T-315, roll 2215, frame 000711–13. College Park, Md.

Häfner, August. Statement of February 8, 1966. Callsen trial. Central Office for War Crimes Investigations, 207 AR-Z 419/1962, Abschlussbericht, 204 AR-Z 269/1960. Ludwigsburg, Germany.

International Military Tribunal at Nuremberg. U.S. National Archives and Records Administration, NARA Doc. No. 1028-PS, 12–13. College Park, Md.

Jeckeln, Friedrich. Interrogations of, December 13 and 14, 1945, United States Holocaust Memorial Museum, USHMM, KGB (FSB) records from Riga, RG 06.025*01. Washington, D.C.

Kriegstagebuch (KTB). Army Group South, meeting in Vinnytsia, August 24–25, 1941, summary notes. U.S. National Archives and Records Administration, NARA RG 242, T-501/R5/000773. College Park, Md.

Krüger, Friedrich-Wilhelm. Report given in the Generalgouvernement conference, December 8, 1939, cited in the Hans Frank diary, PS-2233. Available in Office of United States Counsel for Prosecution of Axis Criminality, *Nazi Conspiracy and Aggression.* 8 vols., 2 suppl. Washington, D.C.: Government Printing Office, 1946–48.

"Łódź Ghetto Conference." *Dokumenty i Materialy* 3 (1946): 241–42.

Mayoral Decrees. 147.501–514 (1944). *Budapesti Közlöny* 135 (June 16, 1944).

———. 148.451–452 (1944). *Budapesti Közlöny* 141 (June 22, 1944).

Meeting notes of September 2, 1941. Document of the Nuremberg Military Tribunals (NMT). U.S. National Archives and Records Administration, NARA RG 238, NOKW-1554. College Park, Md.

Memo from Technischer Kriegsverwaltungsintendant Merkel regarding a conversation with Hans Biebow. March 18, 1941. Federal Records Center, Wirtschaft und Rüstung, Wi/ID 1:40. Alexandria, Va.

"Merkblatt über Sofortaufgaben der Ortskommandanturen." Kriegstagebuch (KTB) SD 454 Anlage zum Div. Befehl Nr. 59. U.S. National Archives and Records Administration, NARA RG 242 T-315, roll 2216, frame 000091–94. College Park, Md.

"Minutes of the Exhibition Jury, March 16, 1943, Vilna Ghetto." YIVO Institute for Jewish Research. Translation of YIVO Document no. 466 by Dina Abramowicz (original document in Yiddish). New York.

"Nakaz #21." Bar poster, Vinnytsia Oblast Archives. United States Holocaust

Memorial Museum, USHMM RG 31.011m, P1358–1c-1, reel 3. Washington, D.C.

Oberkommando des Heeres (OKH). OKH orders of August 19, 1941. U.S. National Archives and Records Administration, NARA RG 242 T-501, roll 5, frame 000805. College Park, Md.

Orpo Battalion 314. About killings and confiscation of Jewish monies, January 24, 1942. Bundesarchiv Berlin-Lichterfelde, R 2104/25. Berlin.

Országos Levéltár (OL). Letter dated November 24, 1944, from Third District councilor to the city mayor. National Archives, Microfilm I collection, reel 18. Budapest.

———. Microfilm I collection, reels 15, 16, 17, and originals, Budapest Fõváros Levéltár (Bp. FL, Budapest City Archives) IX/2781–2792.1944.

Polish Main Commission Warsaw. Reports of commander of the Sipo SD Volhynia-Podolia, August 8, 1942, and August 15, 1942. Martin Dean's private collection.

Quante, Josef. Statement, May 24, 1965. Central Office for War Crimes Investigations, I 204, AR-Z 8/80. Ludwigsburg, Germany.

Raoul Wallenberg Project Archive (RWPA). RWPA F2C/003. Univ. Library, Uppsala, Sweden. A copy is also available at the United States Holocaust Memorial Museum archives, Washington, D.C.

———. RWPA F2C/306. Univ. Library, Uppsala, Sweden.

———. RWPA F2C/307. Univ. Library, Uppsala, Sweden.

———. RWPA F2C/309. Univ. Library, Uppsala, Sweden.

———. RWPA F2C/335. Univ. Library, Uppsala, Sweden.

———. RWPA F2C/340. Univ. Library, Uppsala, Sweden.

———. RWPA F2C/344. Univ. Library, Uppsala, Sweden.

———. RWPA F2C/532. Univ. Library, Uppsala, Sweden.

———. RWPA F2C/558. Univ. Library, Uppsala, Sweden.

Rattenhuber, Hans. Chief of Reich Security Service. Kiev Archives, United States Holocaust Memorial Museum, USHMM RG 31.002M, reel 11, 3676–4–116. Washington, D.C.

"Reichskommissar Koch to Kommissare in Podolia and Volhynia." September 5, 1941. Kiev Archives, United States Holocaust Memorial Museum, USHMM AOR, 3206–1–69. Washington, D.C.

Report. *Rüstungsinspektion* 21 (October 1, 1940-December 31, 1941), pt. 2, 33–34. Federal Records Center, Wirtschaft und Rüstung, Wi/ID 1:20. Alexandria, Va.

RKU Koch and HSSPF Prützmann to the General Commissars and SS Police. Re:

Einrichtung von Ghettos, January 12, 1942. Zhytomyr State Archives, P1151-1-137. Zhytomyr, Ukraine.

RKU orders of February 20, 1942. Kiev Archives, United States Holocaust Memorial Museum, USHMM RG 31.002M, reel 2, 2206-1-65. Washington, D.C.

Rosenberg, Micheal Alexeyevich. Oral testimony, April 25, 1996. Original tape and transcript are with Kira Burova, Office of Jewish Affairs and Emigration. Zhytomyr, Ukraine.

Rumkowski, M. C. "Letters." June 16 and 20, 1940, to the German Ghetto Administration, AZIH (AJHI), Rum. Records, no. 66.

Uj Magyar Központi Levéltár (UMKL, New Hungarian Central Archive). "Announcement Relating to the Jews." UMKL XXXIII-5-c-10, copy of 142/4 Zs. Ü. 1944. Budapest.

———. "The Jewish Council Diary." UMKL XXXIII-5-c-1, XI. 23. Budapest.

———. "Report of the Distribution and Number of Inhabitants in the Ghetto Houses," and June 22 list of "yellow-star houses." UMKL XXXIII-5-c-2. Budapest.

"A város különbözõ helyeire tömöritik a zsidókat" (The Jews will be gathered in various places in the city). *Magyarság* 20 (April 16, 1944).

"Verordnung über die polizeiliche Strafgewalt der Gebietskommissare." August 23, 1941, in the Brown File, 56–57. State Archives of the Russian Federation (GARF) 7021-148-183. Moscow.

Vinnytsia State Archives. Records. United States Holocaust Memorial Museum, USHMM RG 31.011M, reel 4, P1417-3c-1. Washington, D.C.

Von Roques, Karl. Memo of September 1, 1941, Kriegstagebuch (KTB) SD 454. U.S. National Archives and Records Administration, NARA RG 242, T-315, roll 2216, frame 000081. College Park, Md.

Winter, Alfred. Affidavit. U.S. National Archives and Records Administration, NARA RG 238, NO-5448. College Park, Md.

"A zsidók tágas lakásai és villái alkalmasak a kibombázott Magyar családok betelepítésére" (Large flats and villas belonging to Jews are suitable for resettling bombed Hungarian families). *Függetlenség* 12 (April 7, 1944).

Published Works

Adelson, Alan, and Robert Lapides, comps. and eds. *Łódź Ghetto: Inside a Community under Seige.* New York: Penguin, 1989.

Amishai-Maisels, Ziva. "Ben Shahn and the Problem of Jewish Identity." *Jewish Art* 12–13 (1986): 304–19.

Andreas-Friedrich, Ruth. *Der Schattenmann: Tagebuchaufzeichnungen 1938–1945.* Berlin: Suhrkamp, 1947.

Anielewicz, Mordejai [Mordecai]. "La última carta del comandante de la rebelión." In *Guetos, martirio y rebelión,* edited by Asociación Mutual Israelita Argentina (AMIA), 49. Buenos Aires: AMIA, 1969.

Anielewicz, Mordejai [Mordecai], and Organización Judía Combate (OJC). "Llamado a la OJC del gueto de Varsovia, el 23 de abril de 1943." In *Guetos, martirio y rebelión,* edited by Asociación Mutual Israelita Argentina (AMIA), 47–48. Buenos Aires: AMIA, 1969.

Arad, Yitzhak. *Ghetto in Flames: The Struggle and Destruction of the Jews in Vilna in the Holocaust.* New York: Holocaust Library, 1982.

———. *The Partisan: From the Valley of Death to Mount Zion.* New York: Holocaust Library, 1979.

———. "Vilna." In *Encyclopedia of the Holocaust,* 4 vols., edited by Yisrael Gutman, 4: 1571–575. New York: Simon and Schuster, Macmillan, 1990.

Arad, Yitzhak, Yisrael Gutman, and Abraham Margaliot, eds. *Documents on the Holocaust: Selected Sources on the Destruction of the Jews of Germany and Austria, Poland and the Soviet Union.* Jerusalem: Yad Vashem, 1981.

Arad, Yitzhak, Shmuel Krakowski, and Shmuel Spector, eds. *The Einsatzgruppen Reports: Selections from the Dispatches of the Nazi Death Squads' Campaigns Against the Jews, July 1941-January 1943.* New York: Holocaust Library, 1989.

Aussenberg, Adolf. *Kunstenaar in Theresienstadt.* Haarlem, Netherlands: Uitgeverij Tuindorp, Ab Caransa en Zuidhollans Verzetsmuseurn Gouda, 1993.

Baeck, Leo. *The Essence of Judaism.* Rev. ed. Translated by Victor Grubenwieser and Leonard Pearl. New York: Schocken, 1948.

Bajtay, Péter. *Emberirtás, Embermentés: Svéd Követjelentések 1944-bõl. Az Auschwitzi Jegyzõkönyv.* Budapest: Katalizátor Iroda, 1944.

Bak, Samuel. *Bak: Landscapes of the Jewish Experience.* Boston: Pucker Gallery, 1993.

———. *Bak: Landscapes of the Jewish Experience II.* Boston: Pucker Gallery, 1996.

———. *Samuel Bak: The Past Continues.* Boston: Pucker Safrai Gallery, 1988.

Bauer, Yehuda. *A History of the Holocaust.* New York: Franklin Watts, 1982.

Bauman, Zygmunt. "Survival as a Social Construct." In *Cultural Theory and Cultural Change,* edited by Mike Featherstone, 1–36. London: Sage, 1992.

Blatter, Janet, and Sybil Milton. *Art of the Holocaust.* New York: Routledge, 1981.

Bocock, Robert. *Ritual in Industrial Society: A Sociological Analysis of Ritualism in Modern England.* Edinburgh: George Allen and Unwin, 1974.

Braham, Randolph L. "The Holocaust in Hungary: A Retrospective Analysis." In *The Nazi's Last Victims: The Holocaust in Hungary,* edited by Randolph L. Braham and Scott Miller, 27–43. Detroit: Wayne State Univ. Press, 1998.

———. *The Hungarian Labor System 1939–1945.* New York: Columbia Univ. Press, 1977.

———. *A Magyar Holocaust* (The Hungarian Holocaust). Budapest: Gondolat, 1990.

———. *The Politics of Genocide: The Holocaust in Hungary.* 2 vols. New York: Columbia Univ. Press, 1994.

Breitman, Richard. *Official Secrets: What the Nazis Planned, What the British and Americans Knew.* New York: Hill and Wang, 1998.

"Brest." In *The Black Book: The Ruthless Murder of Jews by German-Fascist Invaders Throughout the Temporarily-Occupied Regions of the Soviet Union and in the Death Camps of Poland during the War, 1941–1945,* edited by Ilya Ehrenburg and Vasily Grossman, 213–23. New York: Holocaust Library, 1981.

Browning, Christopher. "Nazi Ghettoization Policy in Poland, 1939–1941." *Central European History* 19, no. 4 (1986): 343–68.

———. *Nazi Policy, Jewish Workers, German Killers.* New York: Cambridge Univ. Press, 2000.

———. *Ordinary Men: Reserve Police Battalion 101 and the Final Solution in Poland.* New York: Harper Perennial, 1998.

Camus, Albert. *The Myth of Sisyphus.* Translated by Justin O'Brien. New York: Random House, 1955.

Cargas, Harry James. *Reflections of a Post-Auschwitz Christian.* Detroit: Wayne State Univ. Press, 1989.

Cole, Tim. "Constructing the 'Jew,' Writing the Holocaust: Hungary 1920–45." *Patterns of Prejudice* 33, no. 3 (1999): 19–27.

Cole, Tim, and Graham Smith. "Ghettoization and the Holocaust in Hungary: Budapest 1944." *Journal of Historical Geography* 21, no. 3 (1995): 300–316.

Constanza, Mary S. *The Living Witness: Art in the Concentration Camps and Ghettos.* New York: Free Press, 1982.

Czerniakow, Adam. *The Warsaw Ghetto Diary of Adam Czerniakow.* Edited by Raul Hilberg, Stanislaw Staron, and Joseph Kermisz. Translated by Stanislaw Staron and staff of Yad Vashem. New York: Stein and Day, 1979.

Dabrowska, Danuta, and Lucjan Dobroszycki. *Kronika getta lodzkiego.* 2 vols. Łódź: Wydawnictwo Lodzkie, 1965.

Daghani, Arnold. *The Grave Is in the Cherry Orchard.* London: Adam International, 1961.

Dawidowicz, Lucy S. *The War Against the Jews, 1933–1945.* New York: Holt, Rinehart, and Winston, 1975.

Dean, Martin. *Collaboration in the Holocaust: Crimes of the Local Police in Belorussia and Ukraine, 1941–1944.* New York: St. Martin's, 2000.

Dobroszycki, Lucjan, ed. *The Chronicle of the Łódź Ghetto, 1941–1944.* Translated by Richard Lourie, Joachim Neugroschel, and others. New Haven, Conn.: Yale Univ. Press, 1984.

Dorembus, Helena Elbaum. "Through Helpless Eyes: A Survivor's Diary of the Warsaw Ghetto Uprising." *Moment* (April 1993): 56–61.

Dorian, Emil. *The Quality of Witness.* Edited by Marguerite Dorian. Translated by Mara Soceanu Vamos. Philadelphia: Jewish Publication Society, 1982.

Dvorzeski, Meir. "Ha'amidah Behaye Yom Yom Begeta'ot U'vemahanaot" (Resistance during daily routines in the ghettos and camps). In *Jewish Resistance during the Holocaust: Proceedings of the Conference on Manifestations of Jewish Resistance, Jerusalem, April 7–11, 1968.* Jerusalem: Yad Vashem, 1970.

Edelman, Marek. *El gueto lucha.* Translated by Israel Laubstein. Buenos Aires: Editorial Milá, 1994.

Ehrenburg, Ilya, and Vasily Grossman, eds. *The Black Book: The Ruthless Murder of Jews by German-Fascist Invaders Throughout the Temporarily-Occupied Regions of the Soviet Union and in the Death Camps of Poland during the War, 1941–1945.* New York: Holocaust Library, 1981.

Ehrmann, Frantisek, Otta Heitlinger, and Rudolf Iltis, eds. *Terezin.* Prague: Council of Jewish Communities in Czech Lands, 1965.

Eichengreen, Lucille, and Rebecca Camhi Fromer. *Rumkowski and the Orphans of Łódź.* San Francisco: Mercury House, 2000.

Eliach, Yaffa. *Hasidic Tales of the Holocaust.* New York: Oxford Univ. Press, 1982.

Fackenheim, Emil L. *God's Presence in History: Jewish Affirmations and Philosophical Reflections.* New York: Harper, 1970.

———. *The Jewish Bible after the Holocaust.* Bloomington: Indiana Univ. Press, 1990.

———. *The Jewish Return into History.* New York: Schocken, 1978.

"A Father's Lament." In *Łódź Ghetto: Inside a Community under Siege,* compiled and edited by Alan Adelson and Robert Lapides, 348–49. London: Penguin, 1989.

Feierstein, Daniel. *Cinco ensayos sobre el Genocidio.* Buenos Aires: Acervo Cultural, 1997.

———. *Seis estudios sobre Genocidio: Analísis de las relaciones sociales: Otredad, exclusion y exterminio.* Buenos Aires: Eudeba, 2000.

Fischler-Martinho, Janina. *Have You Seen My Little Sister?* London: Vallentine Mitchell, 1998.

Forman, Joel J. "Holocaust Numismatic." Available on the Simon Wiesenthal Center Web site, Annual 2: http://motlc.wiesenthal.com/resources/books/annual2/chapO8.html.

Förster, Jürgen. "The Relation Between Operation Barbarossa as an Ideological War of Extermination and the Final Solution." In *The Final Solution: Origins and Implementation,* edited by David Cesarani, 85–102. London: Routledge, 1994.

Foxman, Abraham. "The Resistance Movement in the Vilna Ghetto." In *They Fought Back: The Story of the Jewish Resistance in Nazi Europe,* edited by Yuri Suhl, 148–59. New York: Crown, 1967.

Friedman, Philip. "Jewish Ghettos of the Nazi Era." In *Roads to Extinction: Essays on the Holocaust,* 59–87. New York: Jewish Publication Society of America, 1980.

"From the Diary of the Sculptor Rivosh (Riga)." Translated by John Glad and James S. Levine. In *The Black Book: The Ruthless Murder of Jews by German-Fascist Invaders Throughout the Temporarily-Occupied Regions of the Soviet Union and in the Death Camps of Poland during the War, 1941–1945,* edited by Ilya Ehrenburg and Vasily Grossman, 324–46. New York: Holocaust Library, 1981.

Fuchs, Elinor. "Introduction." In *Plays of the Holocaust: An International Anthology,* edited by Elinor Fuchs, xi–xxii. New York: Theatre Communications Group, 1987.

Furman, Erna. Letter from 1989. In *From Bauhaus to Terezin: Friedl Dicker-Brandeis and Her Pupils,* by Elena Makarova, 38. Jerusalem: Yad Vashem, 1990.

Gens, Jacob. "Address by Gens on the First Anniversary of the Establishment of the Jewish Theater in the Vilna Ghetto, January 15, 1943." In *Documents on the Holocaust: Selected Sources on the Destruction of the Jews of Germany and Austria, Poland and the Soviet Union,* edited by Yitzhak Arad, Yisrael Gutman, and Abraham Margaliot; translated by Lea Ben Dor, 449–50. Jerusalem: Yad Vashem, 1981. Reprint. Oxford: Pergamon, 1987.

Gerlach, Christian. *Kalkulierte Morde: Die deutsche Wirtschafts und Vernichtungspolitik in Weissrussland 1941 bis 1944.* Hamburg: Institut für Sozialforschung, 1999.

Gilbert, Martin. *The Holocaust: History of the Jews of Europe during the Second World War.* New York: Henry Holt, 1985.

———. *The Macmillan Atlas of the Holocaust.* New York: Macmillan, 1982.

Goldberg, Vicky. "As a Feminist, a King; as a Ballerina, a Klutz." *New York Times,* August 8, 1999, sec. 2, 35.

Goykher, Vladimir. *The Tragedy of the Letichev Ghetto.* New York: Vladimir Goykher, 1993.

Gramsci, Antonio. "Análisis de las situaciones: Relaciones de fuerzas." In *Escritos políticos (1917–1933),* translated by Raul Crisafio, 342–51. Mexico City: Siglo XXI, 1990.

Green, Gerald. *The Artists of Terezin.* New York: Hawthorne, 1978.

Grossman, Jaika. *La resistencia clandestina.* Translated by Monica Sifrim. Buenos Aires: Editorial Milá, 1990.

Gutman, Yisrael. "El comienzo de la rebelión en el gueto de Varsovia." In *El Holocausto: Un estudio histórico,* edited by Dan Michman, translated by Gabriel Lerner, 130. Ramat Aviv: Open Univ. of Israel, 1987.

———. *The Jews of Warsaw 1939–1943: Ghetto, Underground, Revolt.* Translated by Ina R. Friedman. Bloomington: Indiana Univ. Press, 1982.

———. "Warsaw: Jews during the Holocaust." In *Encyclopedia of the Holocaust,* 4 vols., edited by Yisrael Gutman, 4: 1601–625. New York: Simon and Schuster, Macmillan, 1990.

Harran, Marilyn, Dieter Kuntz, Russel Lemmons, Robert Ashley Michael, Keith Pickus, and John K. Roth. *The Holocaust Chronicle: A History in Words and Pictures.* Lincolnwood, Ill.: Publications International, 2000.

Heiber, Helmut, ed. *Reichsführer! Briefe an und von Himmler.* Stuttgart: DVA, 1968.

Heppner, Ernest G. *Shanghai Refuge: A Memoir of the World War II Jewish Ghetto.* Lincoln: Univ. of Nebraska Press, 1993.

Heschel, Abraham Joshua. *I Asked for Wonder.* Edited by Samuel H. Dresner. New York: Crossroad, 1983.

Hick, John. *Death and Eternal Life.* London: Harper and Row, 1976.

Hilberg, Raul. *The Destruction of the European Jews.* Chicago: Quadrangle, 1961.

———. *The Destruction of the European Jews: Revised and Definitive Edition.* 3 vols. New York: Holmes and Meier, 1985.

———. *Die Vernichtung der europäischen Juden.* 3 vols. Frankfurt am Main: Fischer, 1990.

Iltis, Rudolph. "Terezin—Its Influence on Czechoslovak Literature, Music, Plastic Arts, and Film." In *Terezin,* edited by Frantisek Ehrmann, Otta Heitlinger, and Rudolf Iltis, 309–16. Prague: Council of Jewish Communities in Czech Lands, 1965.

"In My Hometown (Brailov)." In *The Black Book: The Ruthless Murder of Jews by German-Fascist Invaders Throughout the Temporarily-Occupied Regions of the Soviet Union and in the Death Camps of Poland during the War, 1941–1945,* edited by Ilya Ehrenburg and Vasily Grossman, 39–50. New York: Holocaust Library, 1981.

Ioanid, Radu. *The Holocaust in Romania: The Destruction of Jews and Gypsies under the Antonescu Regime, 1940–1944.* Chicago: Ivan R. Dee, 2000.

Jacobs, Louis. *The Jewish Religion: A Companion.* Oxford: Oxford Univ. Press, 1995.

Jacoby, Roberto. *El asalto al cielo.* Buenos Aires: Cuadernos de CICSO, n.d. (mimeo).

"Jakub Szulman's Notebook." In *Łódź Ghetto: Inside a Community under Siege,* compiled and edited by Alan Adelson and Robert Lapides, 81–89. London: Penguin, 1989.

"J. B. A. [Jerakhmil Bryman], 'The Nature of Ghetto Prayer Services.' " In *Łódź Ghetto: Inside a Community under Siege,* edited by Alan Adelson and Robert Lapides, 399–405. London: Penguin, 1989.

"Jozef Zelkowicz, in *These Nightmarish Days.*" In *Łódź Ghetto: Inside a Community under Siege,* compiled and edited by Alan Adelson and Robert Lapides, 320–26. London: Penguin, 1989.

"Jozef Zelkowicz, Sketches." In *Łódź Ghetto: Inside a Community under Siege,* compiled and edited by Alan Adelson and Robert Lapides, 122–29. London: Penguin, 1989.

Kahane, David. *Lvov Ghetto Diary.* Translated by Jerzy Michalowicz. Amherst: Univ. of Massachusetts Press, 1990.

Kaienburg, Hermann. "Jüdische Arbeitslager an der 'Strasse der SS.' " *Zeitschrift für Sozialgeschichte des 20 Jahrhunderts* 11 (1996): 13–39.

Kantor, Alfred. *The Book of Alfred Kantor.* New York: McGraw Hill, 1971.

Kaplan, Chaim A. *Scroll of Agony: The Warsaw Diary of Chaim A. Kaplan.* Rev. ed. Translated and edited by Abraham I. Katsh. New York: Collier, 1973.

Karsai, Elek, ed. *Vádirat a Nácizmus Ellen.* 3 vols. Budapest: Magyar Izraeliták Országos Képviselete Kiadása, 1967.

Kársai, László, ed. *"Befogadok" Writings Against Antisemitism 1882–1993.* Budapest: Aura, 1993.

———. "The Last Phase of the Hungarian Holocaust: The Szálasi Regime and the Jews." In *The Nazis' Last Victims: The Holocaust in Hungary,* edited by Randolph L. Braham and Scott Miller, 103–16. Detroit: Wayne State Univ. Press, 1998.

Katz, Josef. *One Who Came Back: The Diary of a Jewish Survivor.* Translated by Herzl Reach. New York: Herzl Press and Bergen-Belsen Memorial Press, 1973.

Katznelson, Yitzhak. *Vittel Diary.* 2d ed. Translated by Myer Cohn. Tel Aviv: Hakibbutz Hameuchad, 1972.

Kaufmann, Max. *Die Vernichtung der Juden Lettlands: Churbn Lettland.* Munich: Hartun-Gorre, 1947.

Kersh, Y. M. "Brief fun Churef-Gevorene Yiddishe Shtet un Shtetlech" (Letters from destroyed cities and towns). *Forvertz,* July 11, 1946, 8.

"Kiev, Babi Yar." In *The Black Book: The Ruthless Murder of Jews by German-Fascist Invaders Throughout the Temporarily-Occupied Regions of the Soviet Union and in the Death Camps of Poland during the War, 1941–1945,* edited by Ilya Ehrenburg and Vasily Grossman, 3–12. New York: Holocaust Library, 1981.

Klein, Bernard. "The Judenrat." *Jewish Social Studies* 22, no. 1 (1960): 27–42.

Klein, Dennis B., and the United States Holocaust Memorial Museum (USHMM). *Hidden History of the Kovno Ghetto: A Project of the United States Holocaust Memorial Museum.* Washington, D.C., and New York: USHMM; Bullfinch Press; Little, Brown, 1997.

Komoroczy, Geza, ed. *A Zsido Budapest* (Jewish Budapest). 2 vols. Budapest: MTA Judaisztikai Kutatócsoport, 1995.

Korber, Mirjam. *Deportiert: Jüdische Überlebensschicksale aus Rumänien 1941–1944: Ein Tagebuch.* Translated by Andrei Hoisie. Konstanz: Hartung-Garre, 1993.

Kruglov, Aleksandr. *Unichtozhenie evreiskogo naseleniia Ukrainy v Vinnitskoi oblasti v 1941–44: Khronika sobytii.* Mohyliv-Podil's'kyi, Ukraine: A. I. Kruglov, 1997.

Kruk, Herman. "Diary of the Vilna Ghetto." Translated by Shlomo Noble. *YIVO Annual of Jewish Social Sciences* 13 (1965): 9–78.

———. *The Last Days of the Jerusalem of Lithuania: Chronicles from the Vilna Ghetto and the Camps, 1939–1944.* Edited by Benjamin Harshav. Translated by Barbara Harshav. New Haven, Conn.: Yale Univ. Press, 2002.

Kulka, Otto Dov. "Theresienstadt." In *Encyclopedia of the Holocaust,* 4 vols., edited by Yisrael Gutman, 4: 1460–463. New York: Simon and Schuster, Macmillan, 1990.

Lamm, Norman. "Foreword." In *The Holocaust and the Halakhah,* by Irving J. Rosenbaum, vii-x. New York: KTAV, 1976.

Langer, Lawrence L. *Preempting the Holocaust.* New Haven, Conn.: Yale Univ. Press, 1998.

———. *Versions of Survival: The Holocaust and the Human Spirit.* Albany: State Univ. of New York Press, 1982.

Lasovsky, Nicholas. "Practicing Law in Nazi-Occupied Ukraine." *American Slavic and East European Review* 11 (April 1952): 123–37.

Lehmden, Anton. *Theresienstadt: Vystava Meisterschule Lehmden.* Vienna: Projekt Gedenksienst, 1993.

Levi, Primo. *Survival in Auschwitz: The Nazi Assault on Humanity.* Translated by Stuart Woolf. 1958. Reprint. New York: Macmillan, 1993.

Levinas, Emmanuel. *Existence and Existents.* Translated by Alphonso Lingis. The Hague: Marinus Nijhoff, 1978.

———. *Totality and Infinity.* Translated by Alphonso Lingis. Pittsburgh: Duquesne Univ. Press, 1969.

Levine, Ellen. "Jewish Views and Customs on Death." In *Death and Bereavement across Cultures,* edited by Colin Murray Parkes, Pittu Laungani, and Bill Young, 98–130. London: Routledge, 1997.

Lubetkin, Tzvia. "Días de exterminio y rebelión." In *Guetos, martirio y rebelión,* edited by Asociación Mutual Israelita Argentina (AMIA), 75–94. Buenos Aires: AMIA, 1969.

Lyakhovitsky, Yuri M. *Poprannaya Mezuza: Knyga Drobytskoho Yar* (Trampled Mezuzah: The book of Drobitsky Yar: Evidence, facts, documents concerning the Nazi genocide of the Kharkov Jewish population during 1941–1942). Kharkov, Ukraine: N.p., 1991.

Madaczyk, Czeslaw. *Polityka III Rzeszy w Okupowanej Polsce.* Warsaw: Panstwowe Wydawn Naukowe, 1970.

Makarova, Elena. *From Bauhaus to Terezin: Friedl Dicker-Brandeis and Her Pupils.* Jerusalem: Yad Vashem, 1990.

Mao Tse-tung. *Selection de escritos militares.* [No transltor listed.] Buenos Aires: Editions de la Rosa Blindada, 1972.

Mark, Ber. *La insurrection del gusto de Varsovia.* Buenos Aires: Ediciones Aporte, 1956.

Milgram, Avraham, Carmit Sagui, and Shulamit Imber. *Everyday Life in the Warsaw Ghetto—1941: A Study Unit for Junior High and High School Students.* 2 vols. Translated by Jerzy Michalowicz. Jerusalem: Yad Vashem, 1993.

"The Murder of the Jews in Berdichev." In *The Black Book: The Ruthless Murder of Jews by German-Fascist Invaders Throughout the Temporarily-Occupied Regions of the*

Soviet Union and in the Death Camps of Poland during the War, 1941–1945, edited by Ilya Ehrenburg and Vasily Grossman, 13–24. New York: Holocaust Library, 1981.

Neher, André. *The Exile of the Word: From the Silence of the Bible to the Silence of Auschwitz.* Translated by David Maisel. Philadelphia: Jewish Publication Society, 1981.

———. *The Prophetic Existence.* Translated by William Wolf. New York: A. S. Barnes, 1969.

"Notes on Rumkowski." In *Łódź Ghetto: Inside a Community under Siege,* compiled and edited by Alan Adelson and Robert Lapides, 489–94. New York: Penguin, 1991.

Nyiszli, Miklós. *Auschwitz.* Translated by Tibere Kremer and Richard Seaver. New York: Fawcett Crest, 1960.

Ofer, Dalia. "The Holocaust in Transnistria: A Special Case of Genocide." In *The Holocaust in the Soviet Union: Studies and Sources on the Destruction of the Jews in the Nazi-Occupied Territories of the USSR, 1941–1945,* edited by L. Dobroszycki and J. Gurock, 133–54. New York: M. E. Sharpe, 1993.

Oliver, Myrna. "Sigi Ziering; Tycoon Survived Nazi Camps." *Los Angeles Times,* November 14, 2000, B6.

"Oskar Singer, Sketches." In *Łódź Ghetto: Inside a Community under Siege,* compiled and edited by Alan Adelson and Robert Lapides, 298–308. London: Penguin, 1989.

Pankiewicz, Tadeusz. *The Cracow Ghetto Pharmacy.* Translated by Henry Tilles. 1947. Reprint. New York: Holocaust Library, 1987.

Paquda, Bachya ibn. *Duties of the Heart.* 2 vols. Translated by Moses Hyamson. New York: Feldheim, 1970.

Patraka, Vivian M. *Spectacular Suffering: Theatre, Fascism, and the Holocaust.* Bloomington: Indiana Univ. Press, 1999.

Perechodnik, Calel. *Am I a Murderer? Testament of a Jewish Ghetto Policeman.* Translated and edited by Frank Fox. Boulder, Colo.: Westview, 1996.

Placek, Max. *Double Signature: Portraits of Personalities from the Terezin Ghetto.* Jerusalem: Yad Vashem, 1994.

Pohl, Dieter. *Nationalsozialistische Judenverfolgung in Ostgalizien 1941–1944: Organisation und Durchführung eines staatlichen Massenverbrechens.* Munich: Oldenbourg, 1997.

———. "Schauplatz Ukraine: Der Massenmord an den Juden im Militärverwaltungsgebiet und im Reichskommissariat 1941–1943." In *Ausbeutung, Vernich-*

tung, Öffentlichkeit: Studien zur nationalistischen Verfolgungspolitik, edited by N. Frei, S. Steinbacher, and B. Wagner, 135–73. Munich: Sauer, 2000.

Potok, Chaim. *Wanderings: Chaim Potok's History of the Jews.* New York: Alfred A. Knopf, 1978.

Prescott, Kenneth W. *The Complete Graphic Works of Ben Shahn.* New York: Quadrangle, 1973.

Ringelblum, Emanuel. *Notes from the Warsaw Ghetto: The Journal of Emmanuel Ringelblum.* Translated by Jacob Sloan. 1958. Reprint. New York: Schocken, 1974.

Robertson, Jenny. "Medieval Ghettos." In *Ghetto: Poems of the Warsaw Ghetto 1939–1943,* 21. Oxford: Lion, 1989.

Robinson, Jacob. "Introduction: Some Basic Issues That Faced the Jewish Councils." In *Judenrat: The Jewish Councils in Eastern Europe under Nazi Occupation,* by Isaiah Trunk, xxv-xxxv. New York: Scarborough, 1977. Reprint. Lincoln: Univ. of Nebraska Press, 1996.

Rokem, Freddie. "On the Fantastic in Holocaust Performances." In *Staging the Holocaust: The Shoah in Drama and Performance,* edited by Claude Schumacher, 40–52. Cambridge: Cambridge Univ. Press, 1998.

———. *Performing History: Theatrical Representations of the Past in Contemporary Theatre.* Iowa City: Univ. of Iowa Press, 2000.

Roland, Charles G. *Courage under Siege: Starvation, Disease, and Death in the Warsaw Ghetto.* Oxford: Oxford Univ. Press, 1992.

Rosenfeld, Alvin H. *A Double Dying: Reflections on Holocaust Literature.* Bloomington: Indiana Univ. Press, 1988.

Rosenfeld, Oskar. *In the Beginning Was the Ghetto: Notebooks from Łódź.* Edited by Hanno Loewy. Translated by Brigitte M. Goldstein. Evanston, Ill.: Northwestern Univ. Press, 2002.

Roskies, David G. *The Literature of Destruction: Jewish Responses to Catastrophe.* Philadelphia: Jewish Publication Society, 1989.

Ross, James R. *Escape to Shanghai: A Jewish Community in China.* New York: Free Press, 1994.

Rotem, Simha, with Barbara Harshav. *Memories of a Warsaw Ghetto Fighter: The Past within Me.* New Haven, Conn.: Yale Univ. Press, 1994.

Roth, John K. *Holocaust Politics.* Louisville, Ky.: Westminster John Knox Press, 2001.

Rubin, Susan Goldman. *Fireflies in the Dark: The Story of Friedl Dicker-Brandeis and the Children of Terezin.* New York: Holiday House, 2000.

Rubinowicz, Dawid. *The Diary of Dawid Rubinowicz.* Translated by Derek Bowman. Edmonds, Wash.: Creative Options, 1982.

Rudashevski, Yitskhok. *The Diary of the Vilna Ghetto.* Translated by Percy Matenko. Tel Aviv: Ghetto Fighters' House and Hakibbutz Hameuchad, 1973.

Safrian, Hans. "Komplizen des Genozids: Zum Anteil der Heeresgruppe Süd an der Verfolgung und Ermordung der Juden in der Ukraine 1941." In *Die Wehrmacht im Rassenkreig,* edited by Walter Manoschek, 90–115. Vienna: Picus, 1996.

Safrian, Hans, and Bernd Boll. "Auf dem Weg nach Stalingrad: Die 6 Armee 1941/42." In *Vernichtungskrieg, Verbrechen der Wehrmacht 1941 bis 1944,* exhibition catalog edited by Hannes Heer and Klaus Naumann, 270–76. Hamburg: N.p., 1995.

Scheiber, Sandor, ed. *Evkonyv 1970* (Jewish yearbook 1970). Budapest: Magyarorszagi Izraelitak Orszagos Kepviselete, 1970.

Schindler, Pesach. *Hasidic Responses to the Holocaust in the Light of Hasidic Thought.* Hoboken, N.J.: KTAV, 1990.

———. "Tikkun as Response to Tragedy: *Em Habanim Semeha* of Rabbi Yissakhar Shlomo Teichthal—Budapest, 1943." *Holocaust and Genocide Studies* 4, no. 4 (1989): 413–33.

Seidman, Hillel. *Tog-bukh fon Warshever geto.* New York: Avraham Mitlberg, 1947.

Shahn, Ben. "The Biography of a Painting." 1957. In *Ben Shahn,* edited by John D. Morse, 64–87. New York: Praeger, 1972.

———. "Interview." 1944. In *Ben Shahn,* edited by John D. Morse, 29–31. New York: Praeger, 1972.

Shteir, Rachel. "In Search of Sobol." *Theater* 21, no. 3 (1990): 39–42.

Skloot, Robert. *The Darkness We Carry: The Drama of the Holocaust.* Madison: Univ. of Wisconsin Press, 1988.

Sobol, Joshua. *Ghetto.* Translated by Kathleen Komar. Adapted by Jack Viertel. In *Plays of the Holocaust: An International Anthology,* edited by Elinor Fuchs, 153–225. New York: Theatre Communications Group, 1987.

———. "Postscript: A Theatre in the Wilna Ghetto." Translated by Ami Weinberg. In *Plays of the Holocaust: An International Anthology,* edited by Elinor Fuchs, 227–30. New York: Theatre Communications Group, 1987.

Spector, Shmuel. "The Holocaust of Ukrainian Jews." In *Bitter Legacy: Confronting the Holocaust in the USSR,* edited by Zvi Y. Gitelman, 43–50. Bloomington: Indiana Univ. Press, 1997.

———. *The Holocaust of Volhynian Jews, 1941–1944.* Jerusalem: Yad Vashem, 1990.

Sterling, Eric. "The Ultimate Sacrifice: The Death of Resistance Hero Yitzhak Wittenberg and the Decline of the United Partisan Organization." In *Resisting the Holocaust,* edited by Ruby Rohrlich, 59–76. Oxford: Berg, 1998.

Stern, Samu. " 'A Race with Time': A Statement." In *Hungarian-Jewish Studies,* 3 vols., edited by Randolph L. Braham, 3: 1–47. New York: World Federation of Hungarian Jews, 1973.

Szekeres, József. *A Pesti Gettók 1945 Januári Megmentése.* Budapest: Budapest Fõváros Levéltár, 1997.

Teichthal, Yissachar. *Em Habanim Semeha* (The mother of children is happy). Budapest: Zalman Katz Katzburg, 1943.

Tory, Avraham. *Surviving the Holocaust: The Kovno Ghetto Diary.* Edited by Martin Gilbert. Translated by Jerzy Michalowicz. Cambridge, Mass.: Harvard Univ. Press, 1990.

Trunk, Isaiah. "Epidemics in the Warsaw Ghetto." *YIVO Annual of Jewish Social Sciences* 8 (1953): 82–122.

———. *Judenrat: The Jewish Councils in Eastern Europe under Nazi Occupation.* New York: Macmillan, 1972.

———. *Judenrat: The Jewish Councils in Eastern Europe under Nazi Occupation.* New York: Scarborough, 1977. Reprint. Lincoln: Univ. of Nebraska Press, 1996.

———. *Lodzher geto: A historishe un sotziologishe shtudie* (Łódź ghetto: A historical and sociological study). New York: YIVO, Yad Vashem, 1962.

———. "Mayrev-eyropeishe Yidn in di mizrekh-eyropeishe getos." *Di Goldene Keyt* 15 (1953): 80–102.

Umanskij, Semjon. *Jüdisches Glück: Bericht aus der Ukraine 1933–1944.* Frankfurt: Fischer, 1998.

Vrba, Rudolf. "The Preparations for the Holocaust in Hungary: An Eyewitness Account." In *The Nazis' Last Victims: The Holocaust in Hungary,* edited by Randolph L. Braham and Scott Miller, 55–101. Detroit: Wayne State Univ. Press, 1998.

Weitzman, Leonore J., and Dalia Ofer, eds. *Women in the Holocaust.* New Haven, Conn.: Yale Univ. Press, 1998.

Weitzman, Mark, Daniel Landes, and Adaire Klein. *Dignity and Defiance: The Confrontation of Life and Death in the Warsaw Ghetto.* Los Angeles: Simon Wiesenthal Center, 1993.

Wells, Leon Weliczker. *The Death Brigade = The Janowska Road.* Translated by Leon Weliczker Wells. New York: Holocaust Library, 1978.

Yahil, Leni. *The Holocaust: The Fate of European Jewry, 1932–1945.* Translated by Ina

Friedman and Haya Galai. 1987. Reprint. New York: Oxford Univ. Press, 1990.

Yordon, Judy E. "More Than a Sense of the Other: An Account of the Events Surrounding a Production of Joshua Sobol's *Ghetto*." *Text and Performance Quarterly* 12 (1992): 372–76.

Young, James E. *At Memory's Edge: After-Images of the Holocaust in Contemporary Art and Architecture*. New Haven, Conn.: Yale Univ. Press, 2000.

Zelkowicz, Josef. *In Those Terrible Days: Notes from the Łódź Ghetto*. Edited by Michal Unger. Translated by Naftali Greenwood. Jerusalem: Yad Vashem, 2002.

Zylberberg, Michael. *A Warsaw Diary*. London: Valentine, Mitchell, 1969.

Index

Italic page number denotes illustration.